SOUL EATER

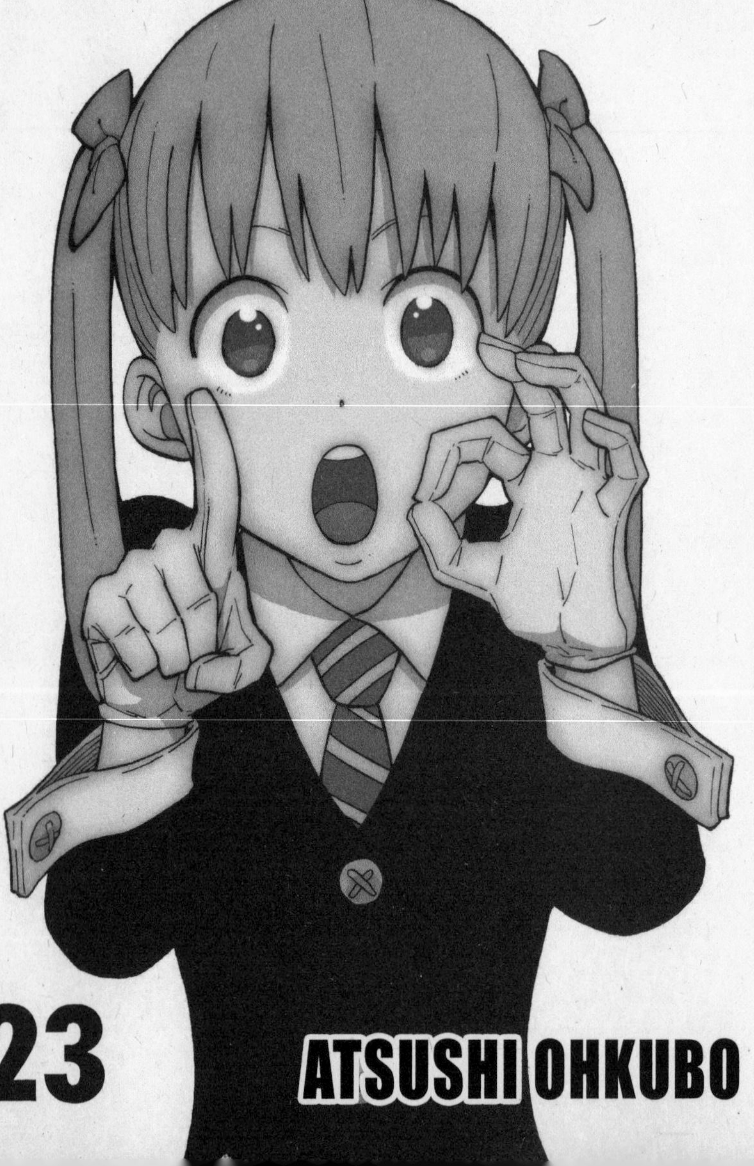

23

ATSUSHI OHKUBO

SOUL EATER

vol. 23
by ATSUSHI OHKUBO

Stand up, DWMA, fight against the insanity

SOUL EATER 23

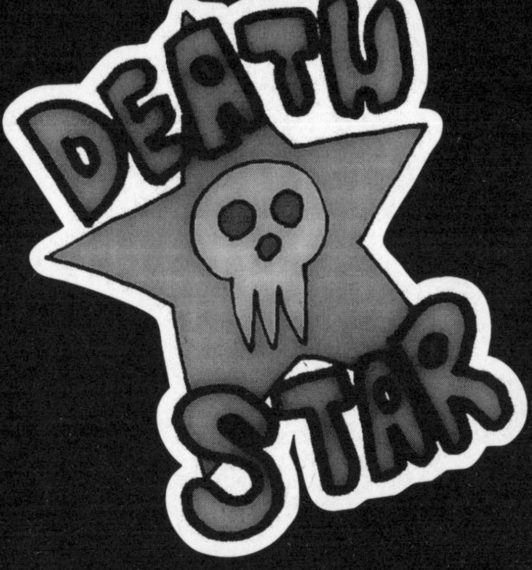
DEATH
STAR

CONTENTS

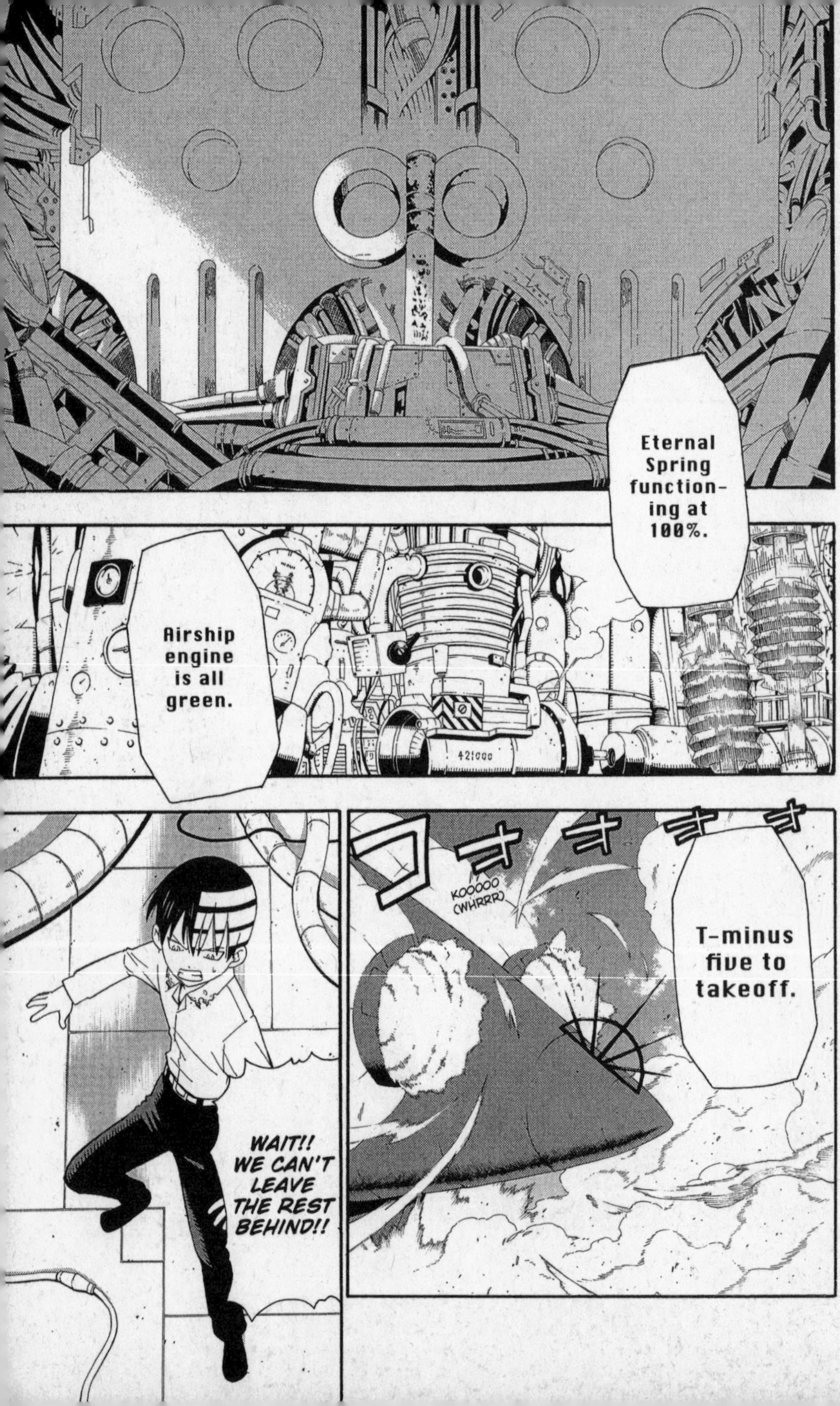
Eternal Spring function-ing at 100%.
Airship engine is all green.
KOOOOO (WHRRR)
T-minus five to takeoff.
WAIT!! WE CAN'T LEAVE THE REST BEHIND!!

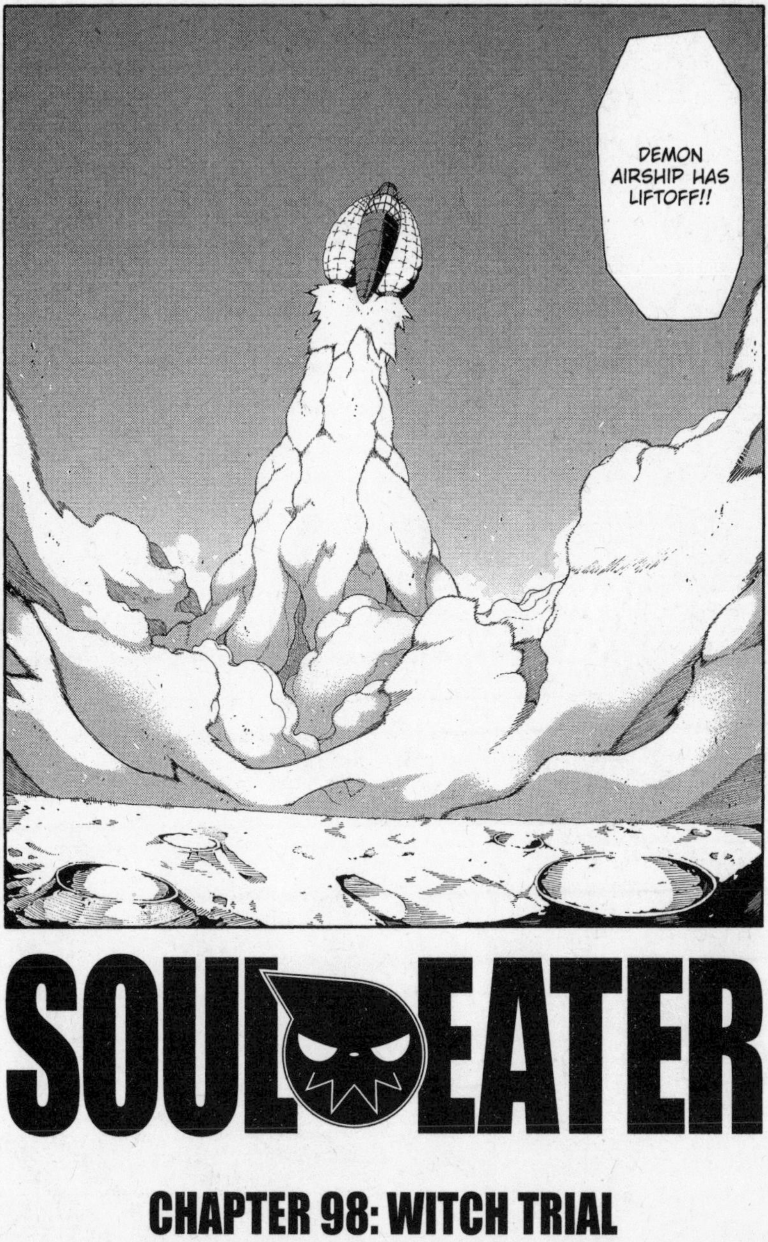
DEMON AIRSHIP HAS LIFTOFF!!

SOUL EATER

CHAPTER 98: WITCH TRIAL

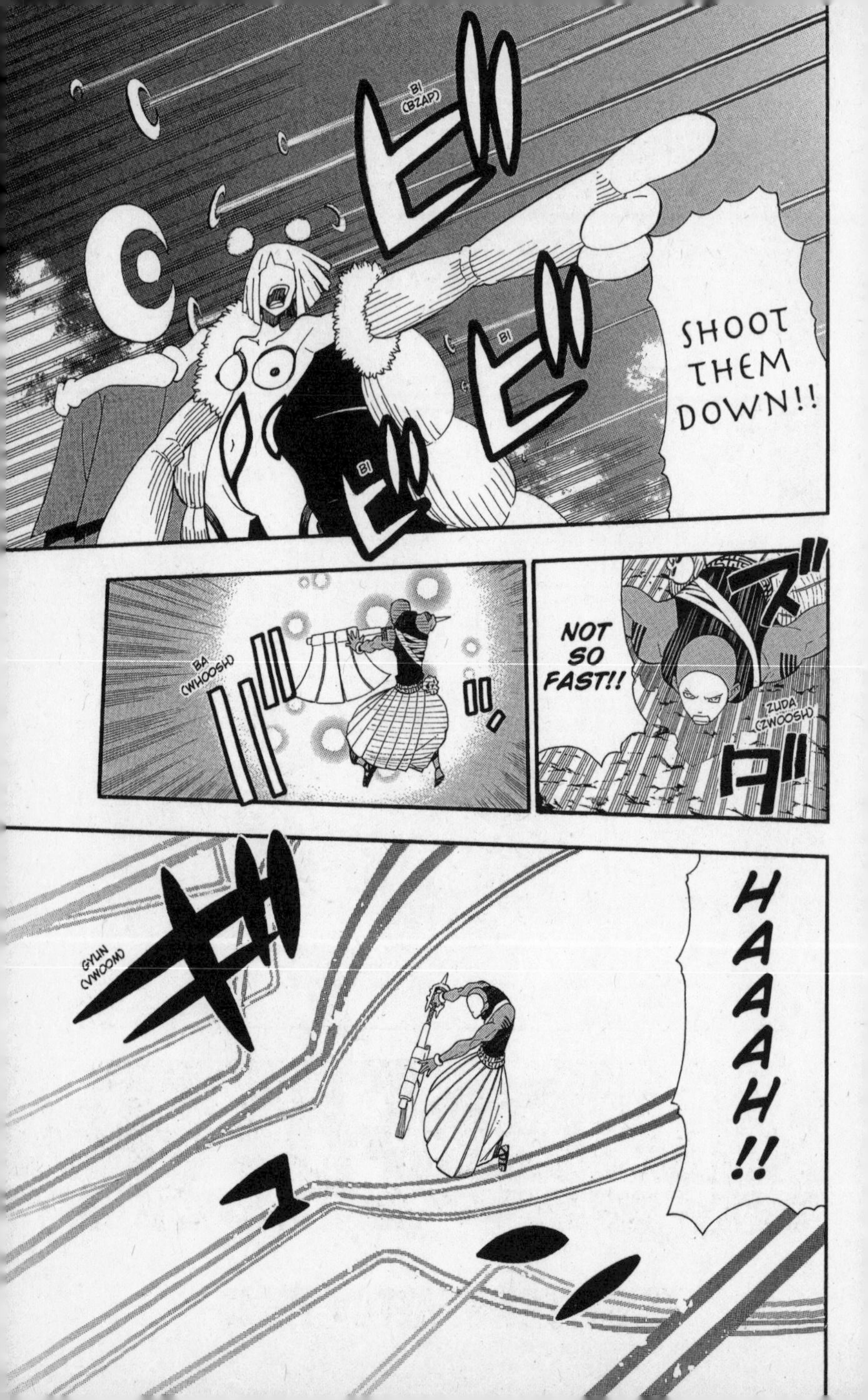
BI (BZAP)
SHOOT THEM DOWN!!
BI
BI
NOT SO FAST!!
ZUDA (ZWOOSH)
BA (WHOOSH)
HAAAAH!!
GYUN (VWOOM)

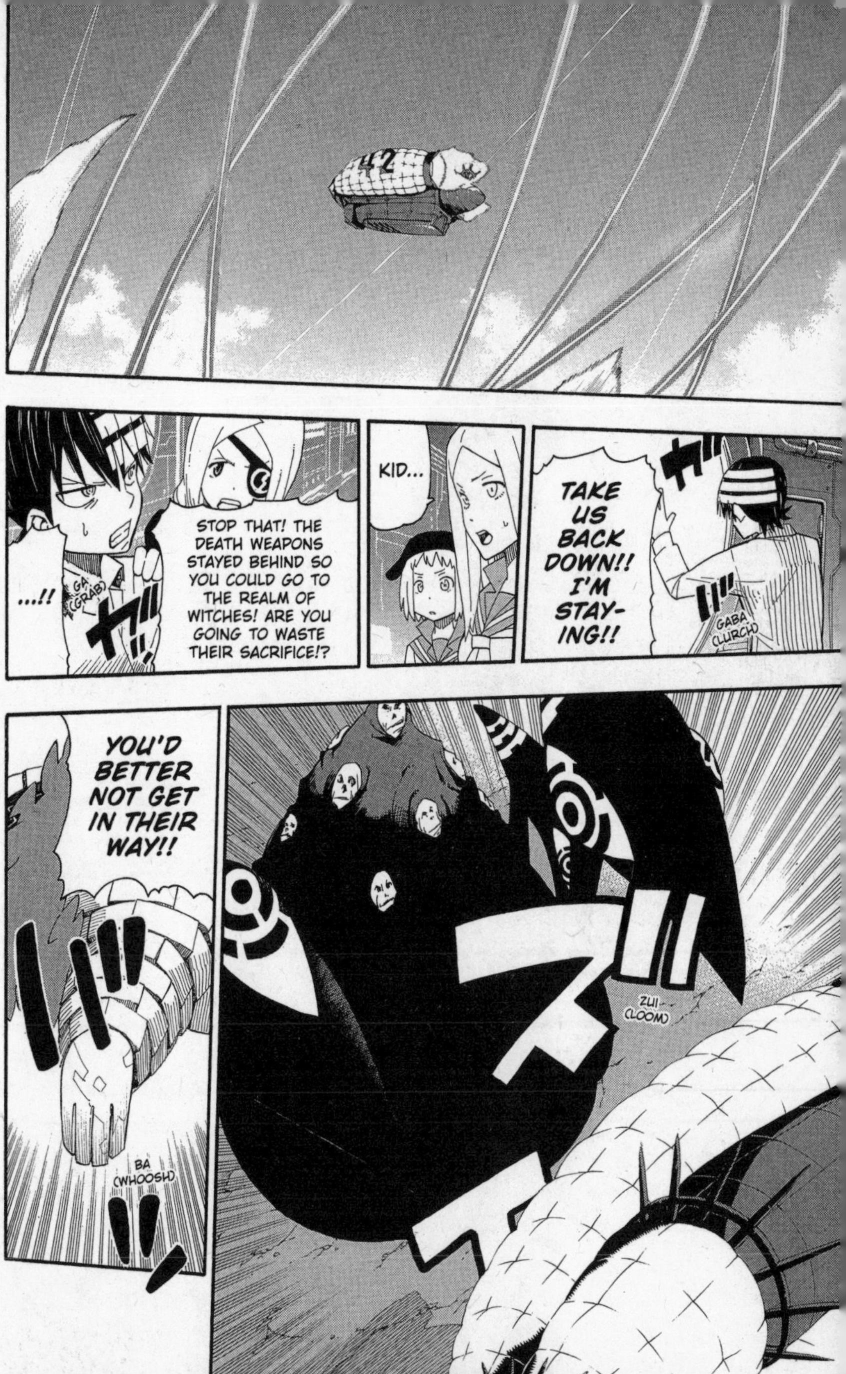
TAKE US BACK DOWN!! I'M STAYING!!
GABA (CLURCH)
KID...
STOP THAT! THE DEATH WEAPONS STAYED BEHIND SO YOU COULD GO TO THE REALM OF WITCHES! ARE YOU GOING TO WASTE THEIR SACRIFICE!?
GA (GRAB)
...!!
ZUI (LOOM)
YOU'D BETTER NOT GET IN THEIR WAY!!
BA (WHOOSH)

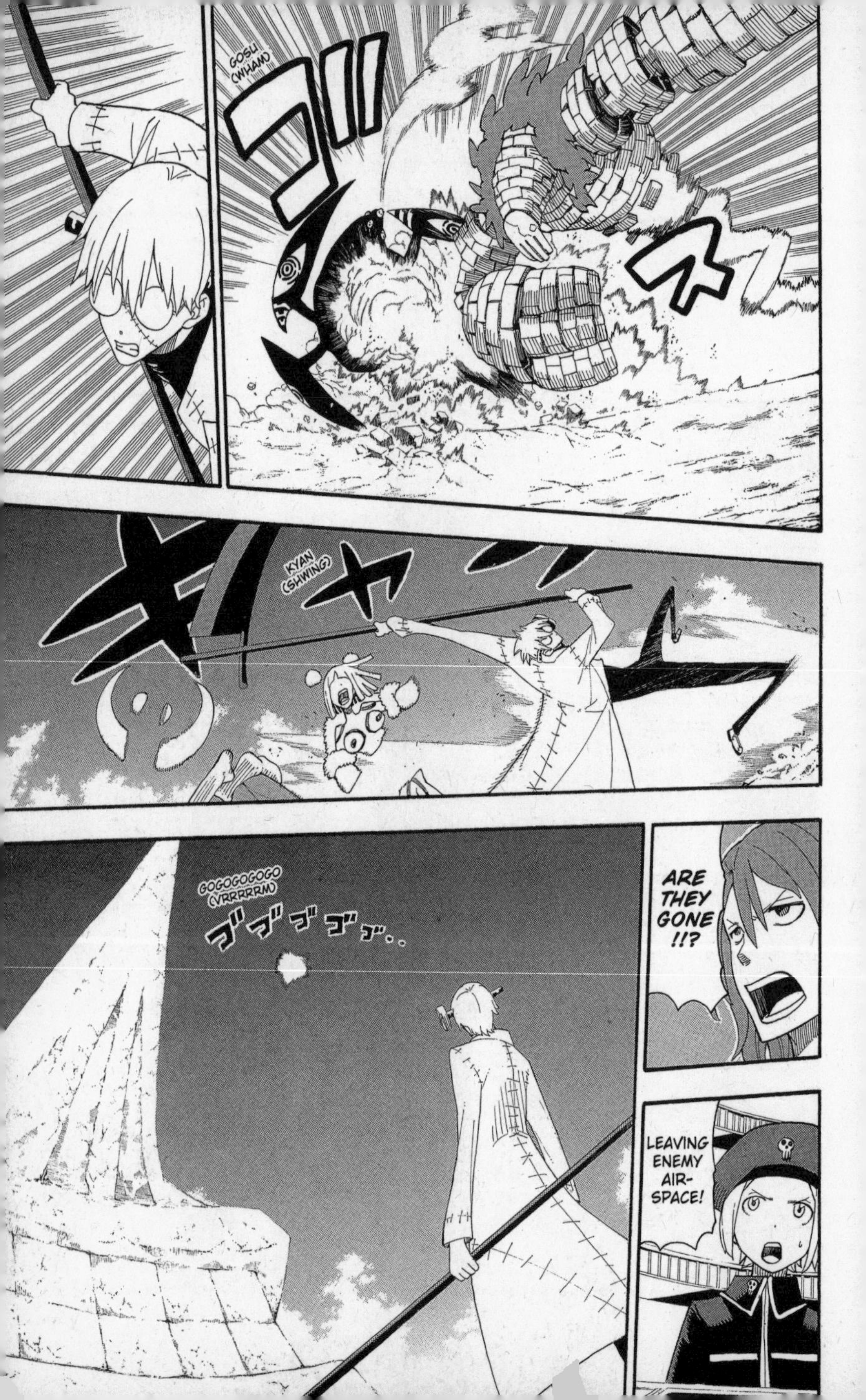
GOSU (WHAM)
ゴッ
KYAN (SHWING)
ギャン
ARE THEY GONE!!?
LEAVING ENEMY AIR-SPACE!
GOGOGOGOGO (VRRRRRM)
ゴゴゴゴゴ・・

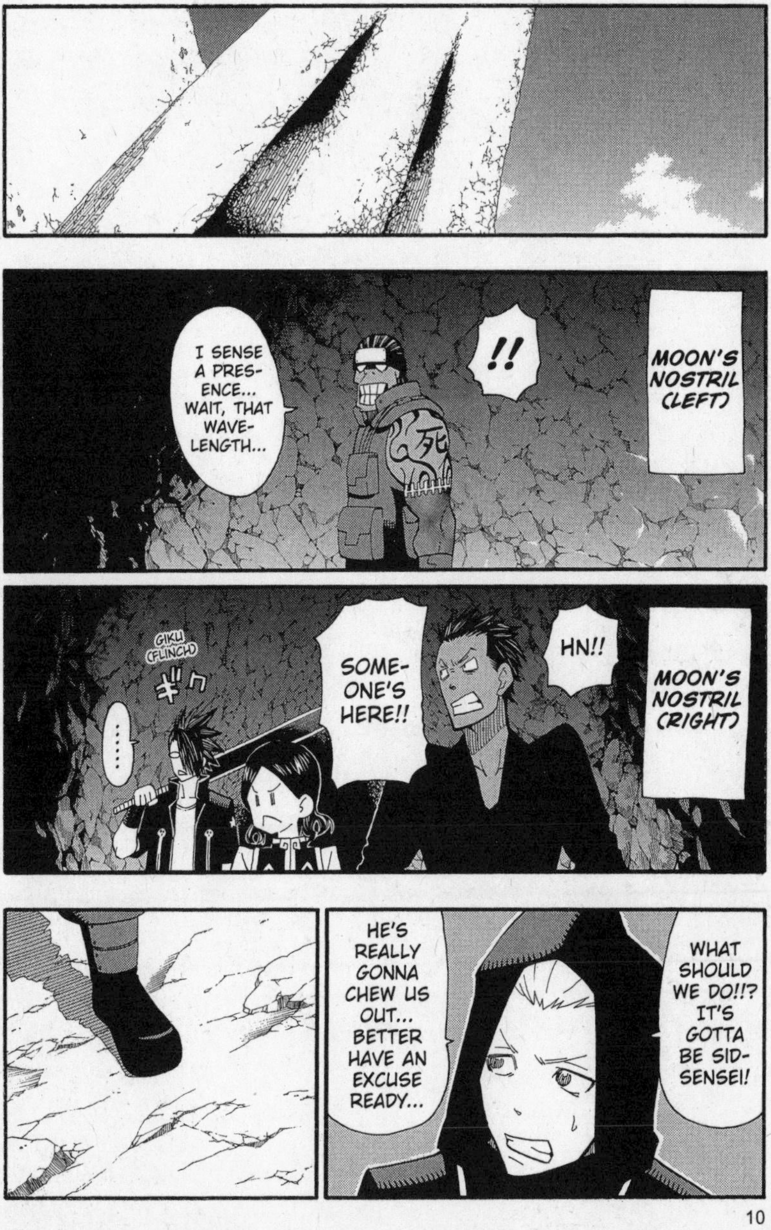
MOON'S NOSTRIL (LEFT)
!!
I SENSE A PRESENCE... WAIT, THAT WAVELENGTH...
MOON'S NOSTRIL (RIGHT)
HN!!
SOMEONE'S HERE!!
GIKU (FLINCH)
ギク
......
WHAT SHOULD WE DO!!? IT'S GOTTA BE SID-SENSEI!
HE'S REALLY GONNA CHEW US OUT... BETTER HAVE AN EXCUSE READY...

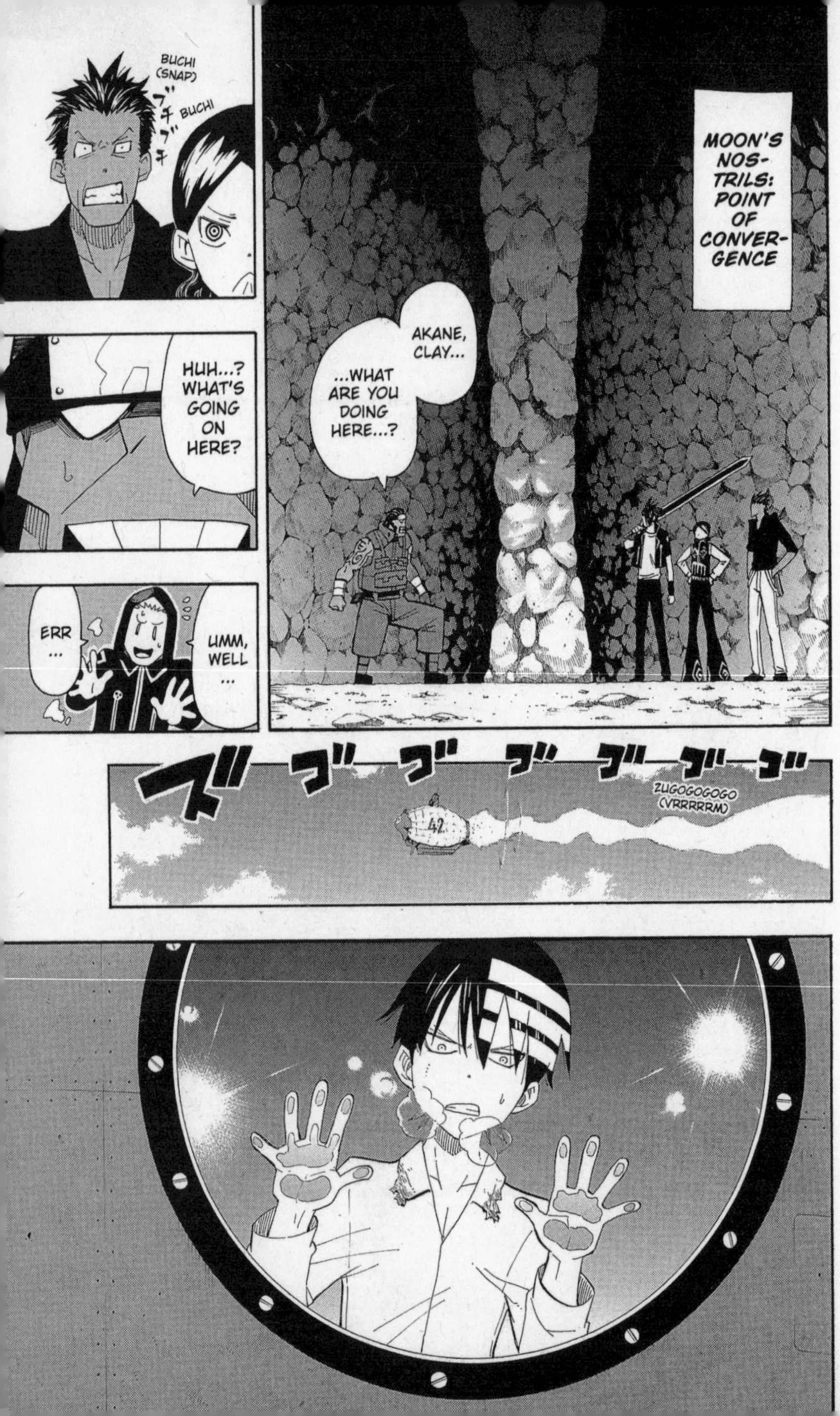
MOON'S NOS-TRILS: POINT OF CONVERGENCE
AKANE, CLAY... ...WHAT ARE YOU DOING HERE...?
BUCHI (SNAP) ブチ BUCHI ブチ
HUH...? WHAT'S GOING ON HERE?
UMM, WELL ...
ERR ...
ズゴゴゴゴゴ
ZUGOGOGOGO (VRRRRRM)

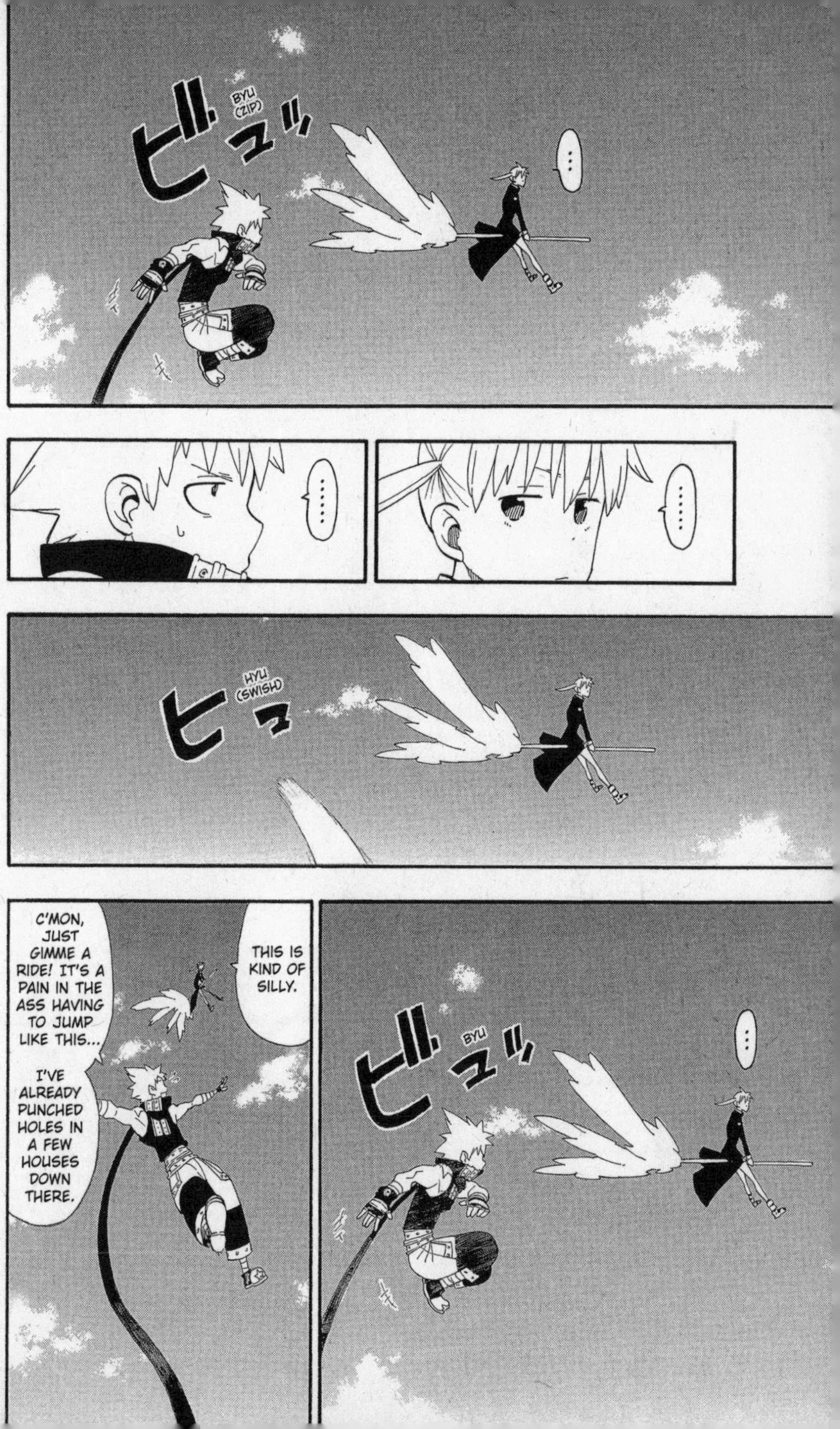
BYU (ZIP)
...
......
......
HYU (SWISH)
...
BYU
THIS IS KIND OF SILLY.
C'MON, JUST GIMME A RIDE! IT'S A PAIN IN THE ASS HAVING TO JUMP LIKE THIS...
I'VE ALREADY PUNCHED HOLES IN A FEW HOUSES DOWN THERE.

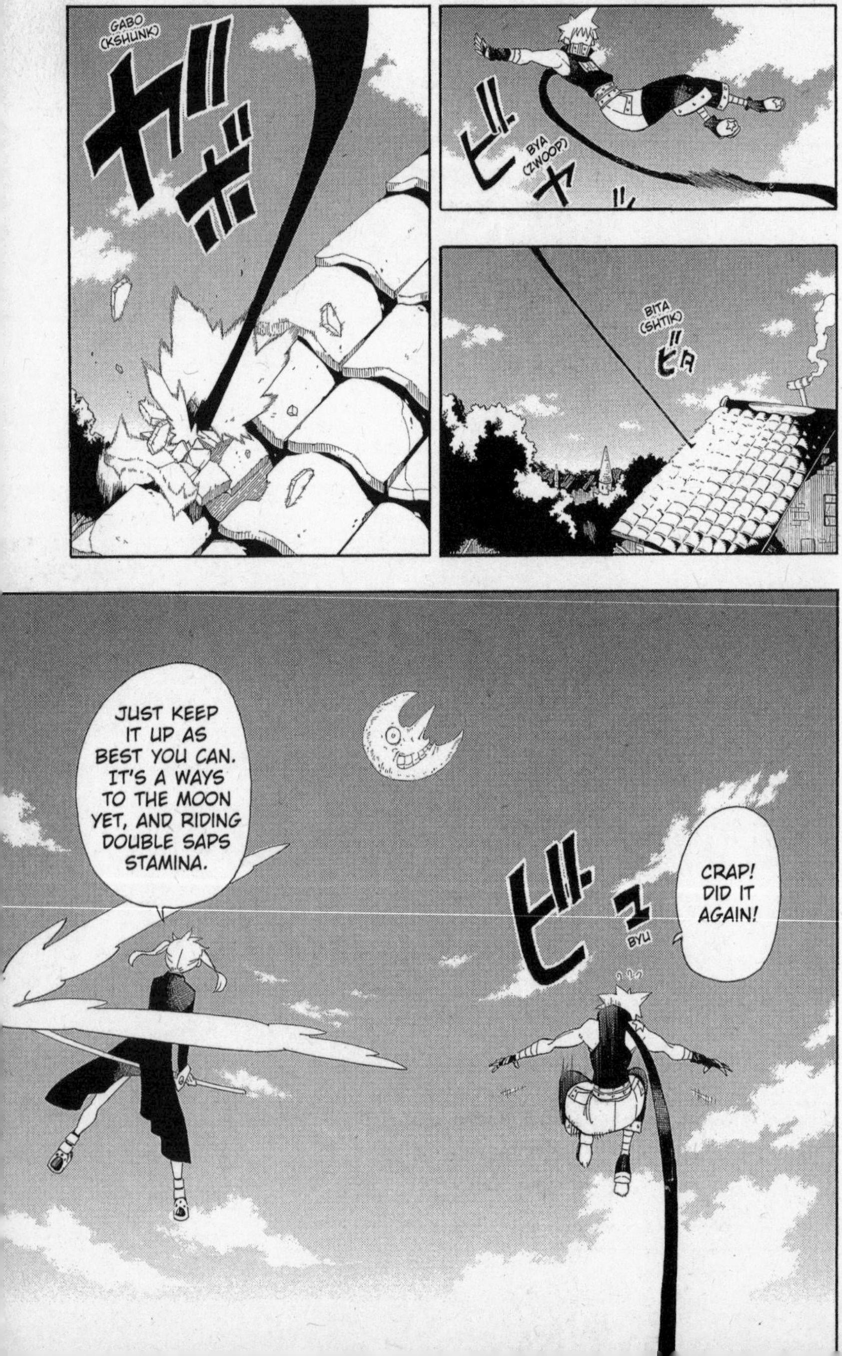
BYA (ZWOOP)
BITA (SHTIK)
GABO (KSHUNK)
CRAP! DID IT AGAIN!
BYU
JUST KEEP IT UP AS BEST YOU CAN. IT'S A WAYS TO THE MOON YET, AND RIDING DOUBLE SAPS STAMINA.

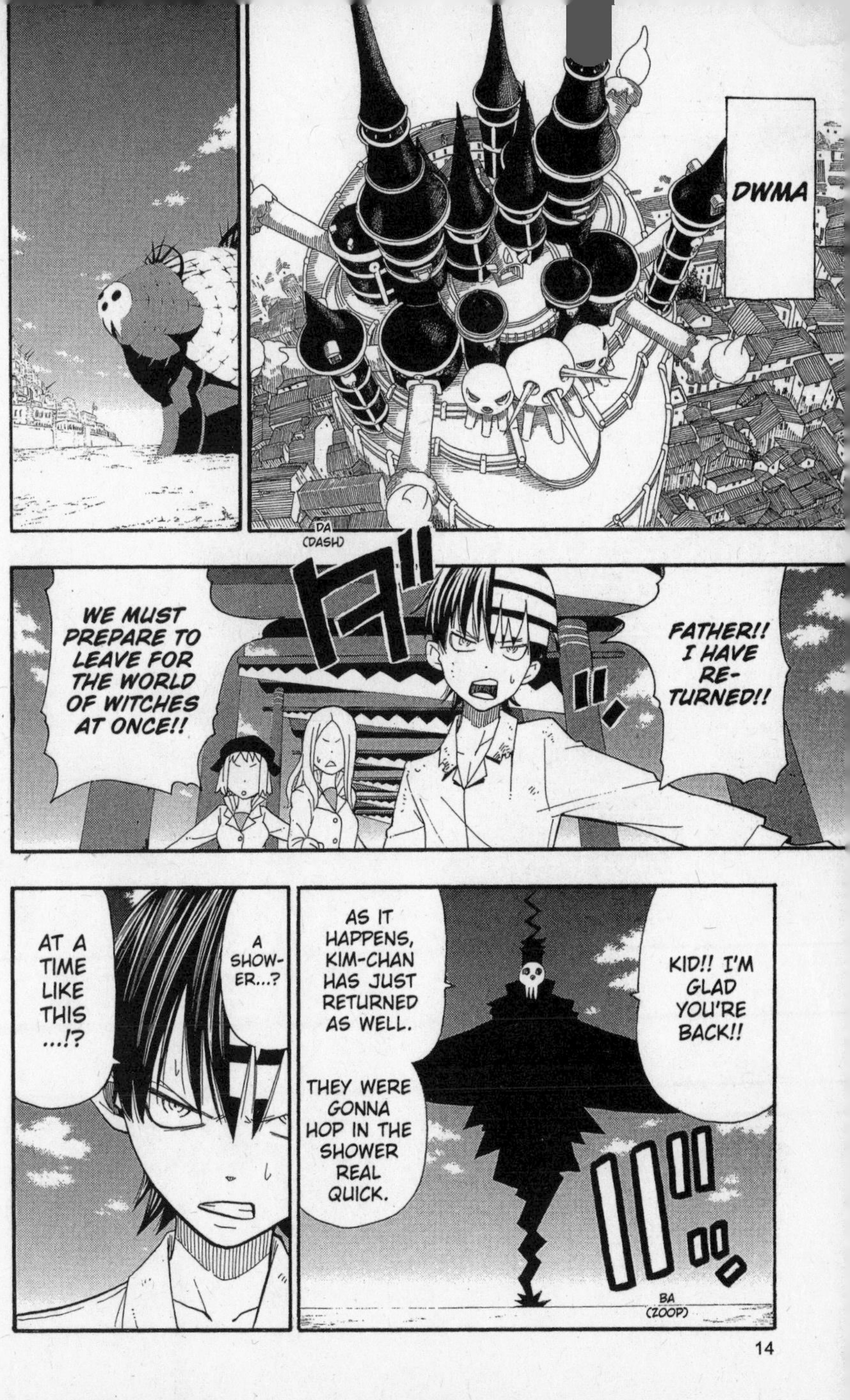
DWMA
DA (DASH)
FATHER!! I HAVE RETURNED!!
WE MUST PREPARE TO LEAVE FOR THE WORLD OF WITCHES AT ONCE!!
KID!! I'M GLAD YOU'RE BACK!!
AS IT HAPPENS, KIM-CHAN HAS JUST RETURNED AS WELL.
THEY WERE GONNA HOP IN THE SHOWER REAL QUICK.
BA (ZOOP)
A SHOWER...?
AT A TIME LIKE THIS...!?

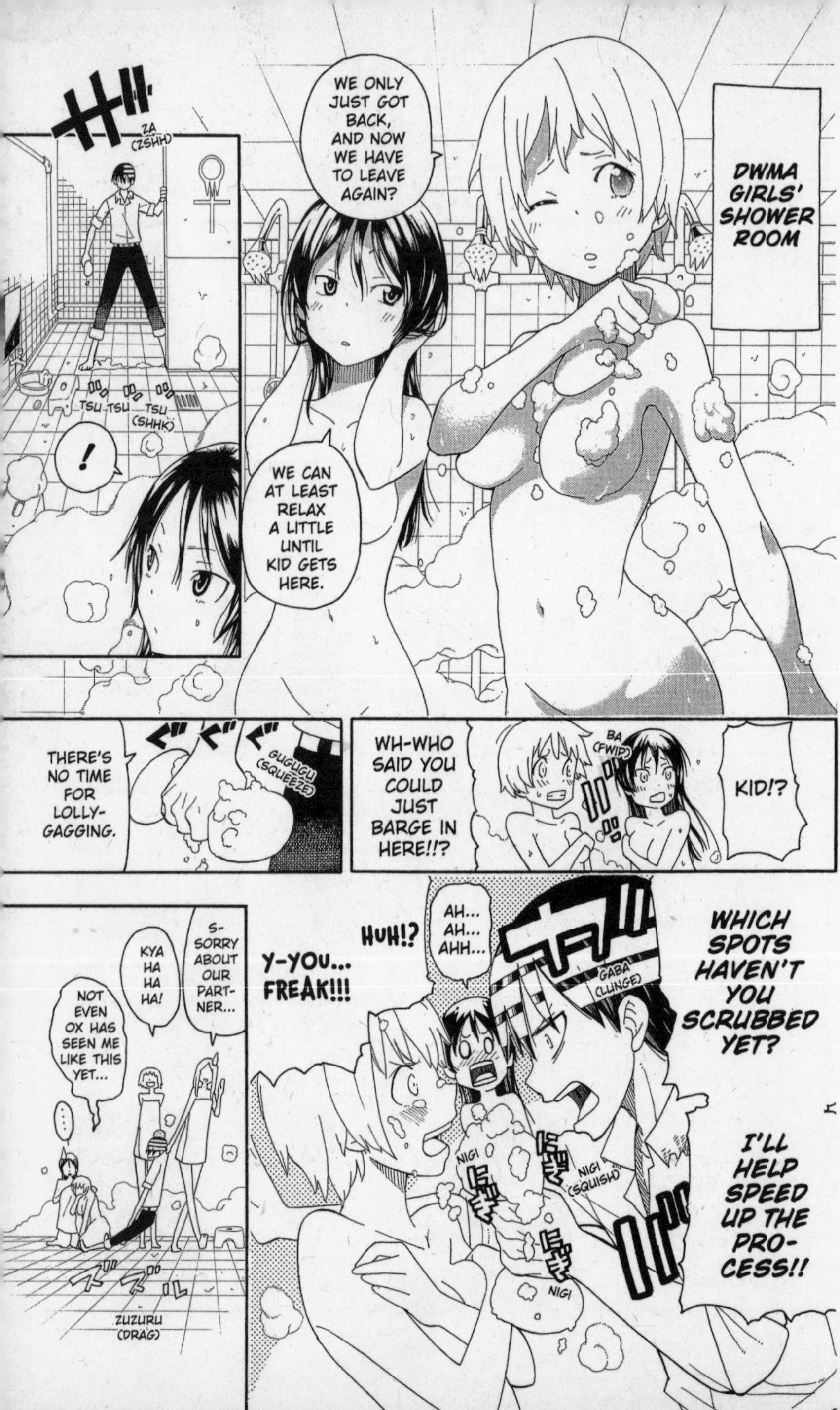
DWMA GIRLS' SHOWER ROOM
WE ONLY JUST GOT BACK, AND NOW WE HAVE TO LEAVE AGAIN?
WE CAN AT LEAST RELAX A LITTLE UNTIL KID GETS HERE.
ZA (ZSHH)
TSU TSU TSU (SHHK)
!
KID!?
BA (FWIP)
WH-WHO SAID YOU COULD JUST BARGE IN HERE!!?
GUGUGU (SQUEEZE)
THERE'S NO TIME FOR LOLLY-GAGGING.
WHICH SPOTS HAVEN'T YOU SCRUBBED YET?
GABA (LUNGE)
AH... AH... AHH...
HUH!?
Y-YOU... FREAK!!!
I'LL HELP SPEED UP THE PRO-CESS!!
NIGI (SQUISH)
NIGI
NIGI
S-SORRY ABOUT OUR PART-NER...
KYA HA HA HA!
NOT EVEN OX HAS SEEN ME LIKE THIS YET...
...
ZUZURU (DRAG)

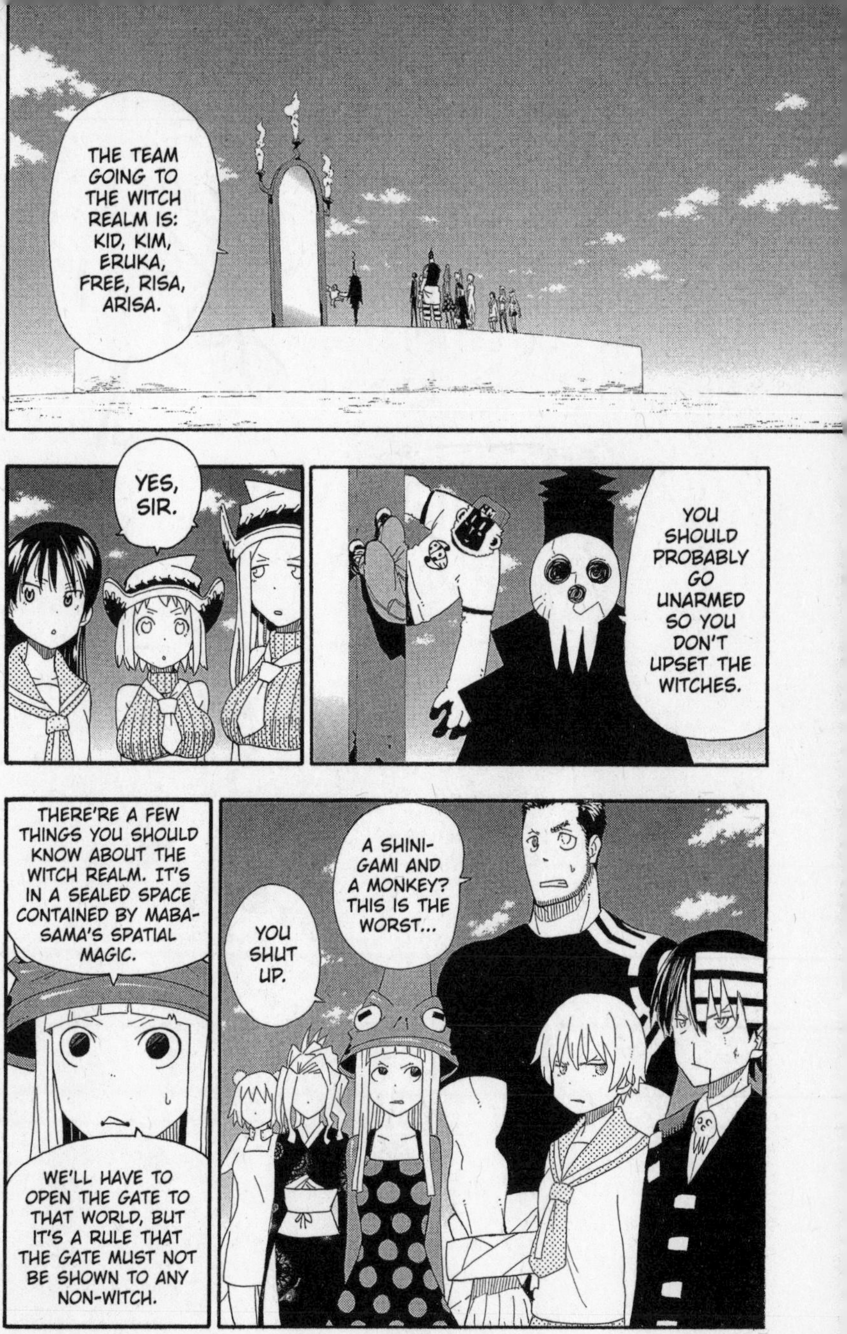
THE TEAM GOING TO THE WITCH REALM IS: KID, KIM, ERUKA, FREE, RISA, ARISA.
YOU SHOULD PROBABLY GO UNARMED SO YOU DON'T UPSET THE WITCHES.
YES, SIR.
A SHINI-GAMI AND A MONKEY? THIS IS THE WORST...
YOU SHUT UP.
THERE'RE A FEW THINGS YOU SHOULD KNOW ABOUT THE WITCH REALM. IT'S IN A SEALED SPACE CONTAINED BY MABA-SAMA'S SPATIAL MAGIC.
WE'LL HAVE TO OPEN THE GATE TO THAT WORLD, BUT IT'S A RULE THAT THE GATE MUST NOT BE SHOWN TO ANY NON-WITCH.

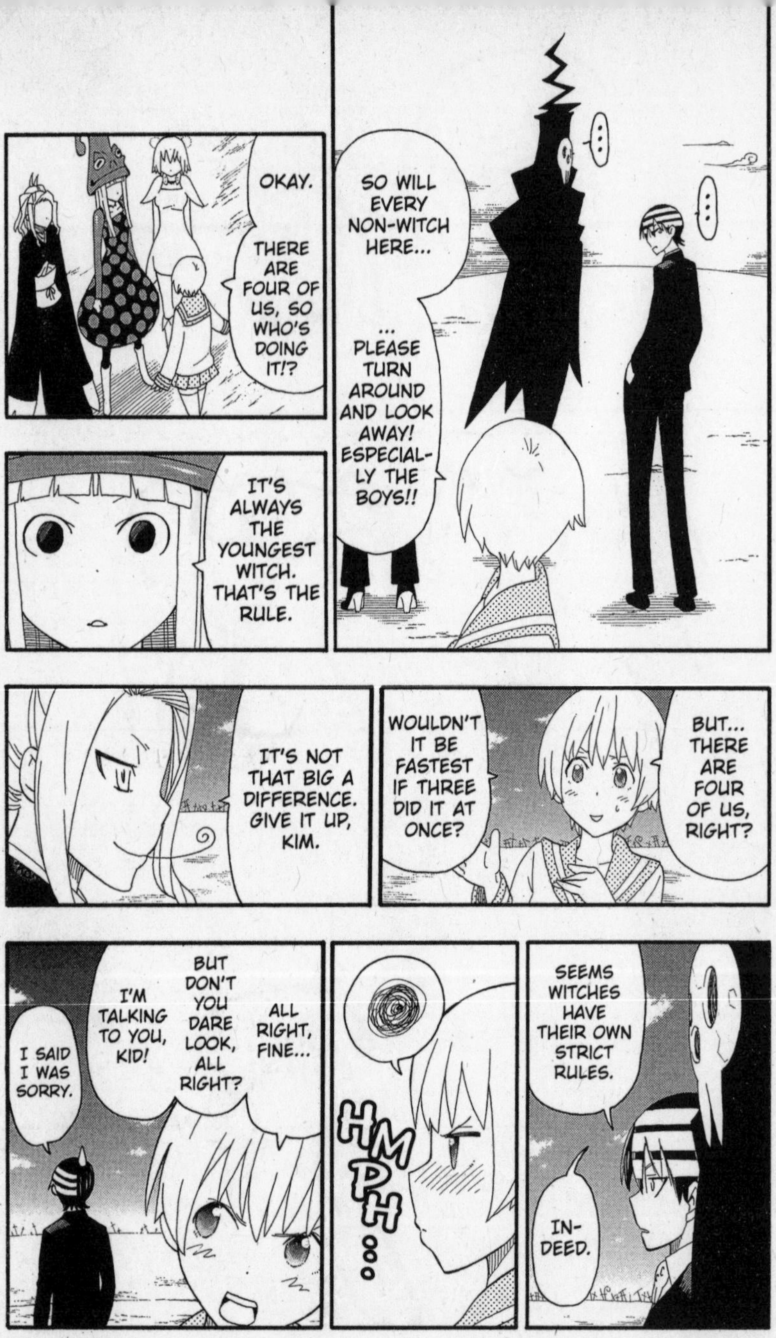
...
...
SO WILL EVERY NON-WITCH HERE...
...PLEASE TURN AROUND AND LOOK AWAY! ESPECIALLY THE BOYS!!
OKAY.
THERE ARE FOUR OF US, SO WHO'S DOING IT!?
IT'S ALWAYS THE YOUNGEST WITCH. THAT'S THE RULE.
BUT... THERE ARE FOUR OF US, RIGHT?
WOULDN'T IT BE FASTEST IF THREE DID IT AT ONCE?
IT'S NOT THAT BIG A DIFFERENCE. GIVE IT UP, KIM.
SEEMS WITCHES HAVE THEIR OWN STRICT RULES.
IN-DEED.
HMPH...
ALL RIGHT, FINE...
BUT DON'T YOU DARE LOOK, ALL RIGHT?
I'M TALKING TO YOU, KID!
I SAID I WAS SORRY.

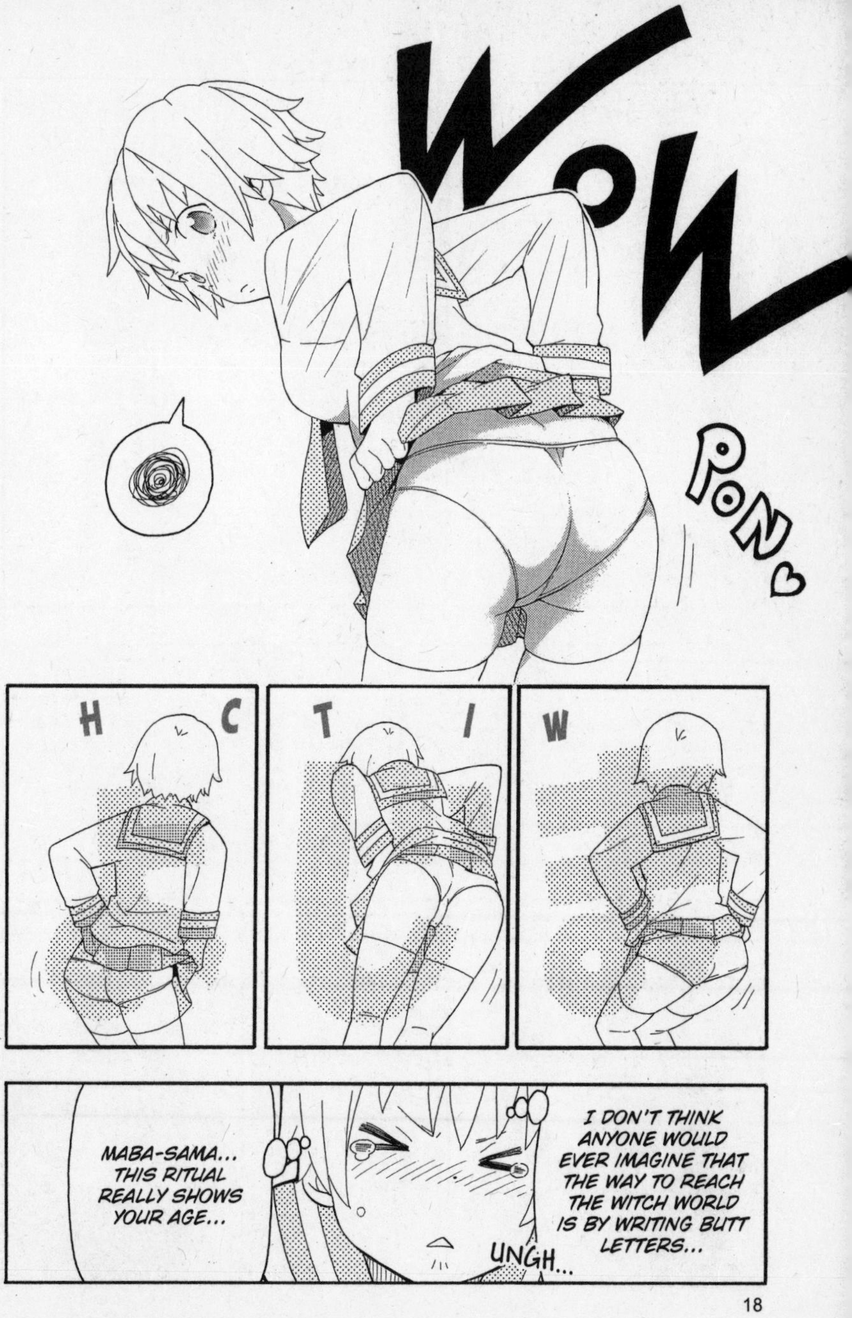
WOW
PON♥
W
I
T
C
H
I DON'T THINK ANYONE WOULD EVER IMAGINE THAT THE WAY TO REACH THE WITCH WORLD IS BY WRITING BUTT LETTERS...
UNGH...
MABA-SAMA... THIS RITUAL REALLY SHOWS YOUR AGE...

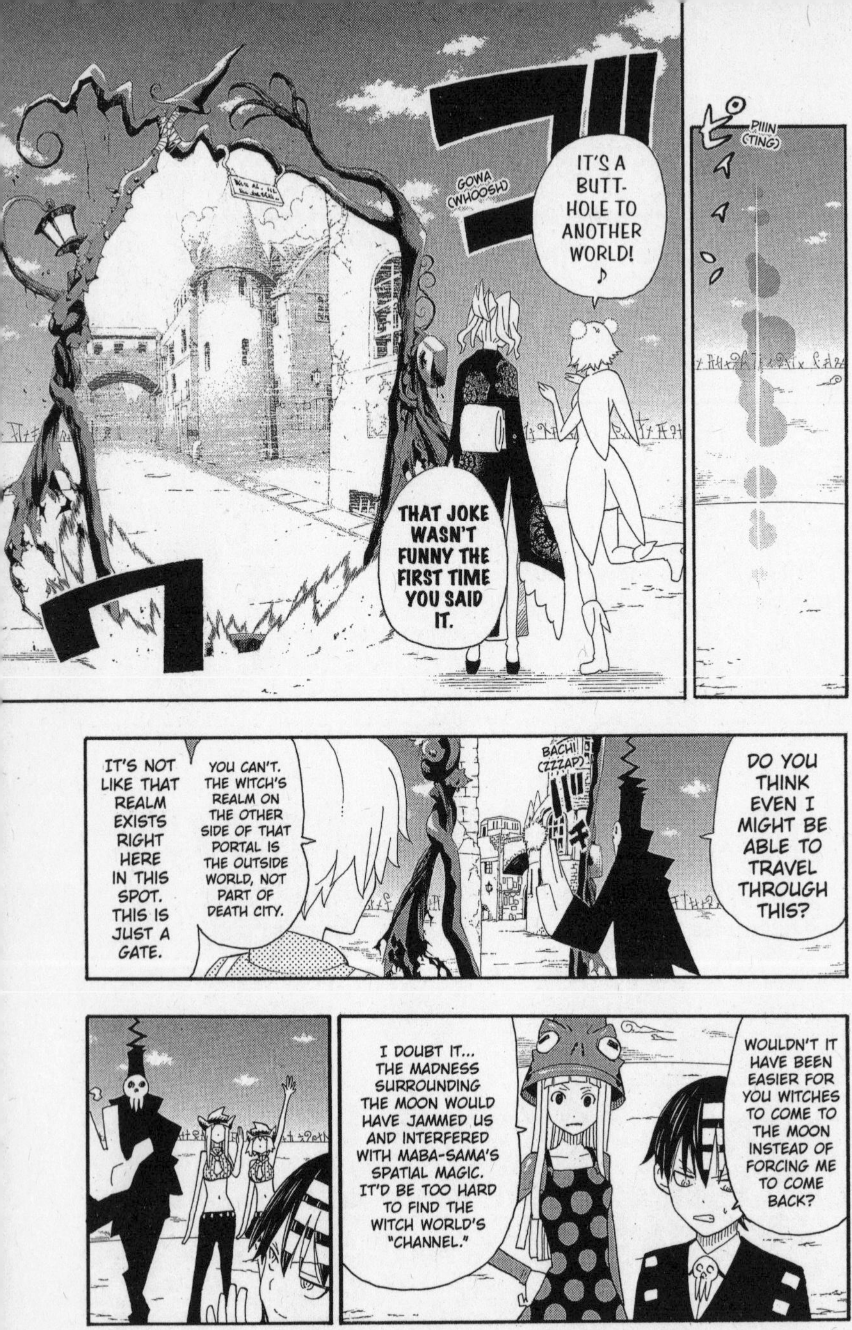
PIIIN (TING)
IT'S A BUTT-HOLE TO ANOTHER WORLD! ♪
GOWA (WHOOSH)
THAT JOKE WASN'T FUNNY THE FIRST TIME YOU SAID IT.
DO YOU THINK EVEN I MIGHT BE ABLE TO TRAVEL THROUGH THIS?
BACHI (ZZZAP)
YOU CAN'T. THE WITCH'S REALM ON THE OTHER SIDE OF THAT PORTAL IS THE OUTSIDE WORLD, NOT PART OF DEATH CITY.
IT'S NOT LIKE THAT REALM EXISTS RIGHT HERE IN THIS SPOT. THIS IS JUST A GATE.
WOULDN'T IT HAVE BEEN EASIER FOR YOU WITCHES TO COME TO THE MOON INSTEAD OF FORCING ME TO COME BACK?
I DOUBT IT... THE MADNESS SURROUNDING THE MOON WOULD HAVE JAMMED US AND INTERFERED WITH MABA-SAMA'S SPATIAL MAGIC. IT'D BE TOO HARD TO FIND THE WITCH WORLD'S "CHANNEL."

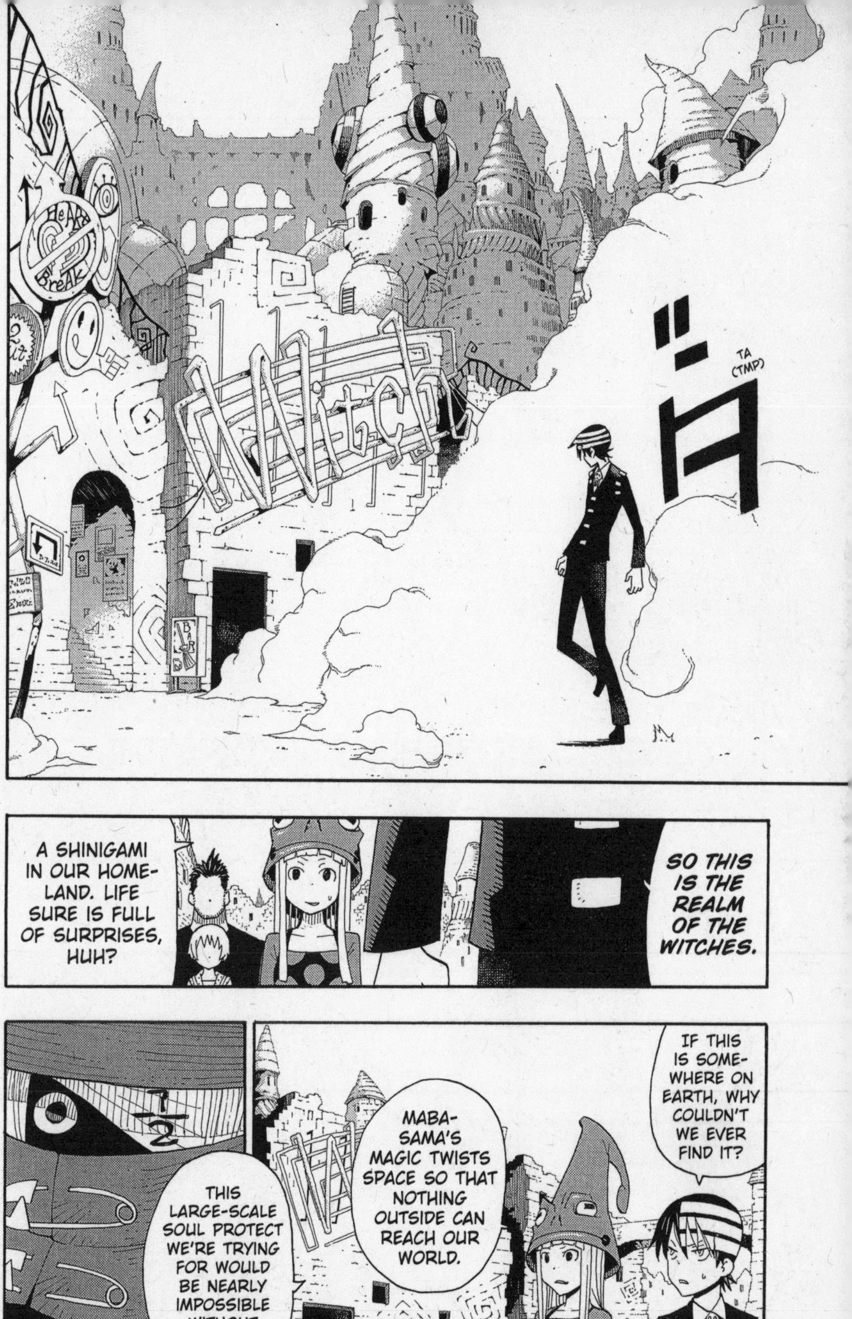
Witch
TA (TMP)
SO THIS IS THE REALM OF THE WITCHES.
A SHINIGAMI IN OUR HOME-LAND. LIFE SURE IS FULL OF SURPRISES, HUH?
IF THIS IS SOME-WHERE ON EARTH, WHY COULDN'T WE EVER FIND IT?
MABA-SAMA'S MAGIC TWISTS SPACE SO THAT NOTHING OUTSIDE CAN REACH OUR WORLD.
THIS LARGE-SCALE SOUL PROTECT WE'RE TRYING FOR WOULD BE NEARLY IMPOSSIBLE WITHOUT HER HELP.

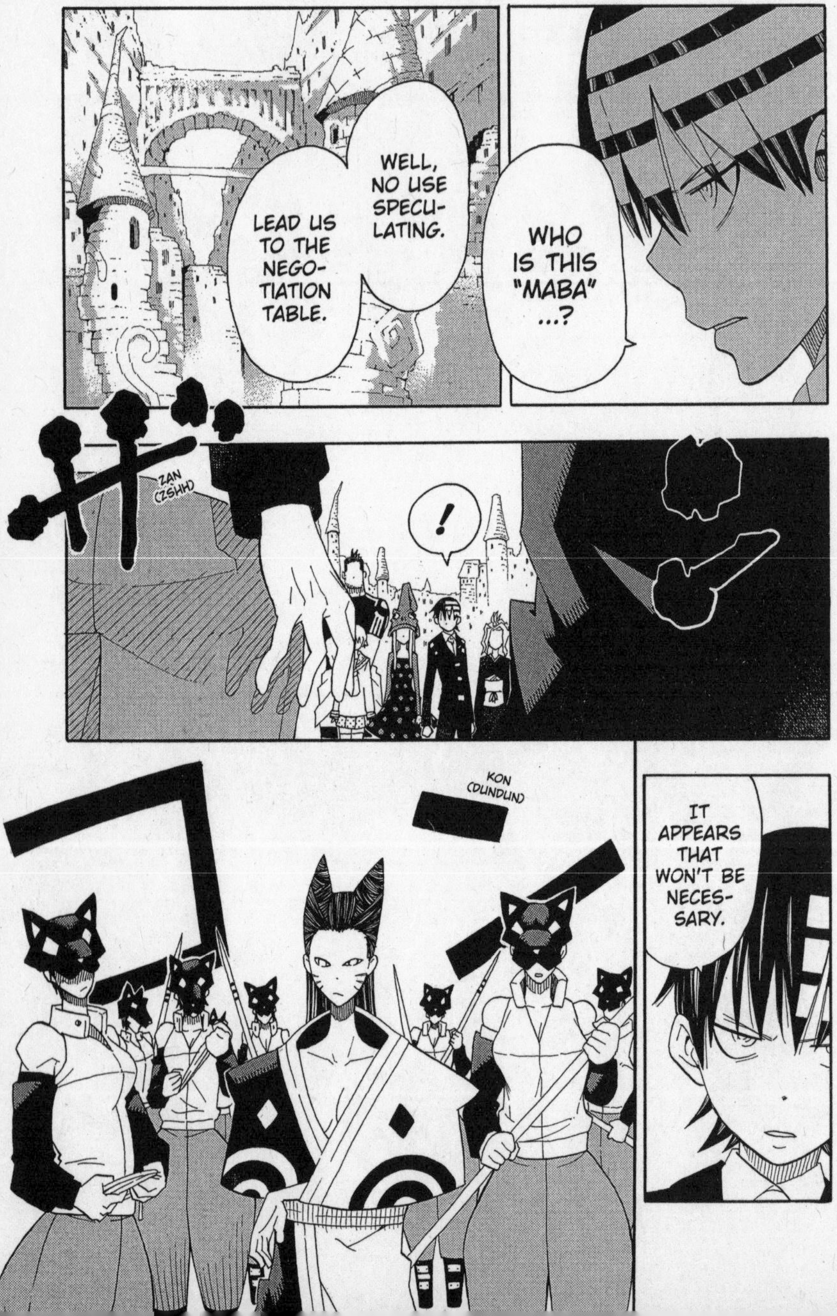
WHO IS THIS "MABA" ...?
WELL, NO USE SPECU-LATING.
LEAD US TO THE NEGO-TIATION TABLE.
ZAN (ZSHH)
!
IT APPEARS THAT WON'T BE NECES-SARY.
KON (DUNDUN)

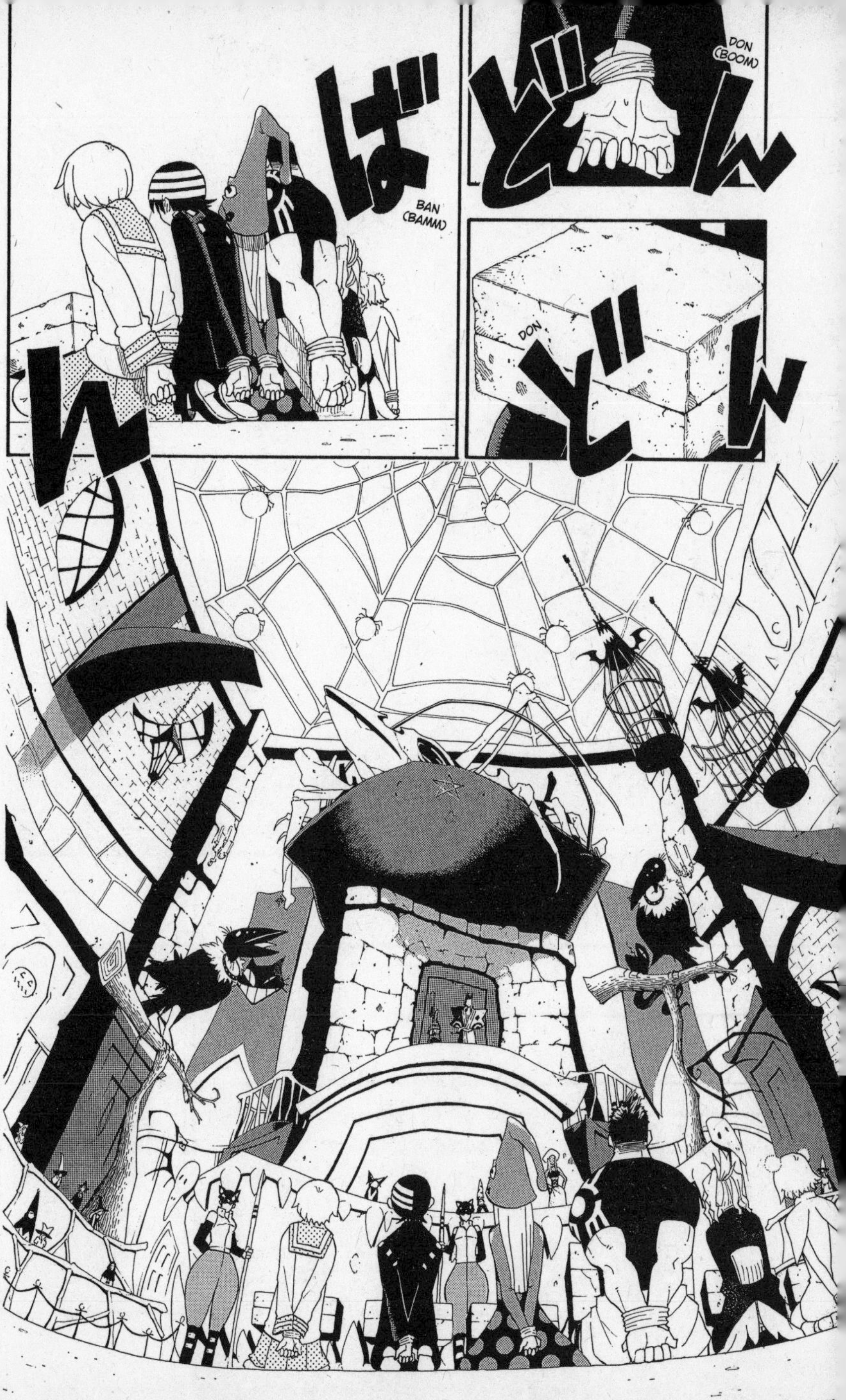
どん
DON (BOOM)
どん
DON
ばん
BAN (BAMM)

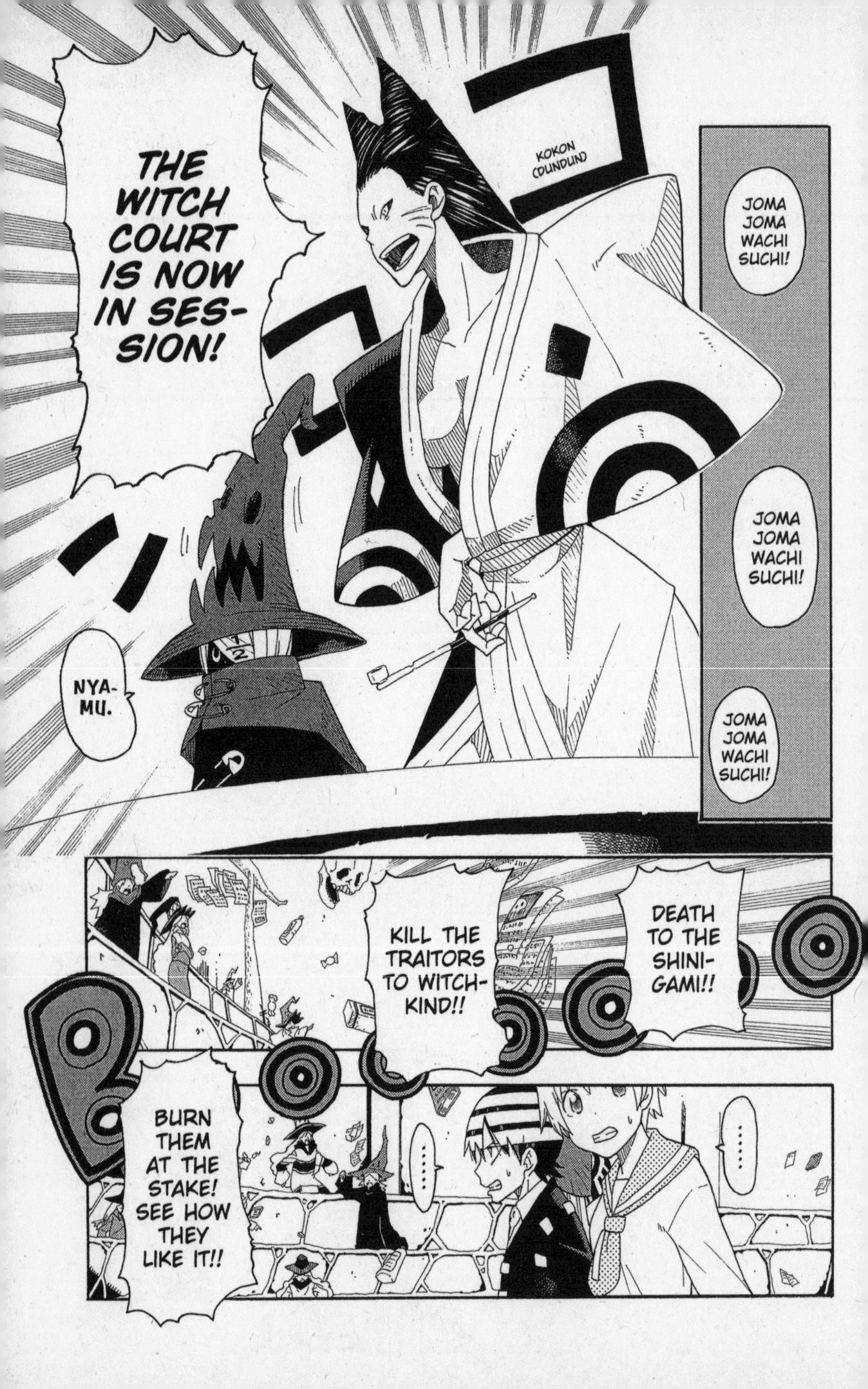
KOKON DUNDUN
JOMA JOMA WACHI SUCHI!
JOMA JOMA WACHI SUCHI!
JOMA JOMA WACHI SUCHI!
THE WITCH COURT IS NOW IN SES-SION!
NYA-MU.
DEATH TO THE SHINI-GAMI!!
KILL THE TRAITORS TO WITCH-KIND!!
BURN THEM AT THE STAKE! SEE HOW THEY LIKE IT!!
......
......

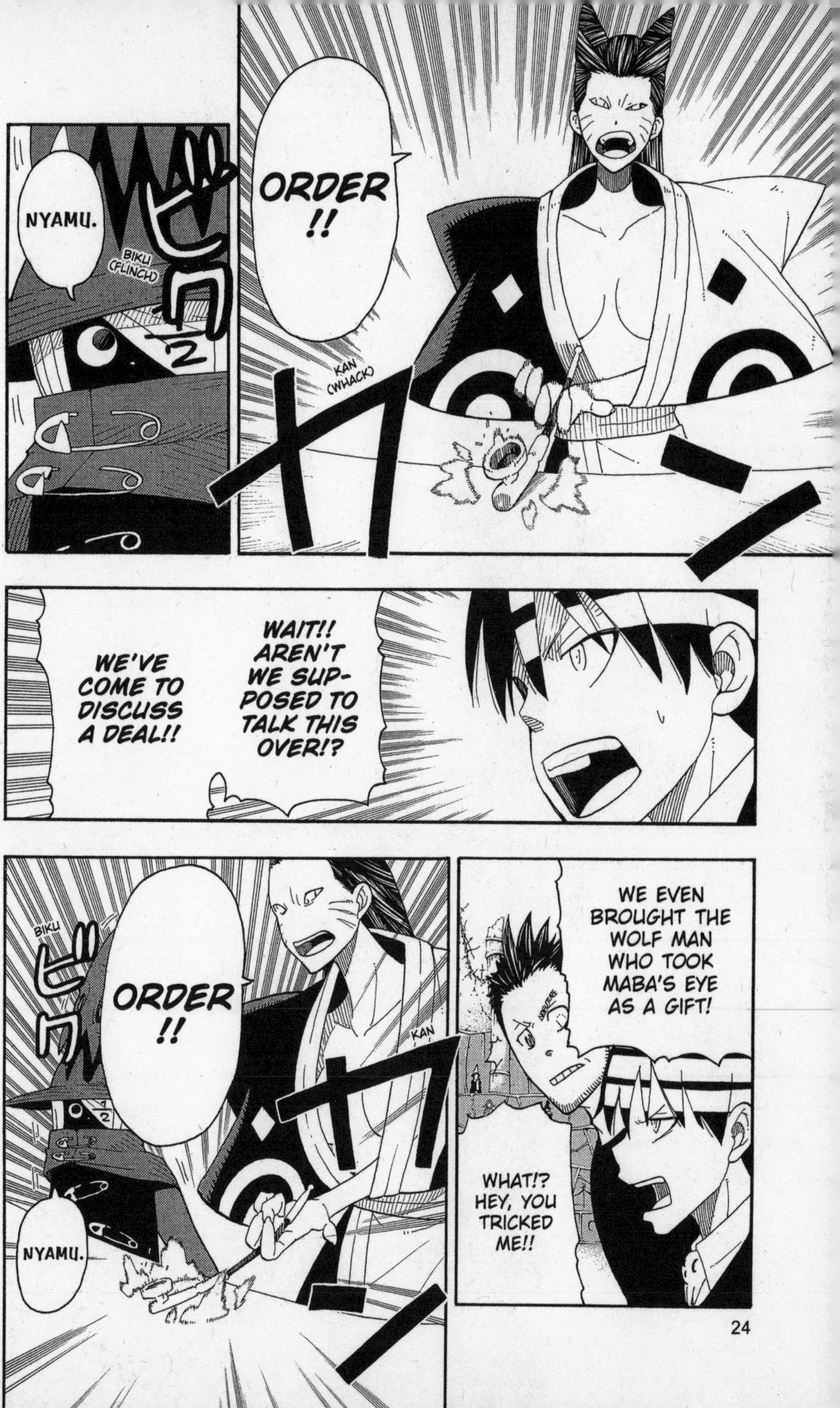
ORDER !!
KAN (WHACK)
BIKU (FLINCH)
NYAMU.
WAIT!! AREN'T WE SUP-POSED TO TALK THIS OVER!?
WE'VE COME TO DISCUSS A DEAL!!
WE EVEN BROUGHT THE WOLF MAN WHO TOOK MABA'S EYE AS A GIFT!
WHAT!? HEY, YOU TRICKED ME!!
ORDER !!
KAN
BIKU
NYAMU.

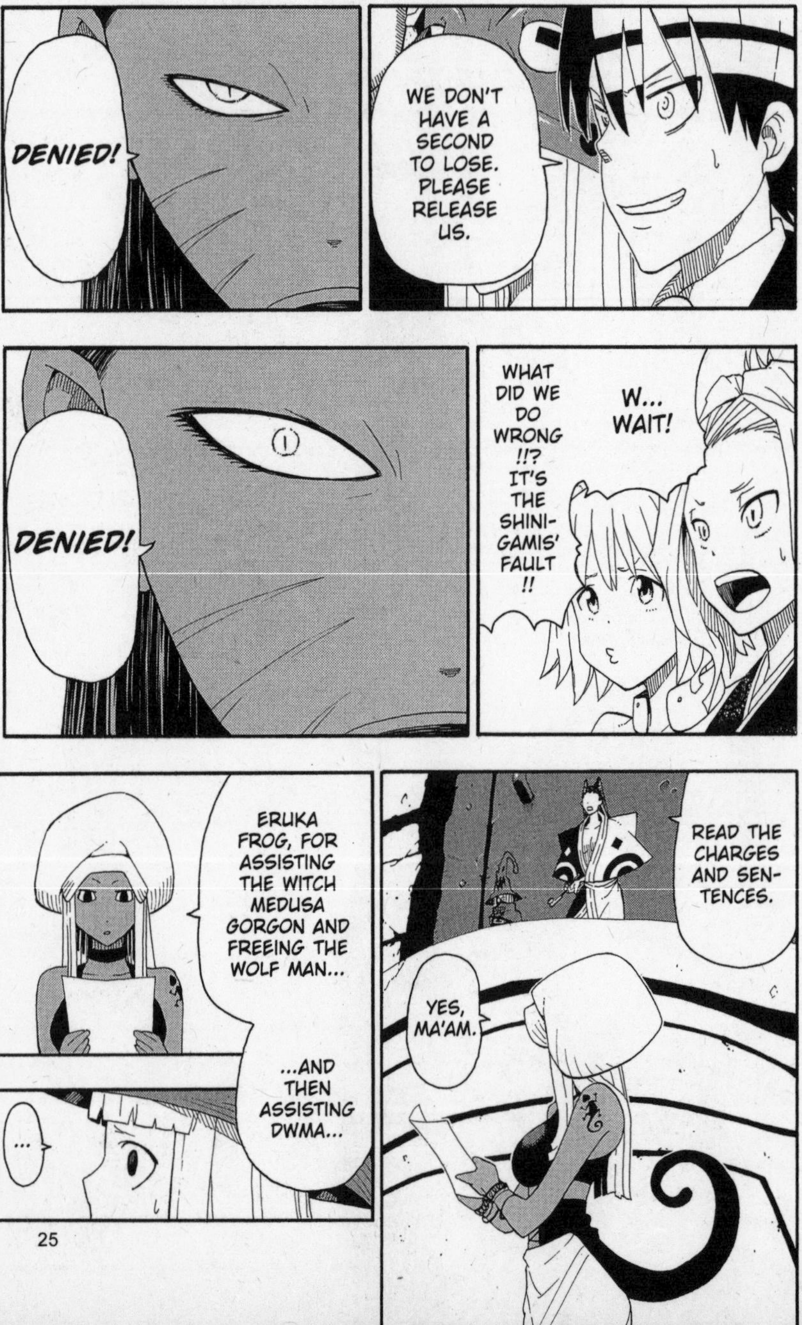
WE DON'T HAVE A SECOND TO LOSE. PLEASE RELEASE US.
DENIED!
W... WAIT!
WHAT DID WE DO WRONG!!? IT'S THE SHINIGAMIS' FAULT!!
DENIED!
READ THE CHARGES AND SENTENCES.
YES, MA'AM.
ERUKA FROG, FOR ASSISTING THE WITCH MEDUSA GORGON AND FREEING THE WOLF MAN...
...AND THEN ASSISTING DWMA...
...

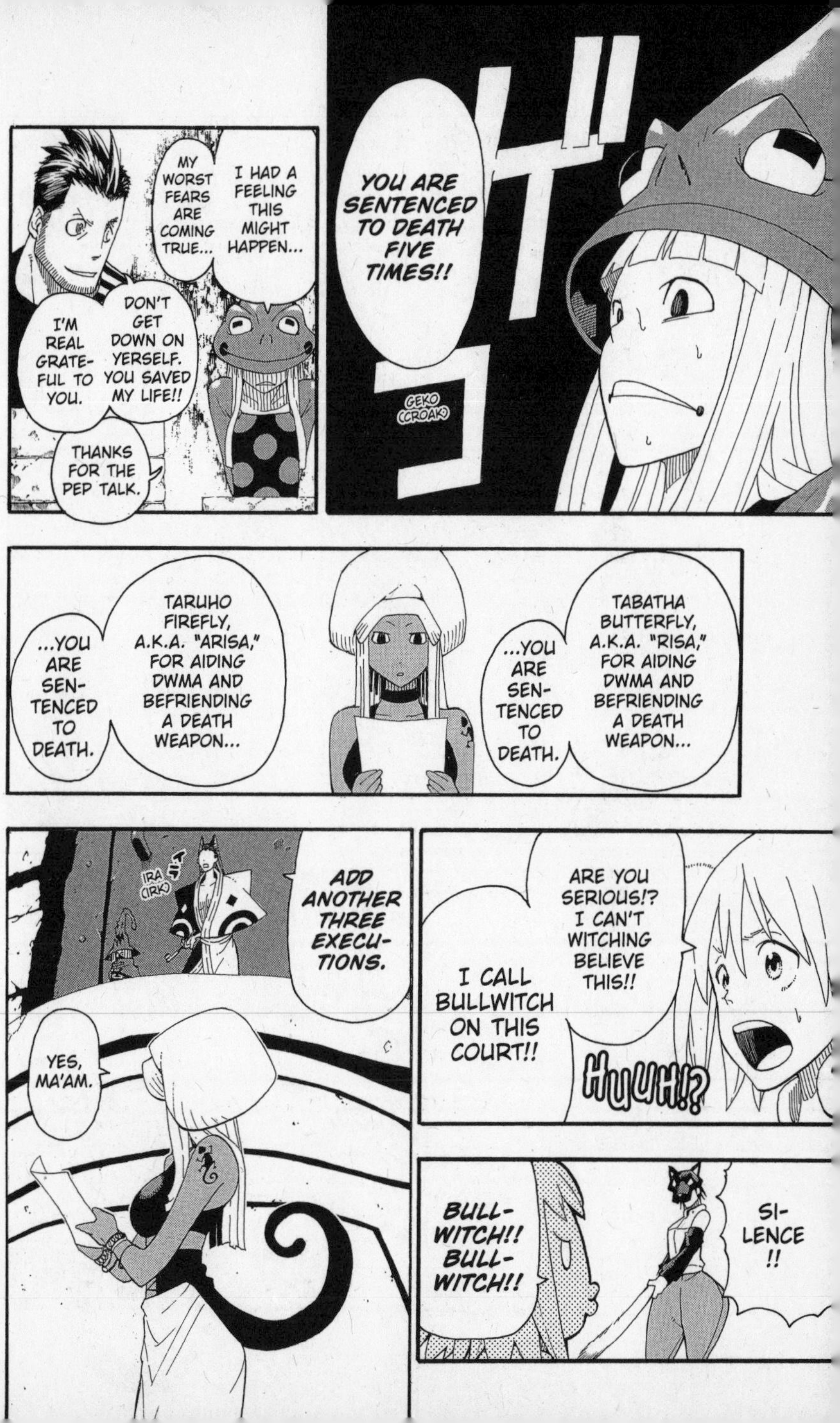
YOU ARE SENTENCED TO DEATH FIVE TIMES!!
GEKO (CROAK)
I HAD A FEELING THIS MIGHT HAPPEN...
MY WORST FEARS ARE COMING TRUE...
DON'T GET DOWN ON YERSELF. YOU SAVED MY LIFE!!
I'M REAL GRATEFUL TO YOU.
THANKS FOR THE PEP TALK.
TABATHA BUTTERFLY, A.K.A. "RISA," FOR AIDING DWMA AND BEFRIENDING A DEATH WEAPON...
...YOU ARE SENTENCED TO DEATH.
TARUHO FIREFLY, A.K.A. "ARISA," FOR AIDING DWMA AND BEFRIENDING A DEATH WEAPON...
...YOU ARE SENTENCED TO DEATH.
ARE YOU SERIOUS!? I CAN'T WITCHING BELIEVE THIS!!
I CALL BULLWITCH ON THIS COURT!!
HUUH!?
SI-LENCE!!
BULL-WITCH!! BULL-WITCH!!
ADD ANOTHER THREE EXECU-TIONS.
IRA (IRK)
YES, MA'AM.

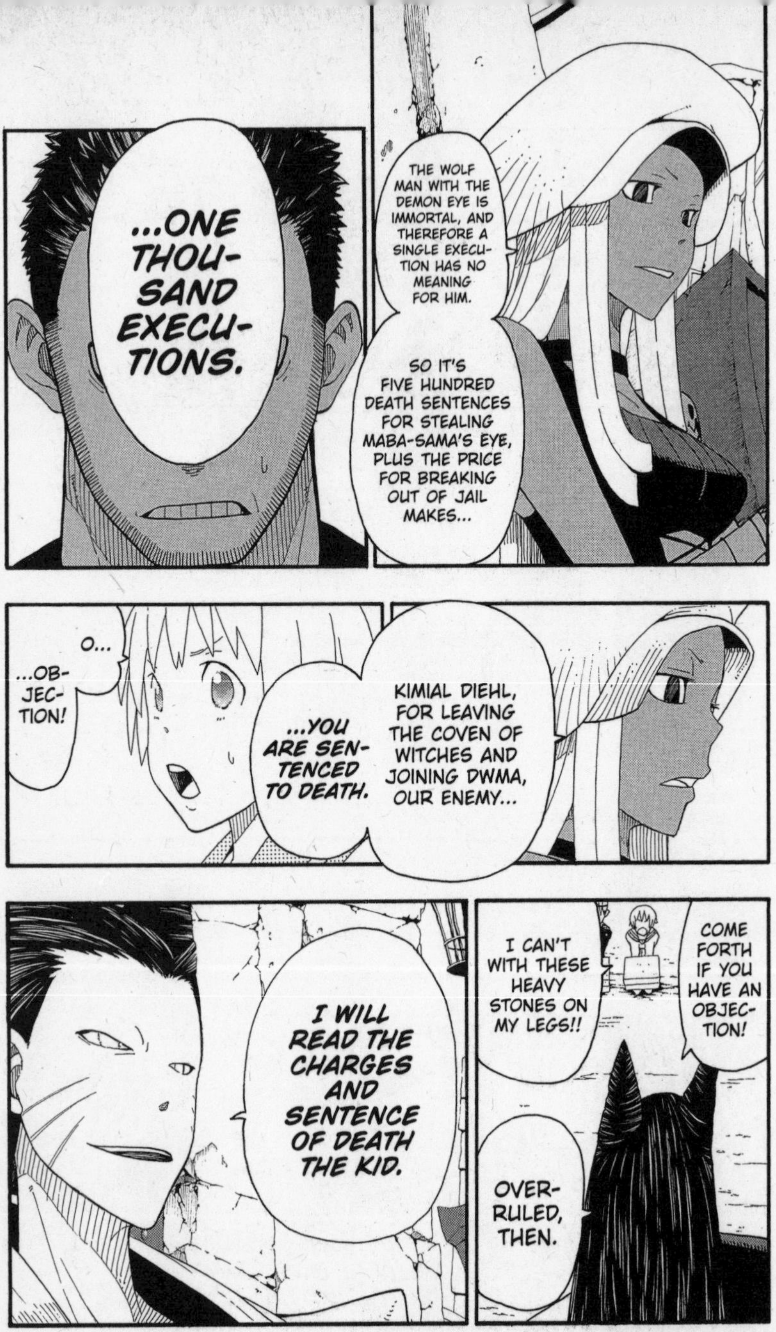
THE WOLF MAN WITH THE DEMON EYE IS IMMORTAL, AND THEREFORE A SINGLE EXECUTION HAS NO MEANING FOR HIM.
SO IT'S FIVE HUNDRED DEATH SENTENCES FOR STEALING MABA-SAMA'S EYE, PLUS THE PRICE FOR BREAKING OUT OF JAIL MAKES...
...ONE THOUSAND EXECUTIONS.
KIMIAL DIEHL, FOR LEAVING THE COVEN OF WITCHES AND JOINING DWMA, OUR ENEMY...
...YOU ARE SENTENCED TO DEATH.
O...
...OBJECTION!
COME FORTH IF YOU HAVE AN OBJECTION!
I CAN'T WITH THESE HEAVY STONES ON MY LEGS!!
OVERRULED, THEN.
I WILL READ THE CHARGES AND SENTENCE OF DEATH THE KID.

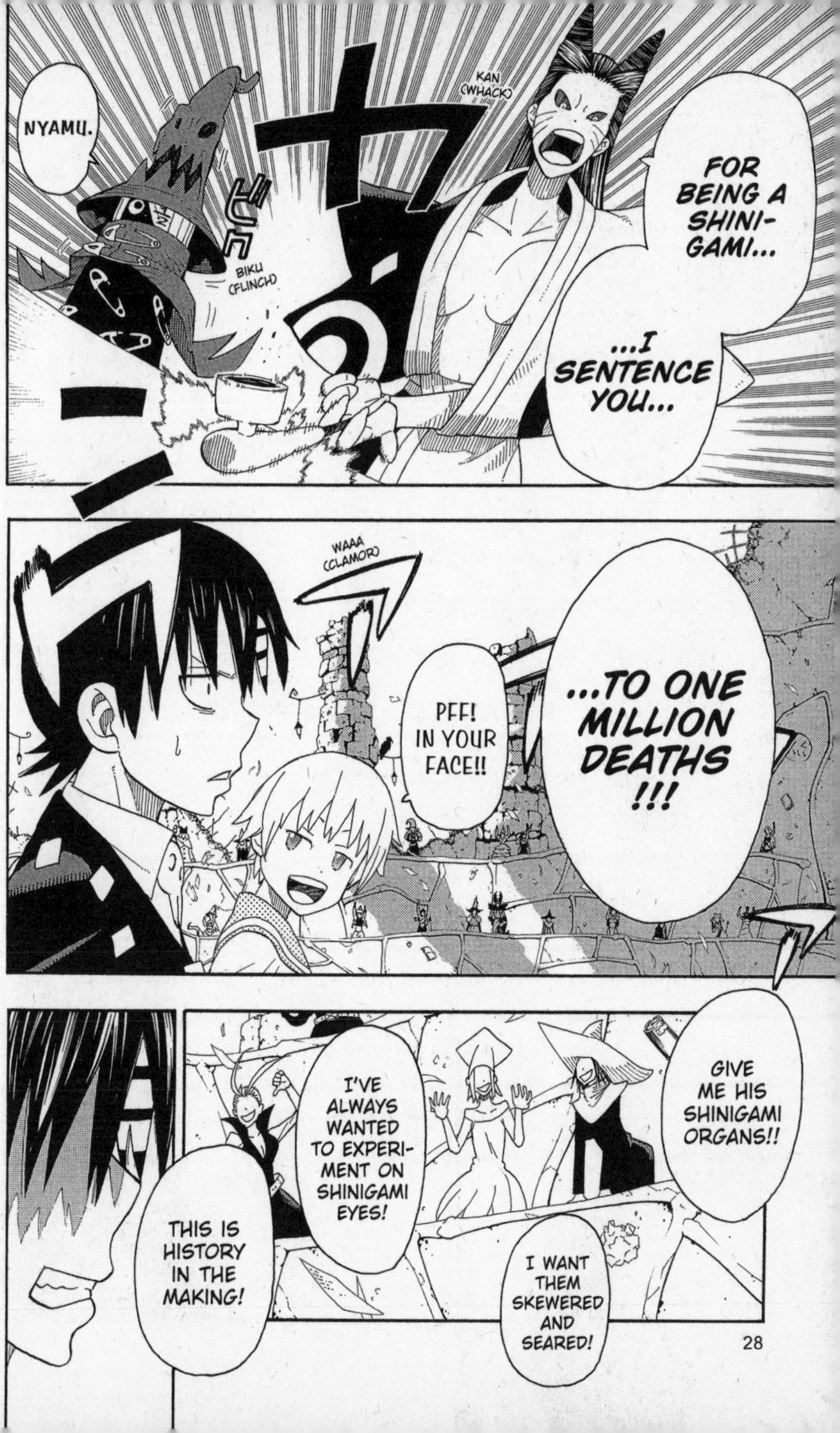
FOR BEING A SHINI-GAMI...
...I SENTENCE YOU...
KAN (WHACK)
NYAMU.
BIKU (FLINCH)
...TO ONE MILLION DEATHS!!!
PFF! IN YOUR FACE!!
WAAA (CLAMOR)
GIVE ME HIS SHINIGAMI ORGANS!!
I'VE ALWAYS WANTED TO EXPERI-MENT ON SHINIGAMI EYES!
I WANT THEM SKEWERED AND SEARED!
THIS IS HISTORY IN THE MAKING!

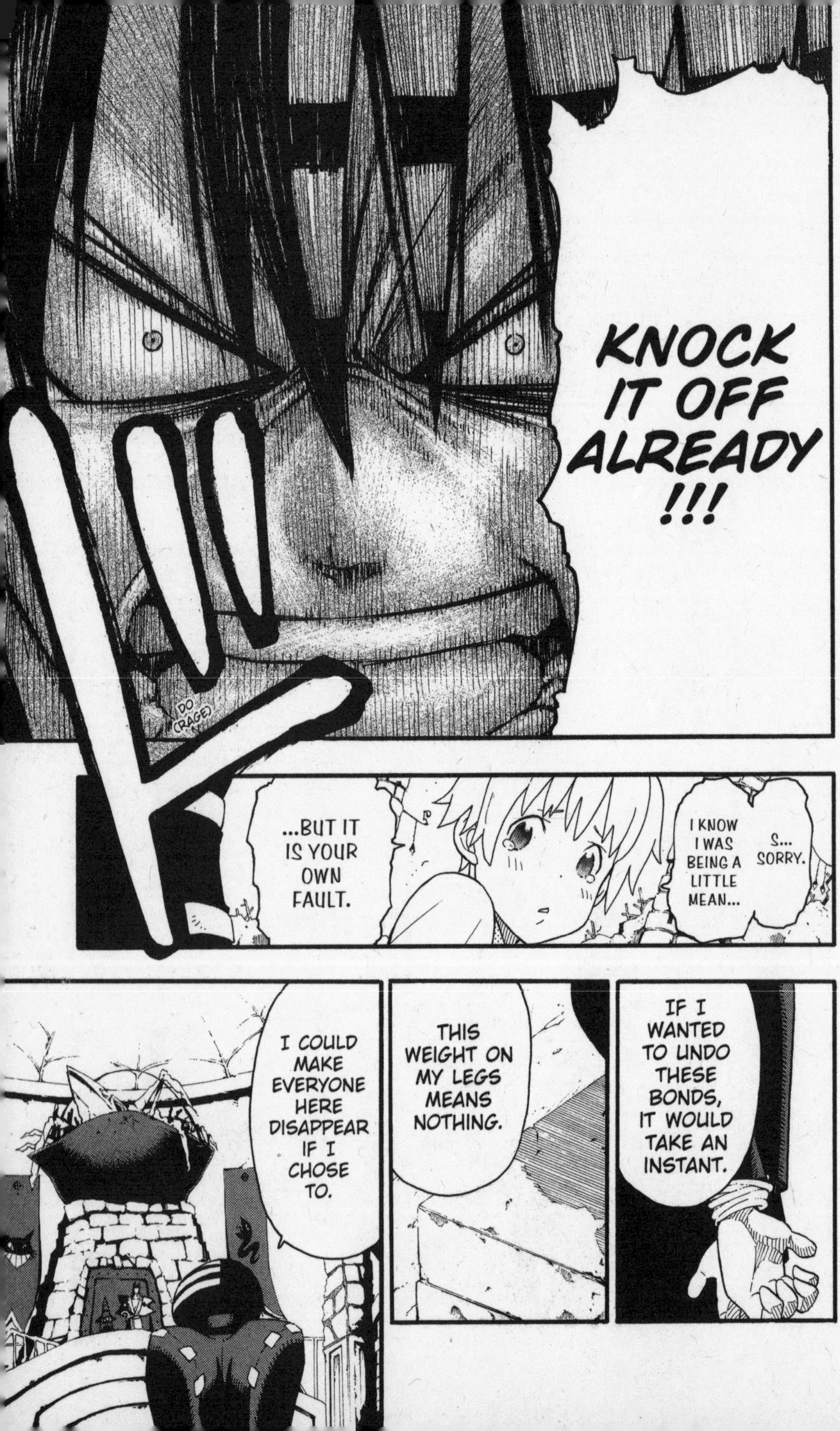
KNOCK IT OFF ALREADY!!!
DO (RAGE)
S... SORRY.
I KNOW I WAS BEING A LITTLE MEAN...
...BUT IT IS YOUR OWN FAULT.
IF I WANTED TO UNDO THESE BONDS, IT WOULD TAKE AN INSTANT.
THIS WEIGHT ON MY LEGS MEANS NOTHING.
I COULD MAKE EVERYONE HERE DISAPPEAR IF I CHOSE TO.

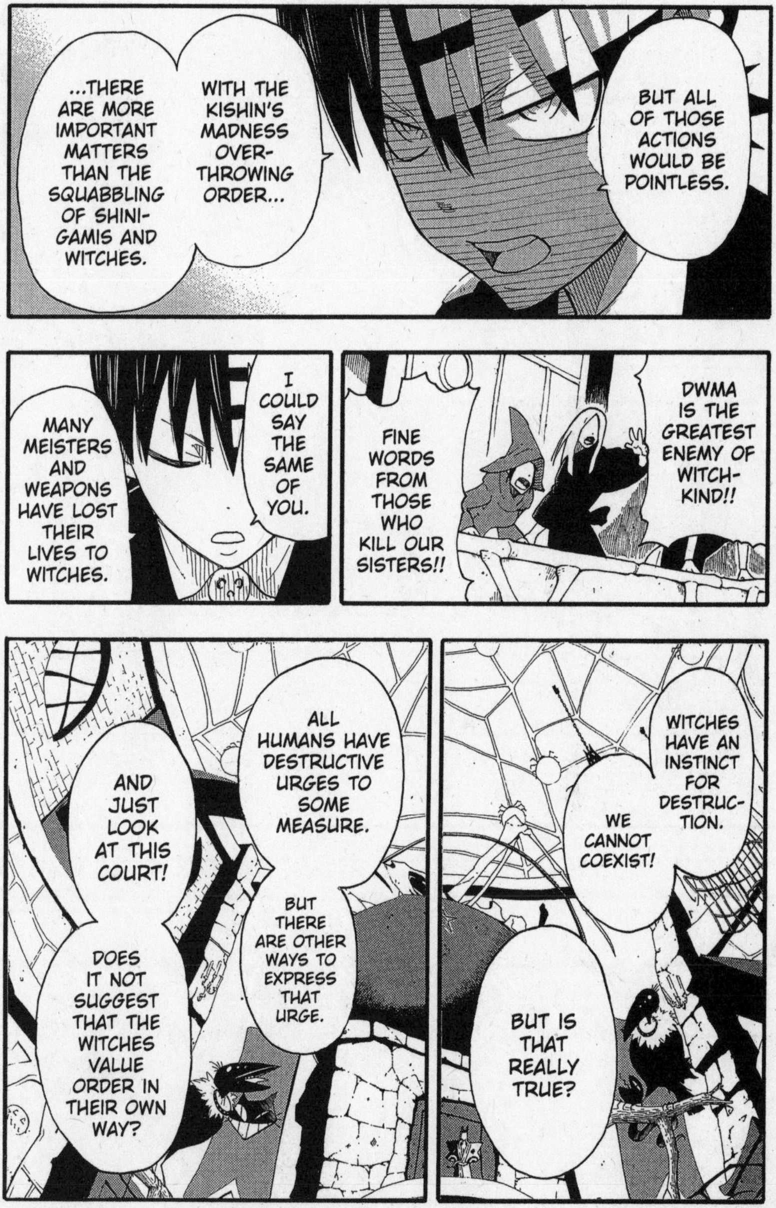
BUT ALL OF THOSE ACTIONS WOULD BE POINTLESS.
WITH THE KISHIN'S MADNESS OVER-THROWING ORDER...
...THERE ARE MORE IMPORTANT MATTERS THAN THE SQUABBLING OF SHINI-GAMIS AND WITCHES.
DWMA IS THE GREATEST ENEMY OF WITCH-KIND!!
FINE WORDS FROM THOSE WHO KILL OUR SISTERS!!
I COULD SAY THE SAME OF YOU.
MANY MEISTERS AND WEAPONS HAVE LOST THEIR LIVES TO WITCHES.
WITCHES HAVE AN INSTINCT FOR DESTRUC-TION.
WE CANNOT COEXIST!
BUT IS THAT REALLY TRUE?
ALL HUMANS HAVE DESTRUCTIVE URGES TO SOME MEASURE.
BUT THERE ARE OTHER WAYS TO EXPRESS THAT URGE.
AND JUST LOOK AT THIS COURT!
DOES IT NOT SUGGEST THAT THE WITCHES VALUE ORDER IN THEIR OWN WAY?

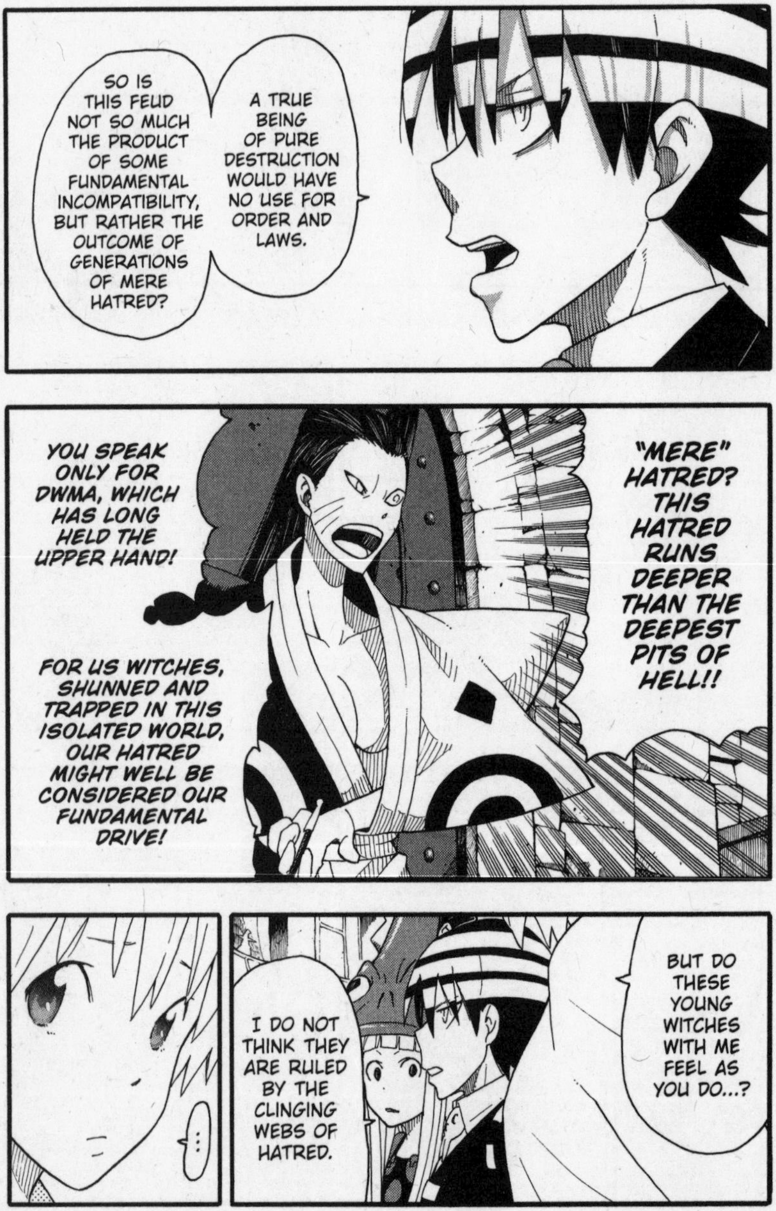
A TRUE BEING OF PURE DESTRUCTION WOULD HAVE NO USE FOR ORDER AND LAWS.
SO IS THIS FEUD NOT SO MUCH THE PRODUCT OF SOME FUNDAMENTAL INCOMPATIBILITY, BUT RATHER THE OUTCOME OF GENERATIONS OF MERE HATRED?
"MERE" HATRED? THIS HATRED RUNS DEEPER THAN THE DEEPEST PITS OF HELL!!
YOU SPEAK ONLY FOR DWMA, WHICH HAS LONG HELD THE UPPER HAND!
FOR US WITCHES, SHUNNED AND TRAPPED IN THIS ISOLATED WORLD, OUR HATRED MIGHT WELL BE CONSIDERED OUR FUNDAMENTAL DRIVE!
BUT DO THESE YOUNG WITCHES WITH ME FEEL AS YOU DO...?
I DO NOT THINK THEY ARE RULED BY THE CLINGING WEBS OF HATRED.
...

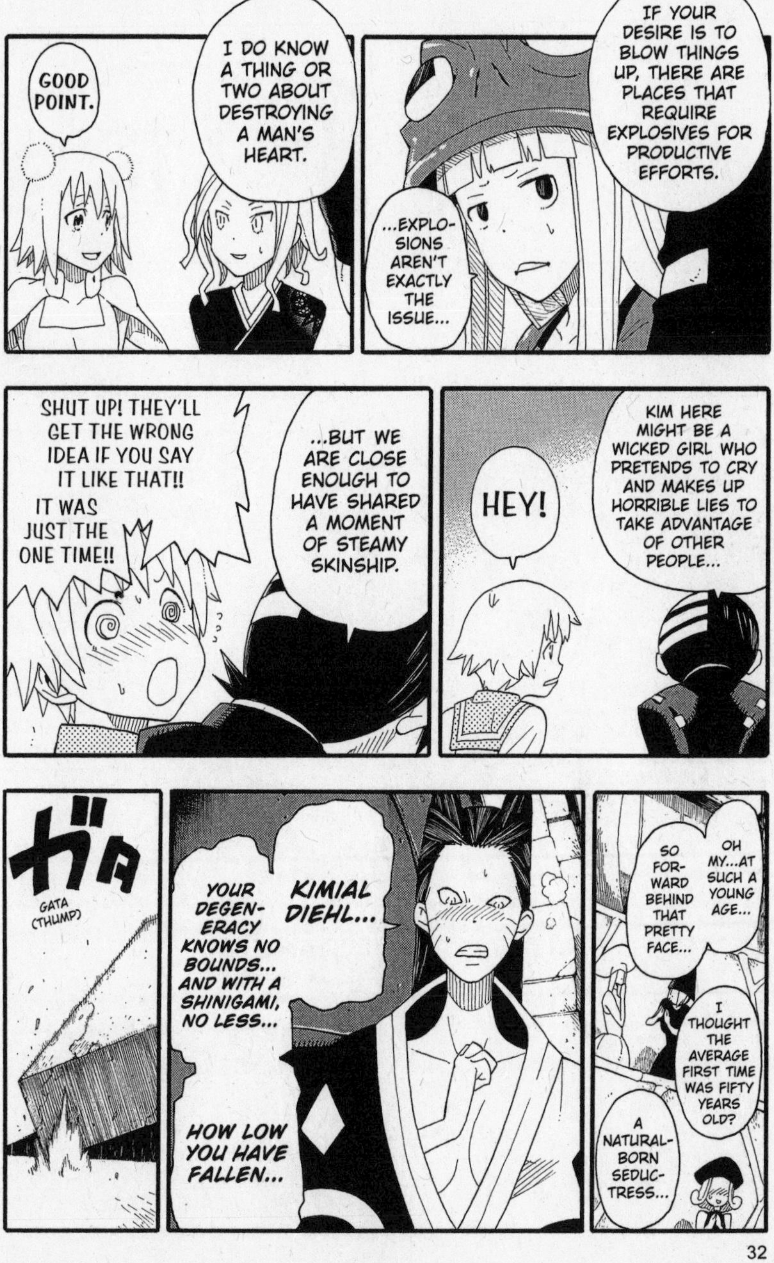
IF YOUR DESIRE IS TO BLOW THINGS UP, THERE ARE PLACES THAT REQUIRE EXPLOSIVES FOR PRODUCTIVE EFFORTS.
...EXPLOSIONS AREN'T EXACTLY THE ISSUE...
I DO KNOW A THING OR TWO ABOUT DESTROYING A MAN'S HEART.
GOOD POINT.
KIM HERE MIGHT BE A WICKED GIRL WHO PRETENDS TO CRY AND MAKES UP HORRIBLE LIES TO TAKE ADVANTAGE OF OTHER PEOPLE...
HEY!
...BUT WE ARE CLOSE ENOUGH TO HAVE SHARED A MOMENT OF STEAMY SKINSHIP.
SHUT UP! THEY'LL GET THE WRONG IDEA IF YOU SAY IT LIKE THAT!!
IT WAS JUST THE ONE TIME!!
OH MY...AT SUCH A YOUNG AGE...
SO FORWARD BEHIND THAT PRETTY FACE...
I THOUGHT THE AVERAGE FIRST TIME WAS FIFTY YEARS OLD?
A NATURAL-BORN SEDUCTRESS...
KIMIAL DIEHL...
YOUR DEGENERACY KNOWS NO BOUNDS... AND WITH A SHINIGAMI, NO LESS...
HOW LOW YOU HAVE FALLEN...
ガタ
GATA (THUMP)

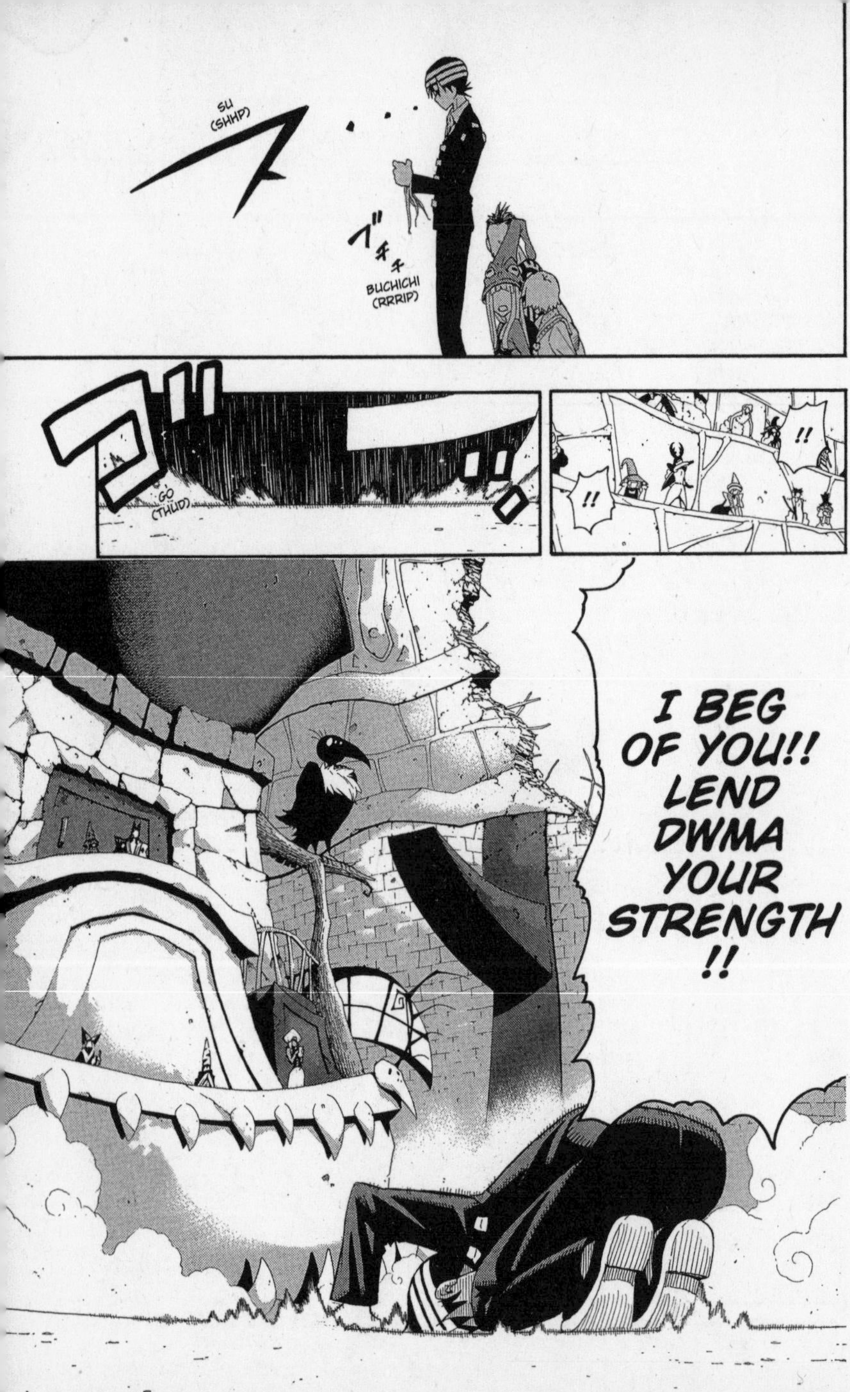
SU (SHHP)
BUCHICHI (RRRIP)
!!
!!
GO (THUD)
I BEG OF YOU!! LEND DWMA YOUR STRENGTH!!

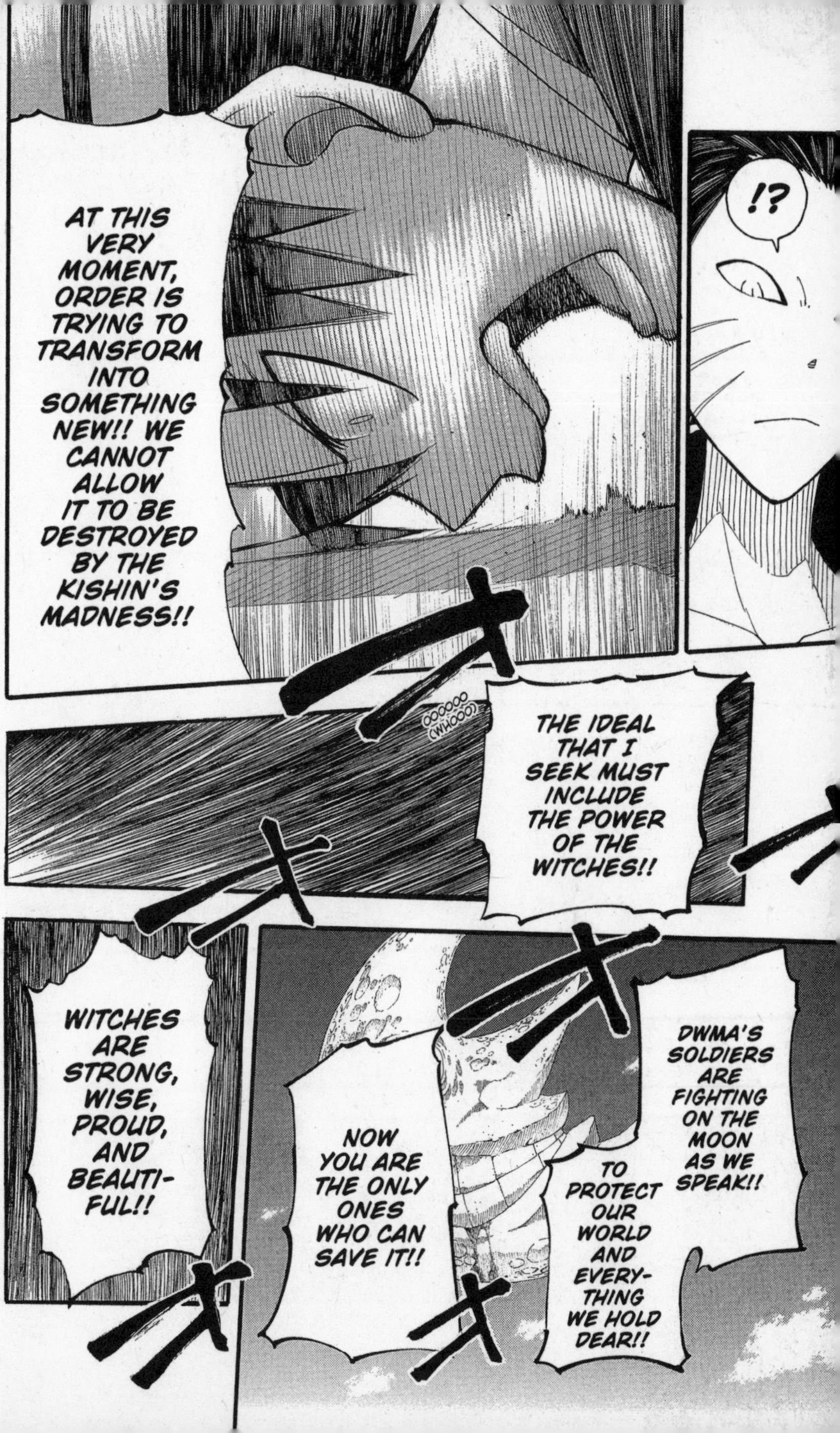
!?
AT THIS VERY MOMENT, ORDER IS TRYING TO TRANSFORM INTO SOMETHING NEW!! WE CANNOT ALLOW IT TO BE DESTROYED BY THE KISHIN'S MADNESS!!
OOOOOO (WHOOO)
THE IDEAL THAT I SEEK MUST INCLUDE THE POWER OF THE WITCHES!!
DWMA'S SOLDIERS ARE FIGHTING ON THE MOON AS WE SPEAK!!
TO PROTECT OUR WORLD AND EVERYTHING WE HOLD DEAR!!
NOW YOU ARE THE ONLY ONES WHO CAN SAVE IT!!
WITCHES ARE STRONG, WISE, PROUD, AND BEAUTIFUL!!

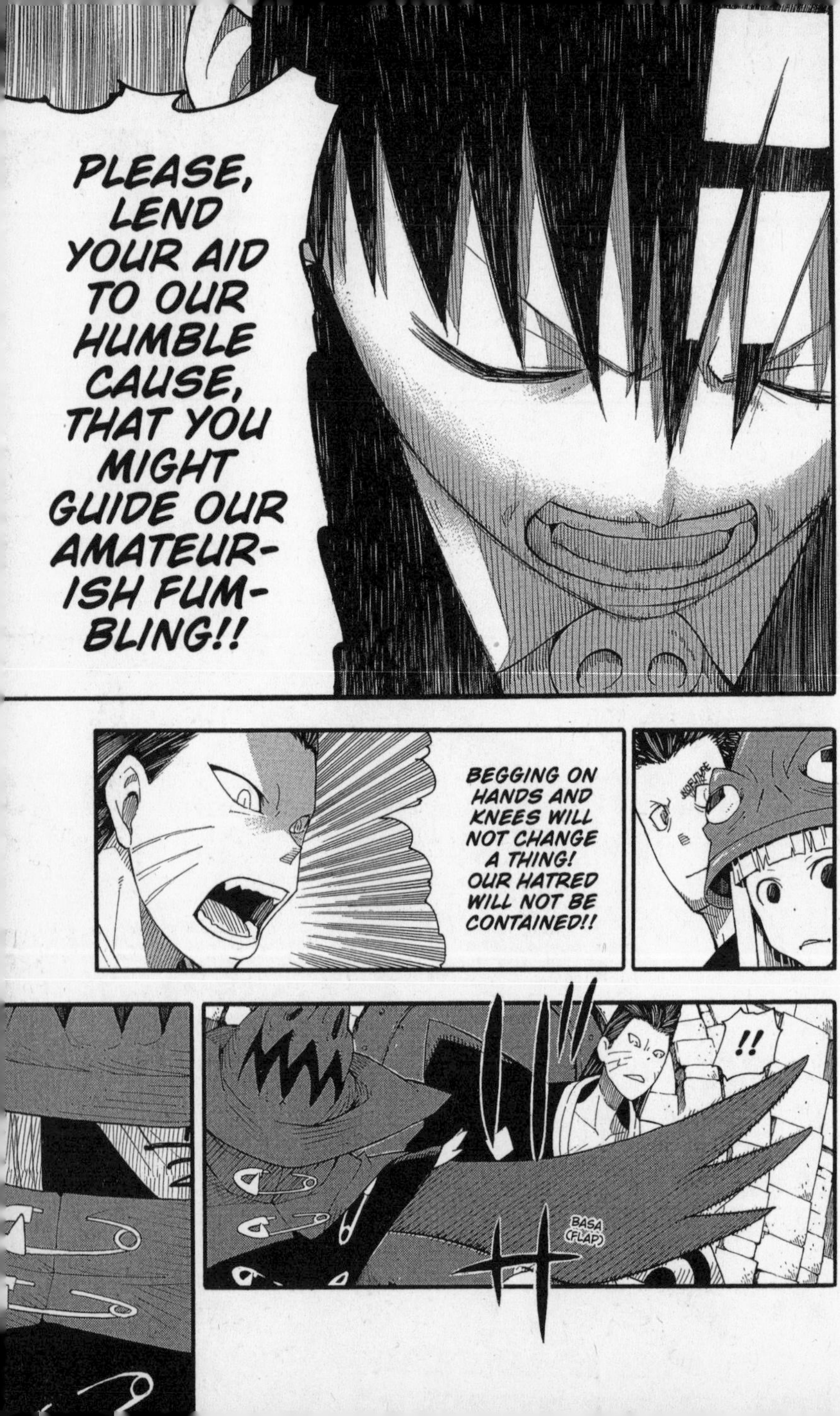
PLEASE, LEND YOUR AID TO OUR HUMBLE CAUSE, THAT YOU MIGHT GUIDE OUR AMATEUR-ISH FUM-BLING!!
BEGGING ON HANDS AND KNEES WILL NOT CHANGE A THING! OUR HATRED WILL NOT BE CONTAINED!!
!!
BASA (FLAP)

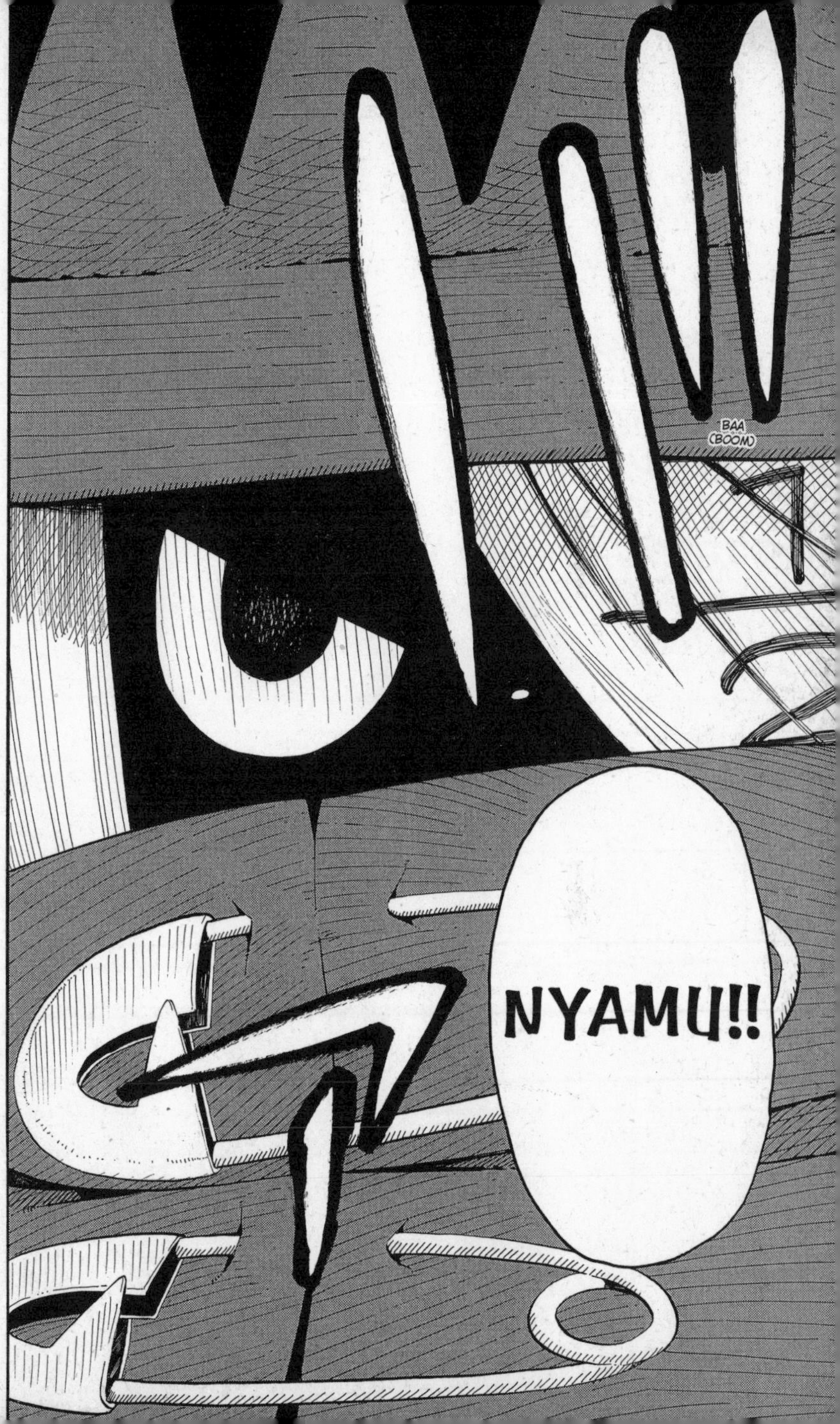
BAA
(BOOM)
NYAMU!!

SOUL EATER

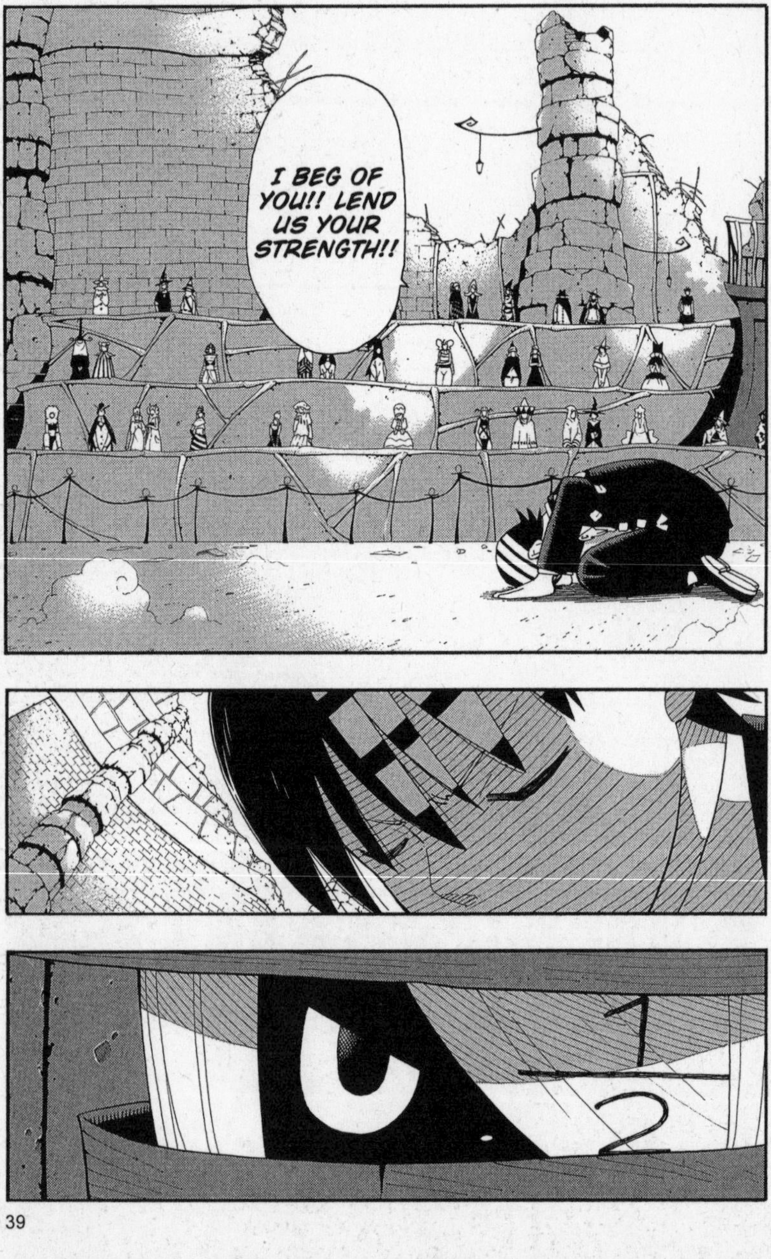
I BEG OF YOU!! LEND US YOUR STRENGTH!!

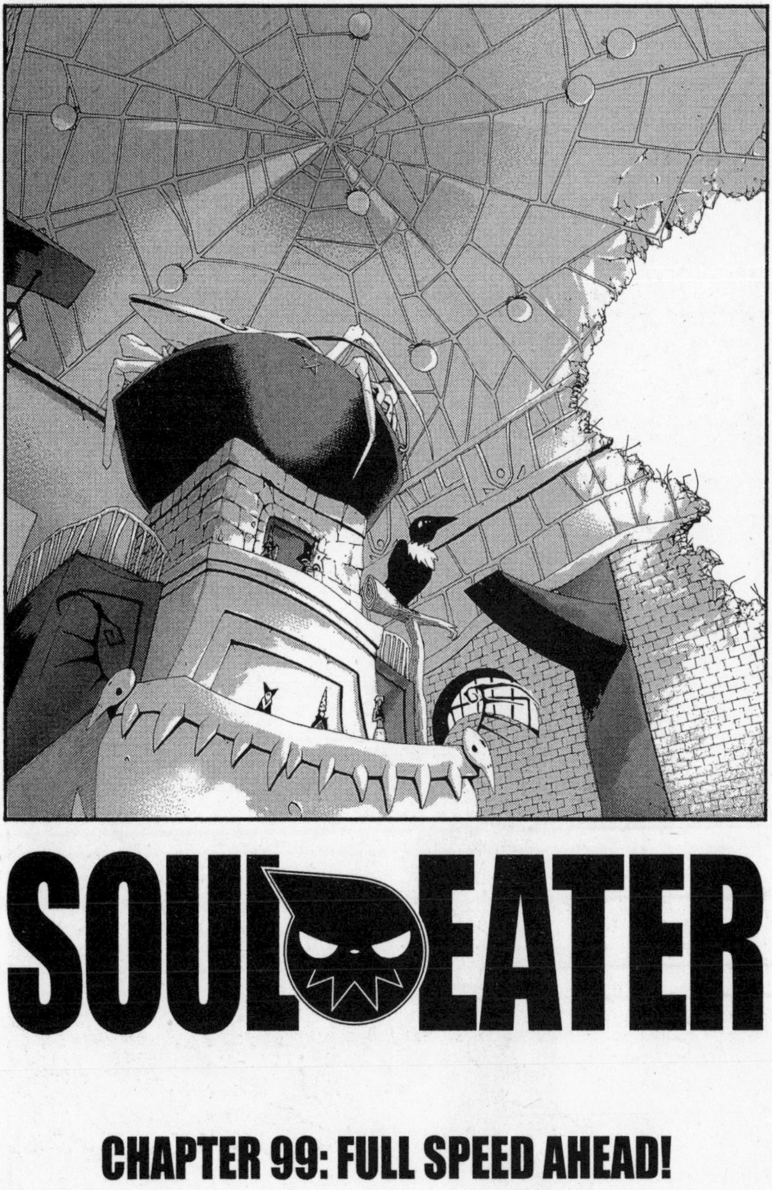

SOUL EATER

CHAPTER 99: FULL SPEED AHEAD!

SILENCE, SHINIGAMI!! THE HATRED OF WITCHES IS DEEP AND POWERFUL!! YOU CANNOT MANIPULATE US WITH YOUR HONEYED WORDS!!

A FEW BOWS AND SCRAPES WILL NOT CHANGE OUR MINDS!!

WE'RE IN TERRIBLE DANGER, AND THERE'S NOT A SECOND TO WASTE... THIS ISN'T THE TIME FOR US TO BE FIGHTING, EVEN IF WE ARE ENEMIES!! ARE YOU SAYING THAT IF WITCHES JOIN THE FIGHT AGAINST THE KISHIN'S MADNESS, YOU'RE GOING TO STOP THEM!?

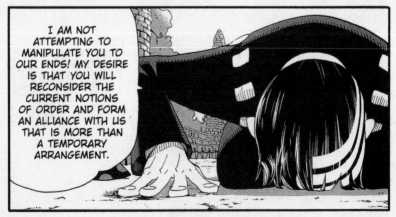

I AM NOT ATTEMPTING TO MANIPULATE YOU TO OUR ENDS! MY DESIRE IS THAT YOU WILL RECONSIDER THE CURRENT NOTIONS OF ORDER AND FORM AN ALLIANCE WITH US THAT IS MORE THAN A TEMPORARY ARRANGEMENT.

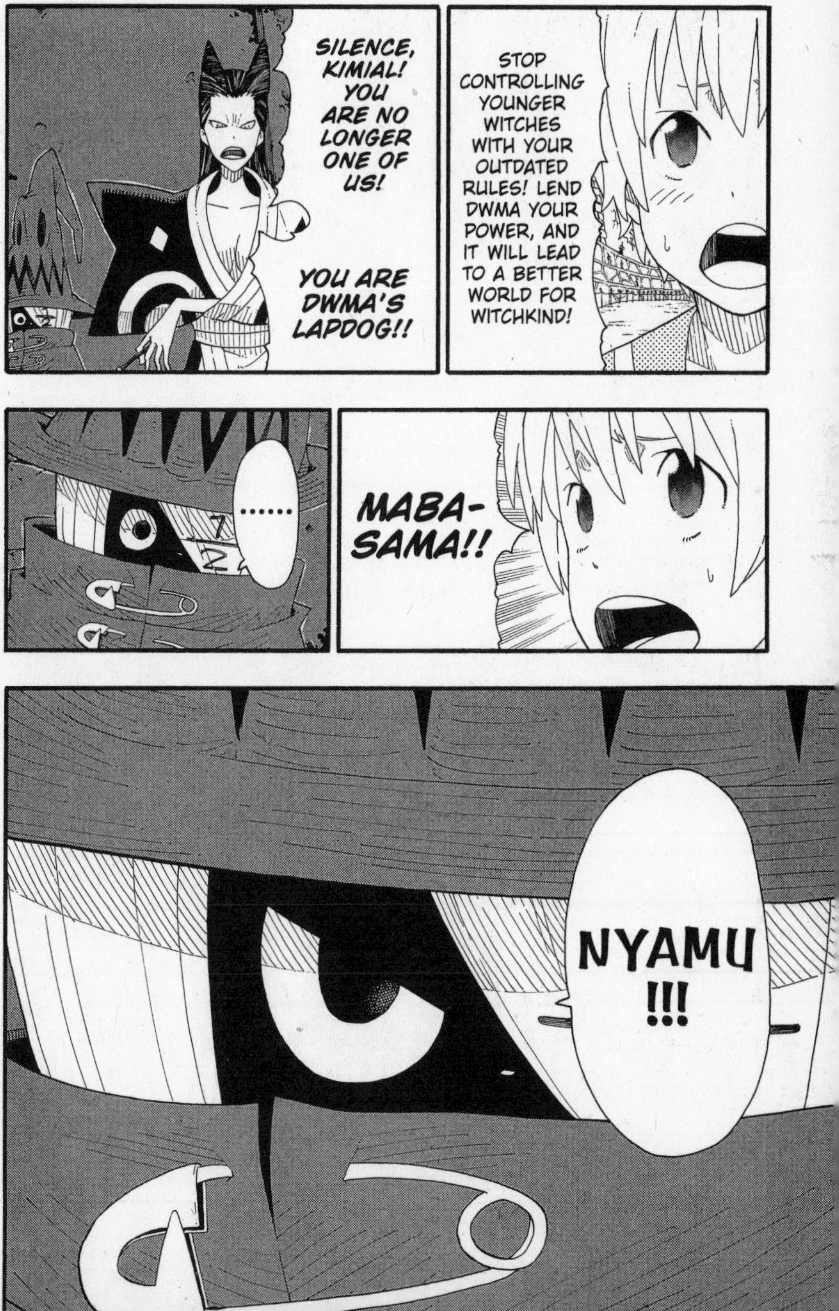
STOP CONTROLLING YOUNGER WITCHES WITH YOUR OUTDATED RULES! LEND DWMA YOUR POWER, AND IT WILL LEAD TO A BETTER WORLD FOR WITCHKIND!
SILENCE, KIMIAL! YOU ARE NO LONGER ONE OF US!
YOU ARE DWMA'S LAPDOG!!
MABA-SAMA!!
......
NYAMU !!!

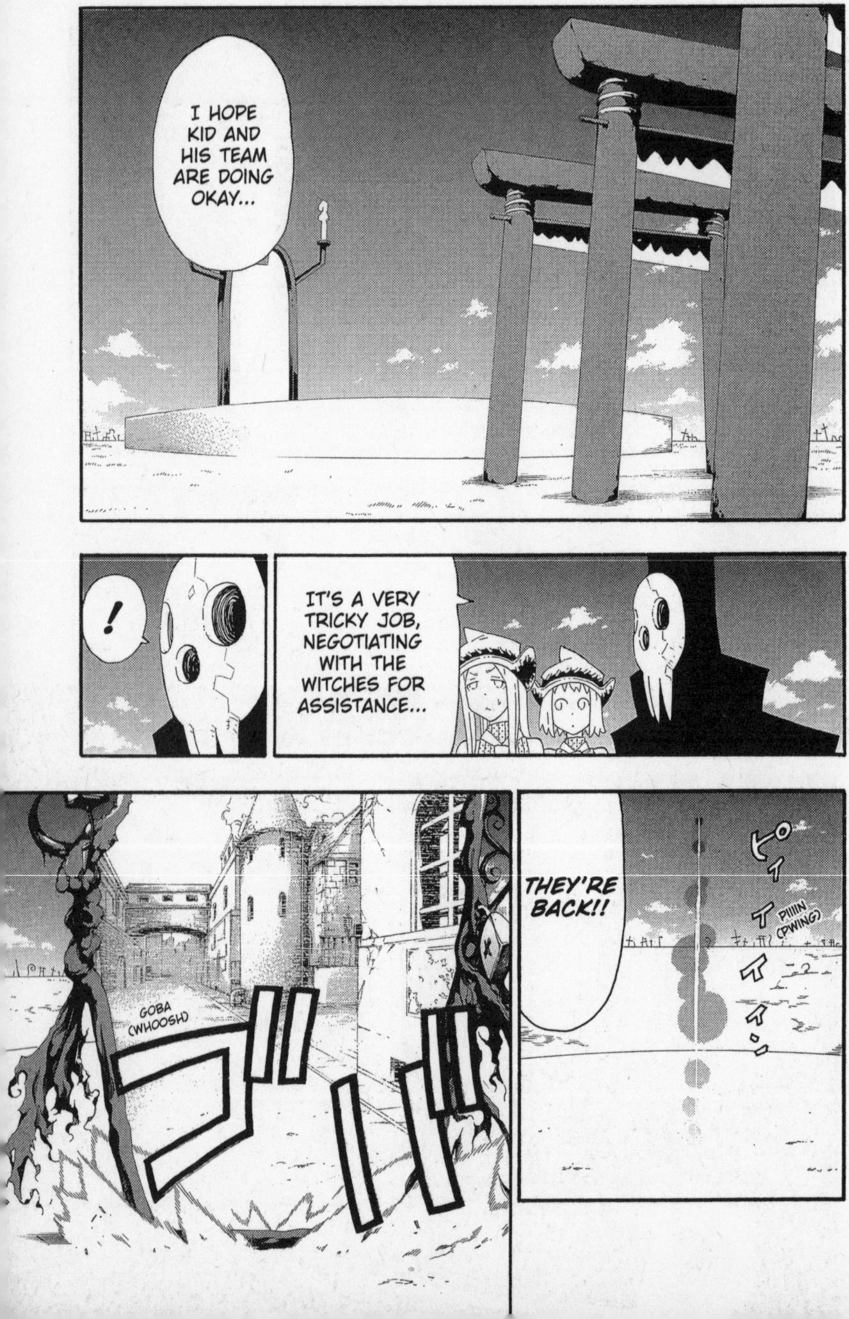
I HOPE KID AND HIS TEAM ARE DOING OKAY...
IT'S A VERY TRICKY JOB, NEGOTIATING WITH THE WITCHES FOR ASSISTANCE...
!
THEY'RE BACK!!
PIIIIN (PWING)
GOBA (WHOOSH)

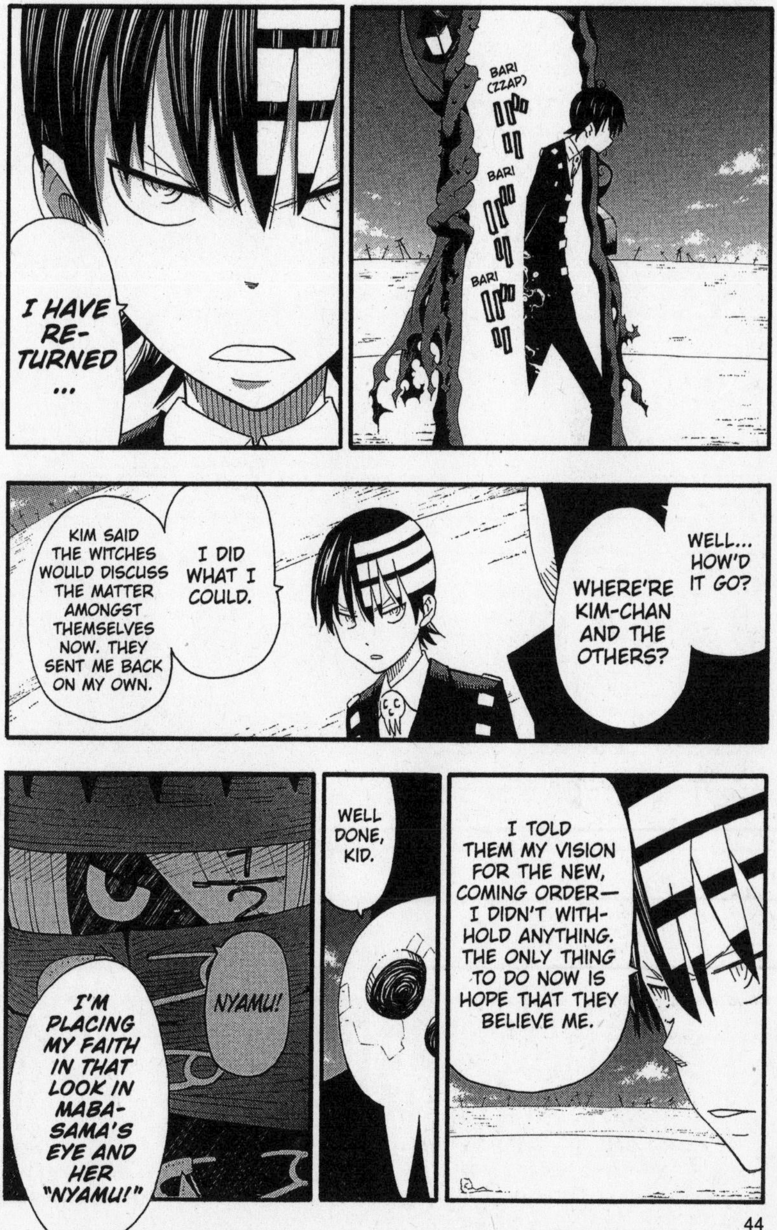

BARI (ZZAP)
BARI
BARI
I HAVE RE-TURNED ...
WELL... HOW'D IT GO?
WHERE'RE KIM-CHAN AND THE OTHERS?
I DID WHAT I COULD.
KIM SAID THE WITCHES WOULD DISCUSS THE MATTER AMONGST THEMSELVES NOW. THEY SENT ME BACK ON MY OWN.
I TOLD THEM MY VISION FOR THE NEW, COMING ORDER— I DIDN'T WITH-HOLD ANYTHING. THE ONLY THING TO DO NOW IS HOPE THAT THEY BELIEVE ME.
WELL DONE, KID.
NYAMU!
I'M PLACING MY FAITH IN THAT LOOK IN MABA-SAMA'S EYE AND HER "NYAMU!"

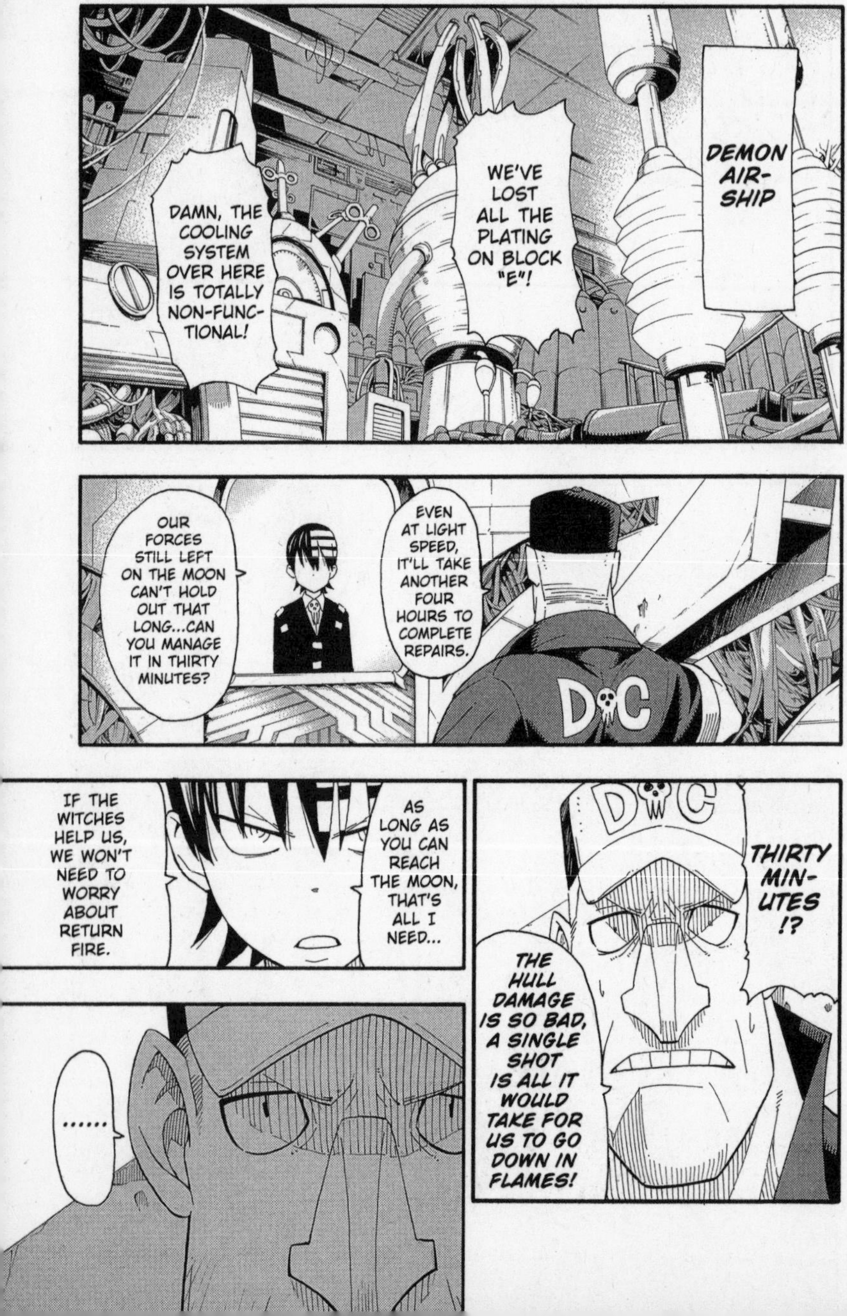
DEMON AIR-SHIP
WE'VE LOST ALL THE PLATING ON BLOCK "E"!
DAMN, THE COOLING SYSTEM OVER HERE IS TOTALLY NON-FUNC-TIONAL!
EVEN AT LIGHT SPEED, IT'LL TAKE ANOTHER FOUR HOURS TO COMPLETE REPAIRS.
OUR FORCES STILL LEFT ON THE MOON CAN'T HOLD OUT THAT LONG...CAN YOU MANAGE IT IN THIRTY MINUTES?
D C
D C
THIRTY MIN-UTES!?
THE HULL DAMAGE IS SO BAD, A SINGLE SHOT IS ALL IT WOULD TAKE FOR US TO GO DOWN IN FLAMES!
AS LONG AS YOU CAN REACH THE MOON, THAT'S ALL I NEED...
IF THE WITCHES HELP US, WE WON'T NEED TO WORRY ABOUT RETURN FIRE.
......

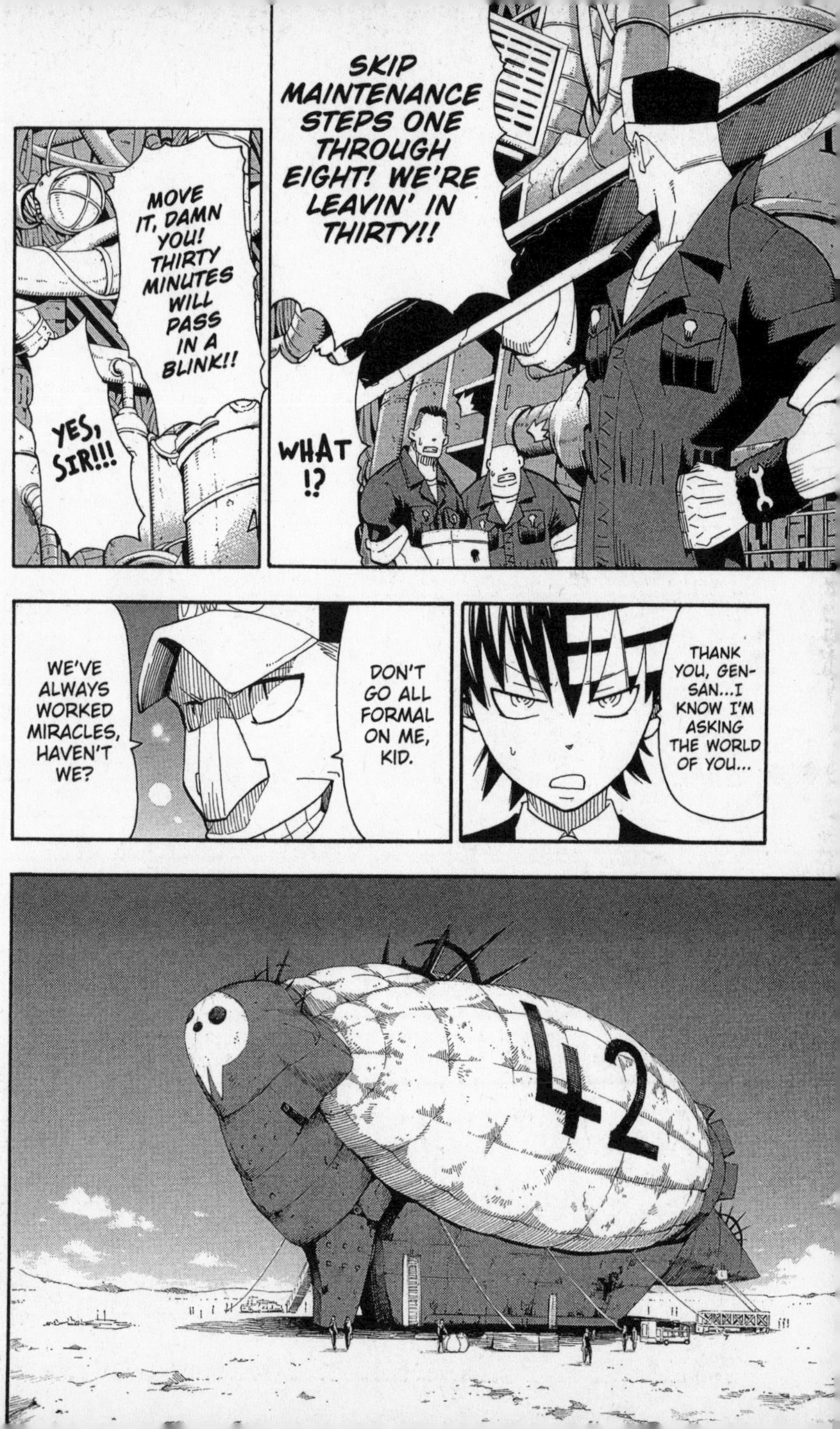
SKIP MAINTENANCE STEPS ONE THROUGH EIGHT! WE'RE LEAVIN' IN THIRTY!!
WHAT !?
MOVE IT, DAMN YOU! THIRTY MINUTES WILL PASS IN A BLINK!!
YES, SIR!!!
THANK YOU, GEN-SAN...I KNOW I'M ASKING THE WORLD OF YOU...
DON'T GO ALL FORMAL ON ME, KID.
WE'VE ALWAYS WORKED MIRACLES, HAVEN'T WE?
42

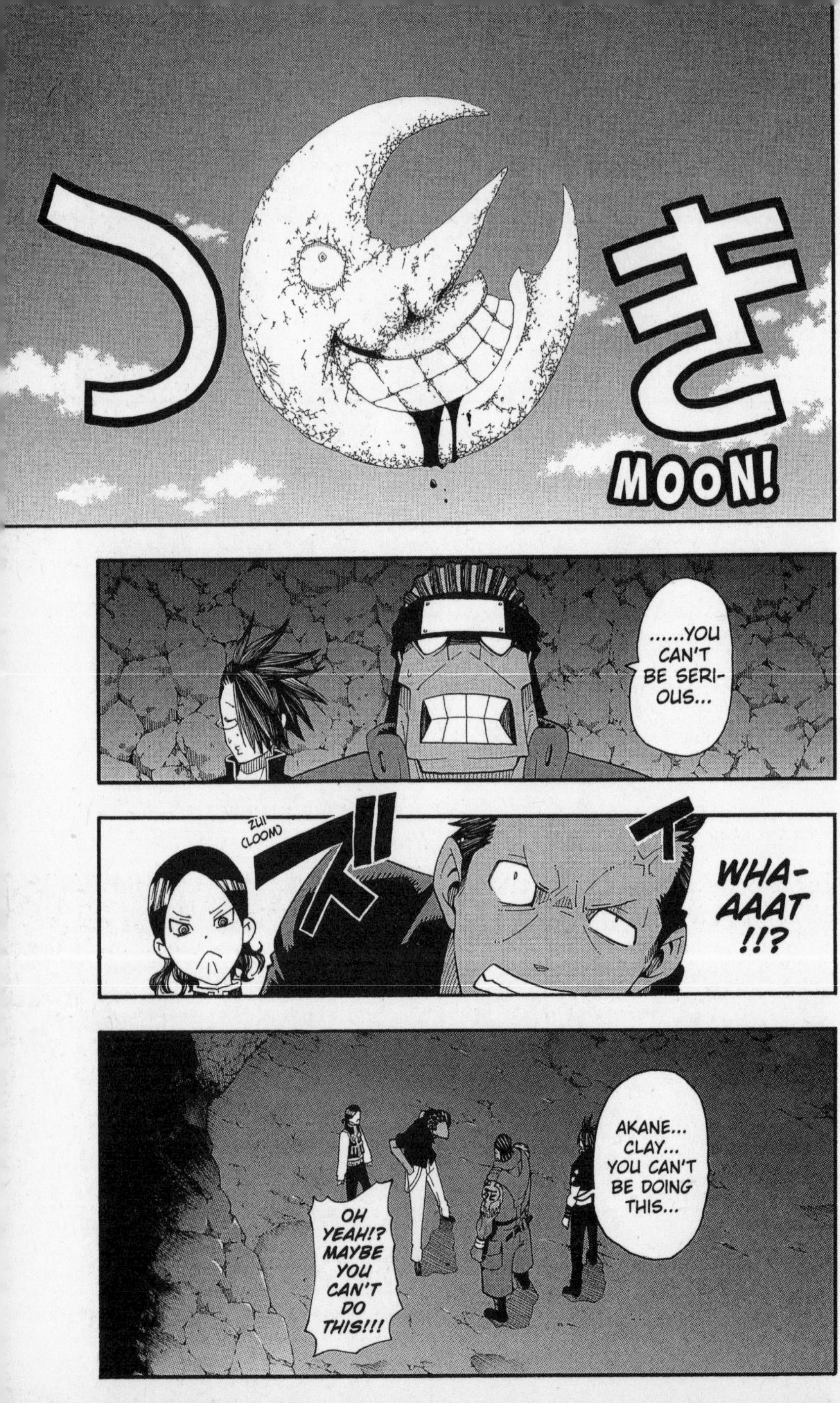つき
MOON!
......YOU CAN'T BE SERI-OUS...
WHA-AAAT!!?
ZUI (LOOM)
AKANE... CLAY... YOU CAN'T BE DOING THIS...
OH YEAH!? MAYBE YOU CAN'T DO THIS!!!

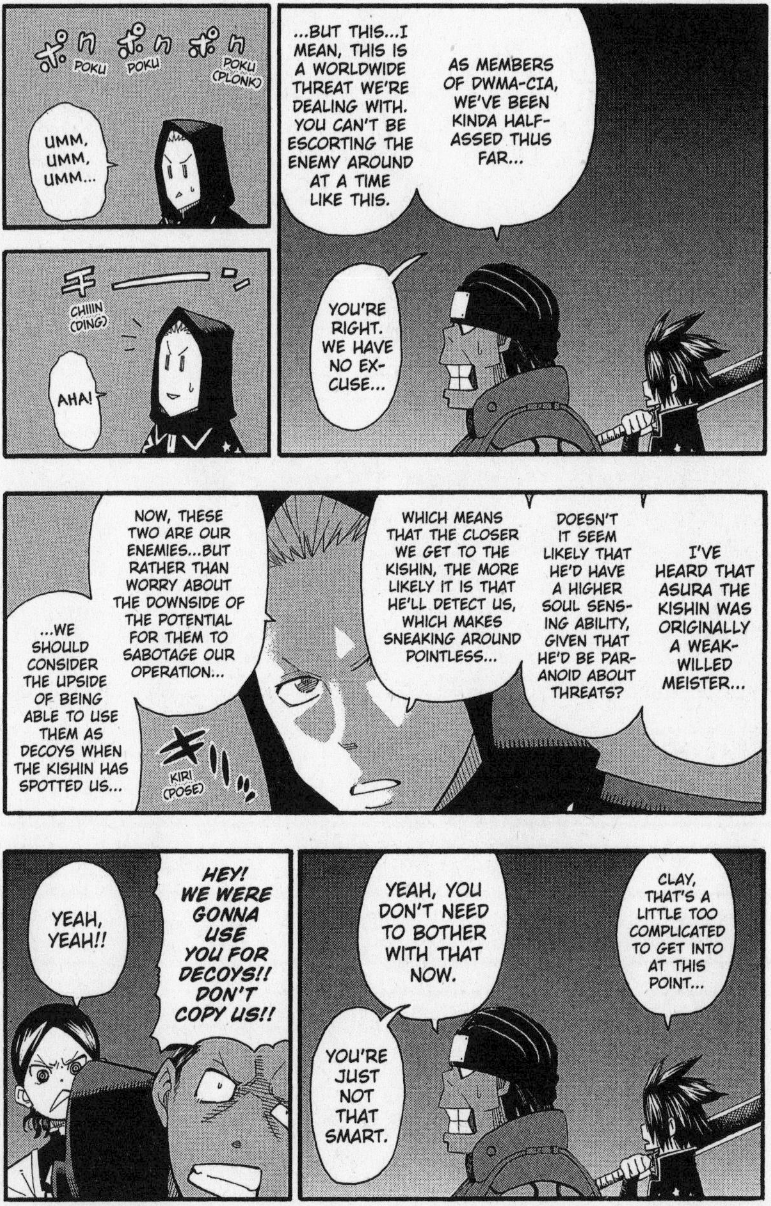
AS MEMBERS OF DWMA-CIA, WE'VE BEEN KINDA HALF-ASSED THUS FAR...
...BUT THIS...I MEAN, THIS IS A WORLDWIDE THREAT WE'RE DEALING WITH. YOU CAN'T BE ESCORTING THE ENEMY AROUND AT A TIME LIKE THIS.
YOU'RE RIGHT. WE HAVE NO EXCUSE...
ポク ポク ポク
POKU POKU POKU (PLONK)
UMM, UMM, UMM...
チーーン
CHIIIN (DING)
AHA!
I'VE HEARD THAT ASURA THE KISHIN WAS ORIGINALLY A WEAK-WILLED MEISTER...
DOESN'T IT SEEM LIKELY THAT HE'D HAVE A HIGHER SOUL SENSING ABILITY, GIVEN THAT HE'D BE PARANOID ABOUT THREATS?
WHICH MEANS THAT THE CLOSER WE GET TO THE KISHIN, THE MORE LIKELY IT IS THAT HE'LL DETECT US, WHICH MAKES SNEAKING AROUND POINTLESS...
NOW, THESE TWO ARE OUR ENEMIES...BUT RATHER THAN WORRY ABOUT THE DOWNSIDE OF THE POTENTIAL FOR THEM TO SABOTAGE OUR OPERATION...
キリッ
KIRI (POSE)
...WE SHOULD CONSIDER THE UPSIDE OF BEING ABLE TO USE THEM AS DECOYS WHEN THE KISHIN HAS SPOTTED US...
CLAY, THAT'S A LITTLE TOO COMPLICATED TO GET INTO AT THIS POINT...
YEAH, YOU DON'T NEED TO BOTHER WITH THAT NOW.
YOU'RE JUST NOT THAT SMART.
HEY! WE WERE GONNA USE YOU FOR DECOYS!! DON'T COPY US!!
YEAH, YEAH!!

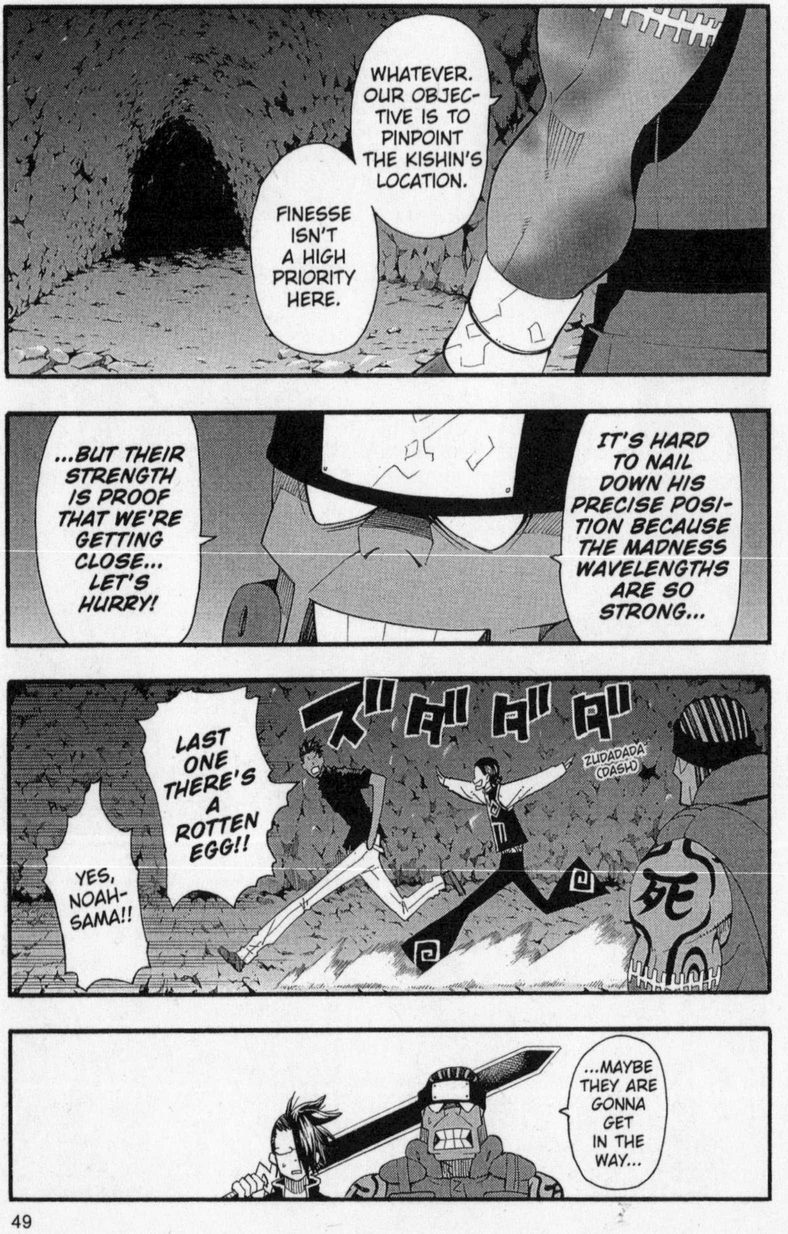
WHATEVER. OUR OBJECTIVE IS TO PINPOINT THE KISHIN'S LOCATION.
FINESSE ISN'T A HIGH PRIORITY HERE.
IT'S HARD TO NAIL DOWN HIS PRECISE POSITION BECAUSE THE MADNESS WAVELENGTHS ARE SO STRONG...
...BUT THEIR STRENGTH IS PROOF THAT WE'RE GETTING CLOSE... LET'S HURRY!
ズダダダ
ZUDADADA (DASH)
LAST ONE THERE'S A ROTTEN EGG!!
YES, NOAH-SAMA!!
...MAYBE THEY ARE GONNA GET IN THE WAY...

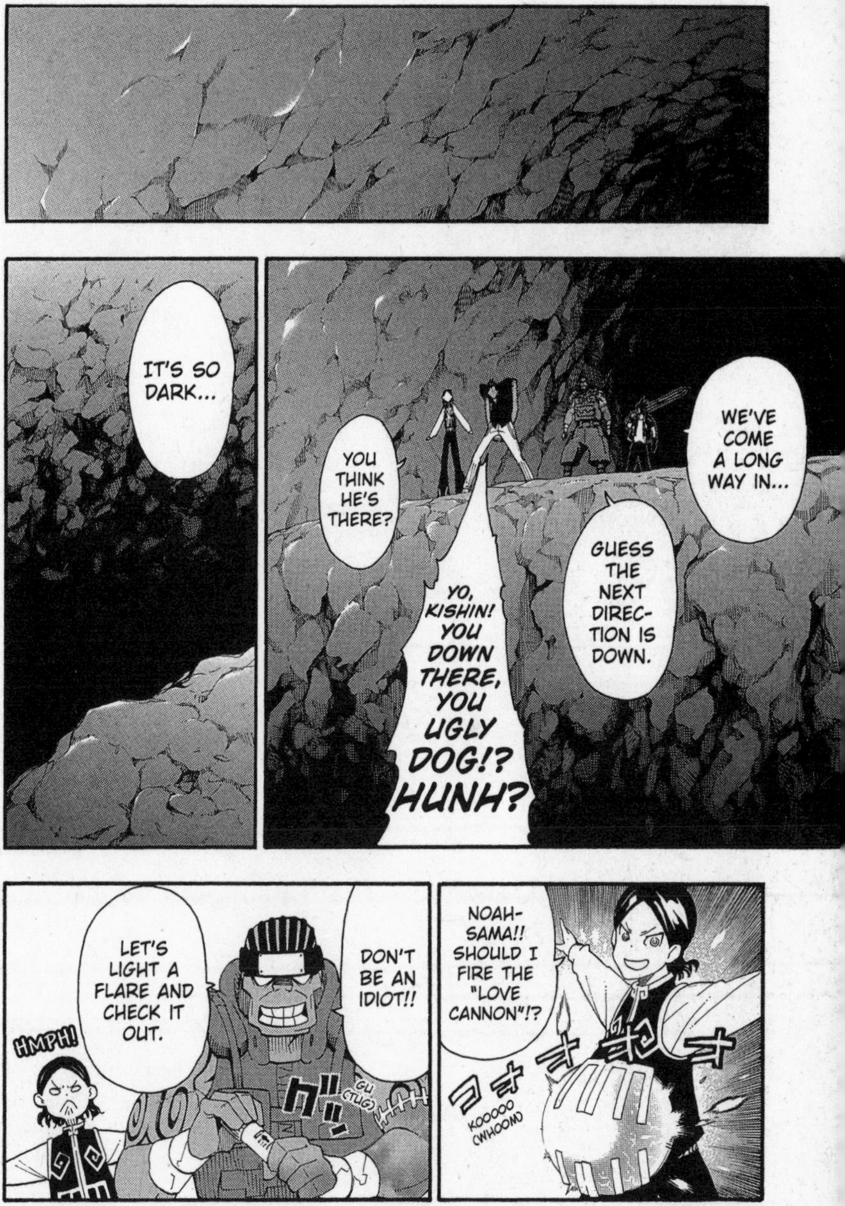
WE'VE COME A LONG WAY IN...
YOU THINK HE'S THERE?
GUESS THE NEXT DIRECTION IS DOWN.
YO, KISHIN! YOU DOWN THERE, YOU UGLY DOG!? HUNH?
IT'S SO DARK...
NOAH-SAMA!! SHOULD I FIRE THE "LOVE CANNON"!?
KOOOOO (WHOOM)
DON'T BE AN IDIOT!!
LET'S LIGHT A FLARE AND CHECK IT OUT.
GU (TUG)
HMPH!

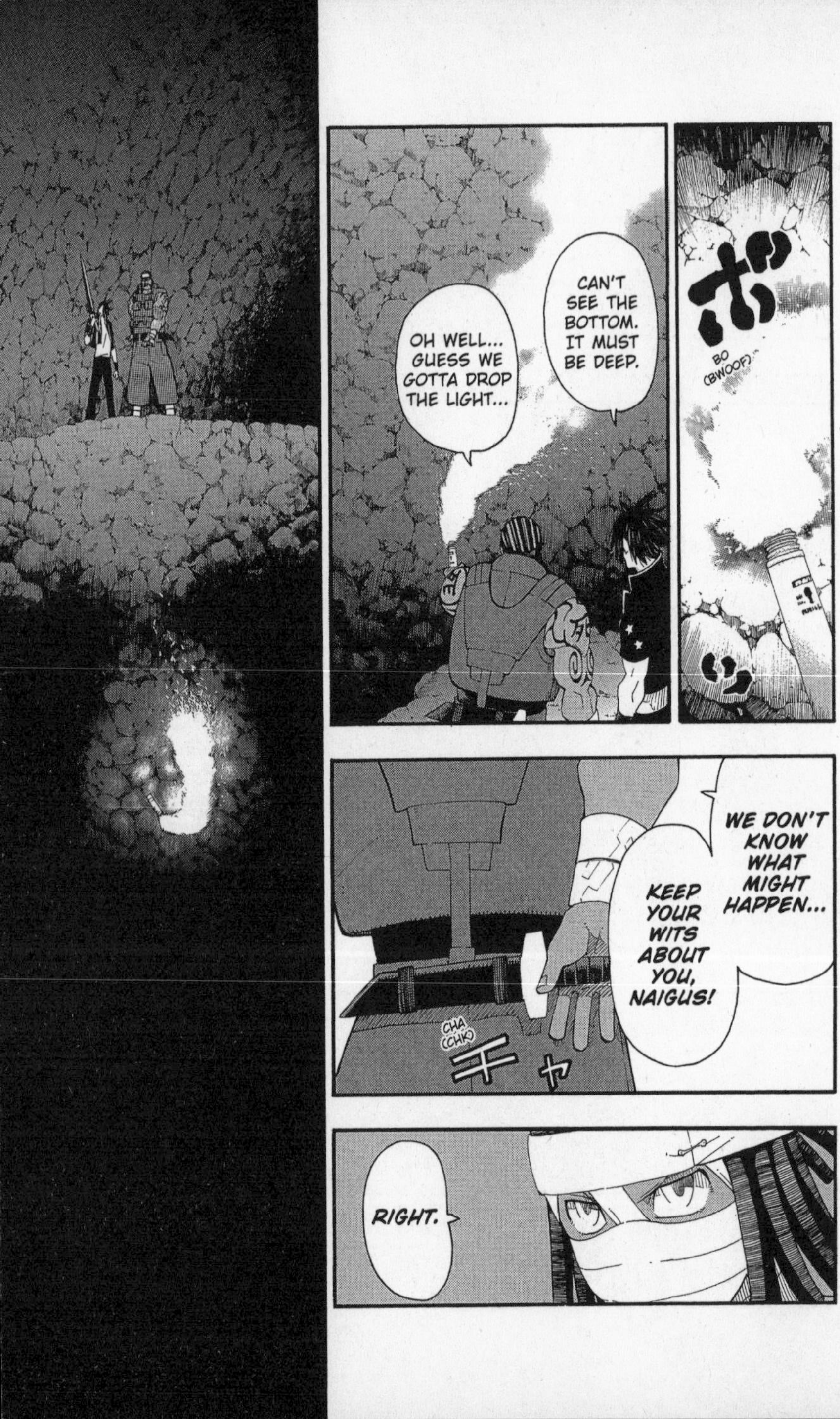
BO (BWOOF)
CAN'T SEE THE BOTTOM. IT MUST BE DEEP.
OH WELL... GUESS WE GOTTA DROP THE LIGHT...
WE DON'T KNOW WHAT MIGHT HAPPEN...
KEEP YOUR WITS ABOUT YOU, NAIGUS!
CHA (CHK)
RIGHT.

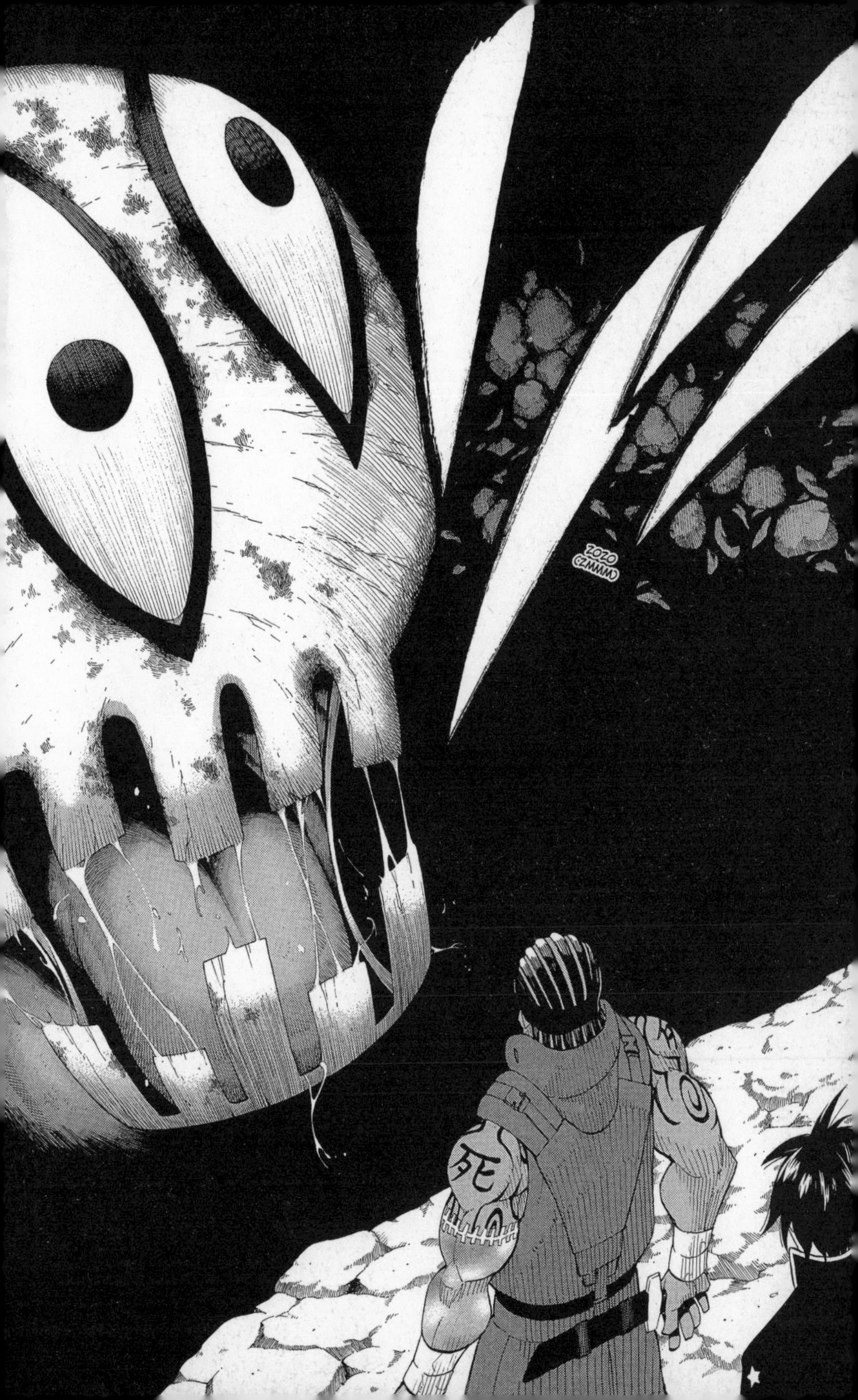
ZOZO
(ZMMM)

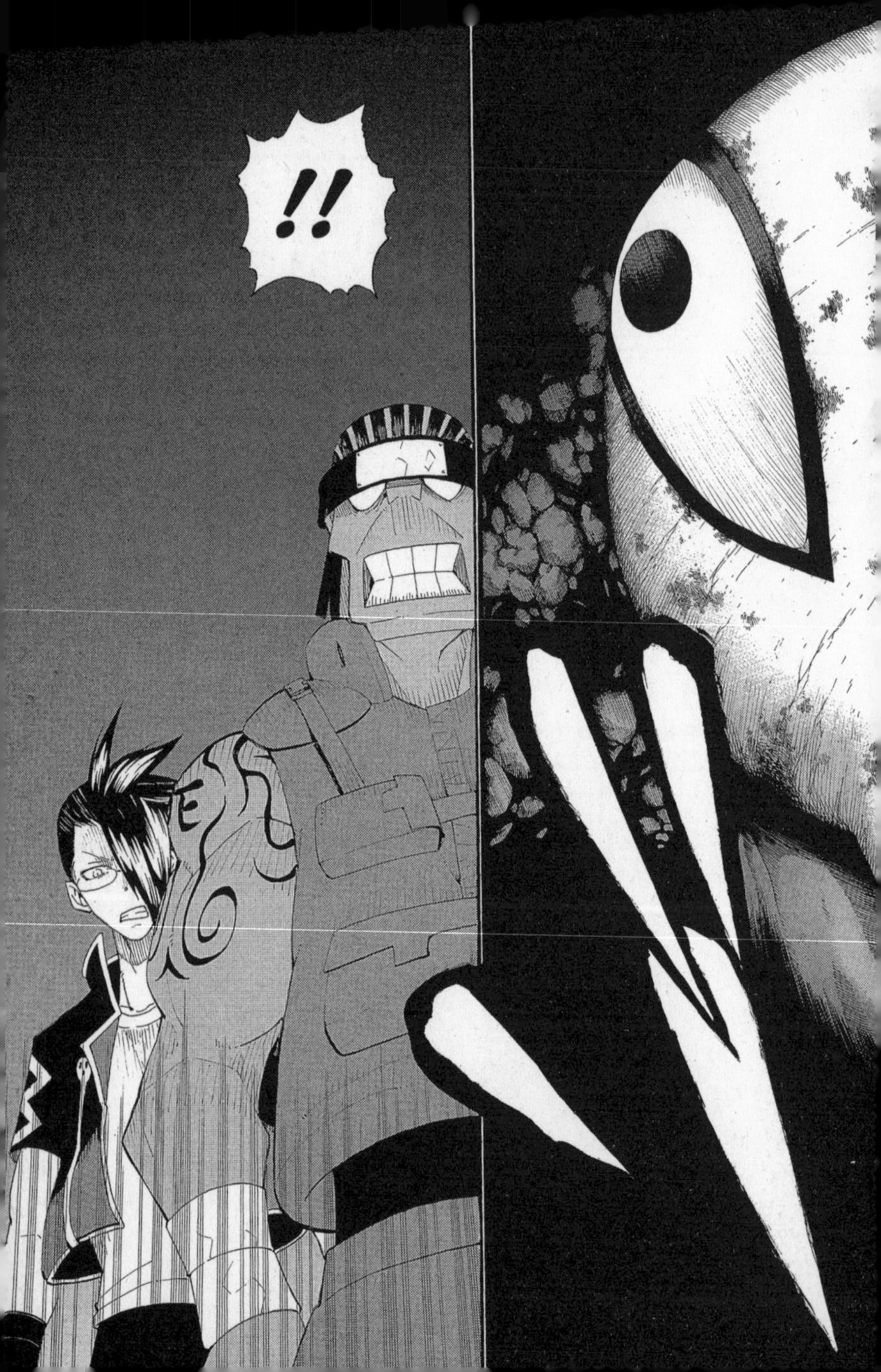
!!

DON
(BOOM)

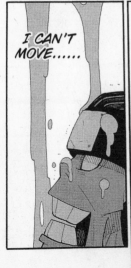

I CAN'T MOVE......

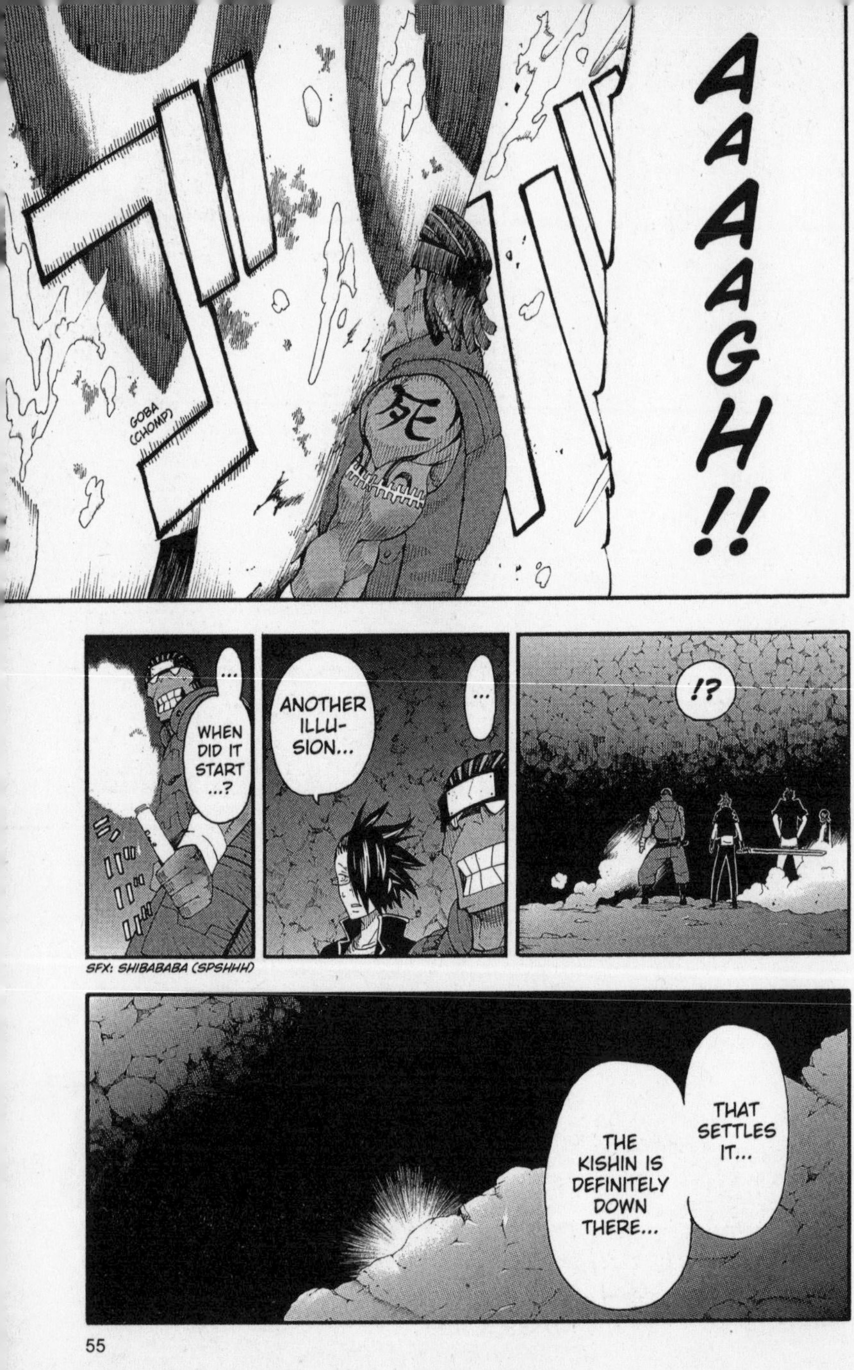
AAAAGH!!
GOBA (CHOMP)
!?
...
ANOTHER ILLUSION...
...
WHEN DID IT START ...?
SFX: SHIBABABA (SPSHHH)
THAT SETTLES IT...
THE KISHIN IS DEFINITELY DOWN THERE...

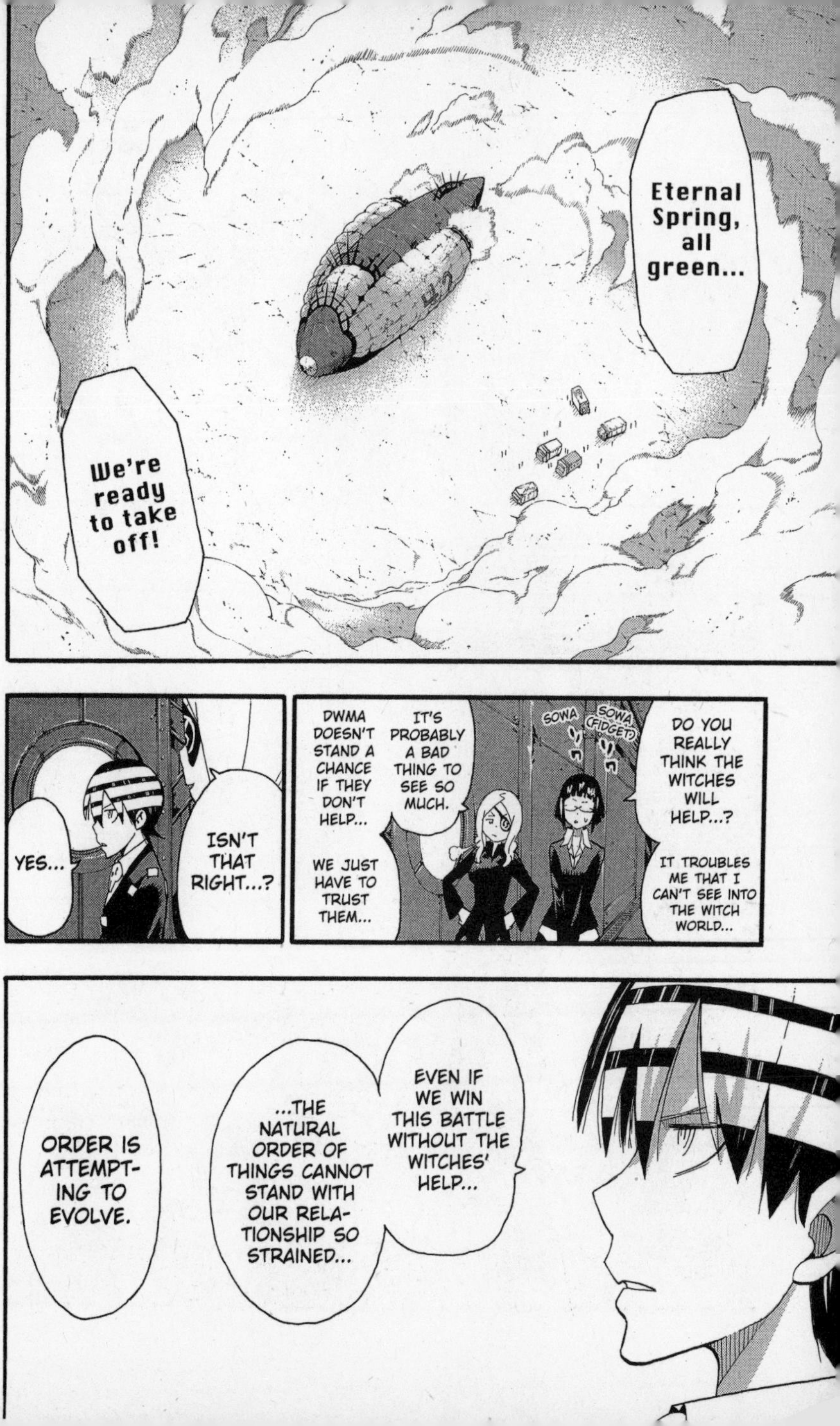
Eternal Spring, all green...
We're ready to take off!
SOWA SOWA (FIDGET)
DO YOU REALLY THINK THE WITCHES WILL HELP...?
IT TROUBLES ME THAT I CAN'T SEE INTO THE WITCH WORLD...
IT'S PROBABLY A BAD THING TO SEE SO MUCH.
DWMA DOESN'T STAND A CHANCE IF THEY DON'T HELP...
WE JUST HAVE TO TRUST THEM...
ISN'T THAT RIGHT...?
YES...
EVEN IF WE WIN THIS BATTLE WITHOUT THE WITCHES' HELP...
...THE NATURAL ORDER OF THINGS CANNOT STAND WITH OUR RELA-TIONSHIP SO STRAINED...
ORDER IS ATTEMPT-ING TO EVOLVE.

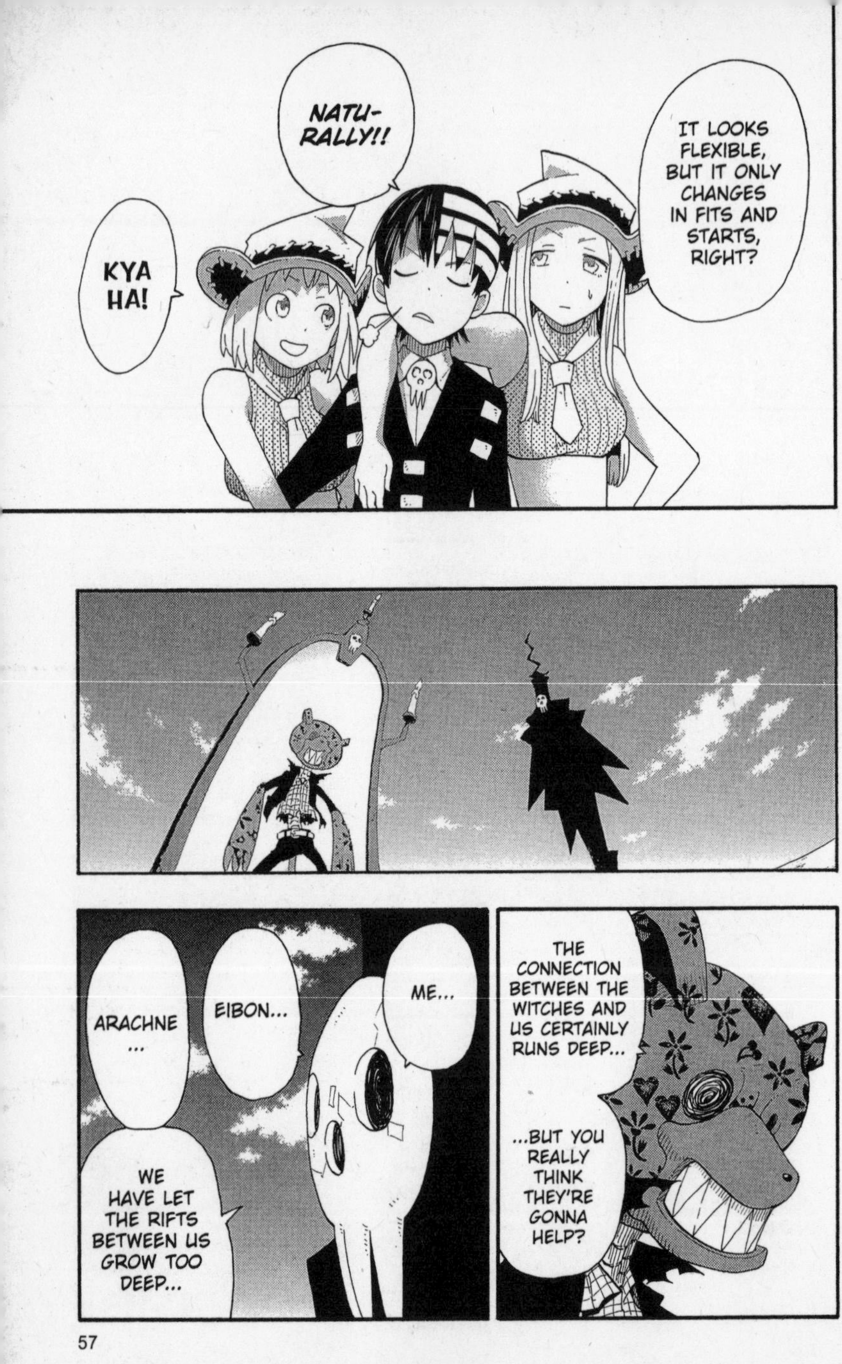
IT LOOKS FLEXIBLE, BUT IT ONLY CHANGES IN FITS AND STARTS, RIGHT?
NATU-RALLY!!
KYA HA!
THE CONNECTION BETWEEN THE WITCHES AND US CERTAINLY RUNS DEEP...
...BUT YOU REALLY THINK THEY'RE GONNA HELP?
ME...
EIBON...
ARACHNE ...
WE HAVE LET THE RIFTS BETWEEN US GROW TOO DEEP...

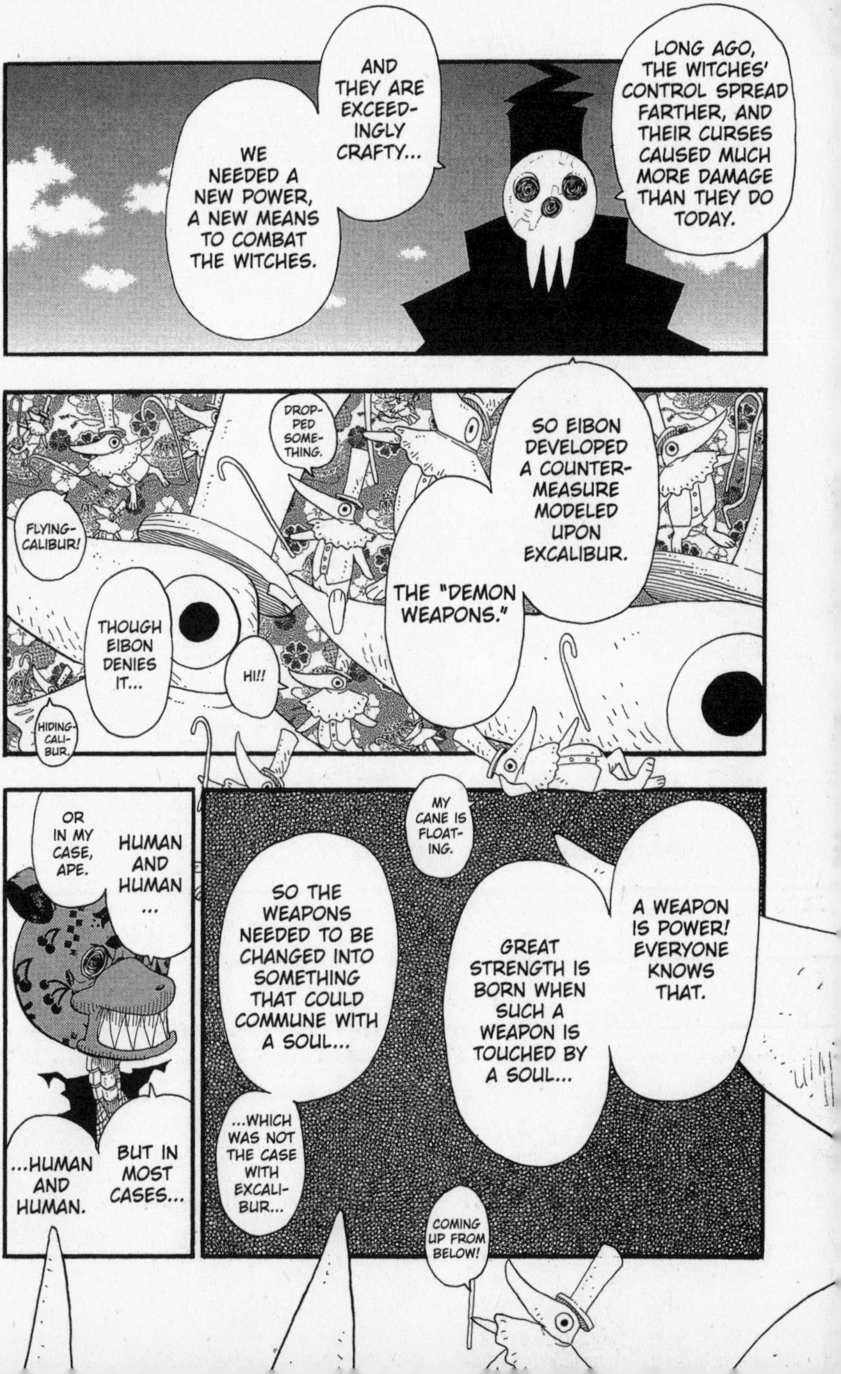
LONG AGO, THE WITCHES' CONTROL SPREAD FARTHER, AND THEIR CURSES CAUSED MUCH MORE DAMAGE THAN THEY DO TODAY.
AND THEY ARE EXCEEDINGLY CRAFTY...
WE NEEDED A NEW POWER, A NEW MEANS TO COMBAT THE WITCHES.
SO EIBON DEVELOPED A COUNTERMEASURE MODELED UPON EXCALIBUR.
THE "DEMON WEAPONS."
DROPPED SOMETHING.
FLYING-CALIBUR!
THOUGH EIBON DENIES IT...
HI!!
HIDING-CALIBUR.
MY CANE IS FLOATING.
A WEAPON IS POWER! EVERYONE KNOWS THAT.
GREAT STRENGTH IS BORN WHEN SUCH A WEAPON IS TOUCHED BY A SOUL...
SO THE WEAPONS NEEDED TO BE CHANGED INTO SOMETHING THAT COULD COMMUNE WITH A SOUL...
...WHICH WAS NOT THE CASE WITH EXCALIBUR...
COMING UP FROM BELOW!
HUMAN AND HUMAN...
OR IN MY CASE, APE.
BUT IN MOST CASES...
...HUMAN AND HUMAN.

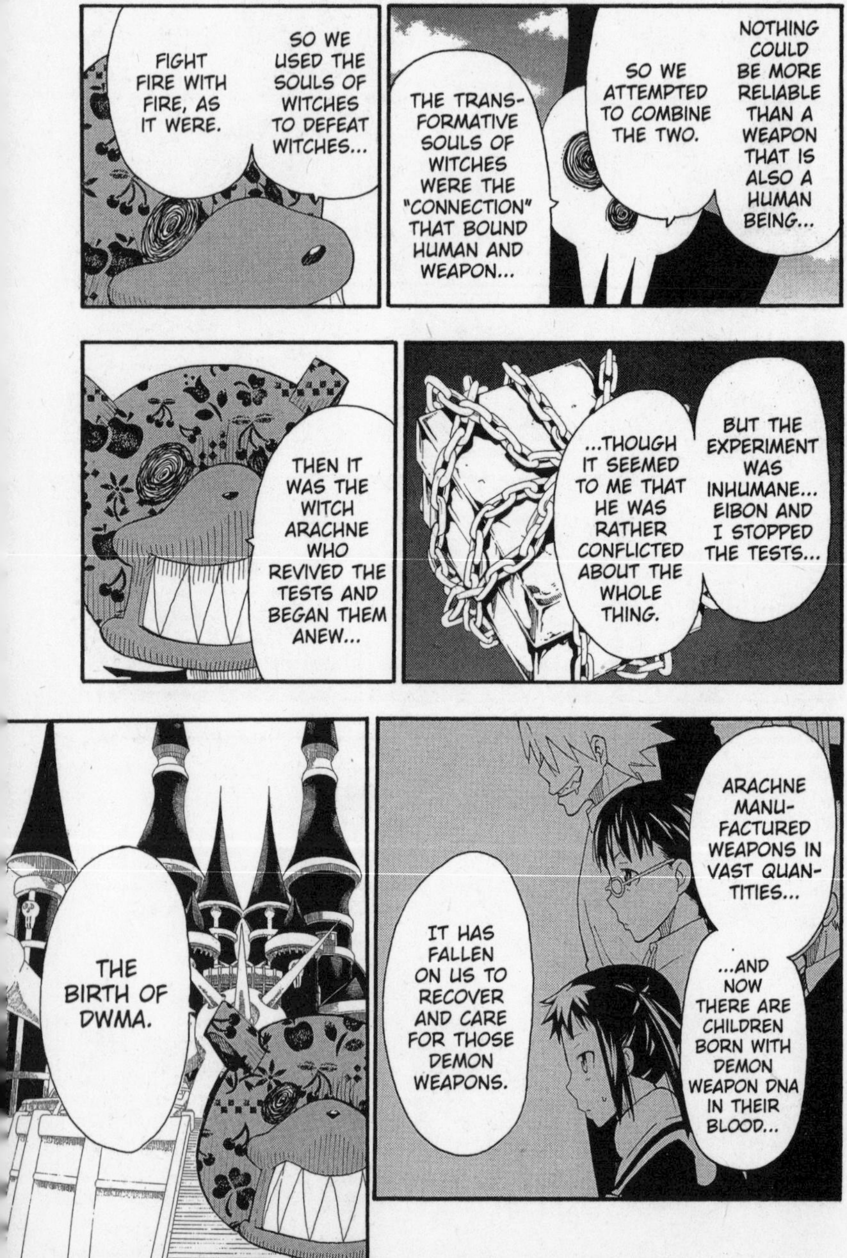
NOTHING COULD BE MORE RELIABLE THAN A WEAPON THAT IS ALSO A HUMAN BEING...
SO WE ATTEMPTED TO COMBINE THE TWO.
THE TRANSFORMATIVE SOULS OF WITCHES WERE THE "CONNECTION" THAT BOUND HUMAN AND WEAPON...
SO WE USED THE SOULS OF WITCHES TO DEFEAT WITCHES...
FIGHT FIRE WITH FIRE, AS IT WERE.
BUT THE EXPERIMENT WAS INHUMANE... EIBON AND I STOPPED THE TESTS...
...THOUGH IT SEEMED TO ME THAT HE WAS RATHER CONFLICTED ABOUT THE WHOLE THING.
THEN IT WAS THE WITCH ARACHNE WHO REVIVED THE TESTS AND BEGAN THEM ANEW...
ARACHNE MANUFACTURED WEAPONS IN VAST QUANTITIES...
...AND NOW THERE ARE CHILDREN BORN WITH DEMON WEAPON DNA IN THEIR BLOOD...
IT HAS FALLEN ON US TO RECOVER AND CARE FOR THOSE DEMON WEAPONS.
THE BIRTH OF DWMA.

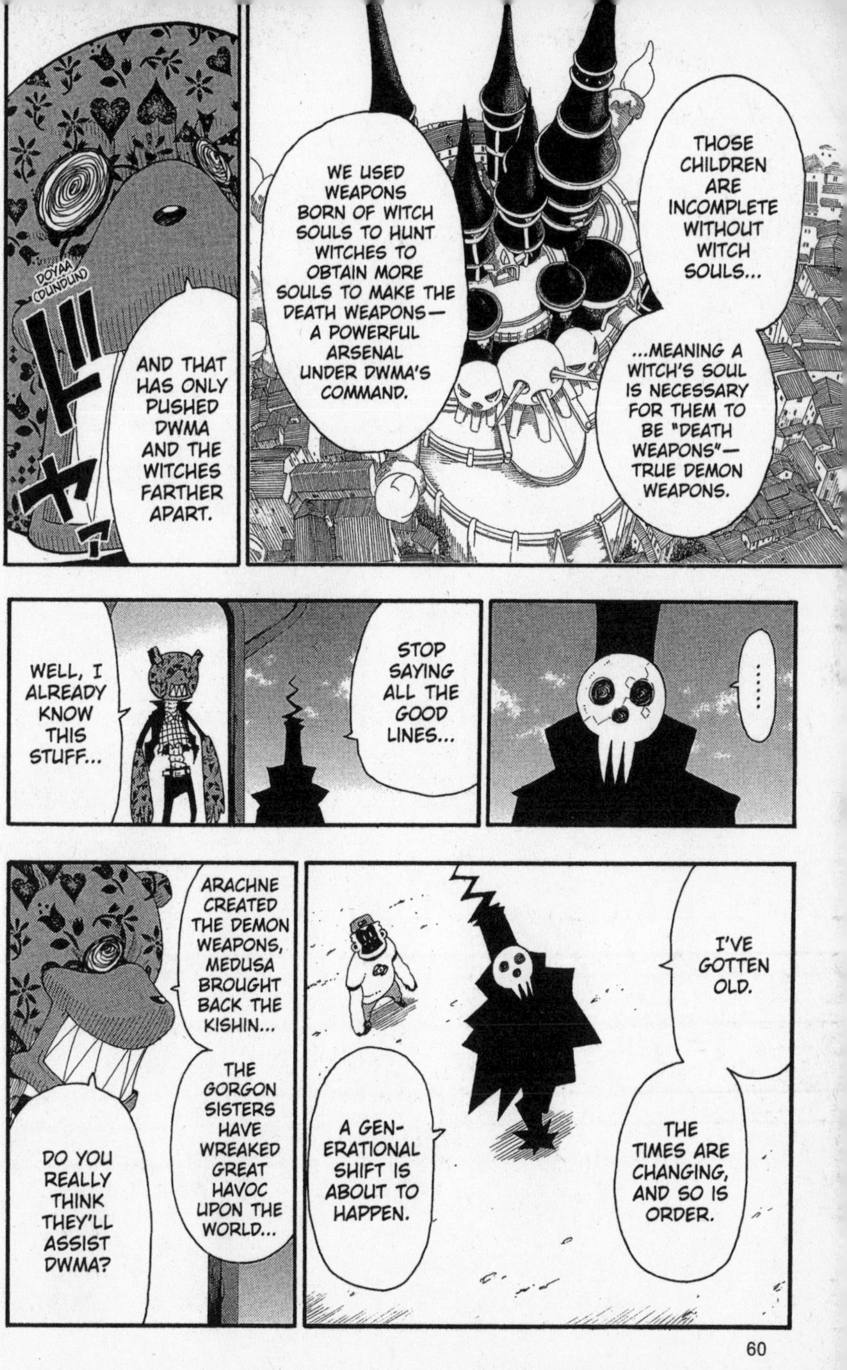
THOSE CHILDREN ARE INCOMPLETE WITHOUT WITCH SOULS...
...MEANING A WITCH'S SOUL IS NECESSARY FOR THEM TO BE "DEATH WEAPONS"—TRUE DEMON WEAPONS.
WE USED WEAPONS BORN OF WITCH SOULS TO HUNT WITCHES TO OBTAIN MORE SOULS TO MAKE THE DEATH WEAPONS—A POWERFUL ARSENAL UNDER DWMA'S COMMAND.
DOYAA (DUNDUN)
AND THAT HAS ONLY PUSHED DWMA AND THE WITCHES FARTHER APART.
......
STOP SAYING ALL THE GOOD LINES...
WELL, I ALREADY KNOW THIS STUFF...
I'VE GOTTEN OLD.
THE TIMES ARE CHANGING, AND SO IS ORDER.
A GEN-ERATIONAL SHIFT IS ABOUT TO HAPPEN.
ARACHNE CREATED THE DEMON WEAPONS, MEDUSA BROUGHT BACK THE KISHIN...
THE GORGON SISTERS HAVE WREAKED GREAT HAVOC UPON THE WORLD...
DO YOU REALLY THINK THEY'LL ASSIST DWMA?

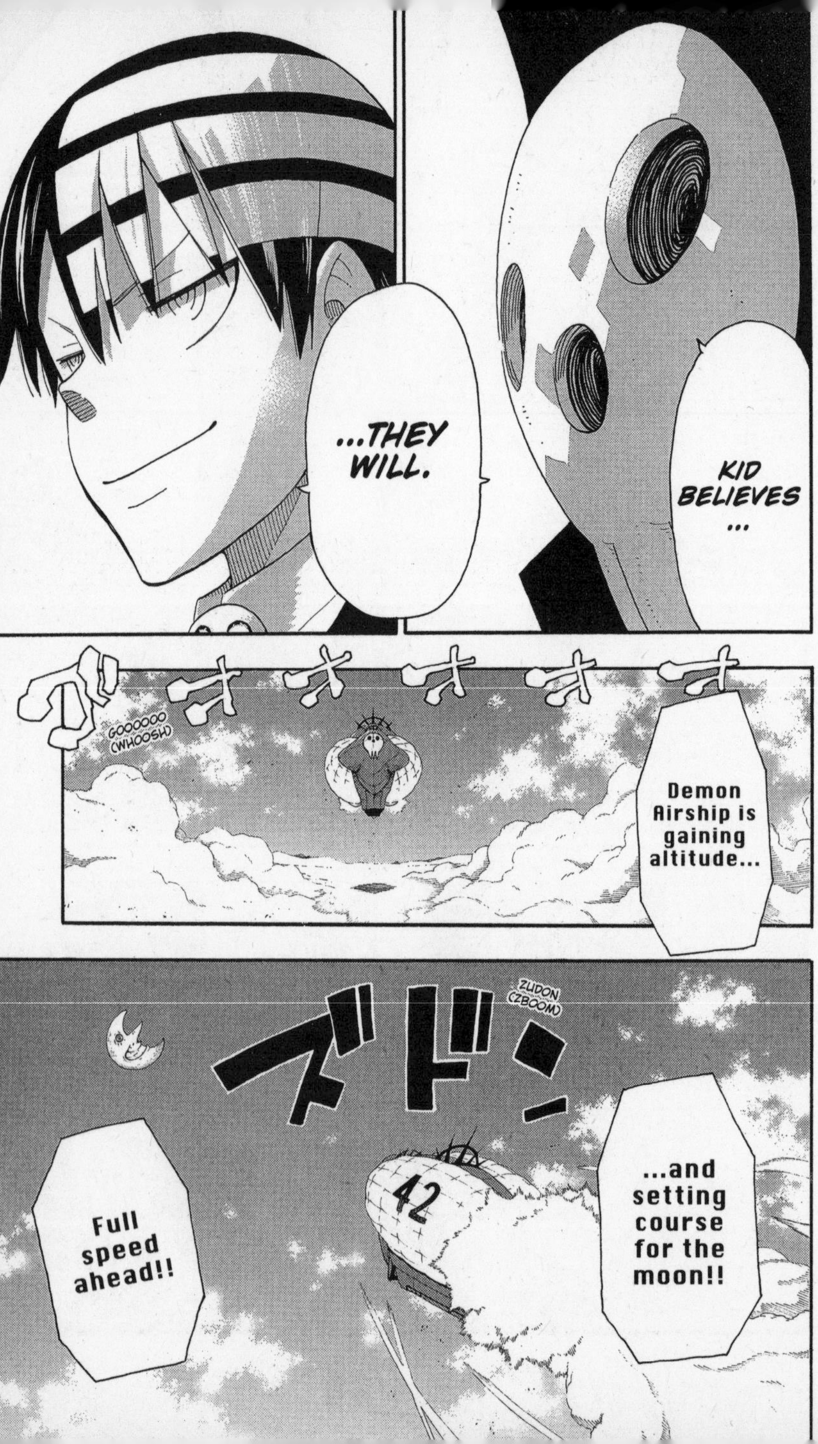
KID BELIEVES ...
...THEY WILL.
GOOOOOO (WHOOSH)
Demon Airship is gaining altitude...
ZUDON (ZBOOM)
...and setting course for the moon!!
42
Full speed ahead!!

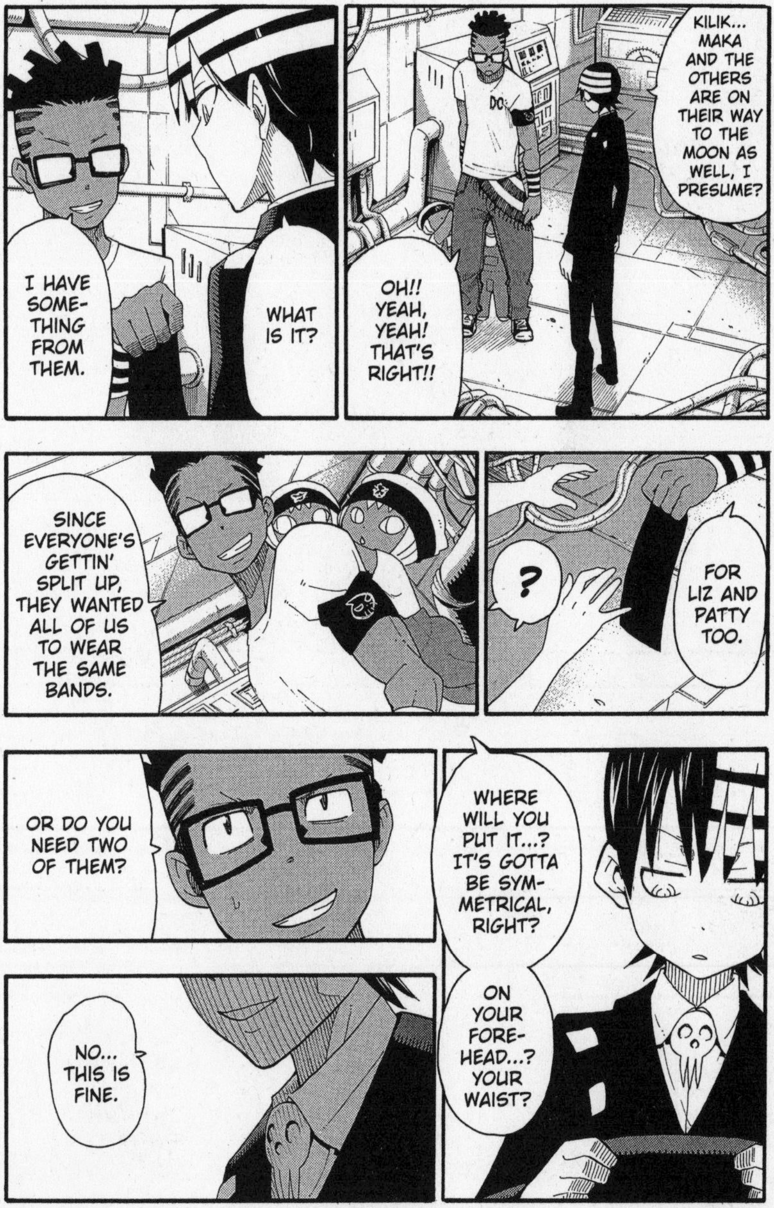
KILIK... MAKA AND THE OTHERS ARE ON THEIR WAY TO THE MOON AS WELL, I PRESUME?
OH!! YEAH, YEAH! THAT'S RIGHT!!
WHAT IS IT?
I HAVE SOME-THING FROM THEM.
FOR LIZ AND PATTY TOO.
?
SINCE EVERYONE'S GETTIN' SPLIT UP, THEY WANTED ALL OF US TO WEAR THE SAME BANDS.
WHERE WILL YOU PUT IT...? IT'S GOTTA BE SYM-METRICAL, RIGHT?
ON YOUR FORE-HEAD...? YOUR WAIST?
OR DO YOU NEED TWO OF THEM?
NO... THIS IS FINE.

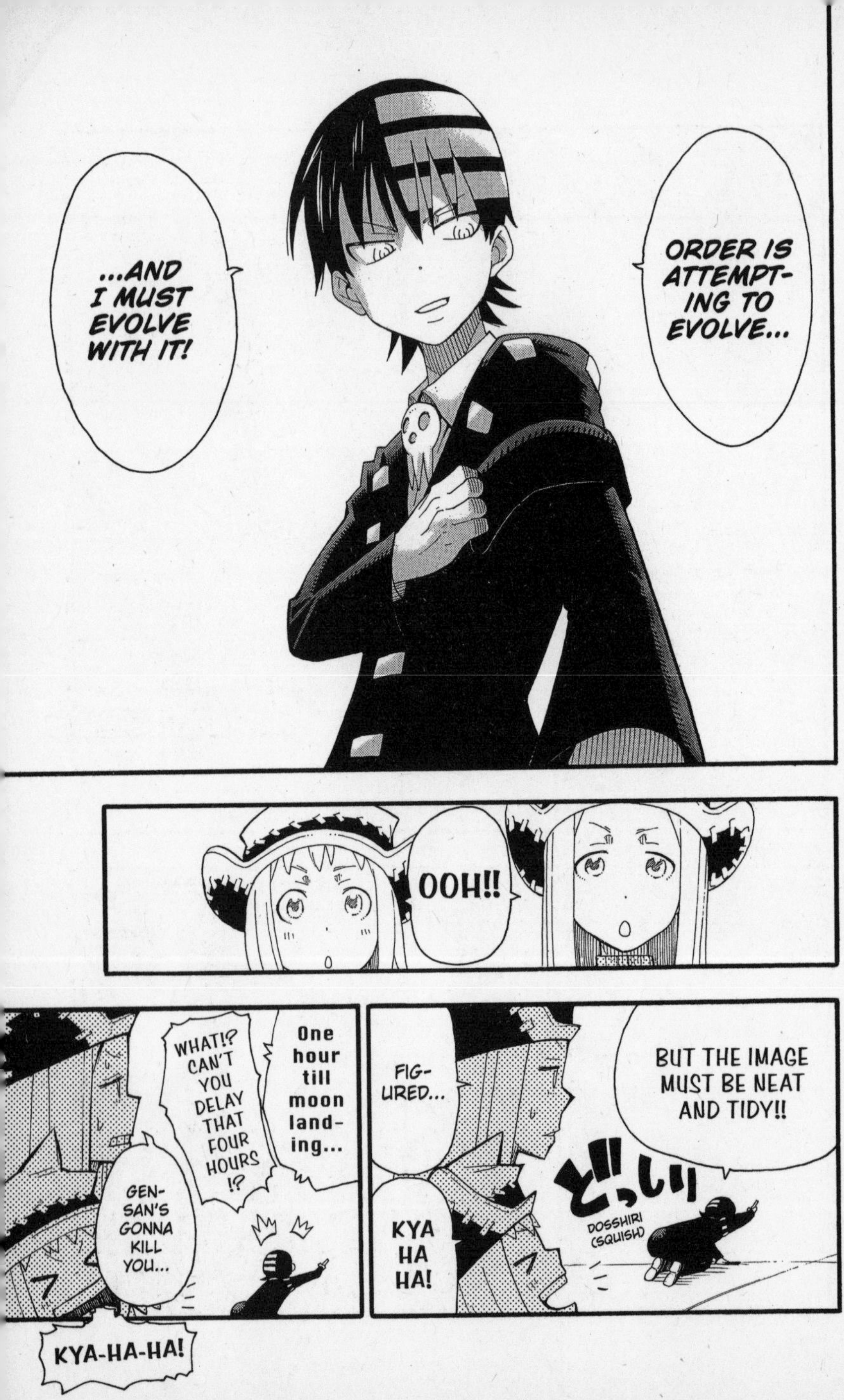
ORDER IS ATTEMPT-ING TO EVOLVE...
...AND I MUST EVOLVE WITH IT!
OOH!!
BUT THE IMAGE MUST BE NEAT AND TIDY!!
FIG-URED...
どっしり
DOSSHIRI (SQUISH)
KYA HA HA!
One hour till moon land-ing...
WHAT!? CAN'T YOU DELAY THAT FOUR HOURS!?
GEN-SAN'S GONNA KILL YOU...
KYA-HA-HA!

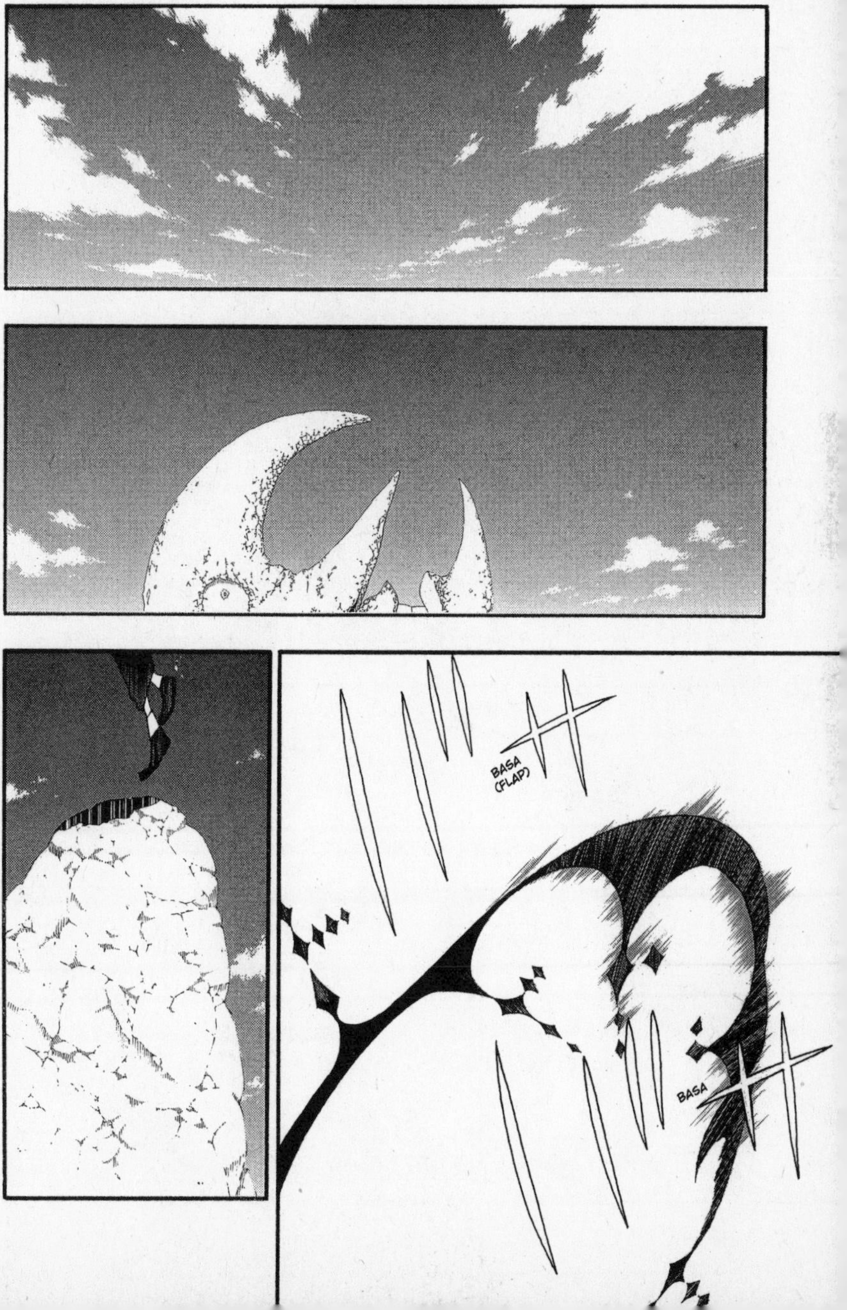
BASA
(FLAP)
BASA

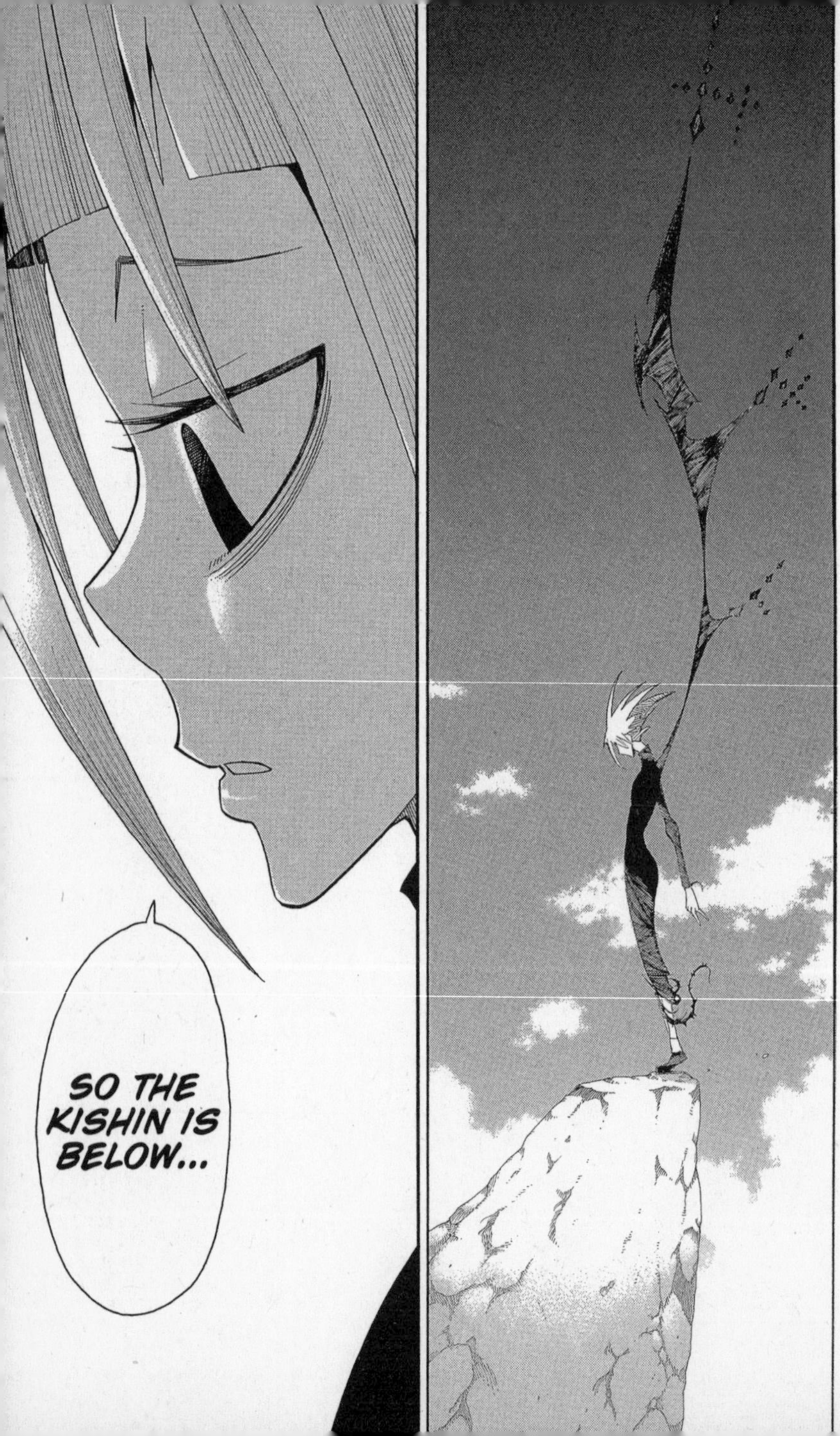
SO THE KISHIN IS BELOW...

OOO
(WHOOSH)

TA
(LEAP)

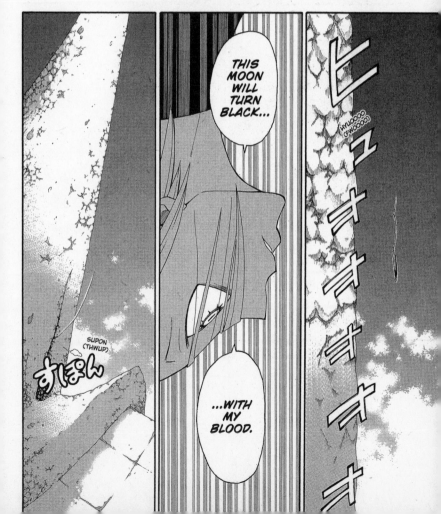

THIS MOON WILL TURN BLACK...

(WHOOO)
(WHOOO)

SUPON
(THWUP)

...WITH MY BLOOD.

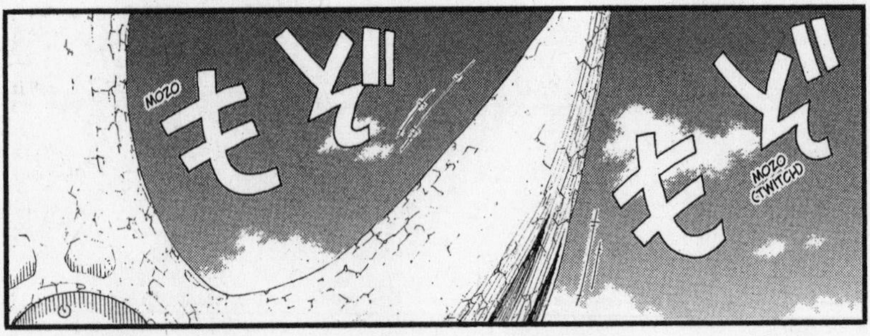
もぞ
MOZO (TWITCH)
もぞ
MOZO

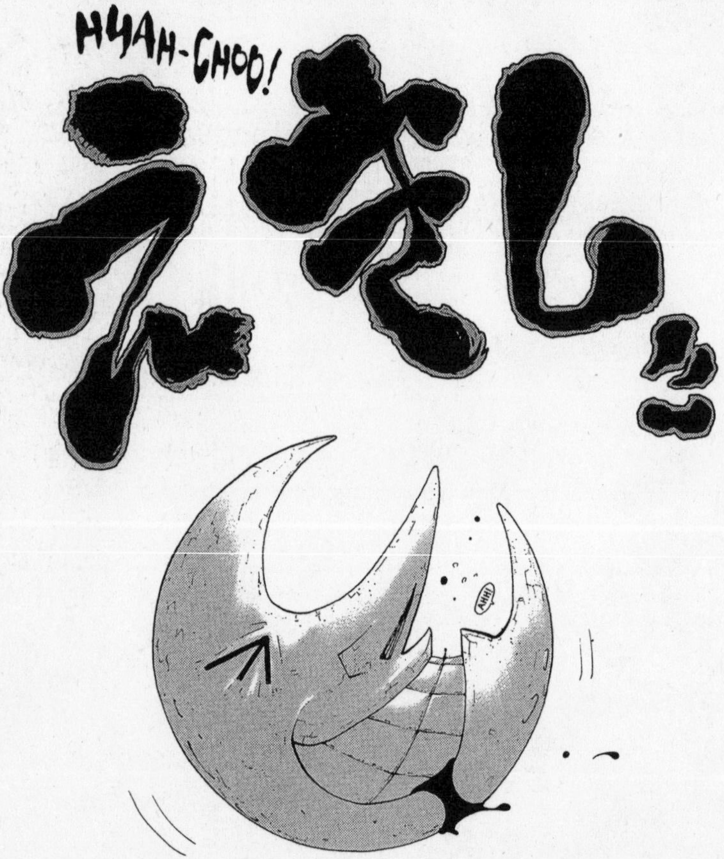
HYAH-CHOO!
AHH!

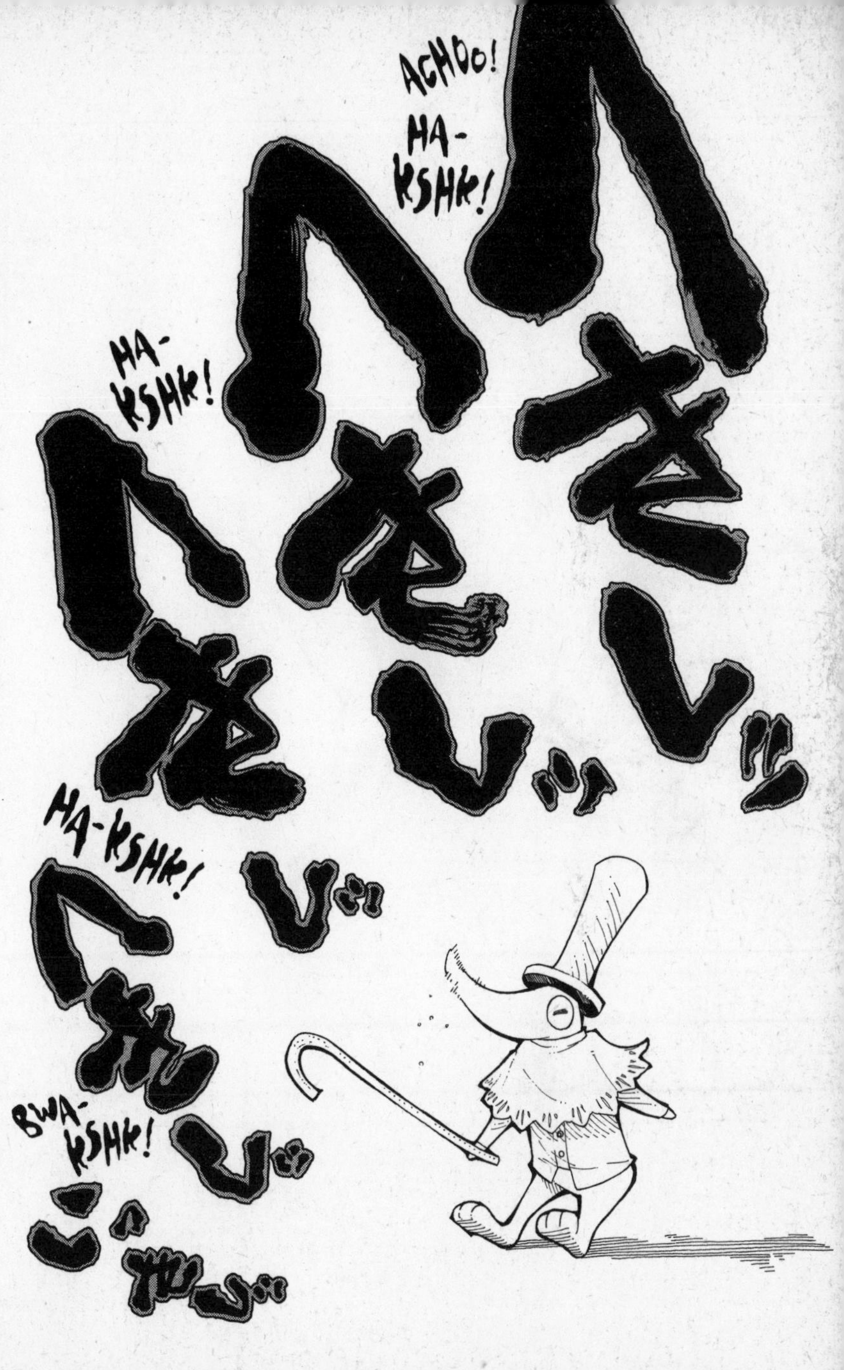
ACHOO!
HA-KSHK!
HA-KSHK!
HA-KSHK!
BWA-KSHK!

SOUL EATER

CHAPTER 100: TO THE MOON

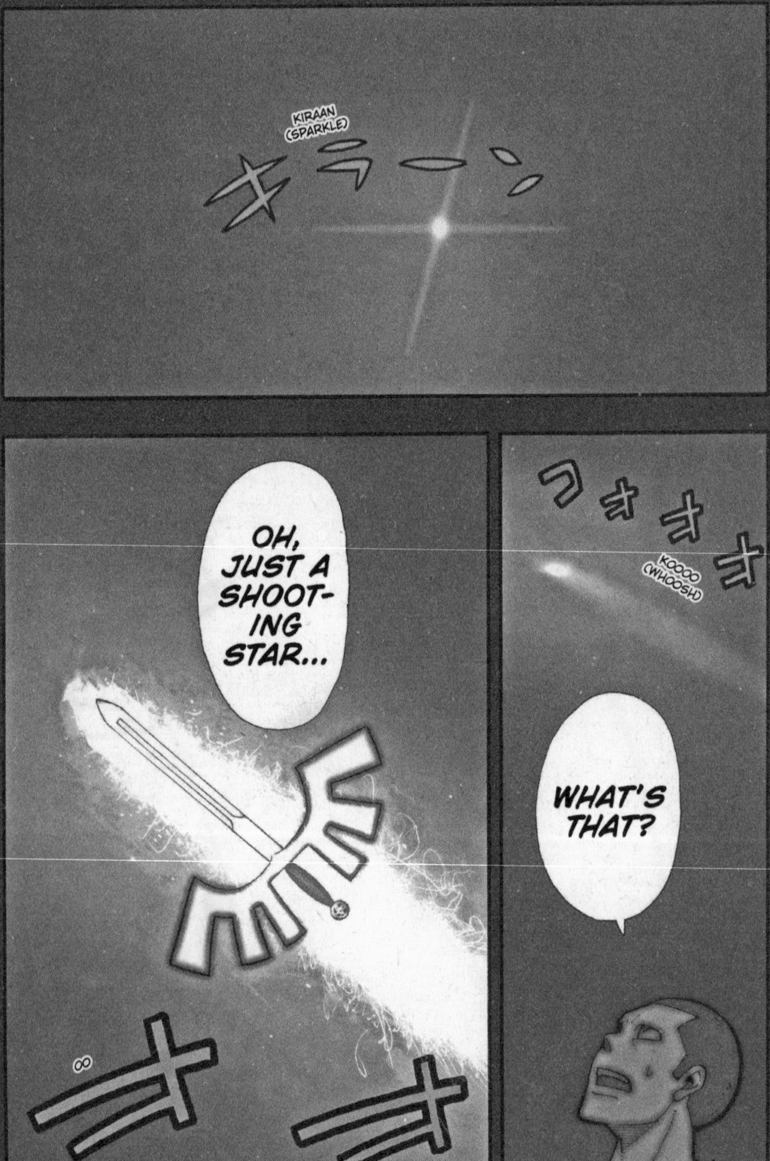
KIRAAN (SPARKLE)
KOOOO (WHOOSH)
WHAT'S THAT?
OH, JUST A SHOOT-ING STAR...

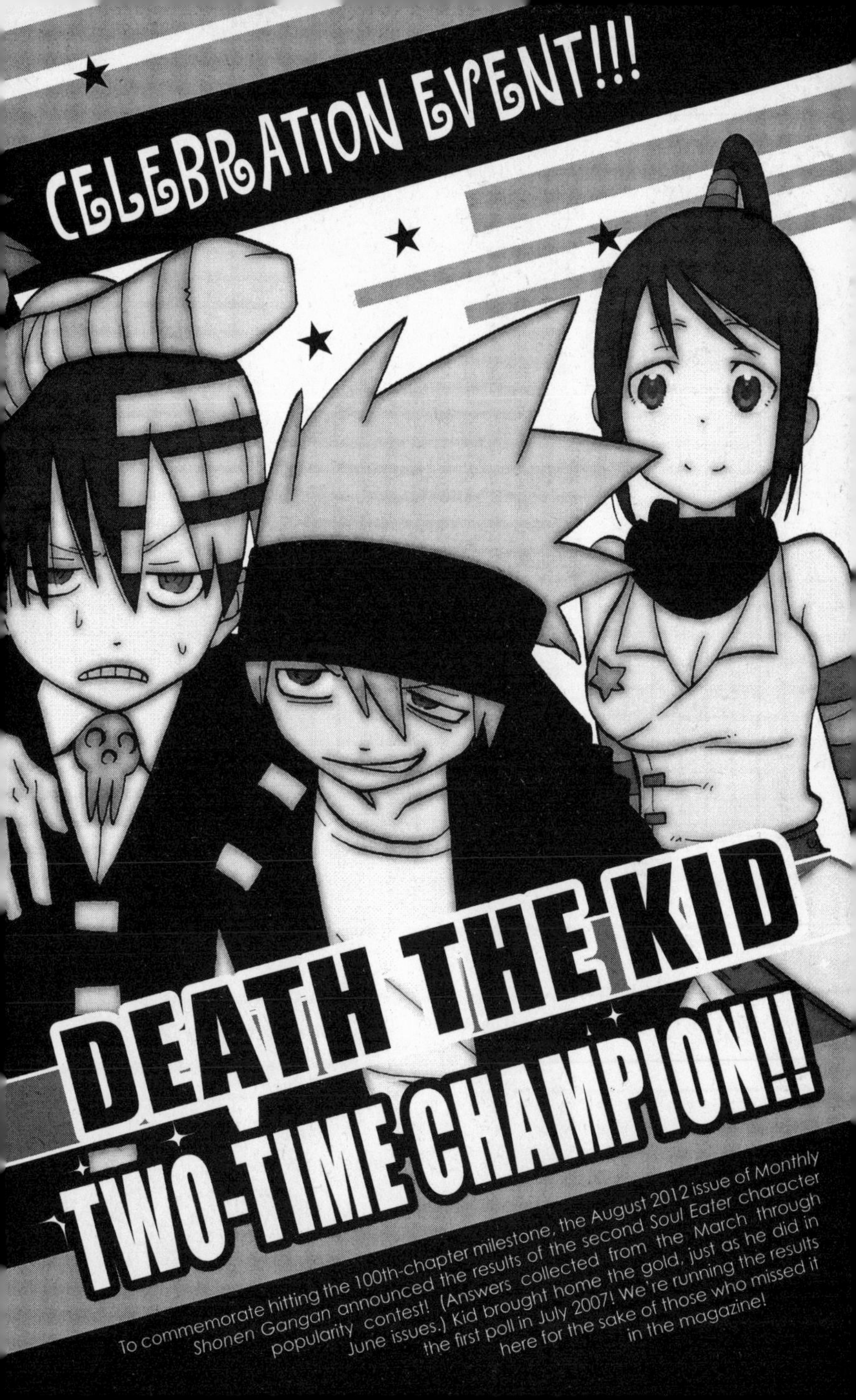
CELEBRATION EVENT!!!
DEATH THE KID
TWO-TIME CHAMPION!!
To commemorate hitting the 100th-chapter milestone, the August 2012 issue of Monthly Shonen Gangan announced the results of the second Soul Eater character popularity contest! (Answers collected from the March through June issues.) Kid brought home the gold, just as he did in the first poll in July 2007! We're running the results here for the sake of those who missed it in the magazine!

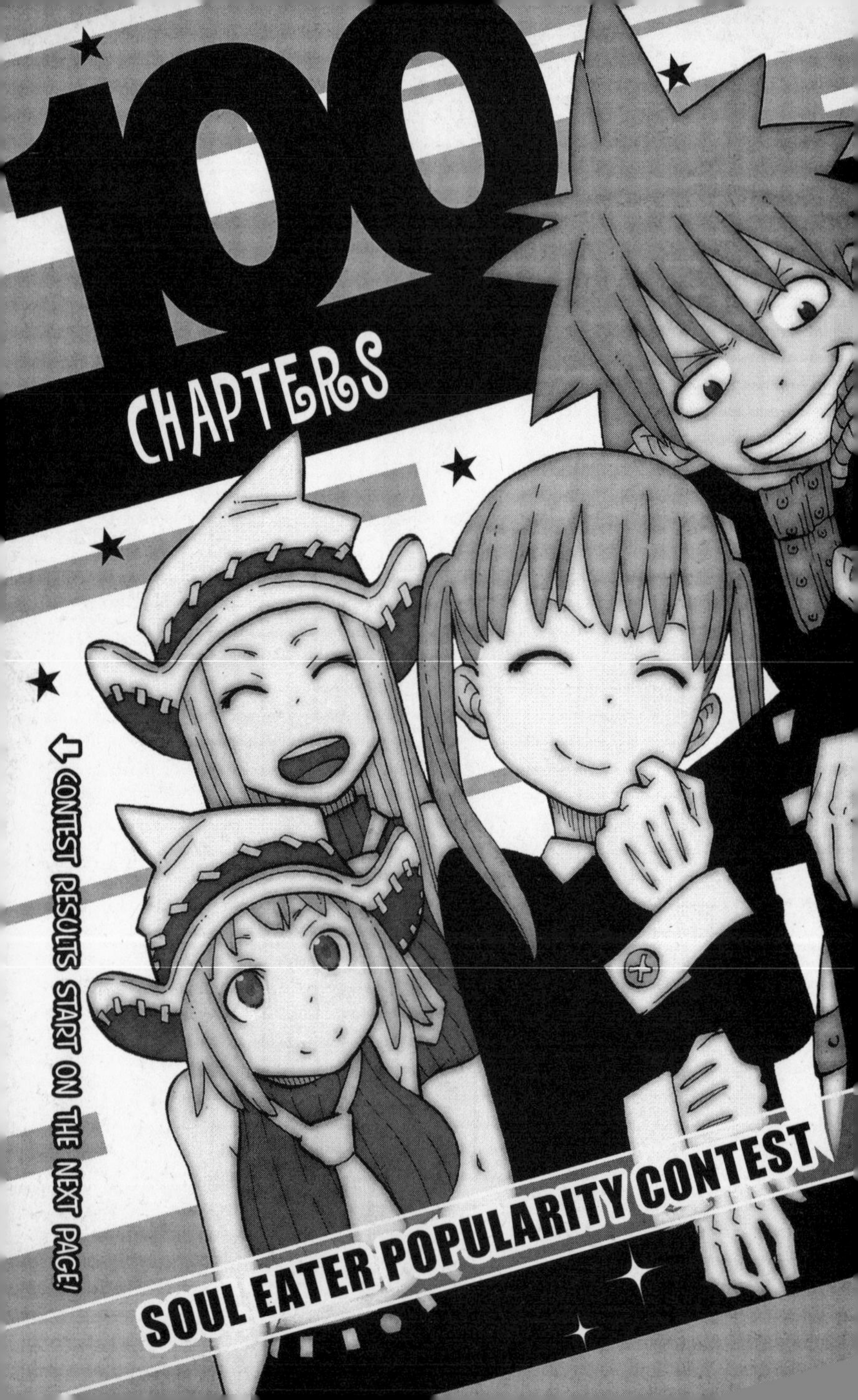
100
CHAPTERS
SOUL EATER POPULARITY CONTEST
CONTEST RESULTS START ON THE NEXT PAGE!

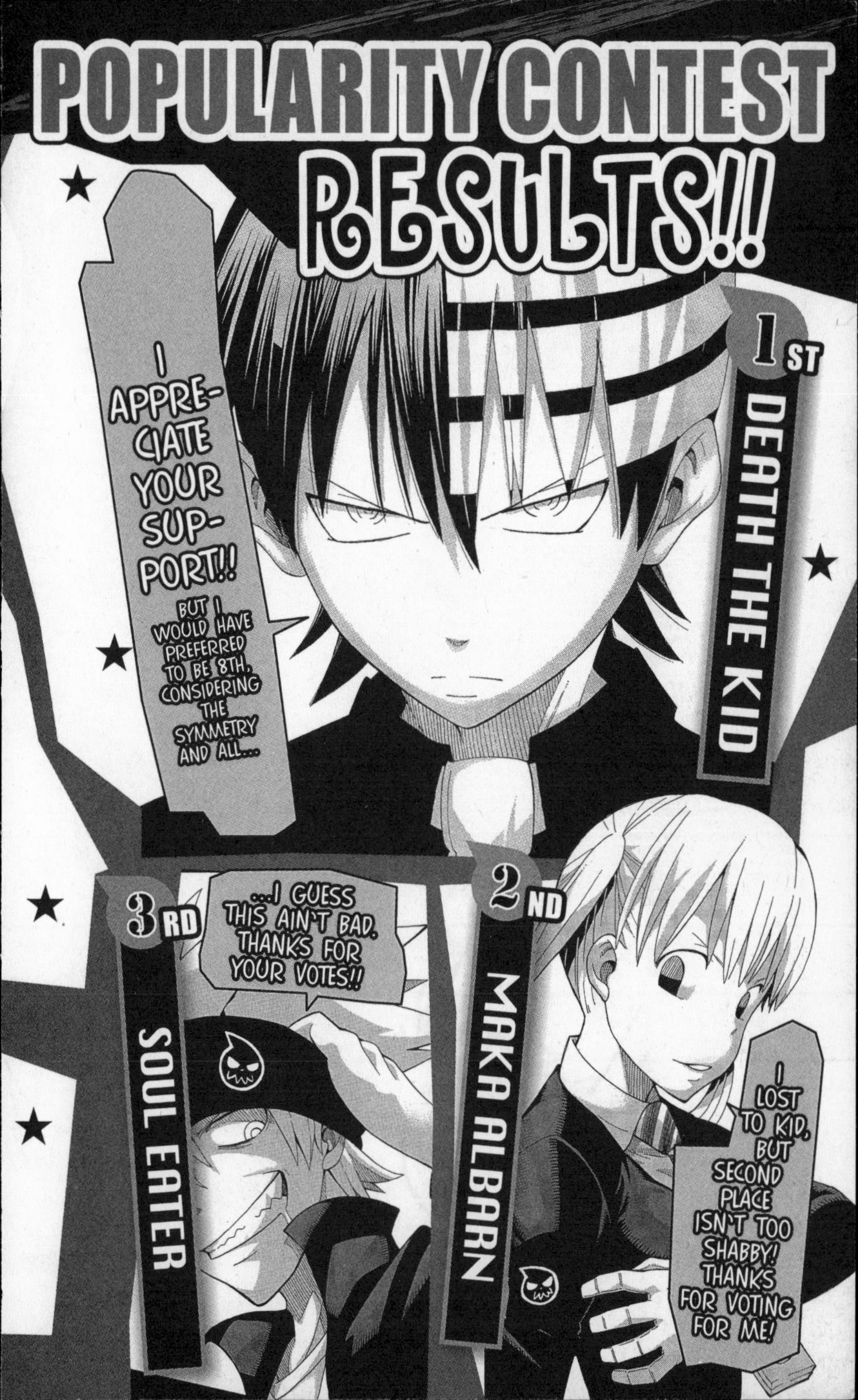

POPULARITY CONTEST RESULTS!!
1ST
DEATH THE KID
I APPRECIATE YOUR SUPPORT!!
BUT I WOULD HAVE PREFERRED TO BE 8TH, CONSIDERING THE SYMMETRY AND ALL...
2ND
MAKA ALBARN
I LOST TO KID, BUT SECOND PLACE ISN'T TOO SHABBY! THANKS FOR VOTING FOR ME!
3RD
SOUL EATER
...I GUESS THIS AIN'T BAD. THANKS FOR YOUR VOTES!!

SOUL EATER CHARACTER

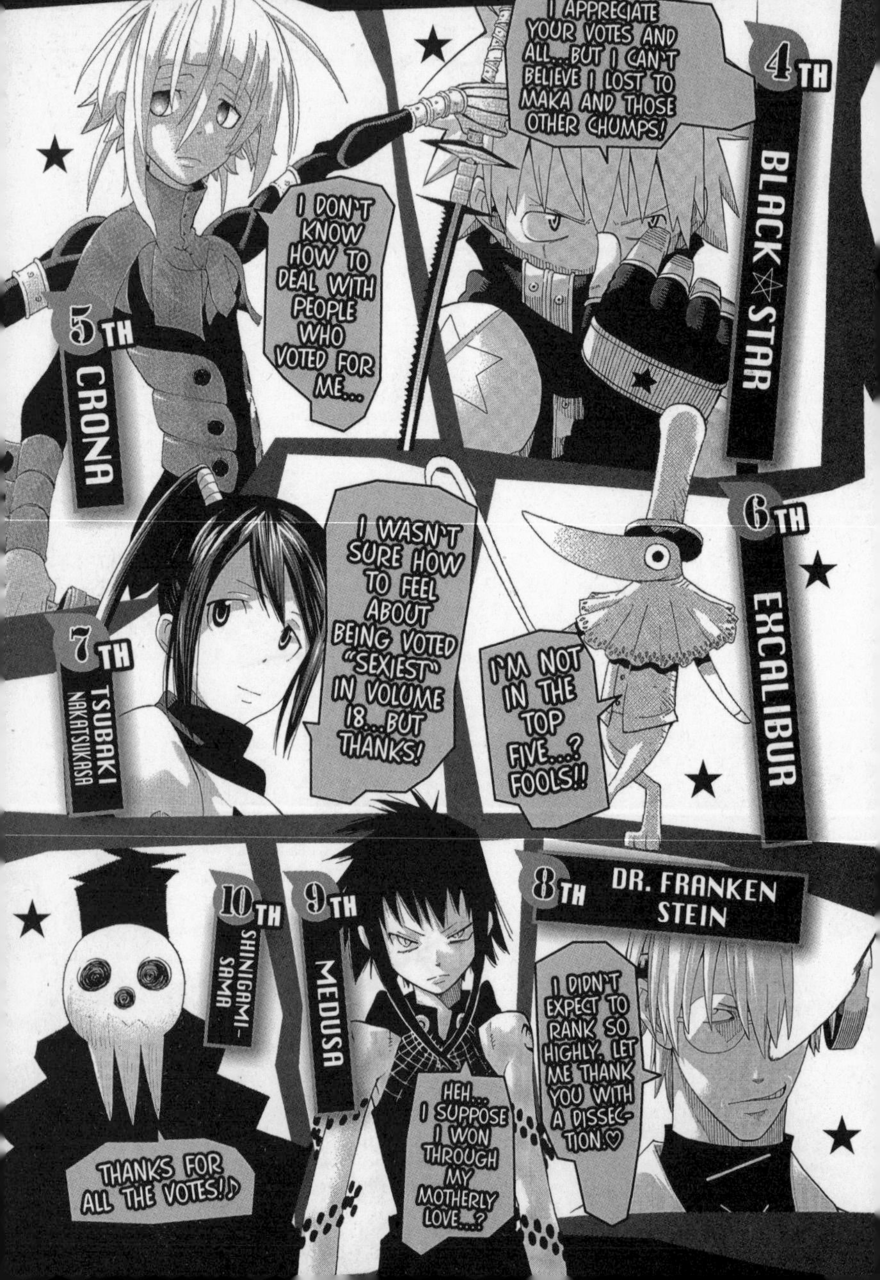

4TH
BLACK☆STAR
I APPRECIATE YOUR VOTES AND ALL...BUT I CAN'T BELIEVE I LOST TO MAKA AND THOSE OTHER CHUMPS!
5TH
CRONA
I DON'T KNOW HOW TO DEAL WITH PEOPLE WHO VOTED FOR ME...
6TH
EXCALIBUR
I'M NOT IN THE TOP FIVE...? FOOLS!!
7TH
TSUBAKI NAKATSUKASA
I WASN'T SURE HOW TO FEEL ABOUT BEING VOTED "SEXIEST" IN VOLUME 18...BUT THANKS!
8TH
DR. FRANKEN STEIN
I DIDN'T EXPECT TO RANK SO HIGHLY. LET ME THANK YOU WITH A DISSEC-TION.♡
9TH
MEDUSA
HEH... I SUPPOSE I WON THROUGH MY MOTHERLY LOVE...?
10TH
SHINIGAMI-SAMA
THANKS FOR ALL THE VOTES!♪

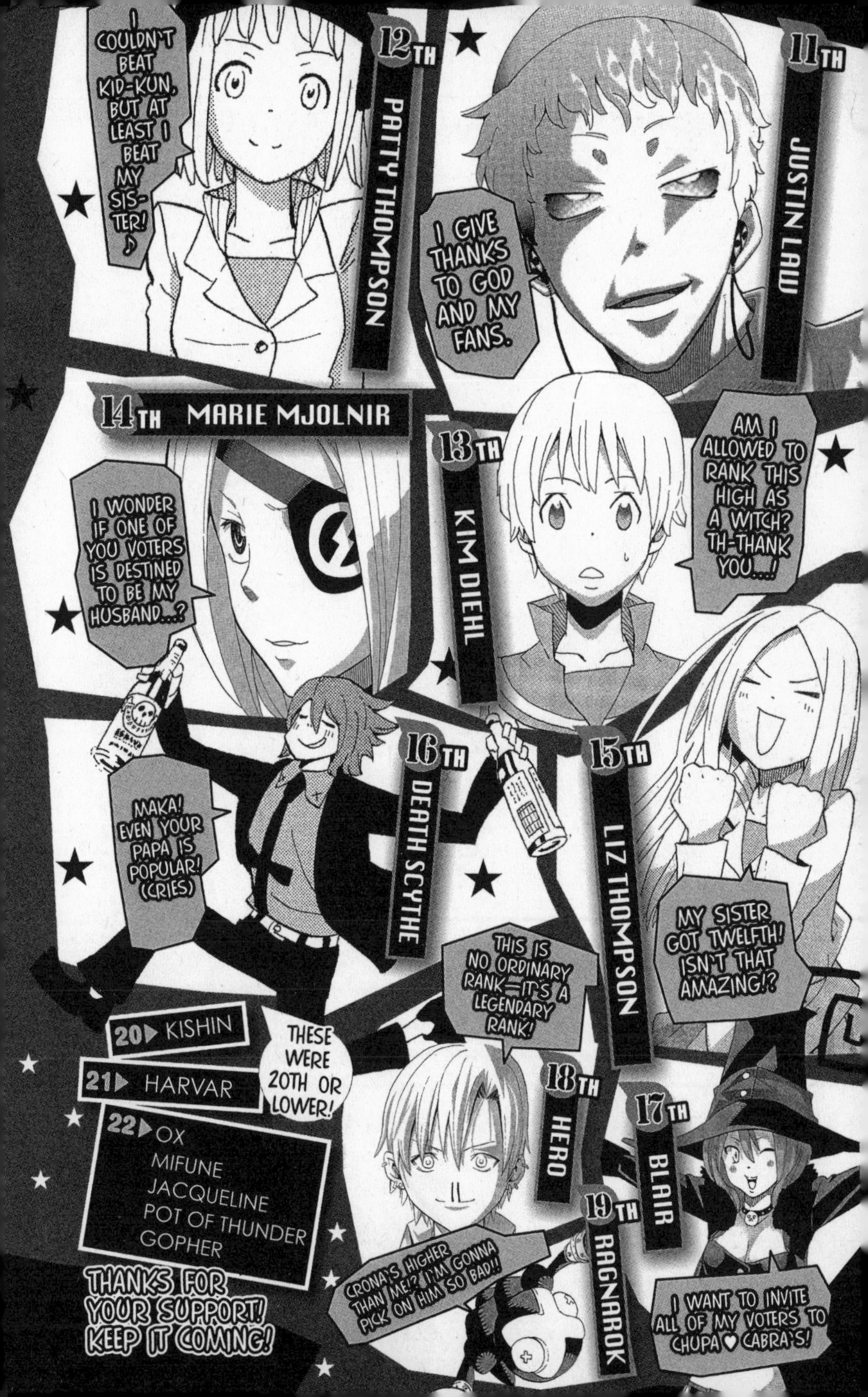
11TH
JUSTIN LAW
I GIVE THANKS TO GOD AND MY FANS.
12TH
PATTY THOMPSON
I COULDN'T BEAT KID-KUN, BUT AT LEAST I BEAT MY SIS-TER! ♪
13TH
KIM DIEHL
AM I ALLOWED TO RANK THIS HIGH AS A WITCH? TH-THANK YOU...!
14TH
MARIE MJOLNIR
I WONDER IF ONE OF YOU VOTERS IS DESTINED TO BE MY HUSBAND...?
15TH
LIZ THOMPSON
MY SISTER GOT TWELFTH! ISN'T THAT AMAZING!?
16TH
DEATH SCYTHE
MAKA! EVEN YOUR PAPA IS POPULAR! (CRIES)
17TH
BLAIR
I WANT TO INVITE ALL OF MY VOTERS TO CHUPA♥CABRA'S!
18TH
HERO
THIS IS NO ORDINARY RANK—IT'S A LEGENDARY RANK!
19TH
RAGNAROK
CRONA'S HIGHER THAN ME!? I'M GONNA PICK ON HIM SO BAD!!
THESE WERE 20TH OR LOWER!
20▶ KISHIN
21▶ HARVAR
22▶ OX
MIFUNE
JACQUELINE
POT OF THUNDER
GOPHER
THANKS FOR YOUR SUPPORT! KEEP IT COMING!

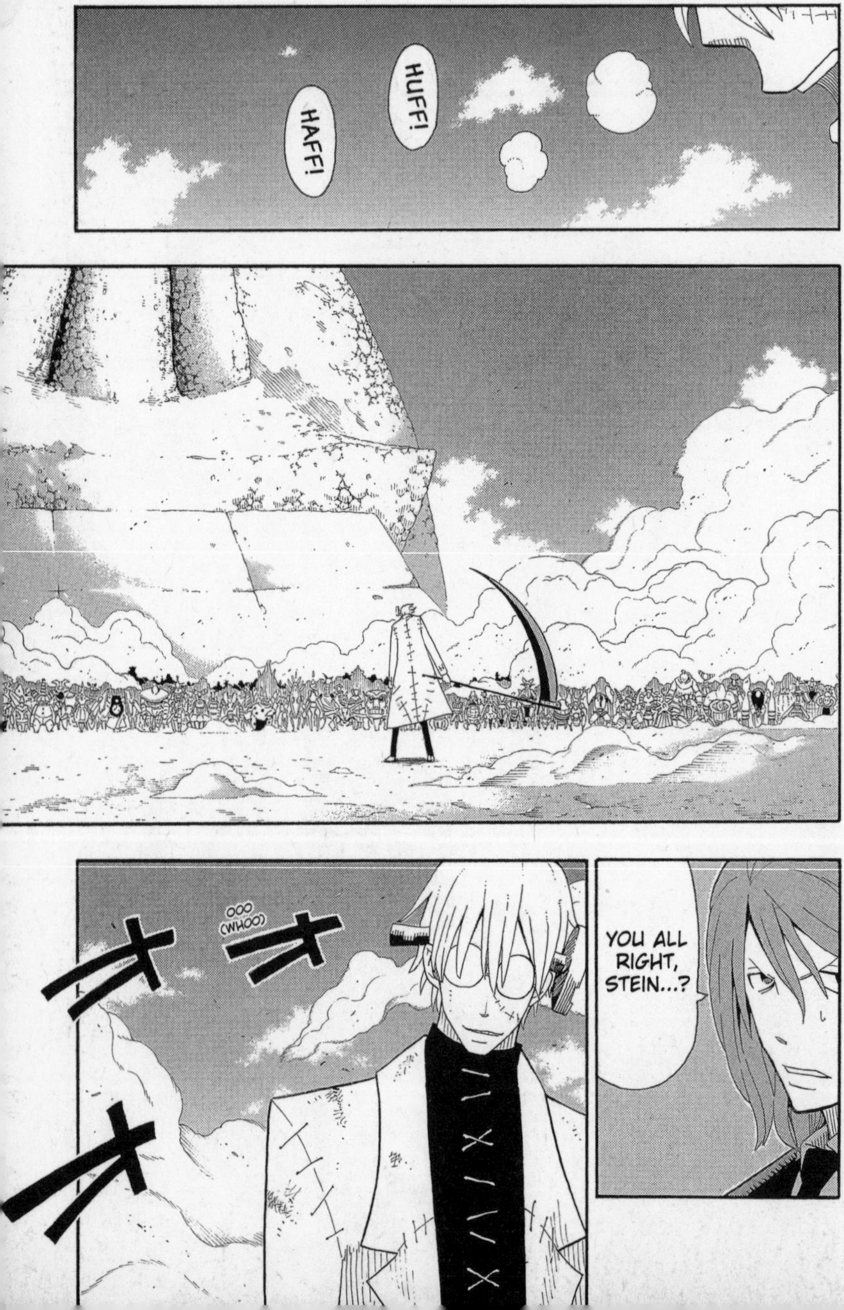
HUFF!
HAFF!
YOU ALL RIGHT, STEIN...?
OOO
(WHOO)

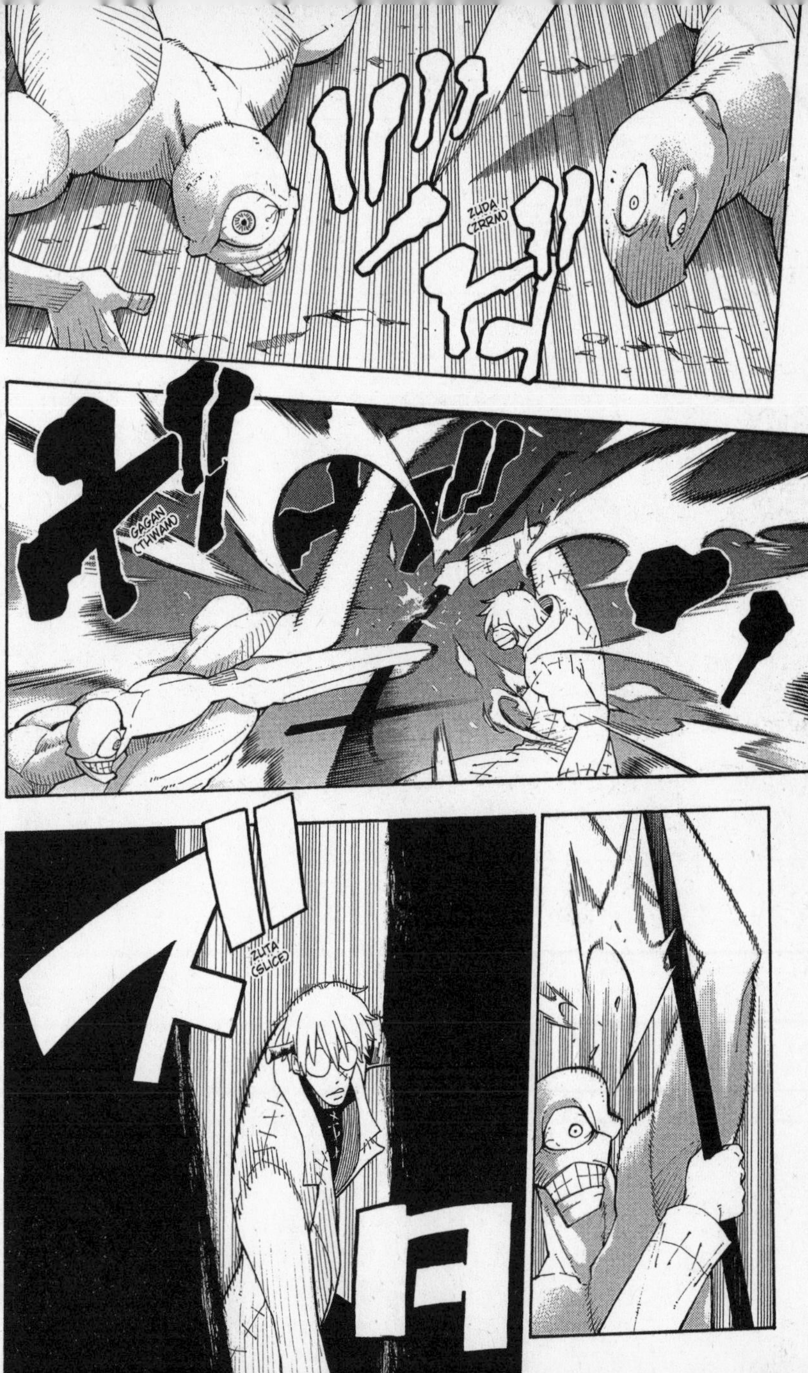
ZUDA (ZRRM)
GAGAN (THWAM)
ZUTA (SLICE)

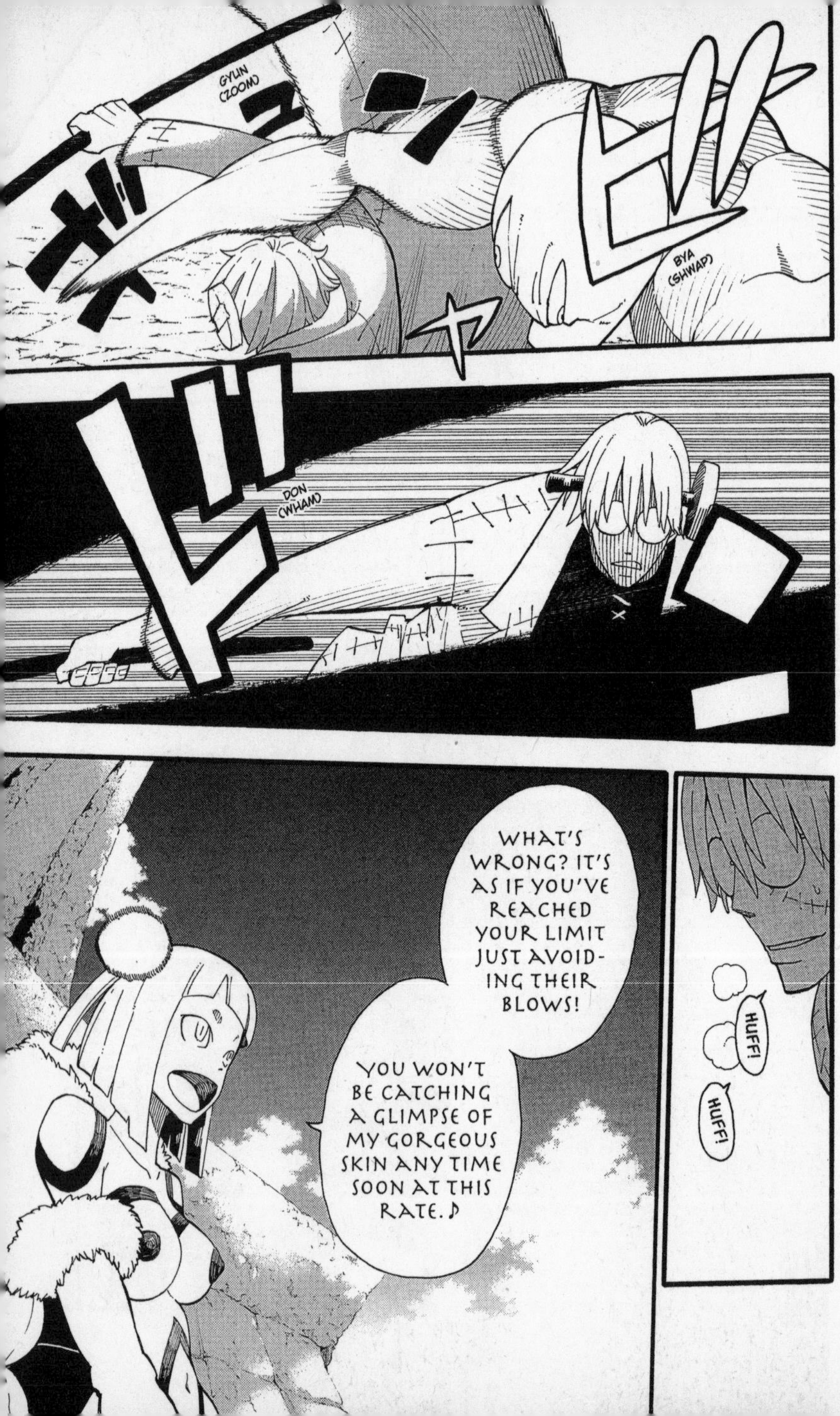
BYA (SHWAP)
GYUN (ZOOM)
DON (WHAM)
HUFF!
HUFF!
WHAT'S WRONG? IT'S AS IF YOU'VE REACHED YOUR LIMIT JUST AVOIDING THEIR BLOWS!
YOU WON'T BE CATCHING A GLIMPSE OF MY GORGEOUS SKIN ANY TIME SOON AT THIS RATE.♪

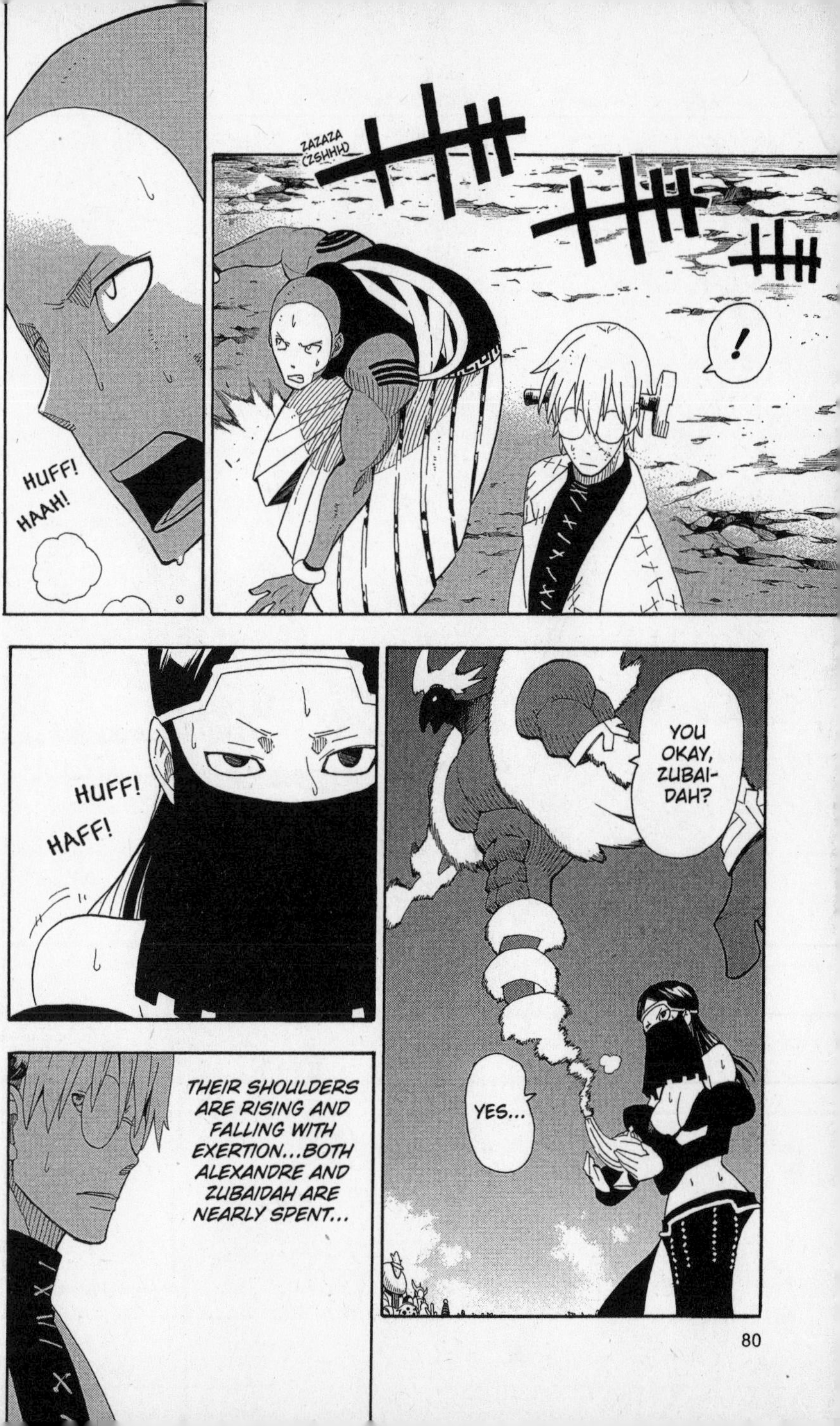
ZAZAZA (ZSHHH)
!
HUFF! HAAH!
YOU OKAY, ZUBAI-DAH?
YES...
HUFF! HAFF!
THEIR SHOULDERS ARE RISING AND FALLING WITH EXERTION...BOTH ALEXANDRE AND ZUBAIDAH ARE NEARLY SPENT...

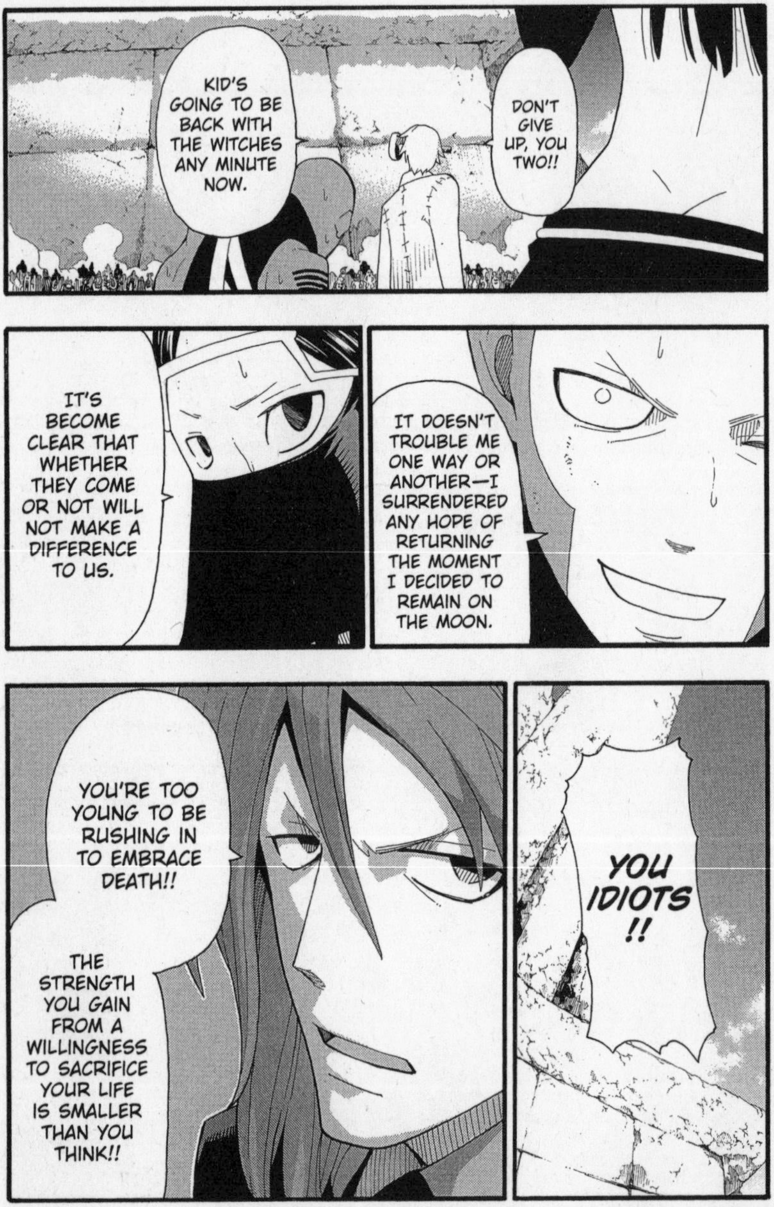
DON'T GIVE UP, YOU TWO!!
KID'S GOING TO BE BACK WITH THE WITCHES ANY MINUTE NOW.
IT DOESN'T TROUBLE ME ONE WAY OR ANOTHER—I SURRENDERED ANY HOPE OF RETURNING THE MOMENT I DECIDED TO REMAIN ON THE MOON.
IT'S BECOME CLEAR THAT WHETHER THEY COME OR NOT WILL NOT MAKE A DIFFERENCE TO US.
YOU IDIOTS!!
YOU'RE TOO YOUNG TO BE RUSHING IN TO EMBRACE DEATH!!
THE STRENGTH YOU GAIN FROM A WILLINGNESS TO SACRIFICE YOUR LIFE IS SMALLER THAN YOU THINK!!

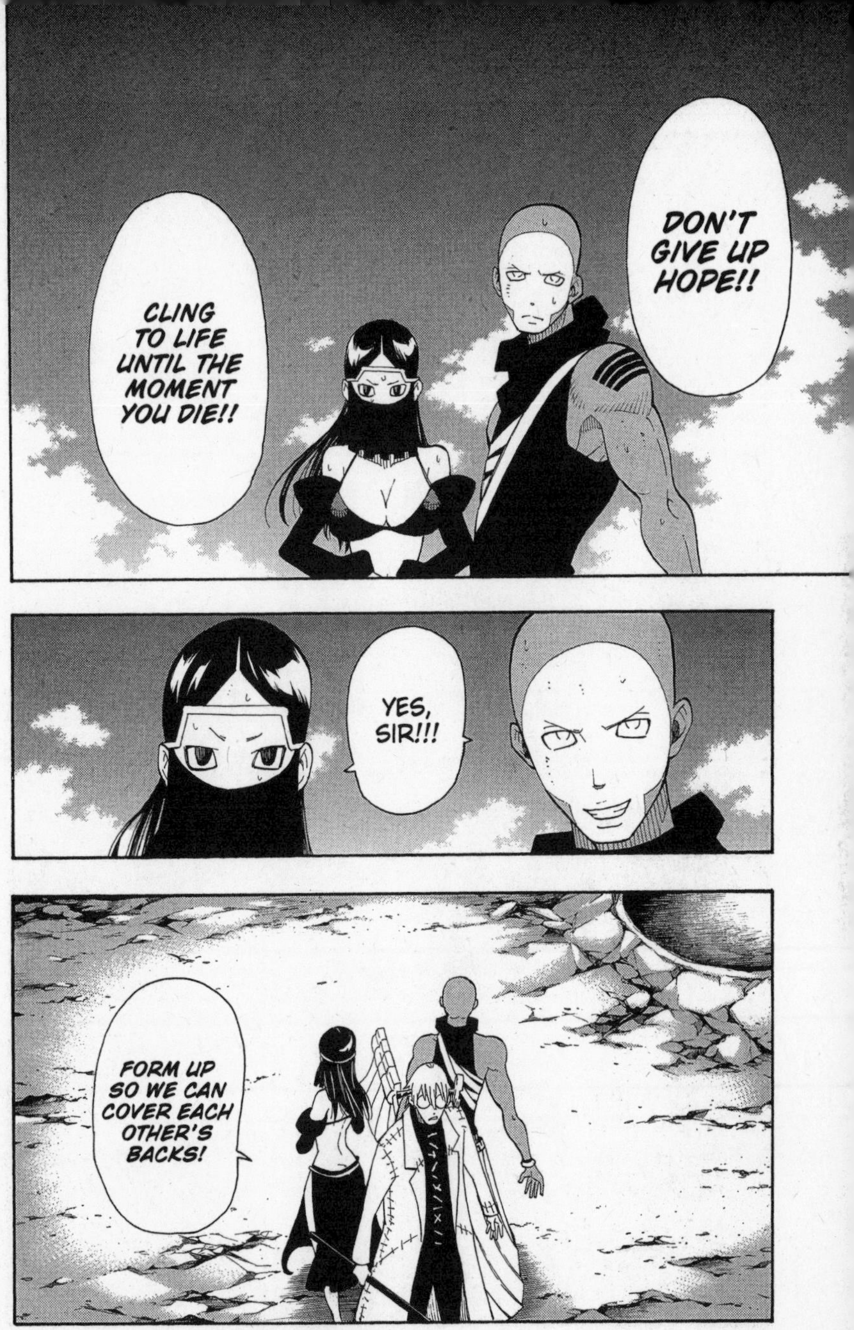
DON'T GIVE UP HOPE!!
CLING TO LIFE UNTIL THE MOMENT YOU DIE!!
YES, SIR!!!
FORM UP SO WE CAN COVER EACH OTHER'S BACKS!

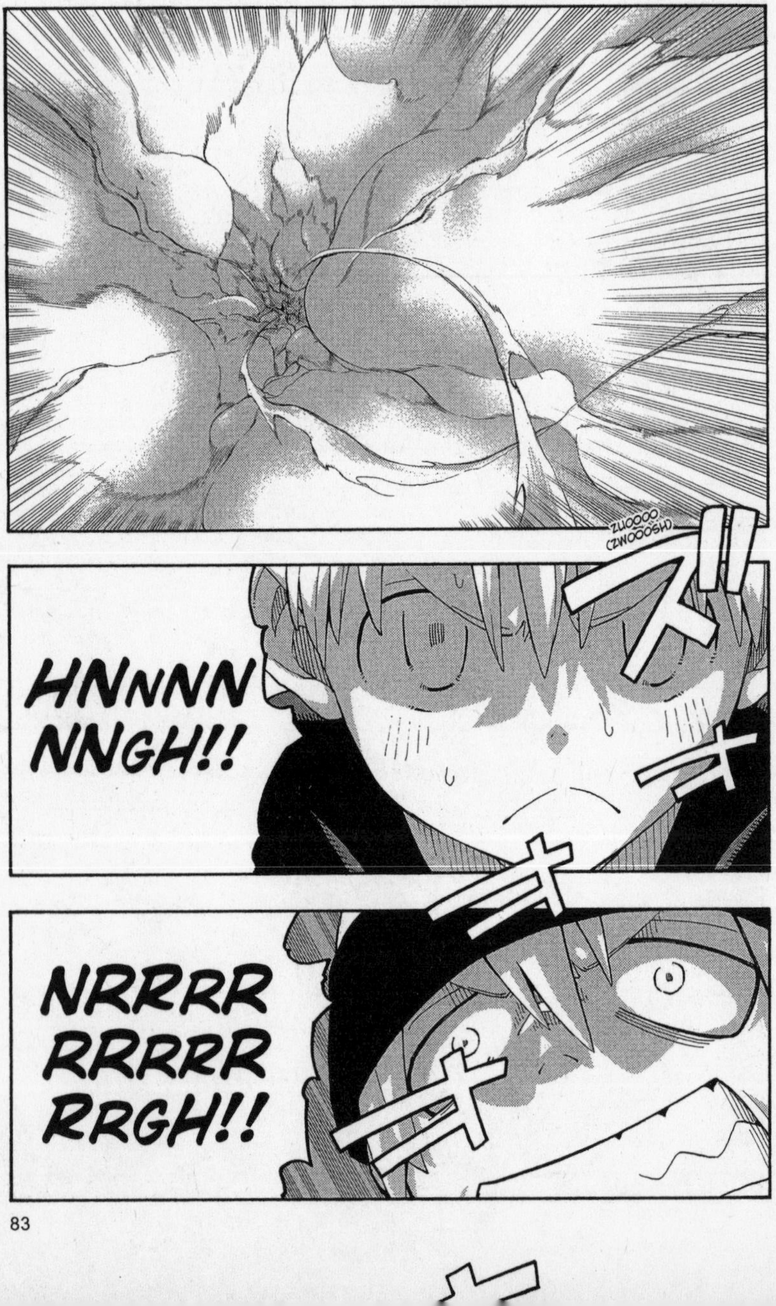
ZUOOOO~
(ZWOOOSH)
HNNNN
NNGH!!
NRRRR
RRRRR
RRGH!!

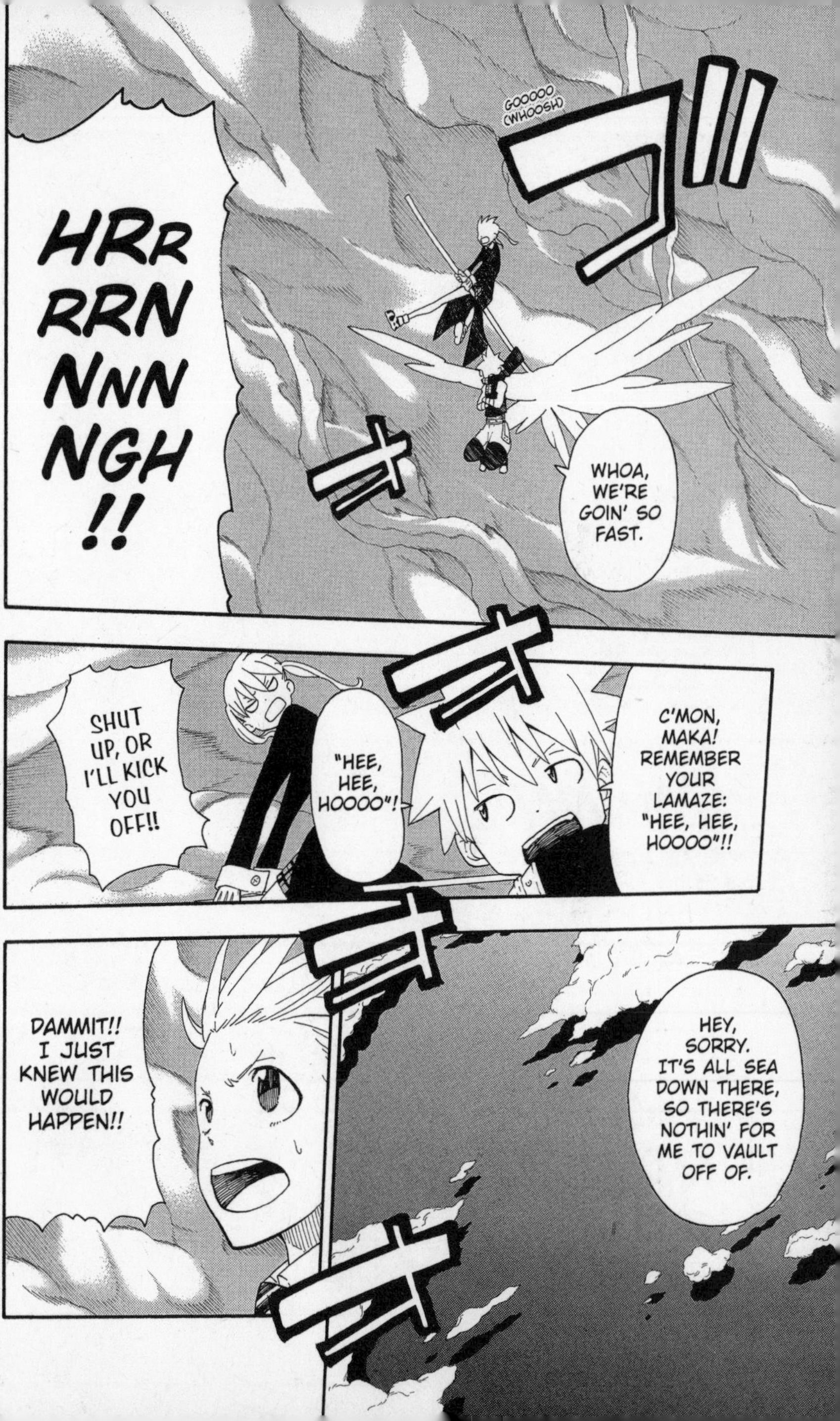
GOOOOO (WHOOSH)
WHOA, WE'RE GOIN' SO FAST.
HRRRRRNNNNNGH!!
C'MON, MAKA! REMEMBER YOUR LAMAZE: "HEE, HEE, HOOOO"!!
"HEE, HEE, HOOOO"!
SHUT UP, OR I'LL KICK YOU OFF!!
HEY, SORRY. IT'S ALL SEA DOWN THERE, SO THERE'S NOTHIN' FOR ME TO VAULT OFF OF.
DAMMIT!! I JUST KNEW THIS WOULD HAPPEN!!

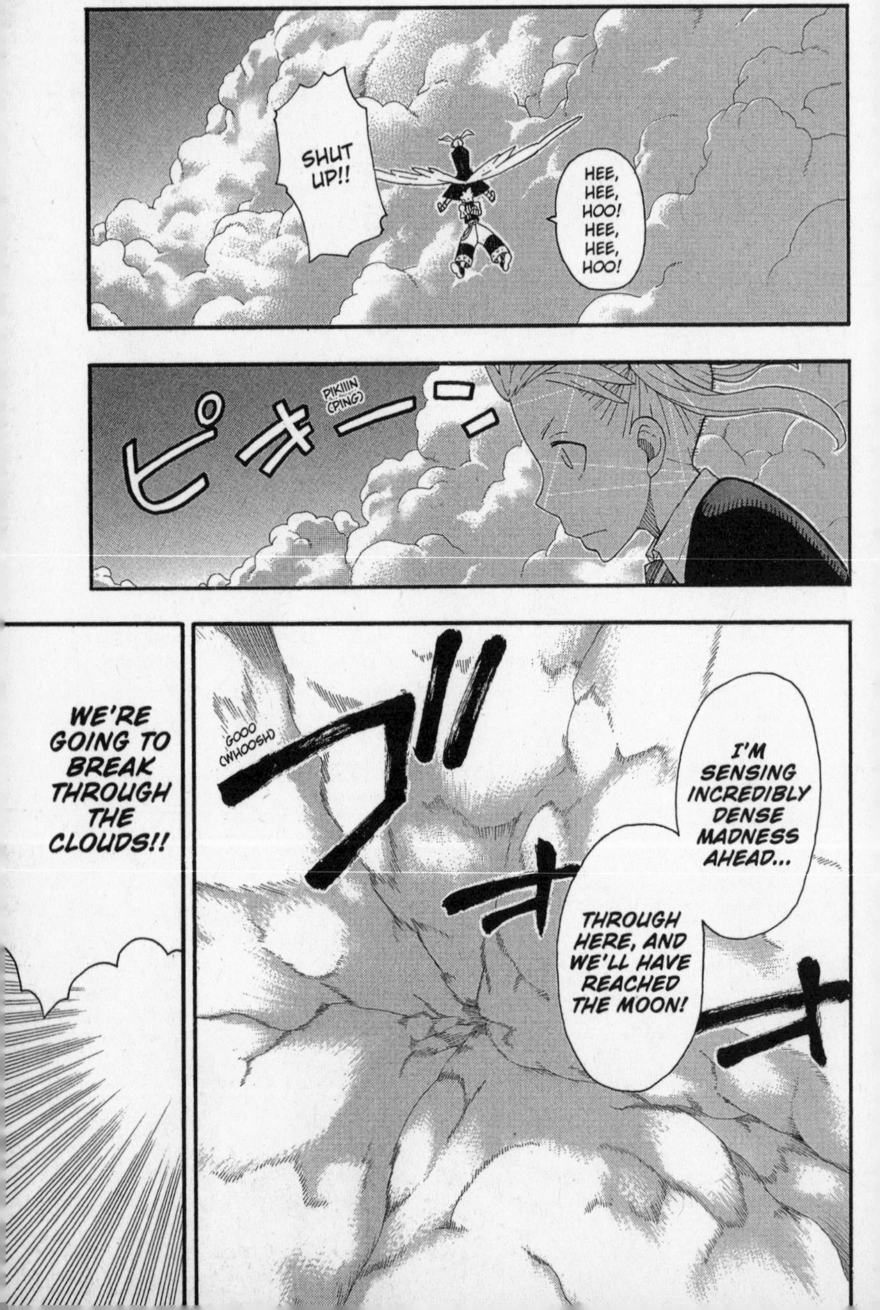
HEE, HEE, HOO! HEE, HEE, HOO!
SHUT UP!!
PIKIIIN (PING)
I'M SENSING INCREDIBLY DENSE MADNESS AHEAD...
THROUGH HERE, AND WE'LL HAVE REACHED THE MOON!
GOOO (WHOOSH)
WE'RE GOING TO BREAK THROUGH THE CLOUDS!!

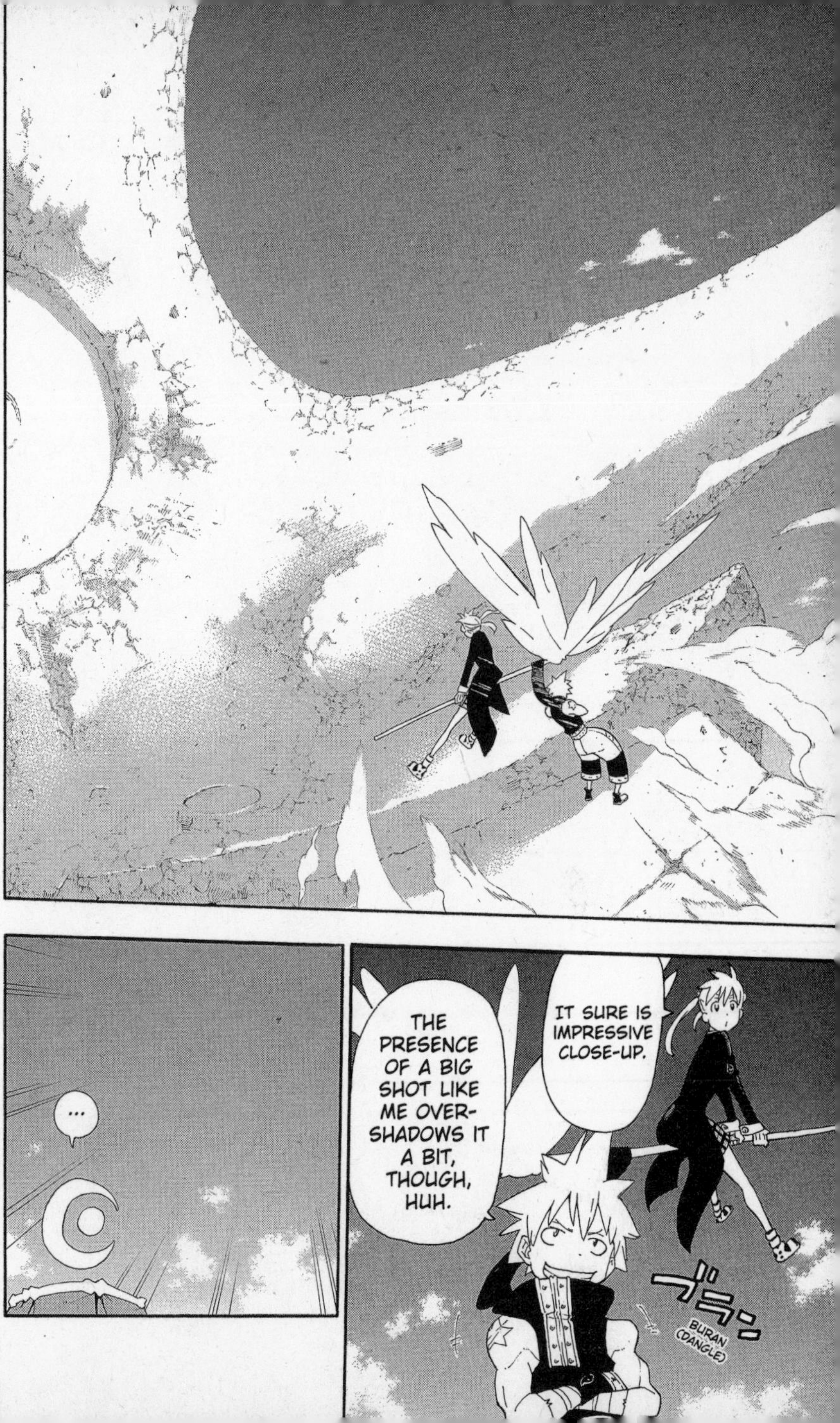
IT SURE IS IMPRESSIVE CLOSE-UP.
THE PRESENCE OF A BIG SHOT LIKE ME OVER-SHADOWS IT A BIT, THOUGH, HUH.
BURAN (DANGLE)
...

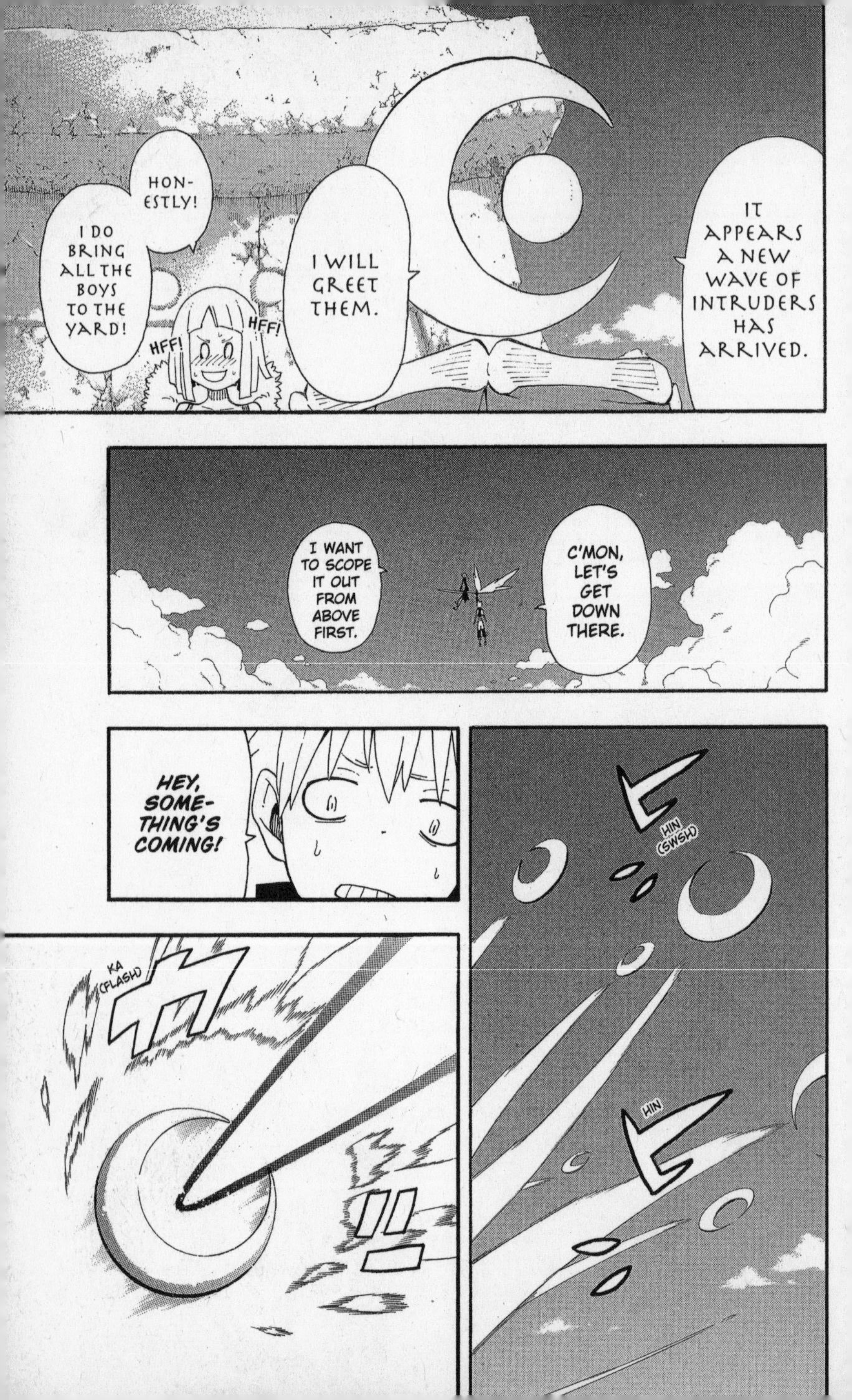
IT APPEARS A NEW WAVE OF INTRUDERS HAS ARRIVED.
I WILL GREET THEM.
HON-ESTLY!
HFF!
HFF!
I DO BRING ALL THE BOYS TO THE YARD!
C'MON, LET'S GET DOWN THERE.
I WANT TO SCOPE IT OUT FROM ABOVE FIRST.
HIN (SWSH)
HIN
HEY, SOME-THING'S COMING!
KA (FLASH)

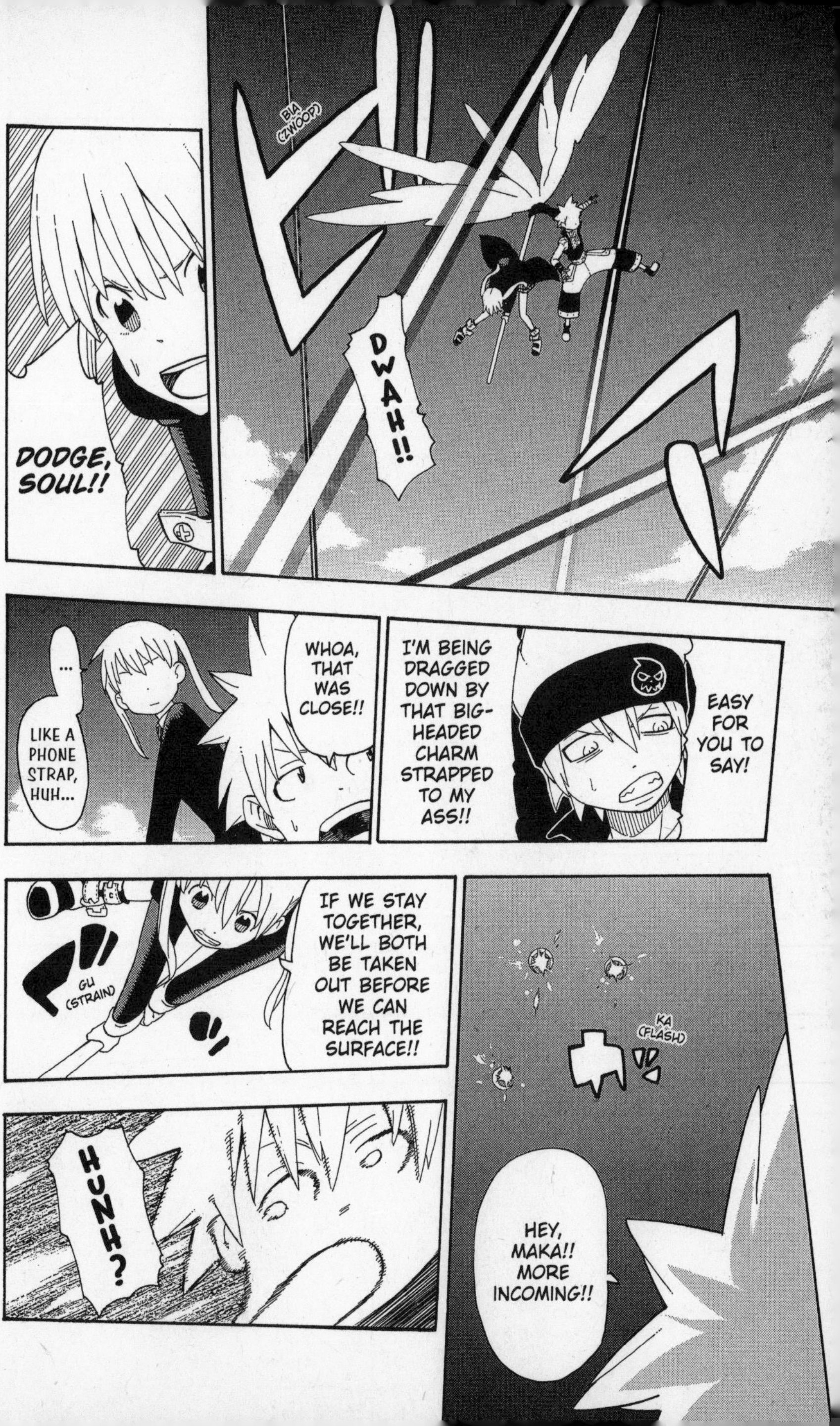
BIA
(ZWOOP)
DWAH!!
DODGE, SOUL!!
EASY FOR YOU TO SAY!
I'M BEING DRAGGED DOWN BY THAT BIG-HEADED CHARM STRAPPED TO MY ASS!!
WHOA, THAT WAS CLOSE!!
...
LIKE A PHONE STRAP, HUH...
KA
(FLASH)
HEY, MAKA!! MORE INCOMING!!
IF WE STAY TOGETHER, WE'LL BOTH BE TAKEN OUT BEFORE WE CAN REACH THE SURFACE!!
GU
(STRAIN)
HUNH?

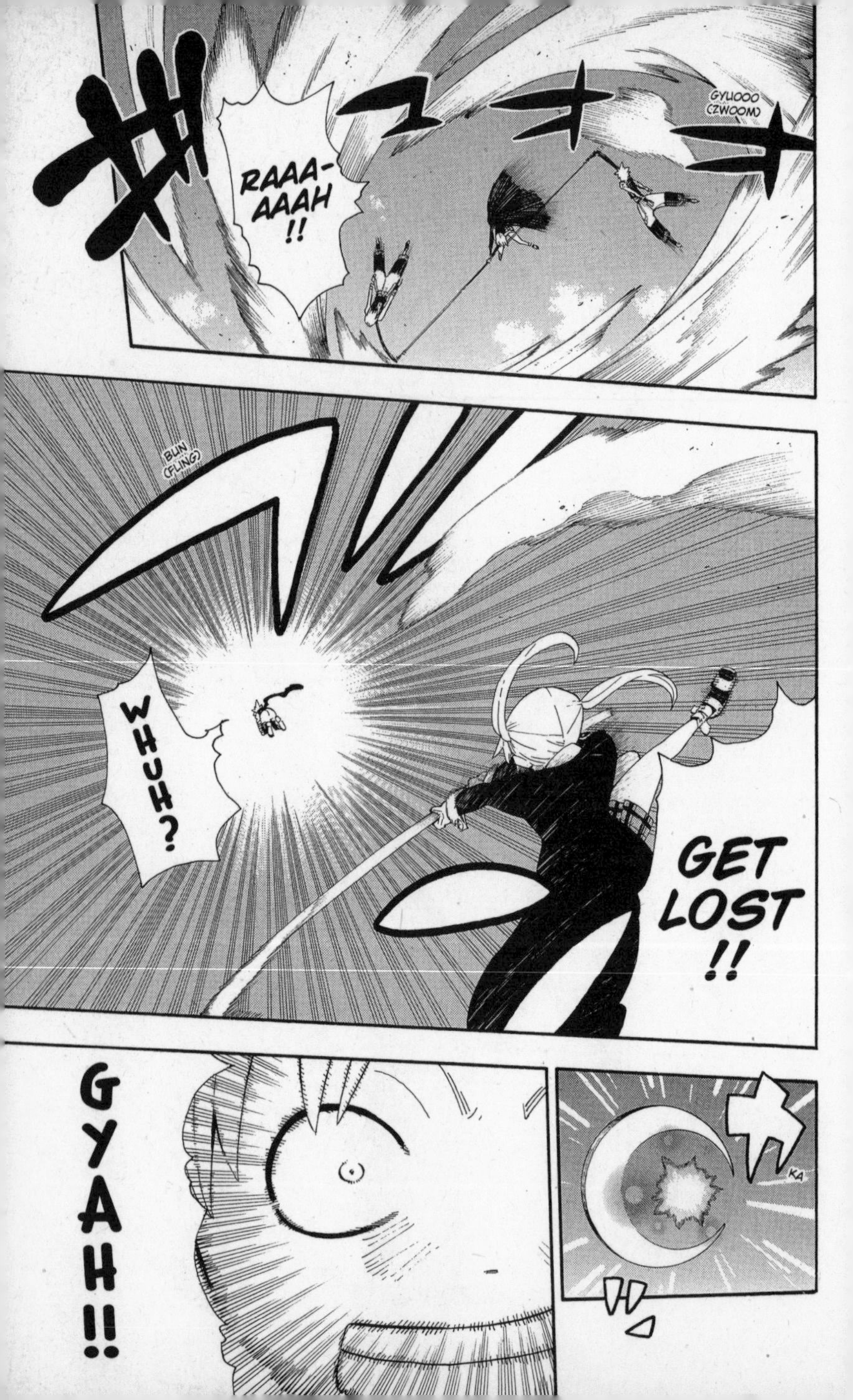
GYUOOO (ZWOOM)
RAAA-AAAH!!
BUN (FLING)
GET LOST!!
WHUH?
KA
GYAH!!

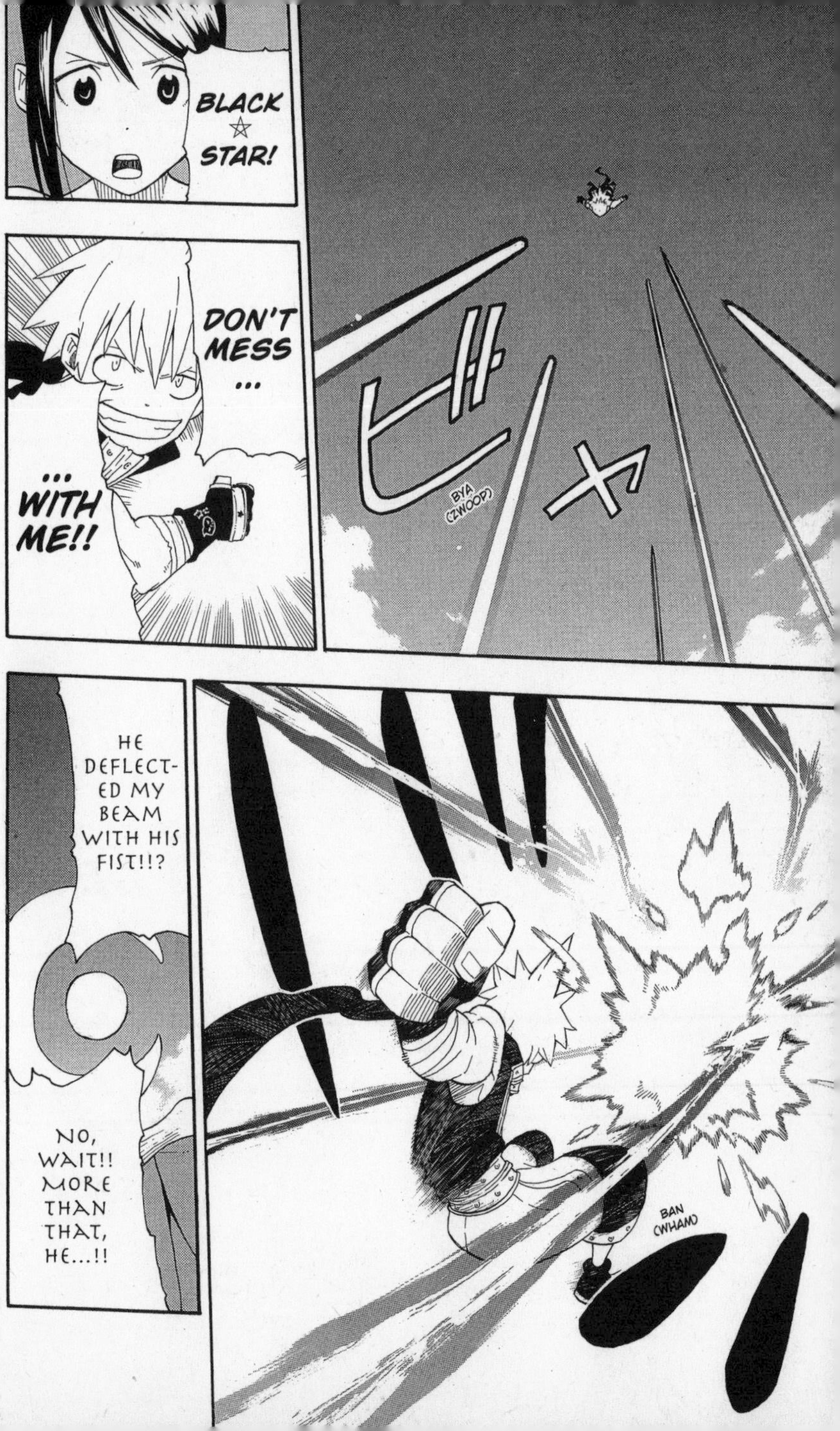
BYA (ZWOOP)
BLACK ☆ STAR!
DON'T MESS ...
... WITH ME!!
BAN (WHAM)
HE DEFLECTED MY BEAM WITH HIS FIST!!?
NO, WAIT!! MORE THAN THAT, HE...!!

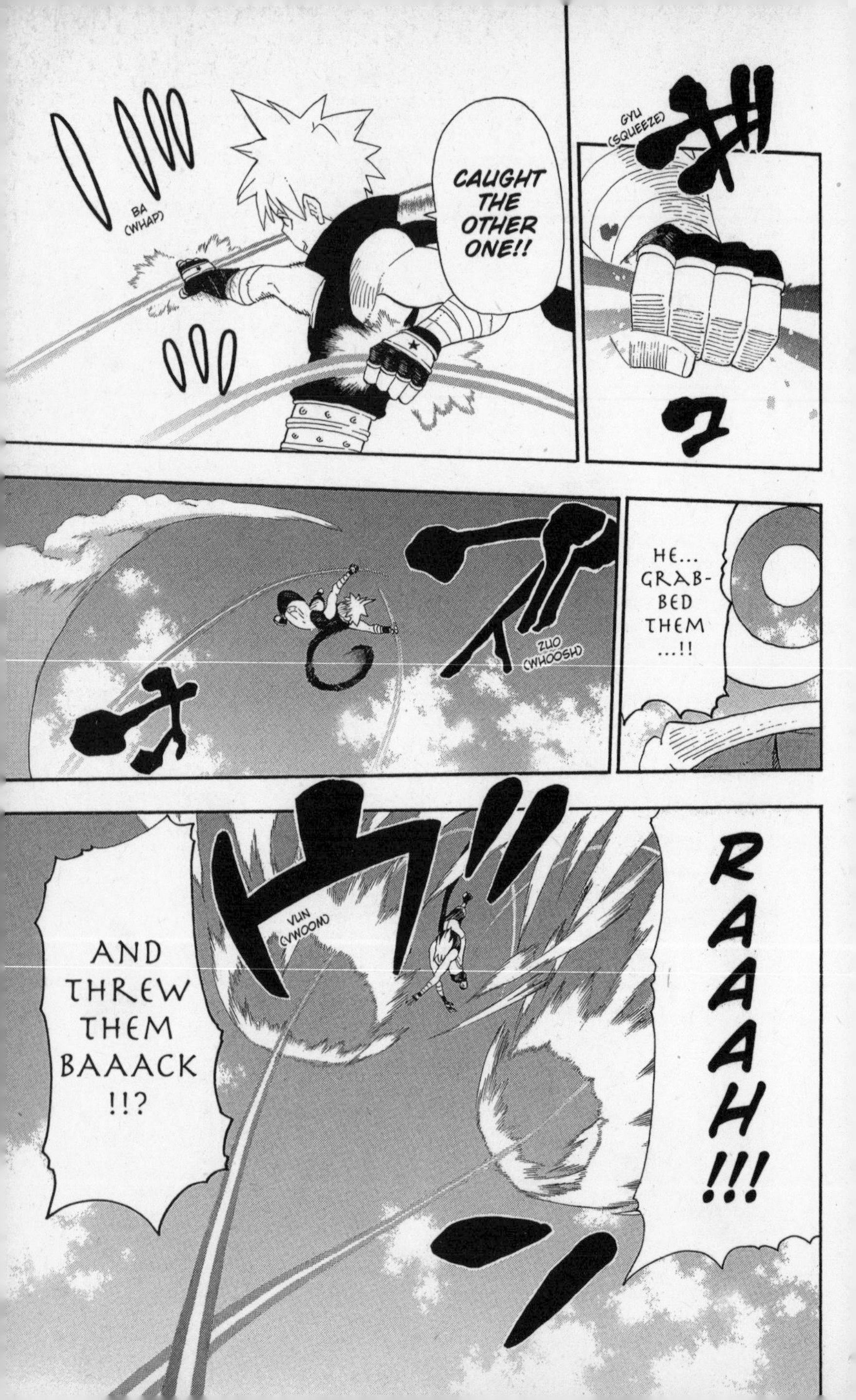
GYU (SQUEEZE)
CAUGHT THE OTHER ONE!!
BA (WHAP)
HE... GRAB-BED THEM ...!!
ZUO (WHOOSH)
RAAAAH!!!
VUN (VWOOM)
AND THREW THEM BAAACK !!?

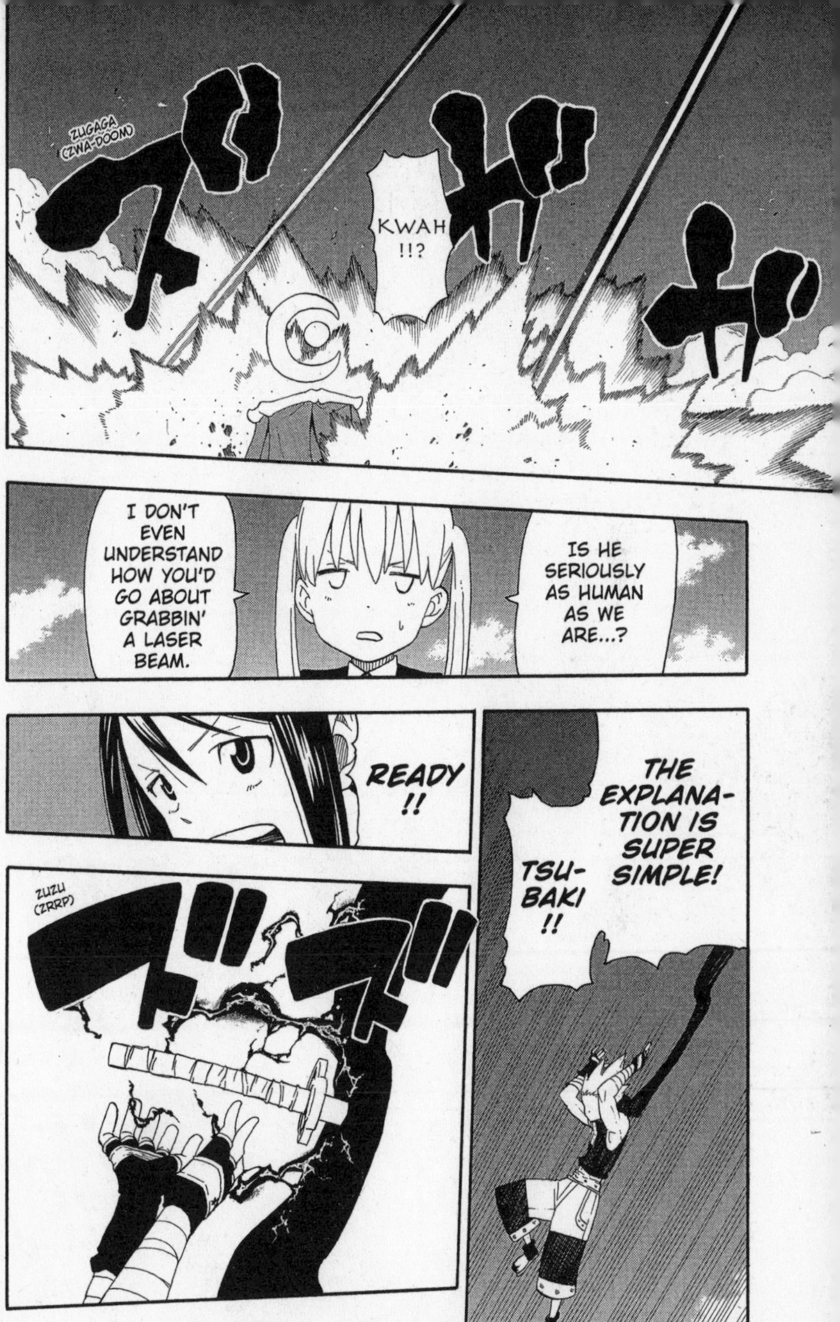
KWAH !!?
ZUGAGA (ZWA-DOOM)
IS HE SERIOUSLY AS HUMAN AS WE ARE...?
I DON'T EVEN UNDERSTAND HOW YOU'D GO ABOUT GRABBIN' A LASER BEAM.
THE EXPLANATION IS SUPER SIMPLE!
TSUBAKI !!
READY !!
ZUZU (ZRRP)

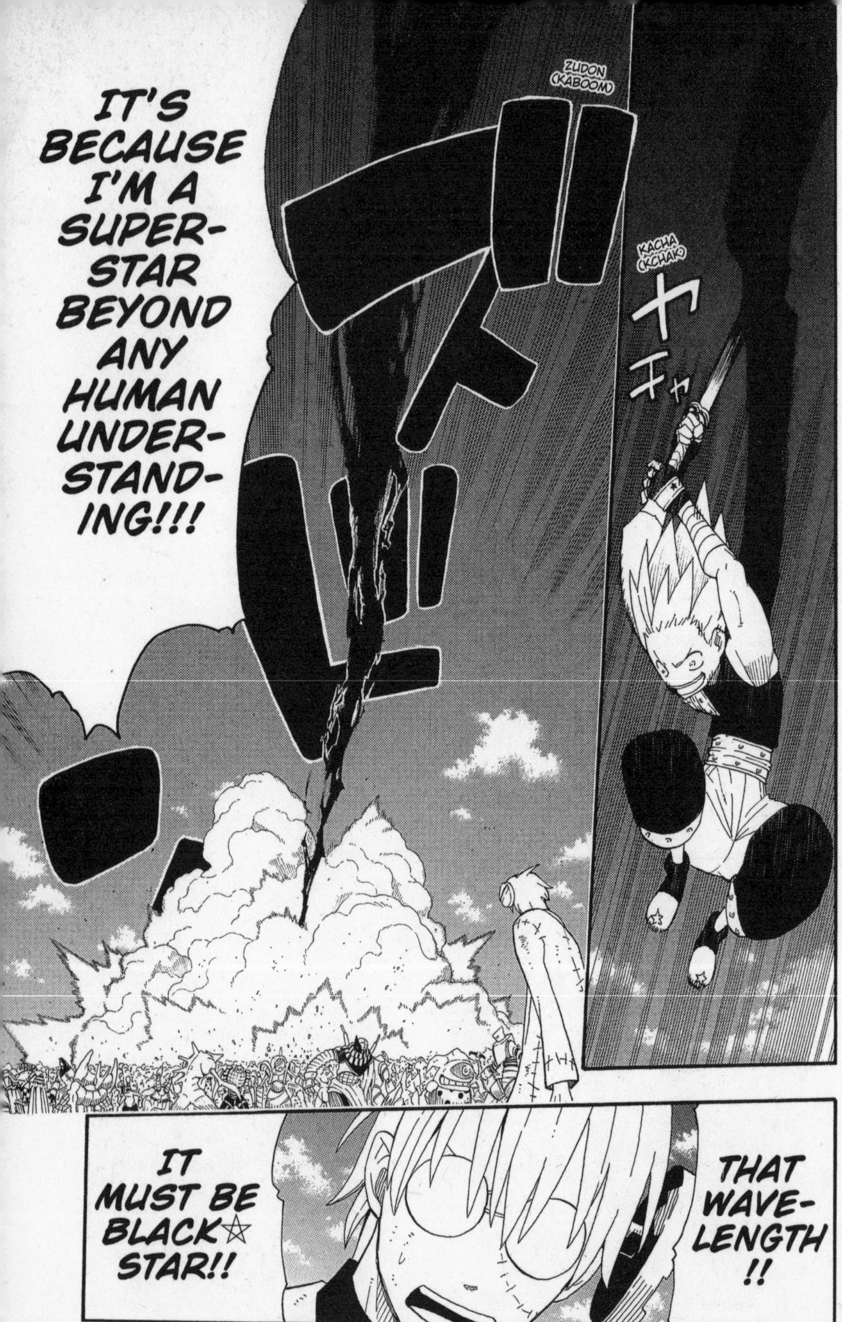
KACHA (KCHAK)
ZUDON (KABOOM)
IT'S BECAUSE I'M A SUPER-STAR BEYOND ANY HUMAN UNDER-STAND-ING!!!
THAT WAVE-LENGTH !!
IT MUST BE BLACK☆STAR!!

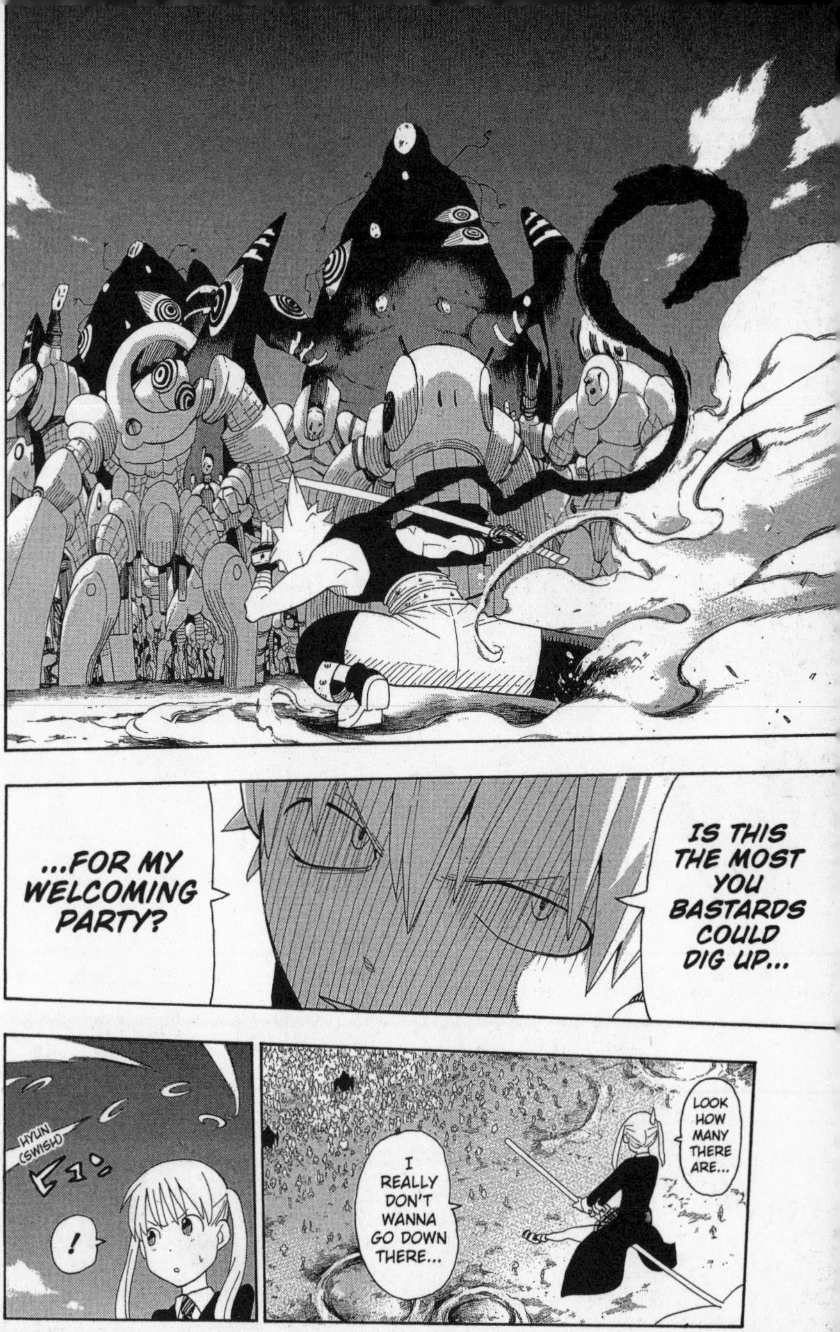
IS THIS THE MOST YOU BASTARDS COULD DIG UP...
...FOR MY WELCOMING PARTY?
LOOK HOW MANY THERE ARE...
I REALLY DON'T WANNA GO DOWN THERE...
HYUN (SWISH)
!

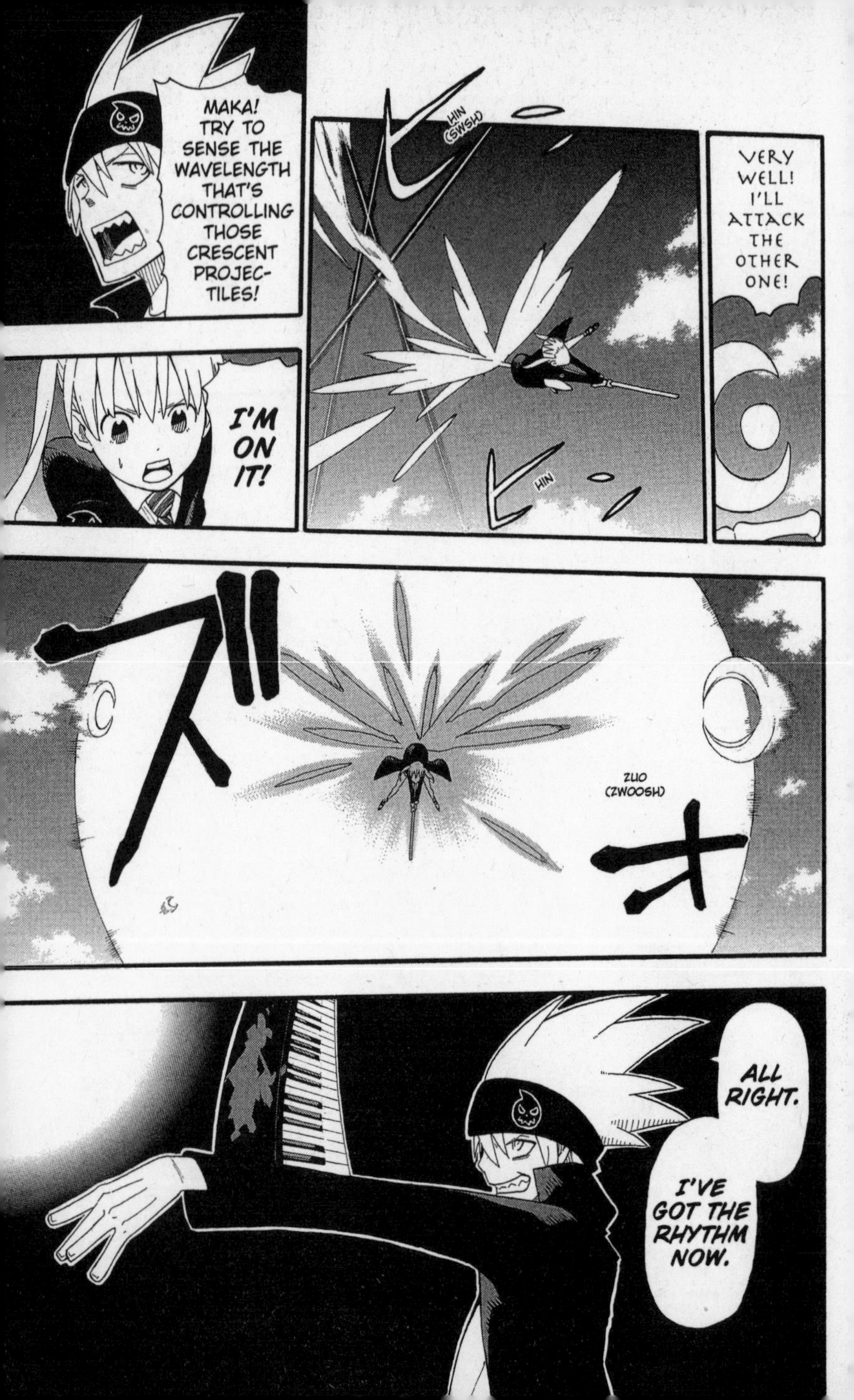
VERY WELL! I'LL ATTACK THE OTHER ONE!
HIN (SWSH)
HIN
MAKA! TRY TO SENSE THE WAVELENGTH THAT'S CONTROLLING THOSE CRESCENT PROJEC-TILES!
I'M ON IT!
ZUO (ZWOOSH)
ALL RIGHT.
I'VE GOT THE RHYTHM NOW.

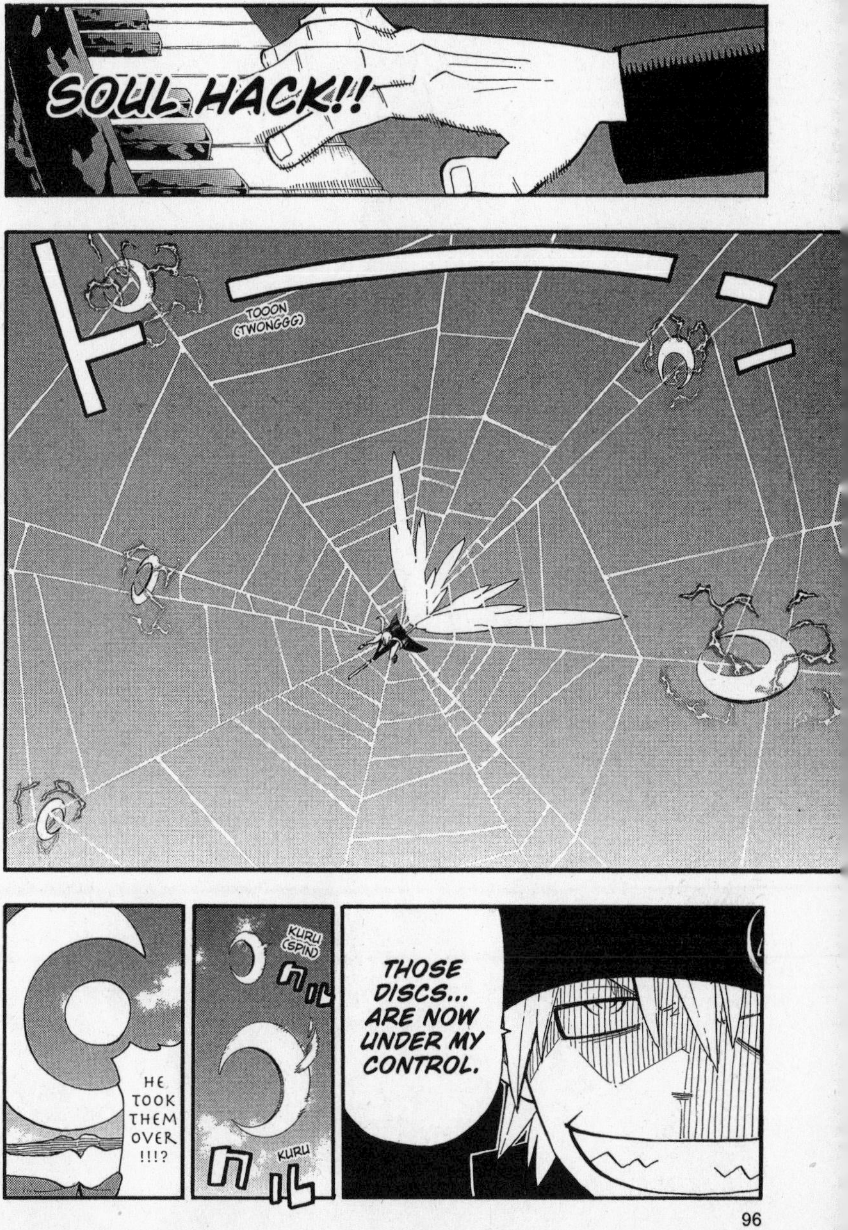
SOUL HACK!!
TOOON (TWONGGG)
THOSE DISCS... ARE NOW UNDER MY CONTROL.
KURU (SPIN)
KURU
HE TOOK THEM OVER!!!?

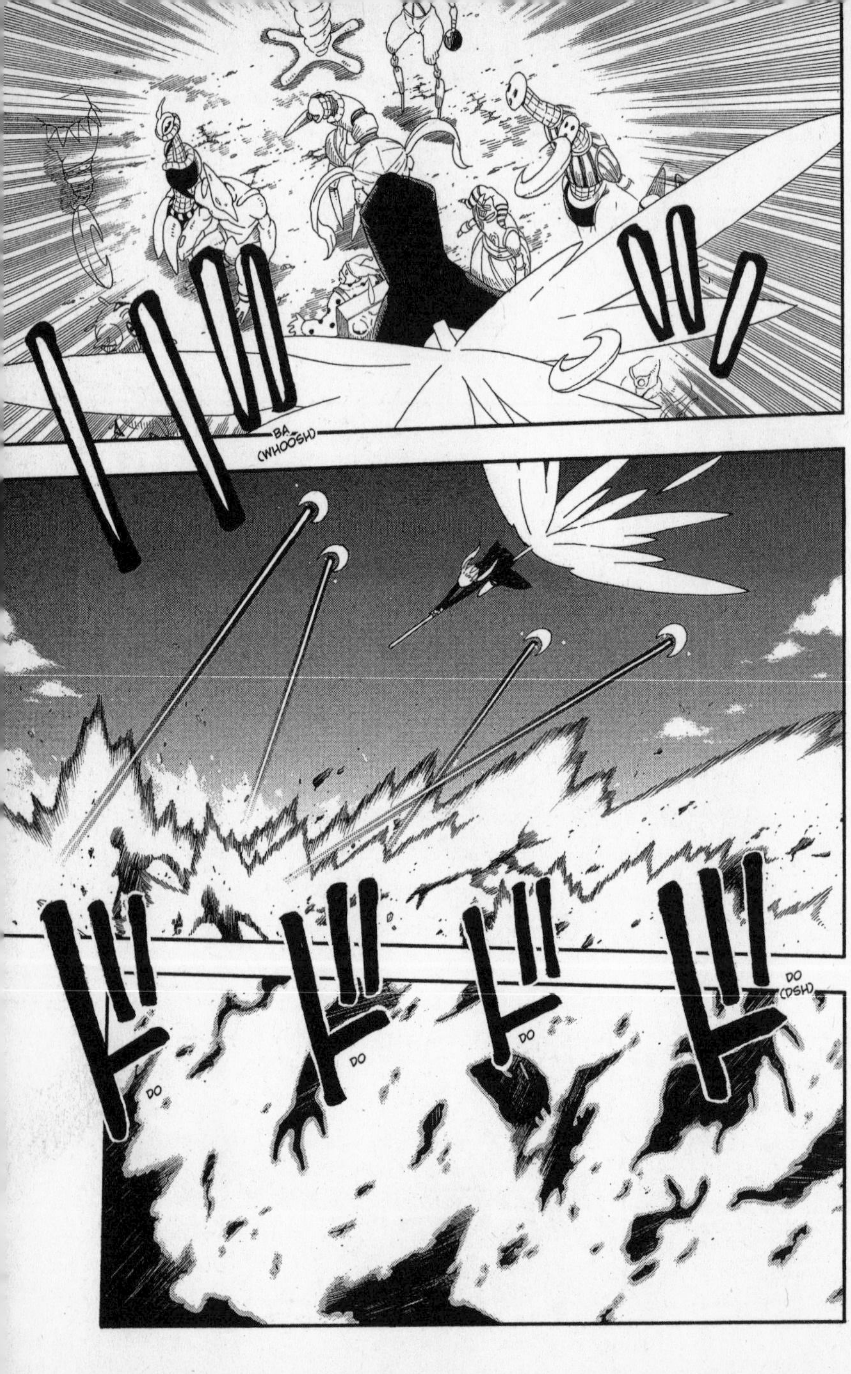
BA
(WHOOSH)
DO
(DSH)
DO
DO
DO

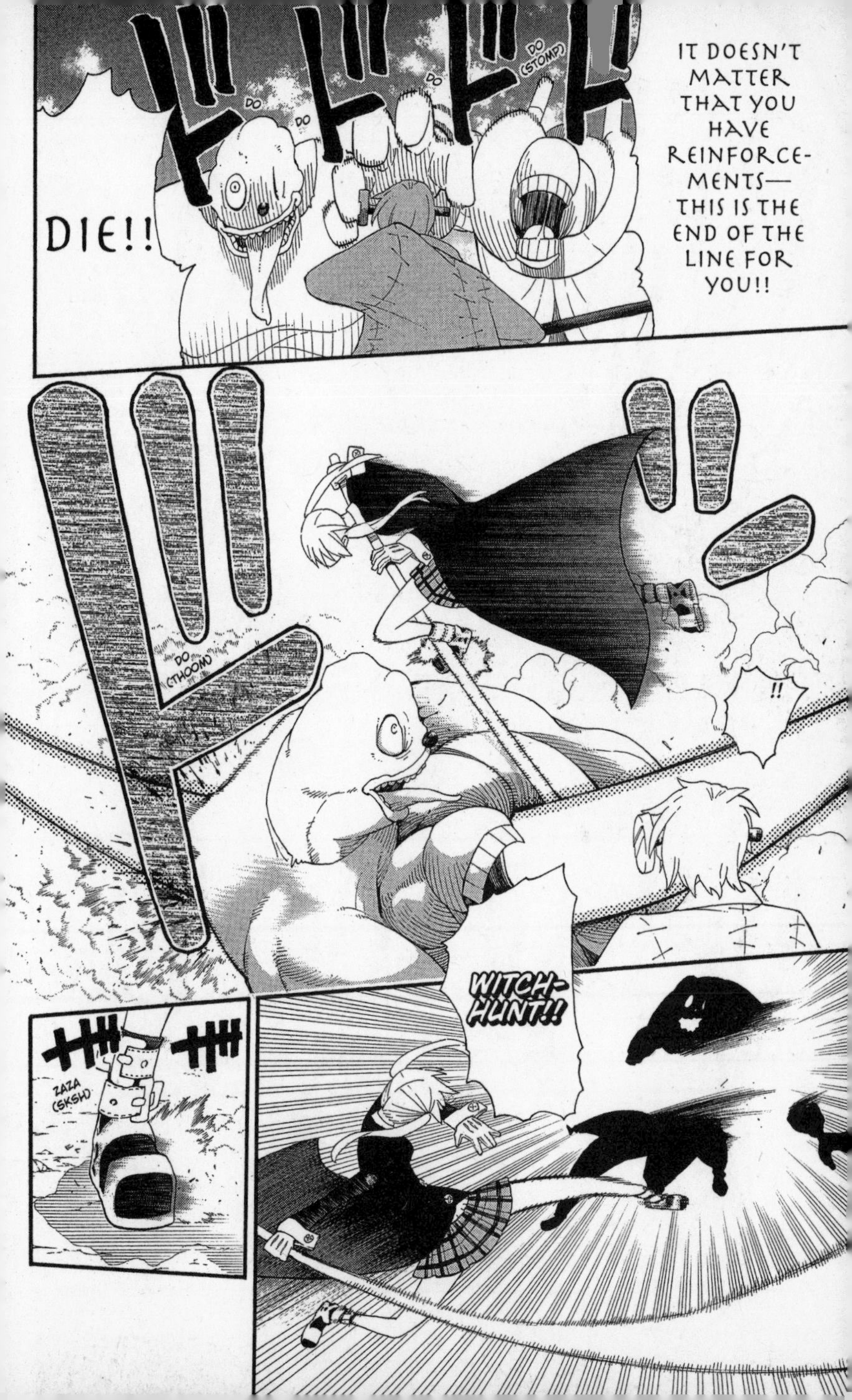
DO (STOMP)
DO
DO
DO
IT DOESN'T MATTER THAT YOU HAVE REINFORCEMENTS—THIS IS THE END OF THE LINE FOR YOU!!
DIE!!
!!
DO (THOOM)
WITCH-HUNT!!
ZAZA (SKSH)

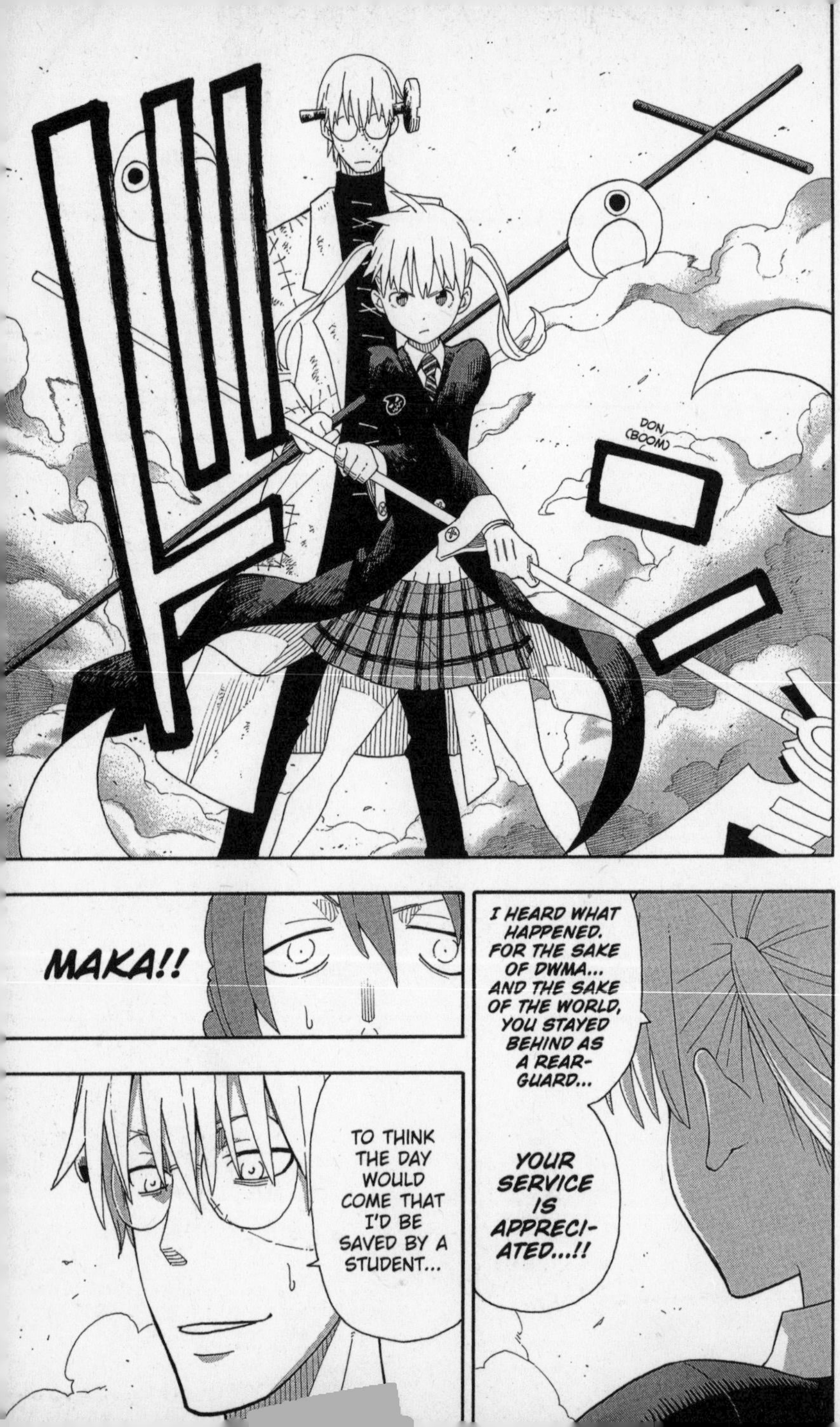
DON (BOOM)
I HEARD WHAT HAPPENED. FOR THE SAKE OF DWMA... AND THE SAKE OF THE WORLD, YOU STAYED BEHIND AS A REAR-GUARD...
YOUR SERVICE IS APPRECI-ATED...!!
MAKA!!
TO THINK THE DAY WOULD COME THAT I'D BE SAVED BY A STUDENT...

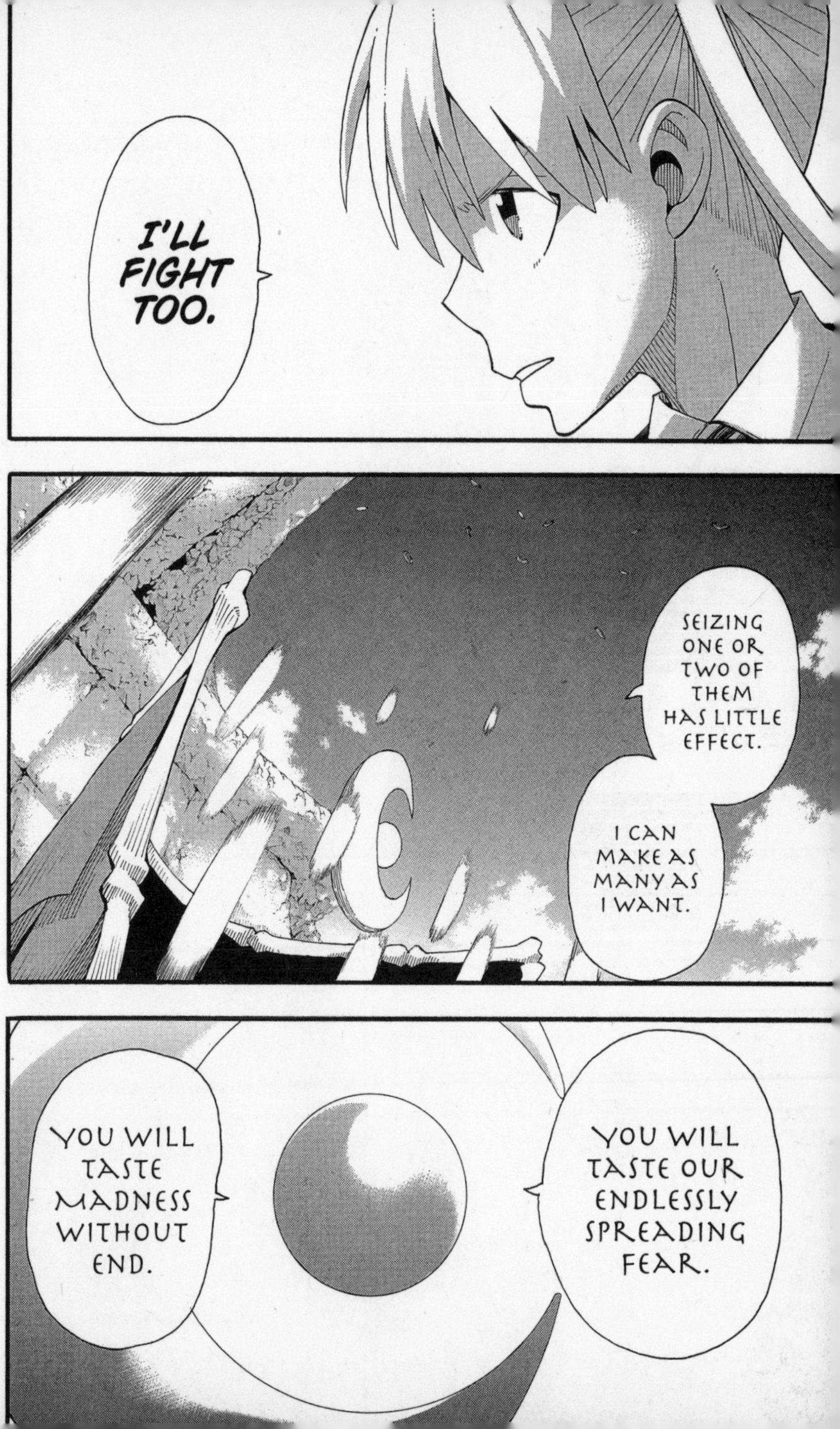
I'LL FIGHT TOO.
SEIZING ONE OR TWO OF THEM HAS LITTLE EFFECT.
I CAN MAKE AS MANY AS I WANT.
YOU WILL TASTE OUR ENDLESSLY SPREADING FEAR.
YOU WILL TASTE MADNESS WITHOUT END.

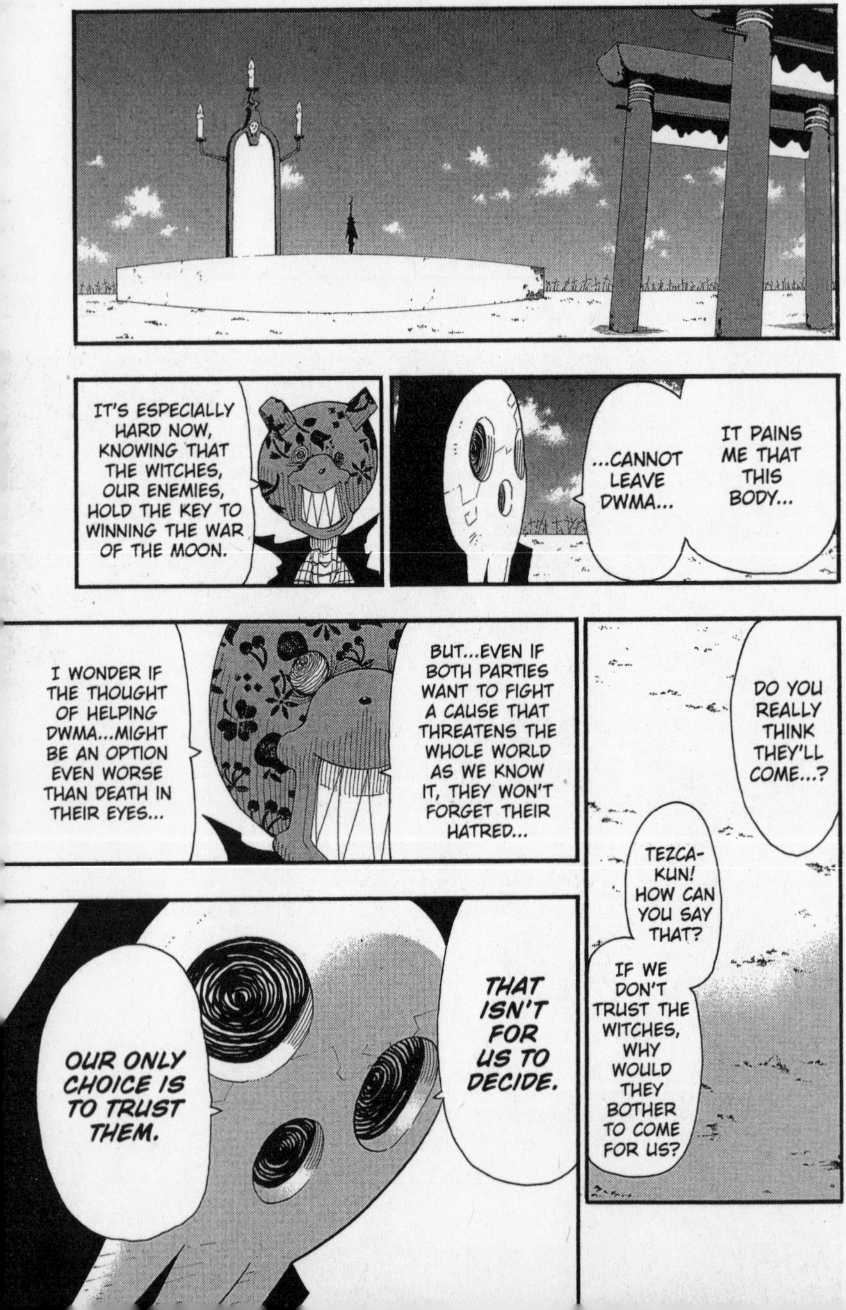
IT PAINS ME THAT THIS BODY...
...CANNOT LEAVE DWMA...
IT'S ESPECIALLY HARD NOW, KNOWING THAT THE WITCHES, OUR ENEMIES, HOLD THE KEY TO WINNING THE WAR OF THE MOON.
DO YOU REALLY THINK THEY'LL COME...?
TEZCA-KUN! HOW CAN YOU SAY THAT?
IF WE DON'T TRUST THE WITCHES, WHY WOULD THEY BOTHER TO COME FOR US?
BUT...EVEN IF BOTH PARTIES WANT TO FIGHT A CAUSE THAT THREATENS THE WHOLE WORLD AS WE KNOW IT, THEY WON'T FORGET THEIR HATRED...
I WONDER IF THE THOUGHT OF HELPING DWMA...MIGHT BE AN OPTION EVEN WORSE THAN DEATH IN THEIR EYES...
THAT ISN'T FOR US TO DECIDE.
OUR ONLY CHOICE IS TO TRUST THEM.

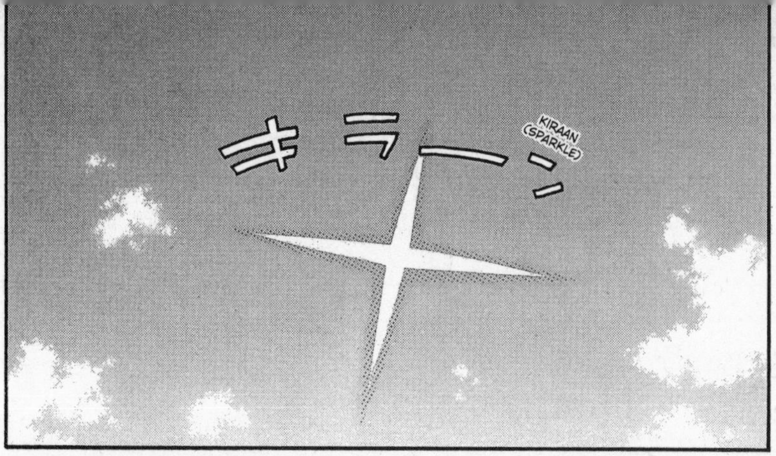
キラーーン
KIRAAN (SPARKLE)
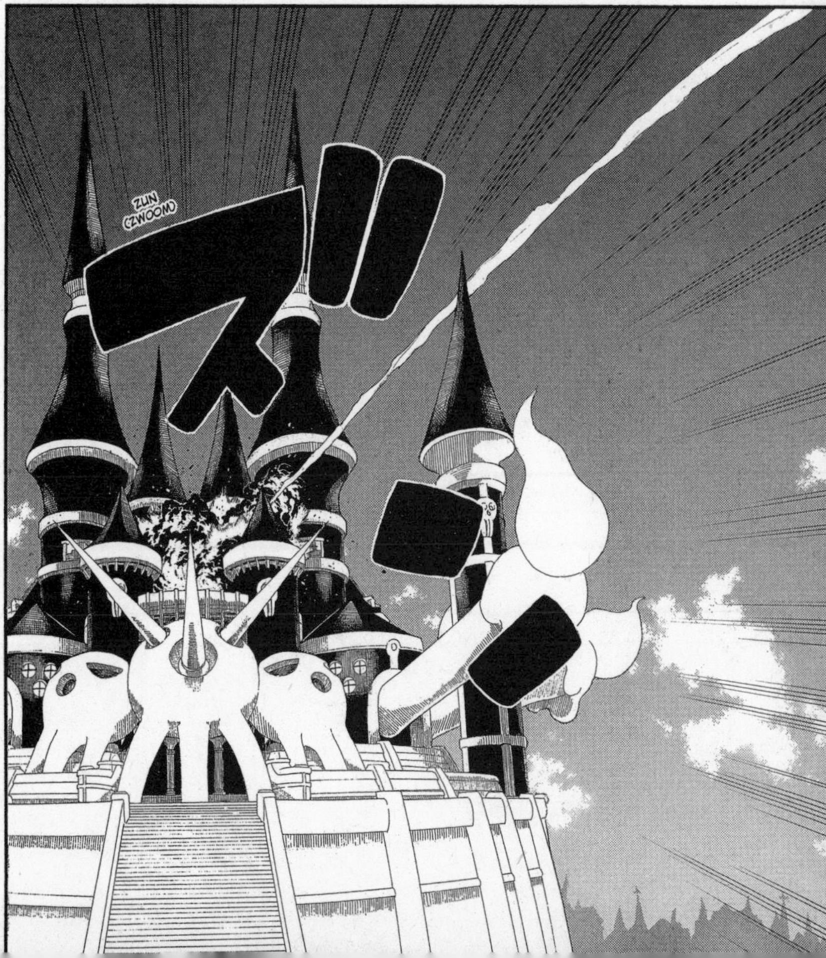
ズン
ZUN (ZWOOM)

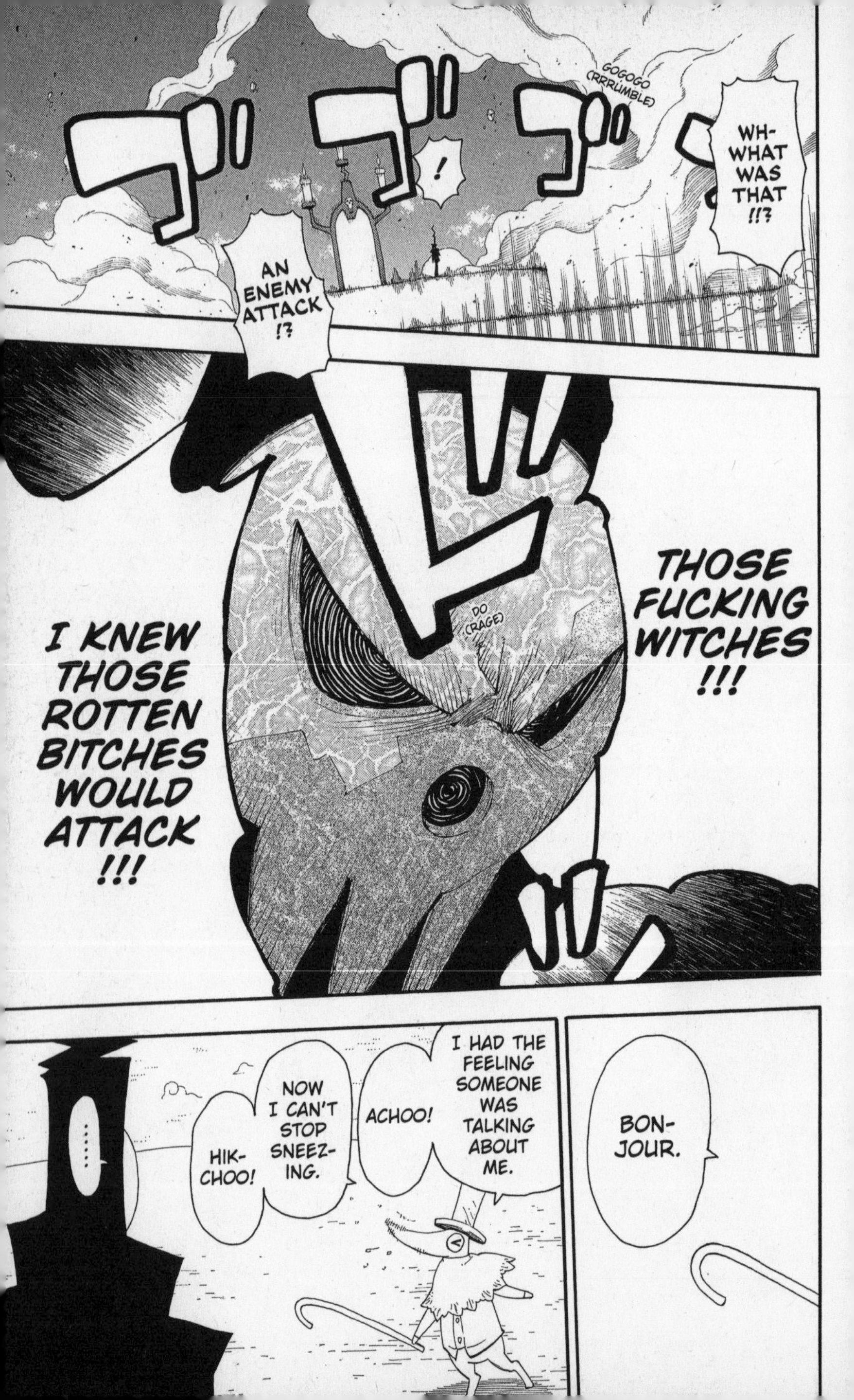
WH- WHAT WAS THAT !!?
GOGOGO (RRRUMBLE)
!
AN ENEMY ATTACK !?
THOSE FUCKING WITCHES !!!
DO (RAGE)
I KNEW THOSE ROTTEN BITCHES WOULD ATTACK !!!
BON- JOUR.
I HAD THE FEELING SOMEONE WAS TALKING ABOUT ME.
ACHOO!
NOW I CAN'T STOP SNEEZ- ING.
HIK- CHOO!
......

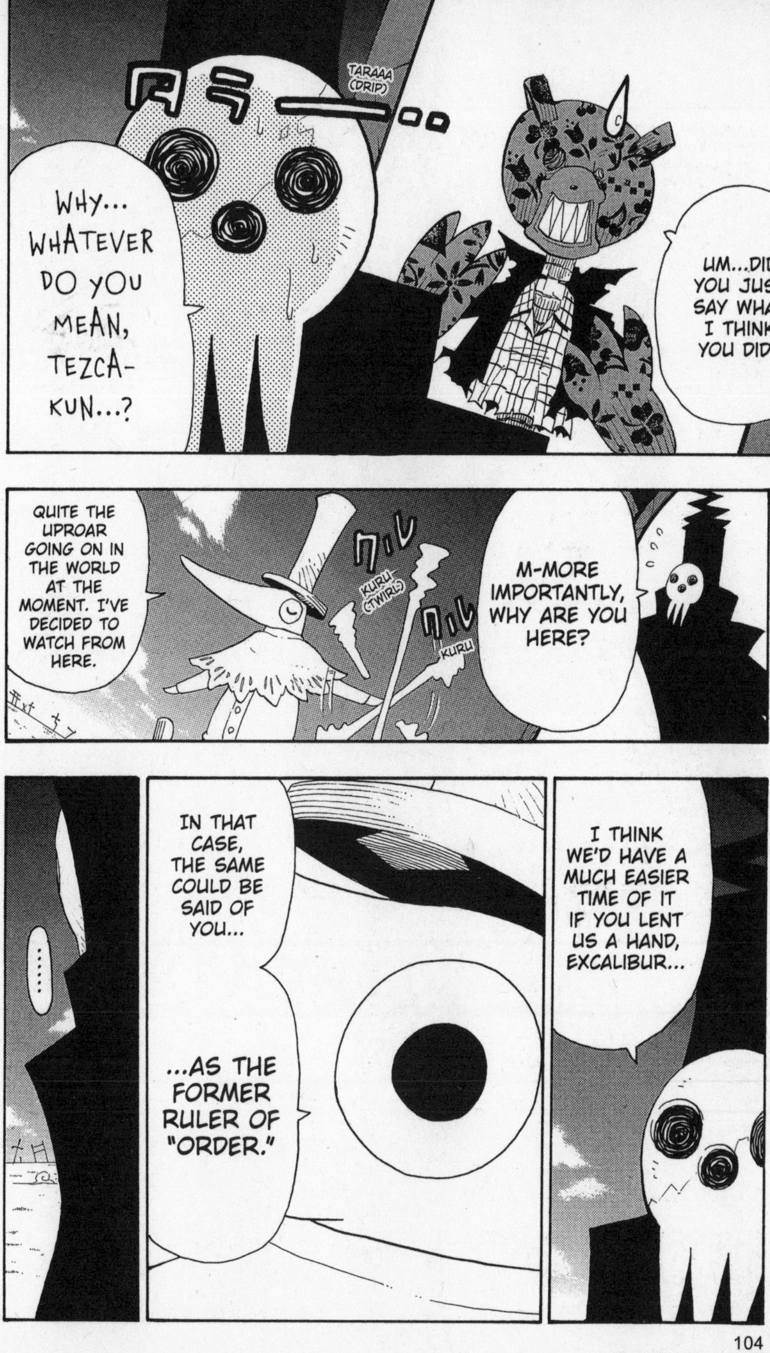
UM...DID YOU JUST SAY WHAT I THINK YOU DID?
TARAAA (DRIP)
WHY... WHATEVER DO YOU MEAN, TEZCA-KUN...?
M-MORE IMPORTANTLY, WHY ARE YOU HERE?
KURU
KURU (TWIRL)
QUITE THE UPROAR GOING ON IN THE WORLD AT THE MOMENT. I'VE DECIDED TO WATCH FROM HERE.
I THINK WE'D HAVE A MUCH EASIER TIME OF IT IF YOU LENT US A HAND, EXCALIBUR...
IN THAT CASE, THE SAME COULD BE SAID OF YOU...
...AS THE FORMER RULER OF "ORDER."
......

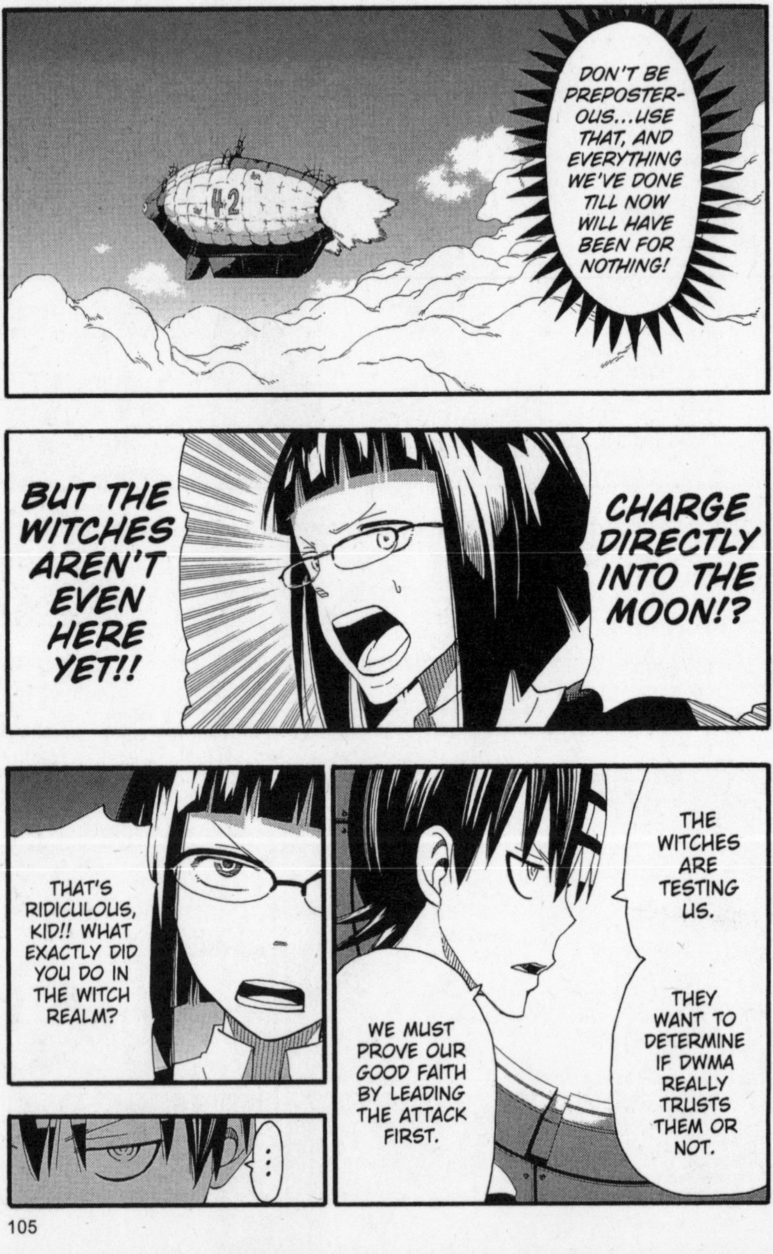
DON'T BE PREPOSTEROUS...USE THAT, AND EVERYTHING WE'VE DONE TILL NOW WILL HAVE BEEN FOR NOTHING!
CHARGE DIRECTLY INTO THE MOON!?
BUT THE WITCHES AREN'T EVEN HERE YET!!
THE WITCHES ARE TESTING US.
THEY WANT TO DETERMINE IF DWMA REALLY TRUSTS THEM OR NOT.
WE MUST PROVE OUR GOOD FAITH BY LEADING THE ATTACK FIRST.
THAT'S RIDICULOUS, KID!! WHAT EXACTLY DID YOU DO IN THE WITCH REALM?
...

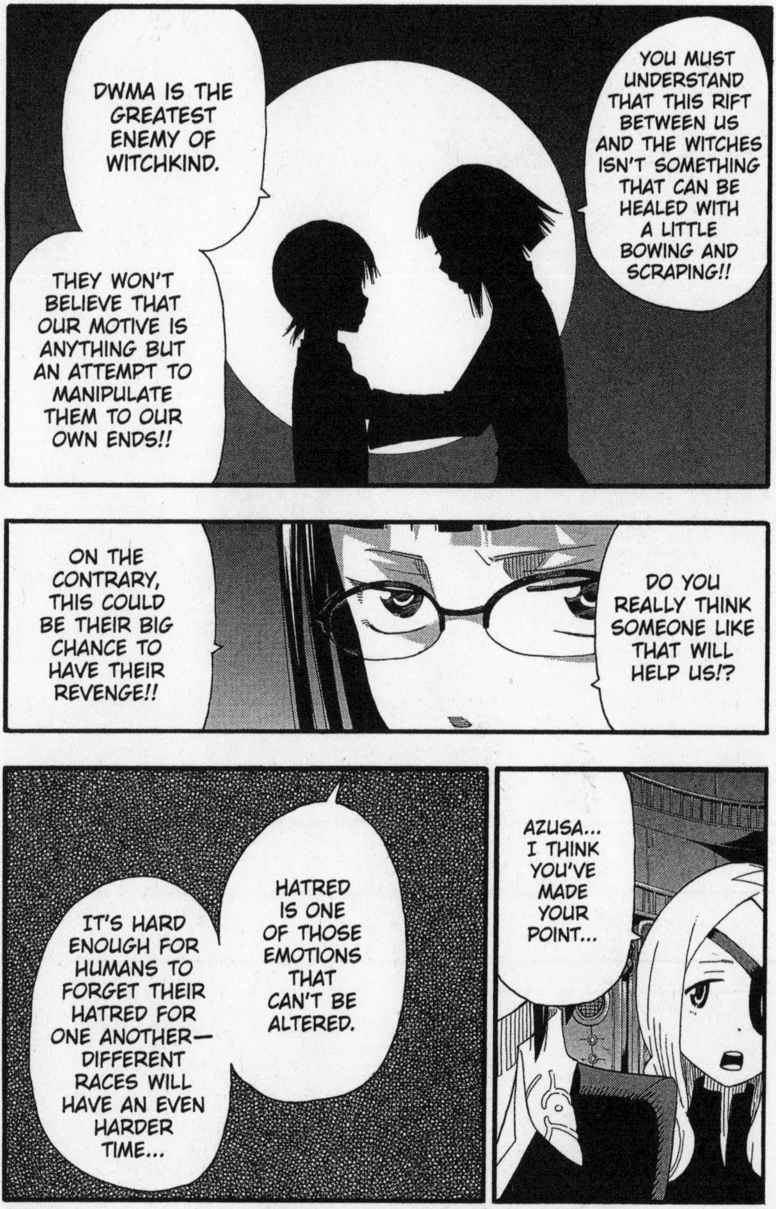
YOU MUST UNDERSTAND THAT THIS RIFT BETWEEN US AND THE WITCHES ISN'T SOMETHING THAT CAN BE HEALED WITH A LITTLE BOWING AND SCRAPING!!
DWMA IS THE GREATEST ENEMY OF WITCHKIND.
THEY WON'T BELIEVE THAT OUR MOTIVE IS ANYTHING BUT AN ATTEMPT TO MANIPULATE THEM TO OUR OWN ENDS!!
DO YOU REALLY THINK SOMEONE LIKE THAT WILL HELP US!?
ON THE CONTRARY, THIS COULD BE THEIR BIG CHANCE TO HAVE THEIR REVENGE!!
AZUSA... I THINK YOU'VE MADE YOUR POINT...
HATRED IS ONE OF THOSE EMOTIONS THAT CAN'T BE ALTERED.
IT'S HARD ENOUGH FOR HUMANS TO FORGET THEIR HATRED FOR ONE ANOTHER—DIFFERENT RACES WILL HAVE AN EVEN HARDER TIME...

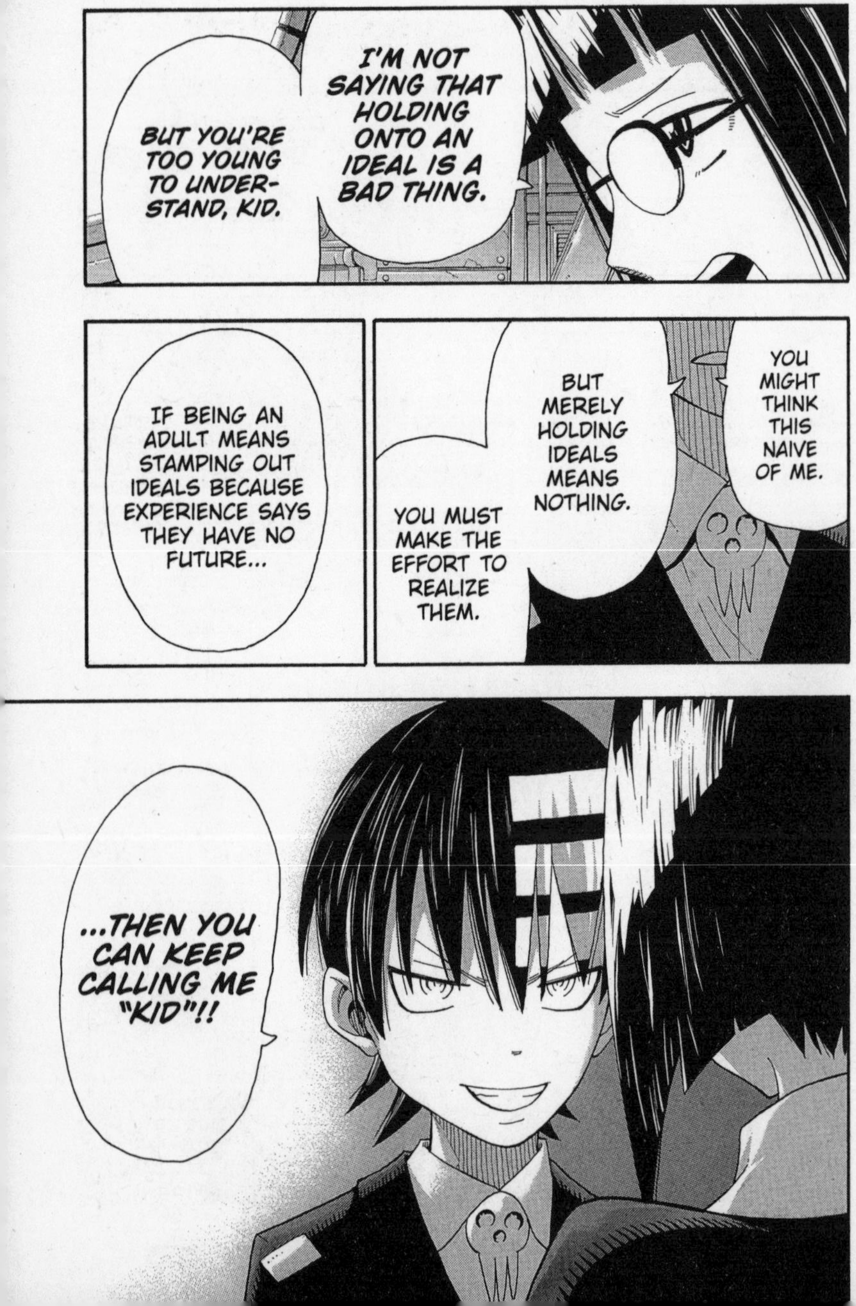
I'M NOT SAYING THAT HOLDING ONTO AN IDEAL IS A BAD THING.
BUT YOU'RE TOO YOUNG TO UNDER-STAND, KID.
YOU MIGHT THINK THIS NAIVE OF ME.
BUT MERELY HOLDING IDEALS MEANS NOTHING.
YOU MUST MAKE THE EFFORT TO REALIZE THEM.
IF BEING AN ADULT MEANS STAMPING OUT IDEALS BECAUSE EXPERIENCE SAYS THEY HAVE NO FUTURE...
...THEN YOU CAN KEEP CALLING ME "KID"!!

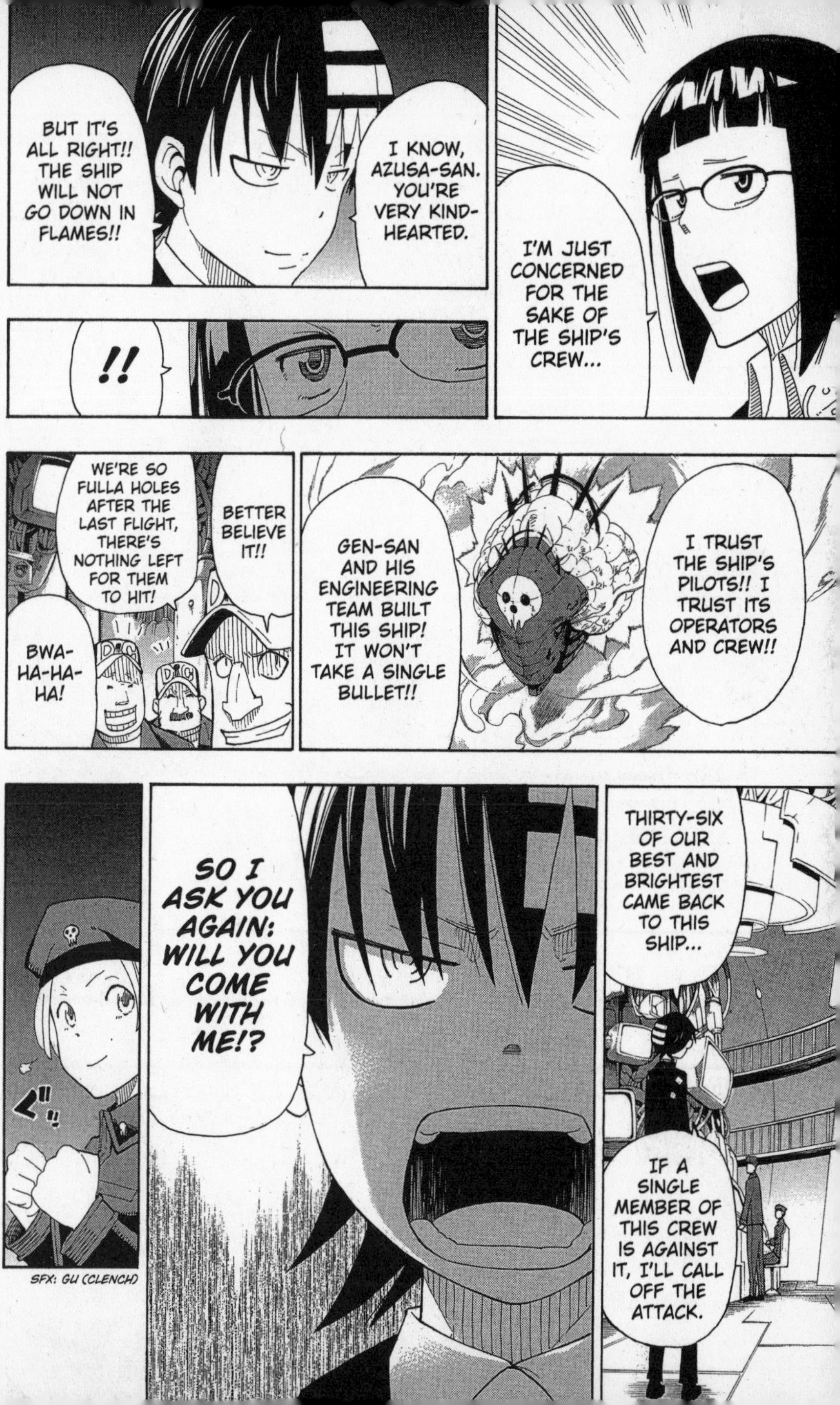
I'M JUST CONCERNED FOR THE SAKE OF THE SHIP'S CREW...
I KNOW, AZUSA-SAN. YOU'RE VERY KIND-HEARTED.
BUT IT'S ALL RIGHT!! THE SHIP WILL NOT GO DOWN IN FLAMES!!
!!
I TRUST THE SHIP'S PILOTS!! I TRUST ITS OPERATORS AND CREW!!
GEN-SAN AND HIS ENGINEERING TEAM BUILT THIS SHIP! IT WON'T TAKE A SINGLE BULLET!!
BETTER BELIEVE IT!!
WE'RE SO FULLA HOLES AFTER THE LAST FLIGHT, THERE'S NOTHING LEFT FOR THEM TO HIT!
BWA-HA-HA-HA!
THIRTY-SIX OF OUR BEST AND BRIGHTEST CAME BACK TO THIS SHIP...
IF A SINGLE MEMBER OF THIS CREW IS AGAINST IT, I'LL CALL OFF THE ATTACK.
SO I ASK YOU AGAIN: WILL YOU COME WITH ME!?
SFX: GU (CLENCH)

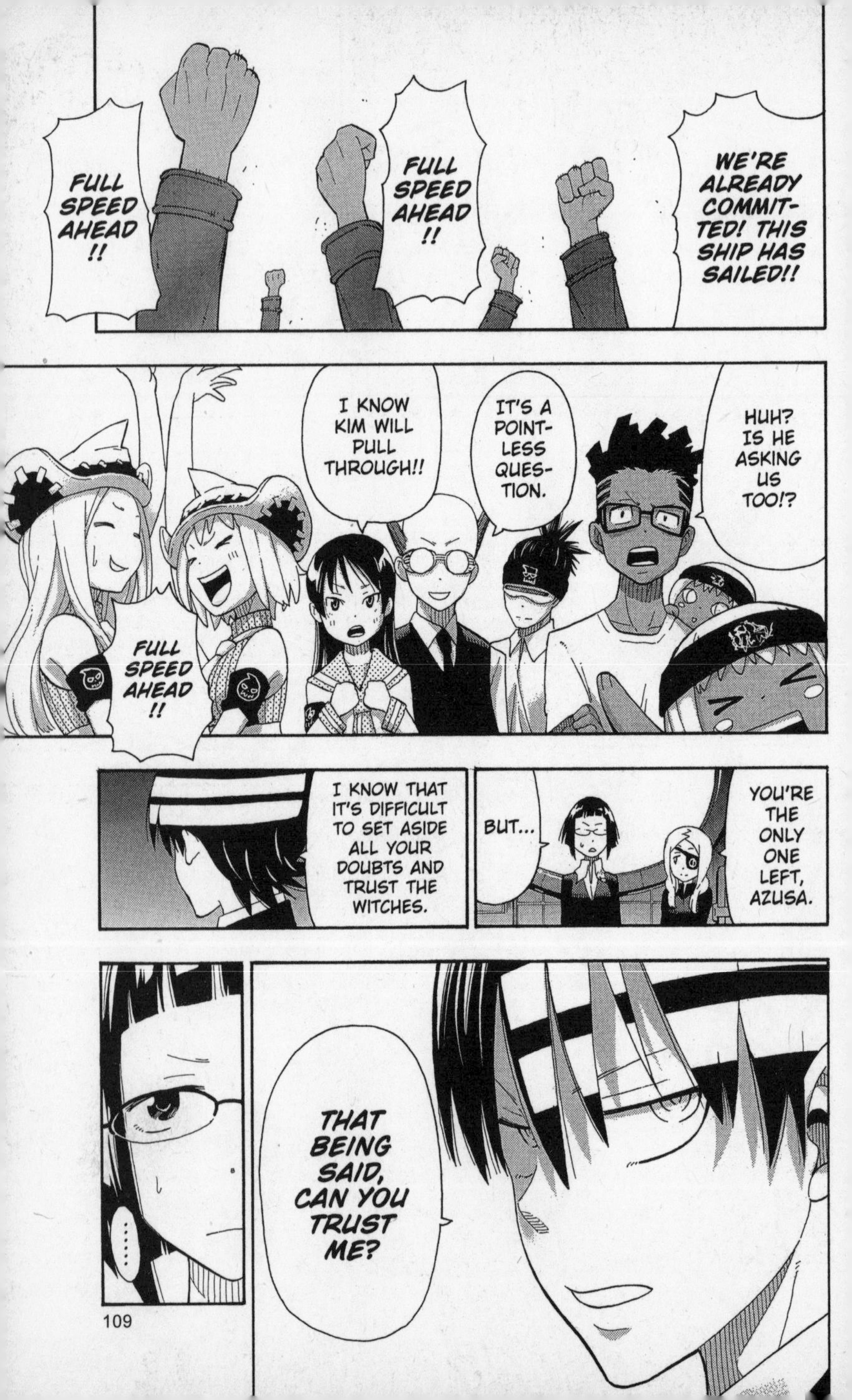
WE'RE ALREADY COMMITTED! THIS SHIP HAS SAILED!!
FULL SPEED AHEAD!!
FULL SPEED AHEAD!!
HUH? IS HE ASKING US TOO!?
IT'S A POINTLESS QUESTION.
I KNOW KIM WILL PULL THROUGH!!
FULL SPEED AHEAD!!
YOU'RE THE ONLY ONE LEFT, AZUSA.
BUT...
I KNOW THAT IT'S DIFFICULT TO SET ASIDE ALL YOUR DOUBTS AND TRUST THE WITCHES.
THAT BEING SAID, CAN YOU TRUST ME?
......

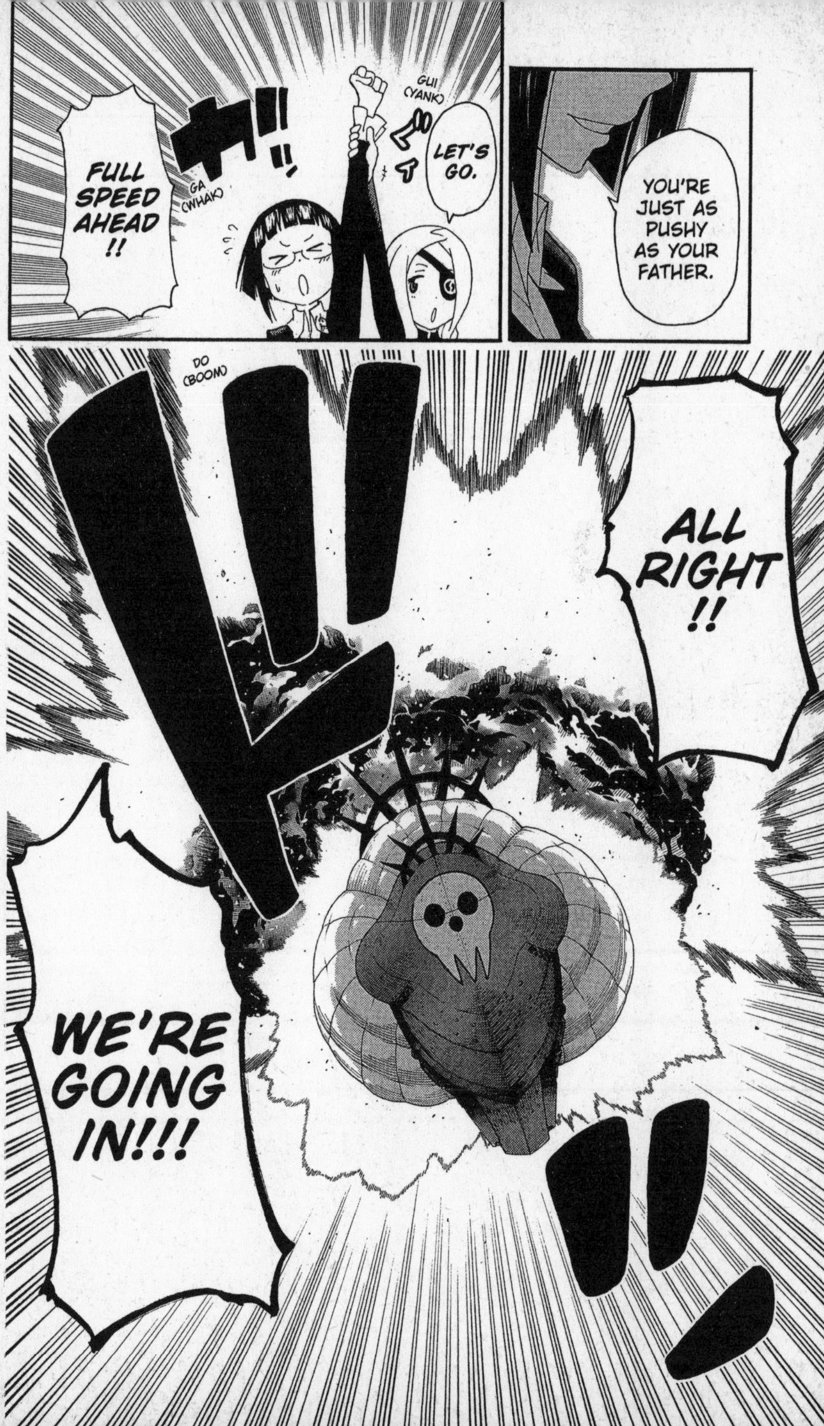
YOU'RE JUST AS PUSHY AS YOUR FATHER.
GUI (YANK)
LET'S GO.
GA (WHAK)
FULL SPEED AHEAD !!
DO (BOOM)
ALL RIGHT !!
WE'RE GOING IN!!!

SOUL EATER

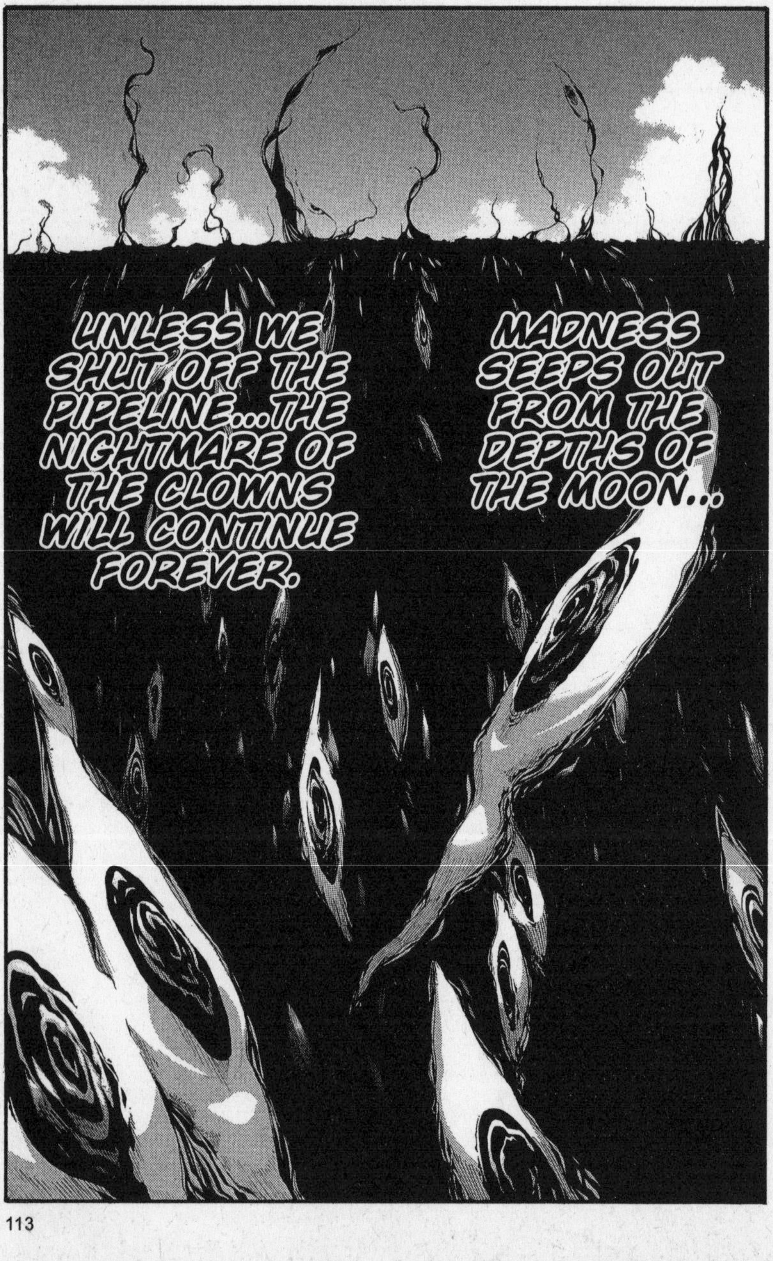
MADNESS SEEPS OUT FROM THE DEPTHS OF THE MOON...
UNLESS WE SHUT OFF THE PIPELINE...THE NIGHTMARE OF THE CLOWNS WILL CONTINUE FOREVER.

THE
WITCHES
WILL COME
TO THE
MOON!!

OOOO
(WHOO)

ブブブ
ZUZUZU
(OOOZE)

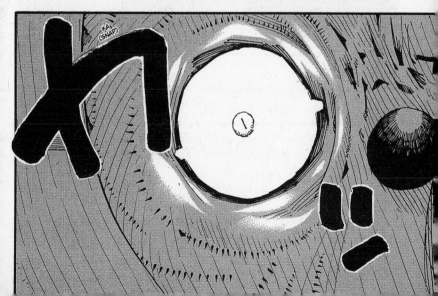

KA!
(SNAP)

わ

ドド

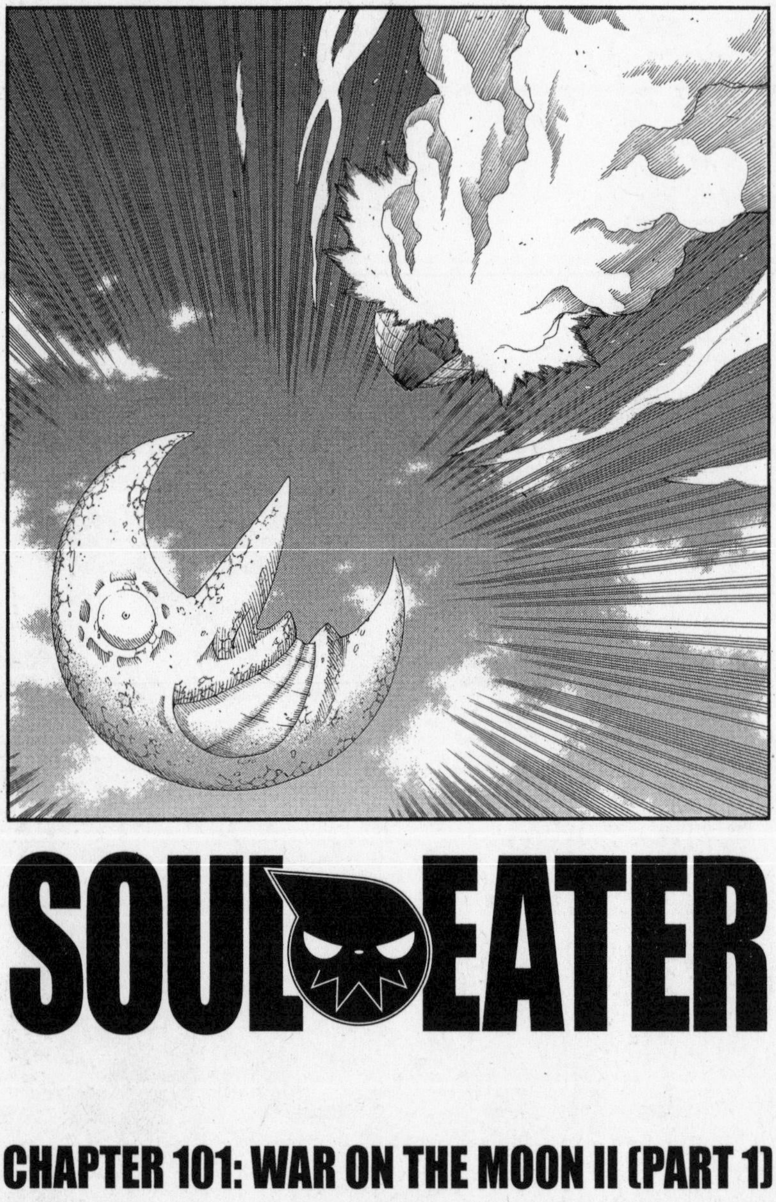

SOUL EATER

CHAPTER 101: WAR ON THE MOON II (PART 1)

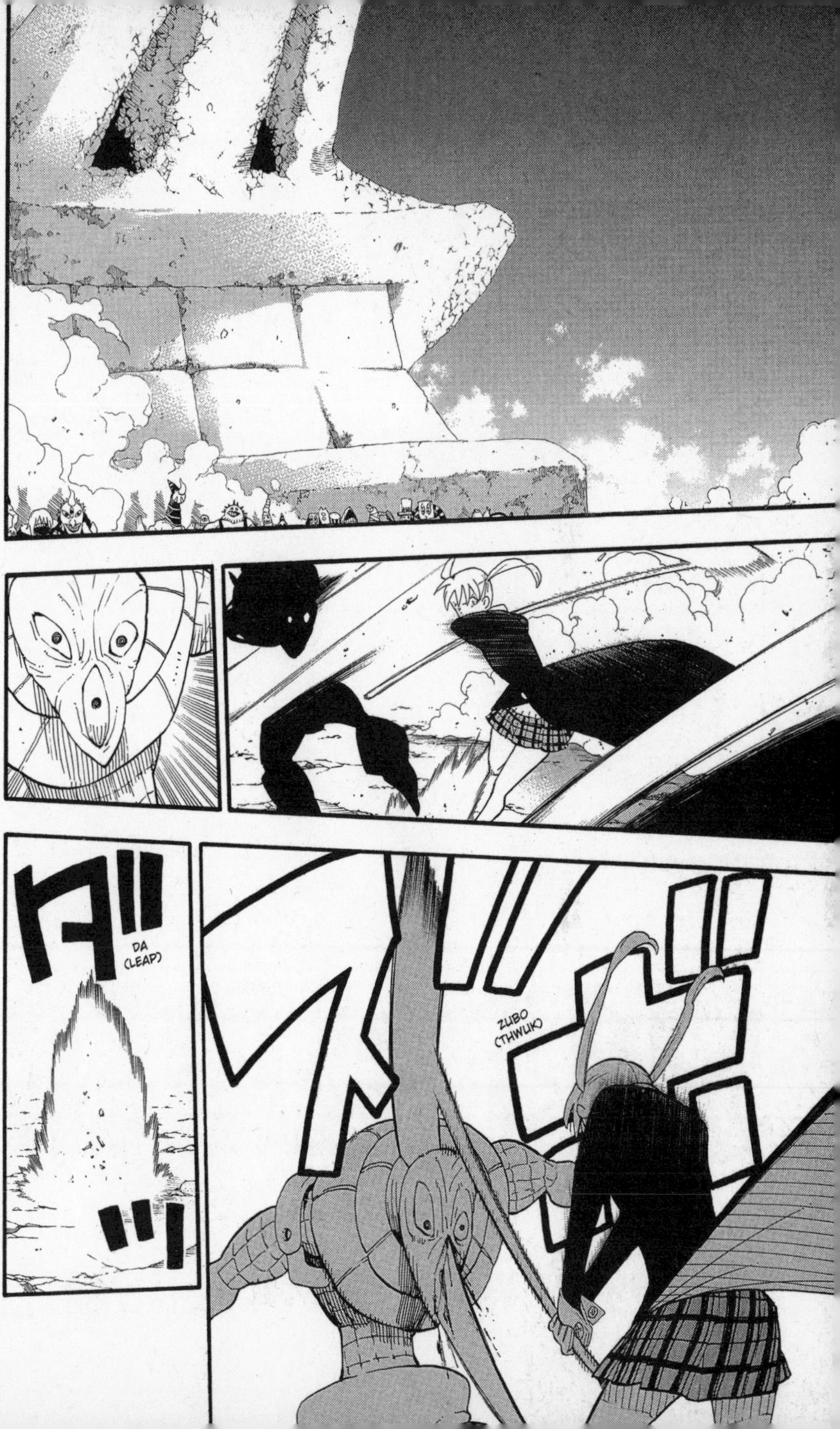
ZUBO
(THWUK)
DA
(LEAP)

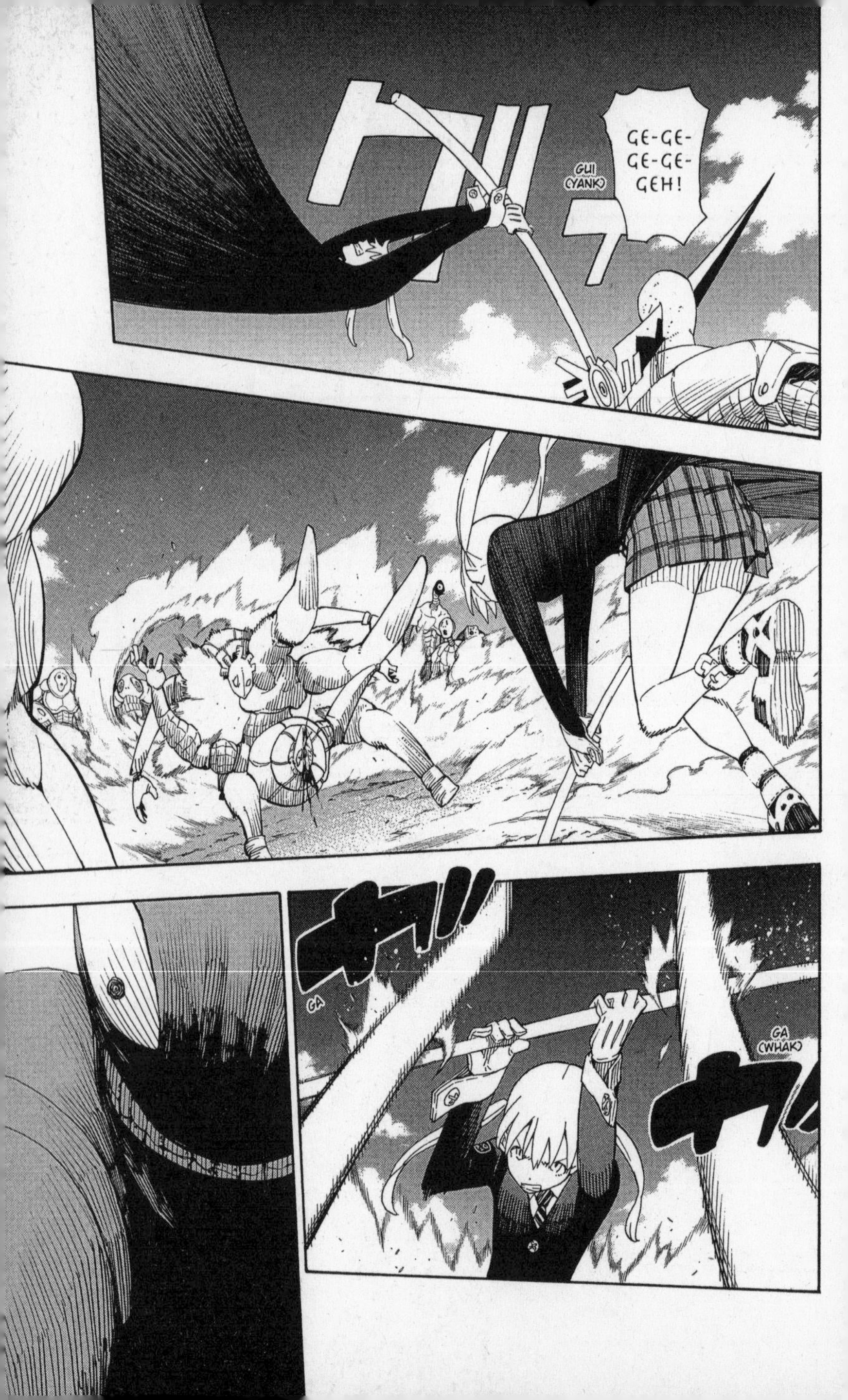
GE-GE-
GE-GE-
GEH!
GUI
(YANK)
GA
(WHAK)
GA

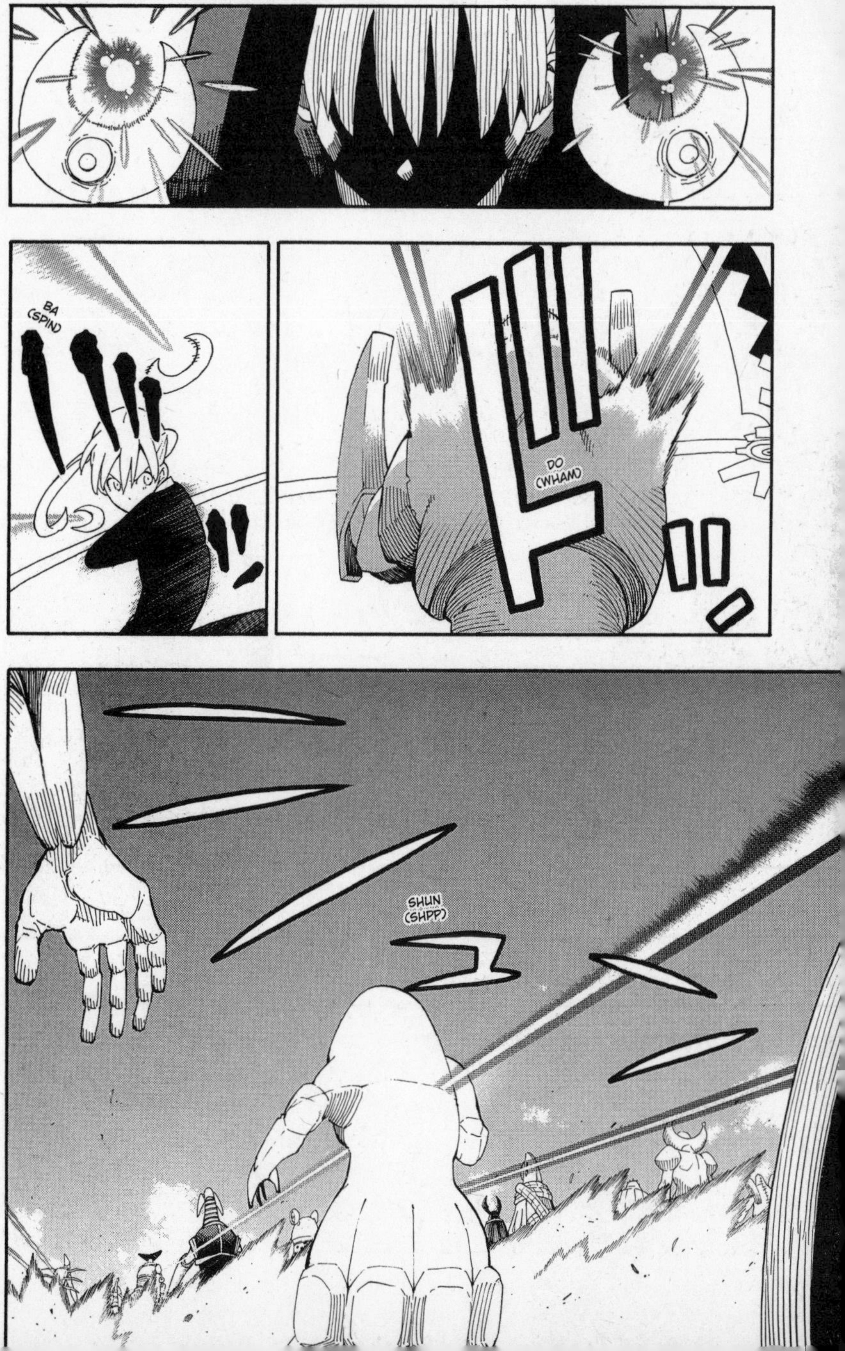
DO
(WHAM)
BA
(SPIN)
SHUN
(SHPP)

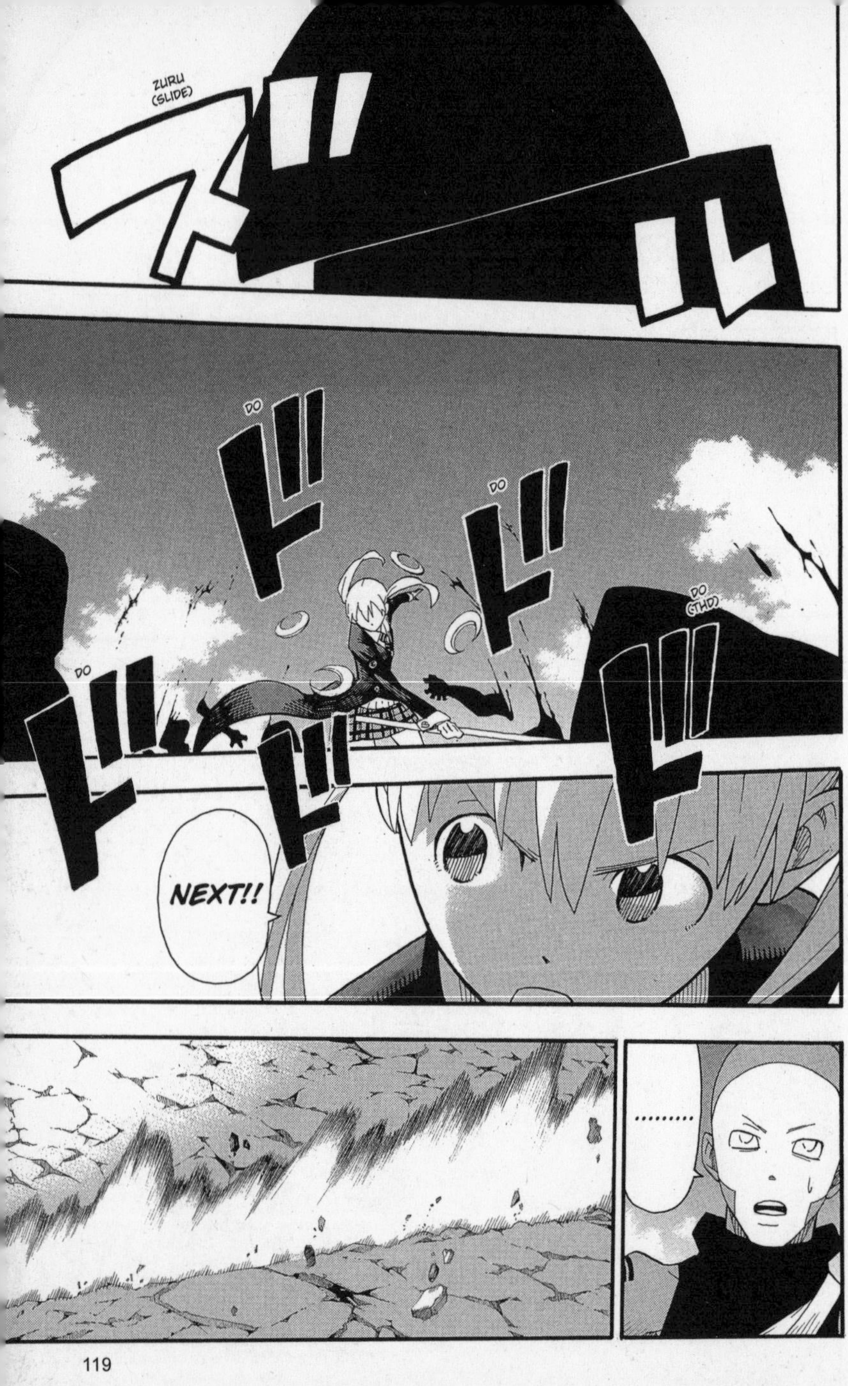
ZURU (SLIDE)
DO (THD)
DO
DO
DO
NEXT!!
....

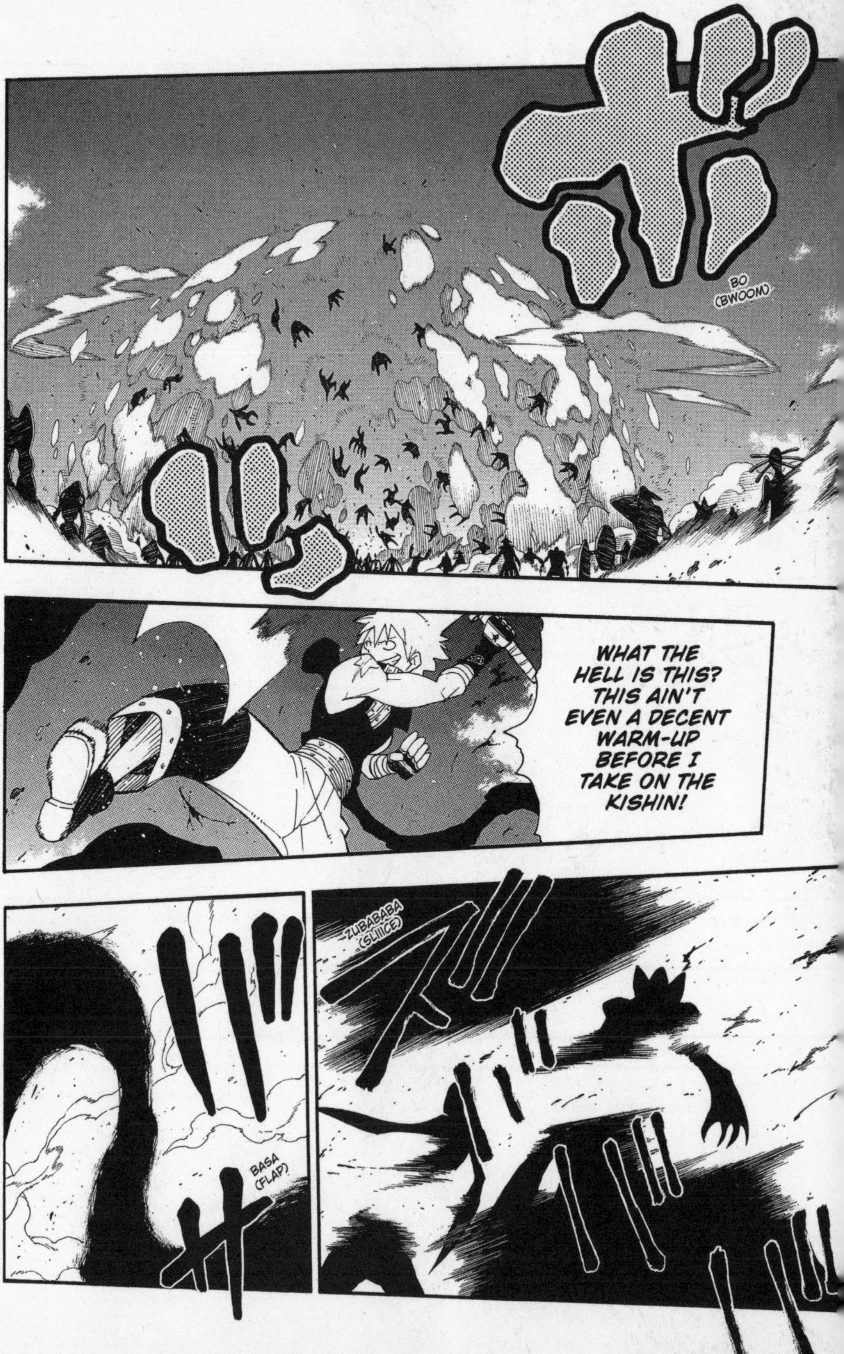
BO
(BWOOM)
WHAT THE HELL IS THIS? THIS AIN'T EVEN A DECENT WARM-UP BEFORE I TAKE ON THE KISHIN!
-ZUBABABA
(SLIIICE)
BASA
(FLAP)

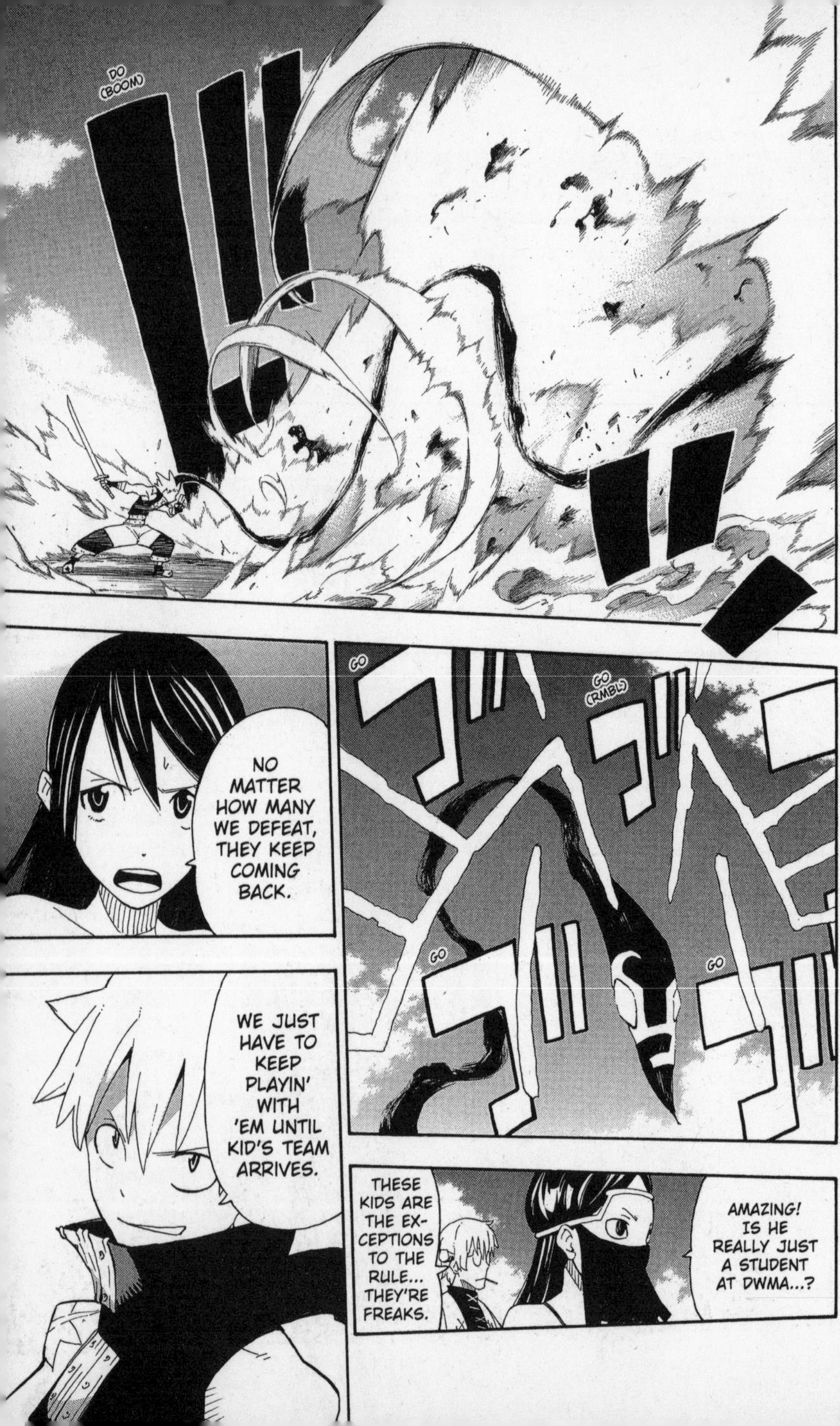
DO (BOOM)
GO
GO (RMBL)
GO
GO
NO MATTER HOW MANY WE DEFEAT, THEY KEEP COMING BACK.
WE JUST HAVE TO KEEP PLAYIN' WITH 'EM UNTIL KID'S TEAM ARRIVES.
AMAZING! IS HE REALLY JUST A STUDENT AT DWMA...?
THESE KIDS ARE THE EX-CEPTIONS TO THE RULE... THEY'RE FREAKS.

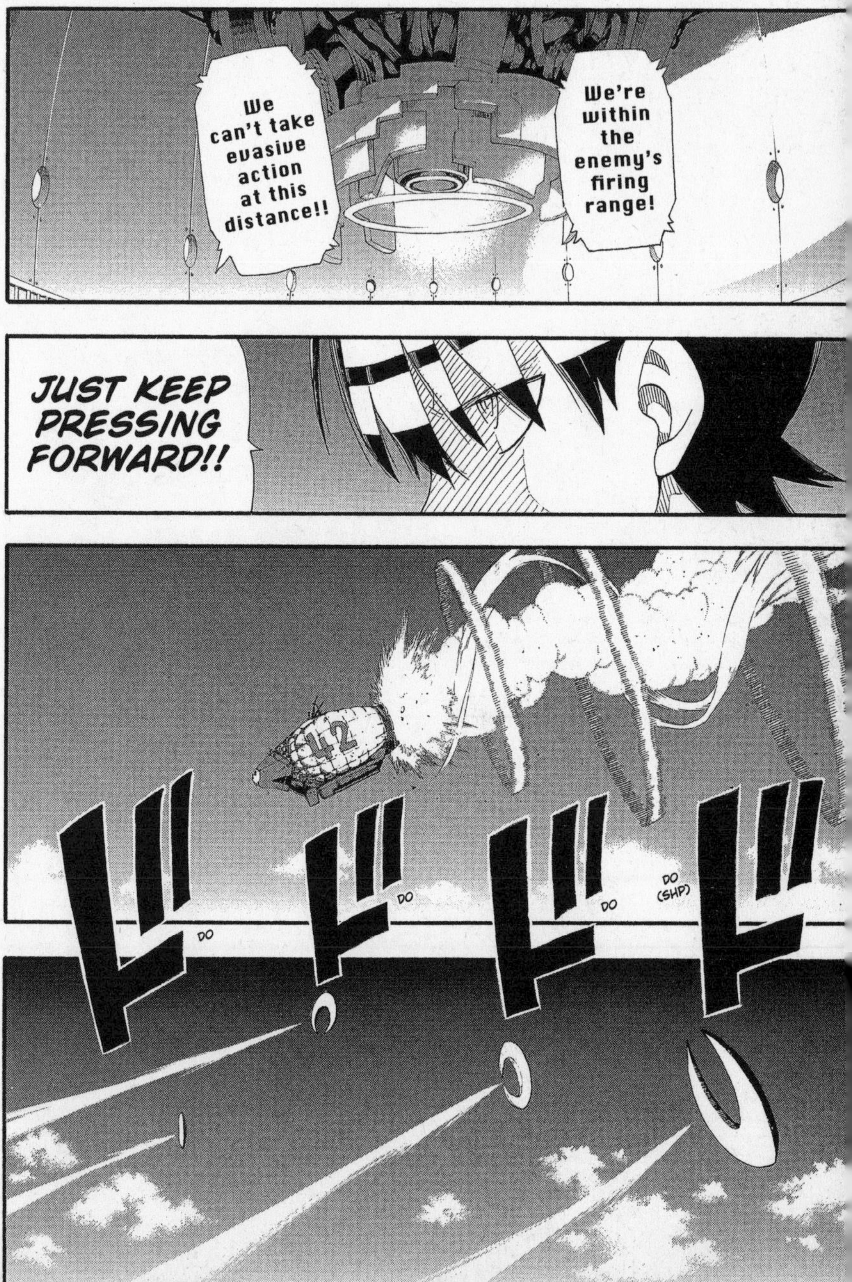
We're within the enemy's firing range!
We can't take evasive action at this distance!!
JUST KEEP PRESSING FORWARD!!
DO (SHP)
DO
DO
DO

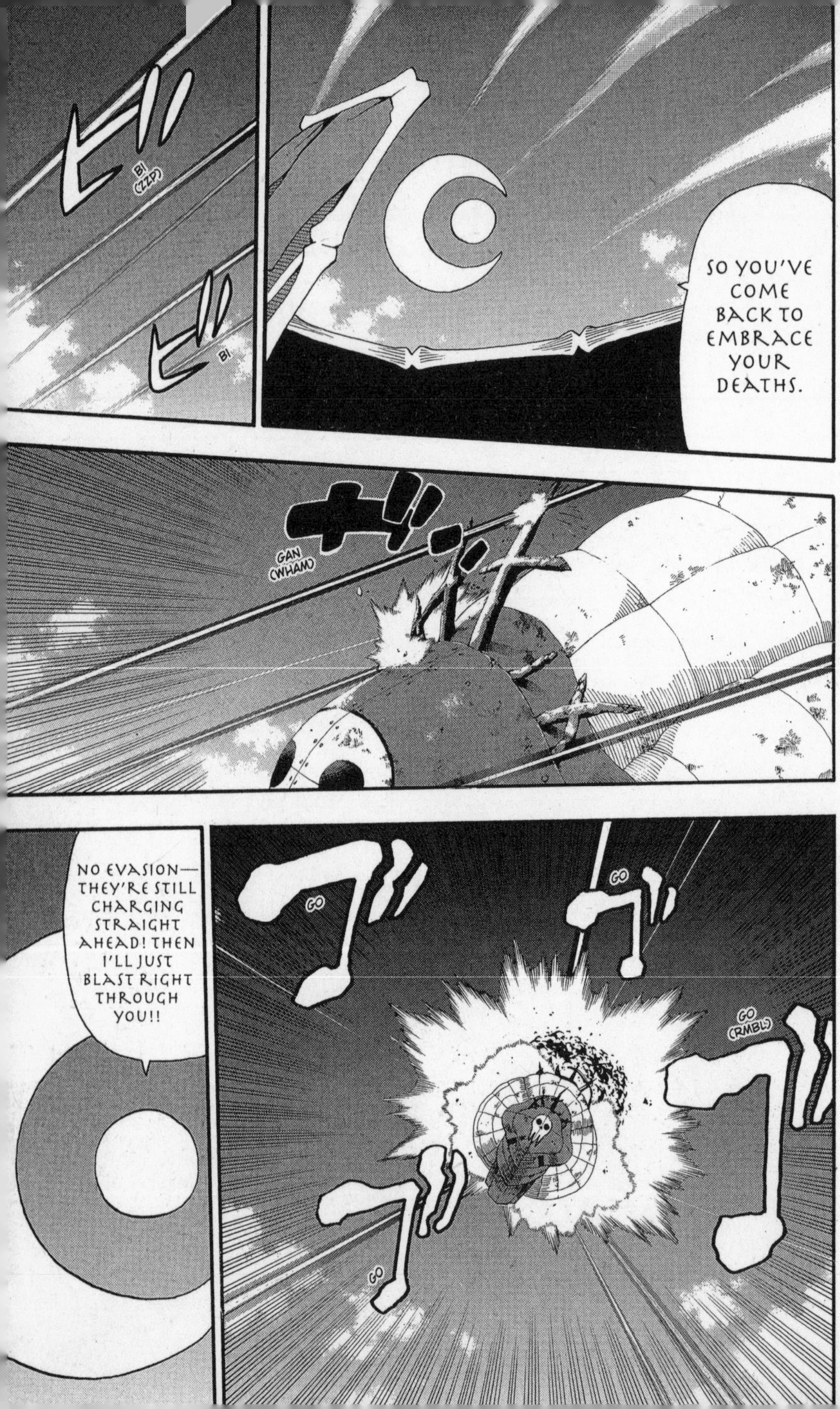
SO YOU'VE COME BACK TO EMBRACE YOUR DEATHS.
BI (ZZZP)
BI
GAN (WHAM)
GO
GO
GO (RMBL)
GO
NO EVASION— THEY'RE STILL CHARGING STRAIGHT AHEAD! THEN I'LL JUST BLAST RIGHT THROUGH YOU!!

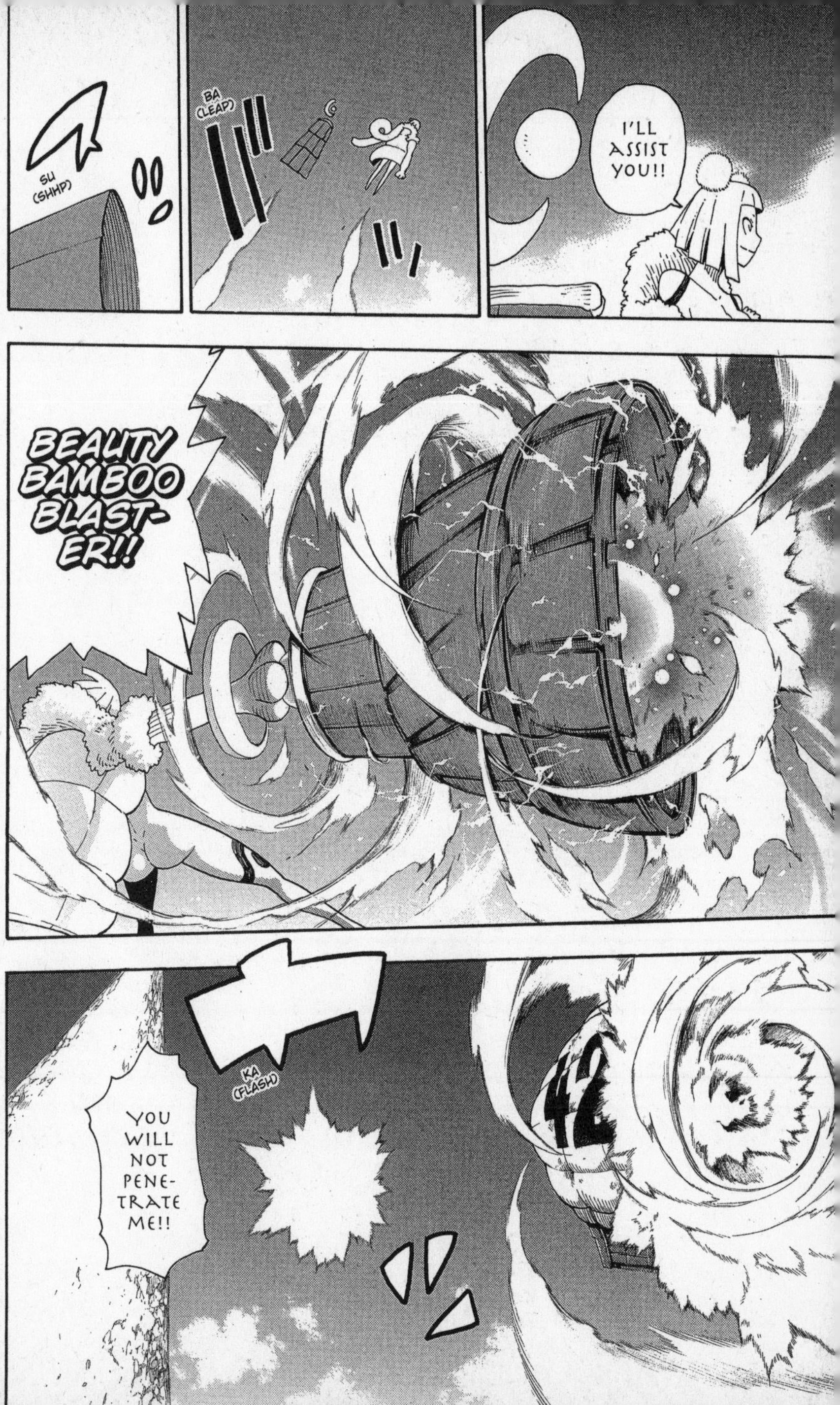
I'LL ASSIST YOU!!
BA (LEAP)
SU (SHHP)
BEAUTY BAMBOO BLAST-ER!!
KA (FLASH)
YOU WILL NOT PENE-TRATE ME!!

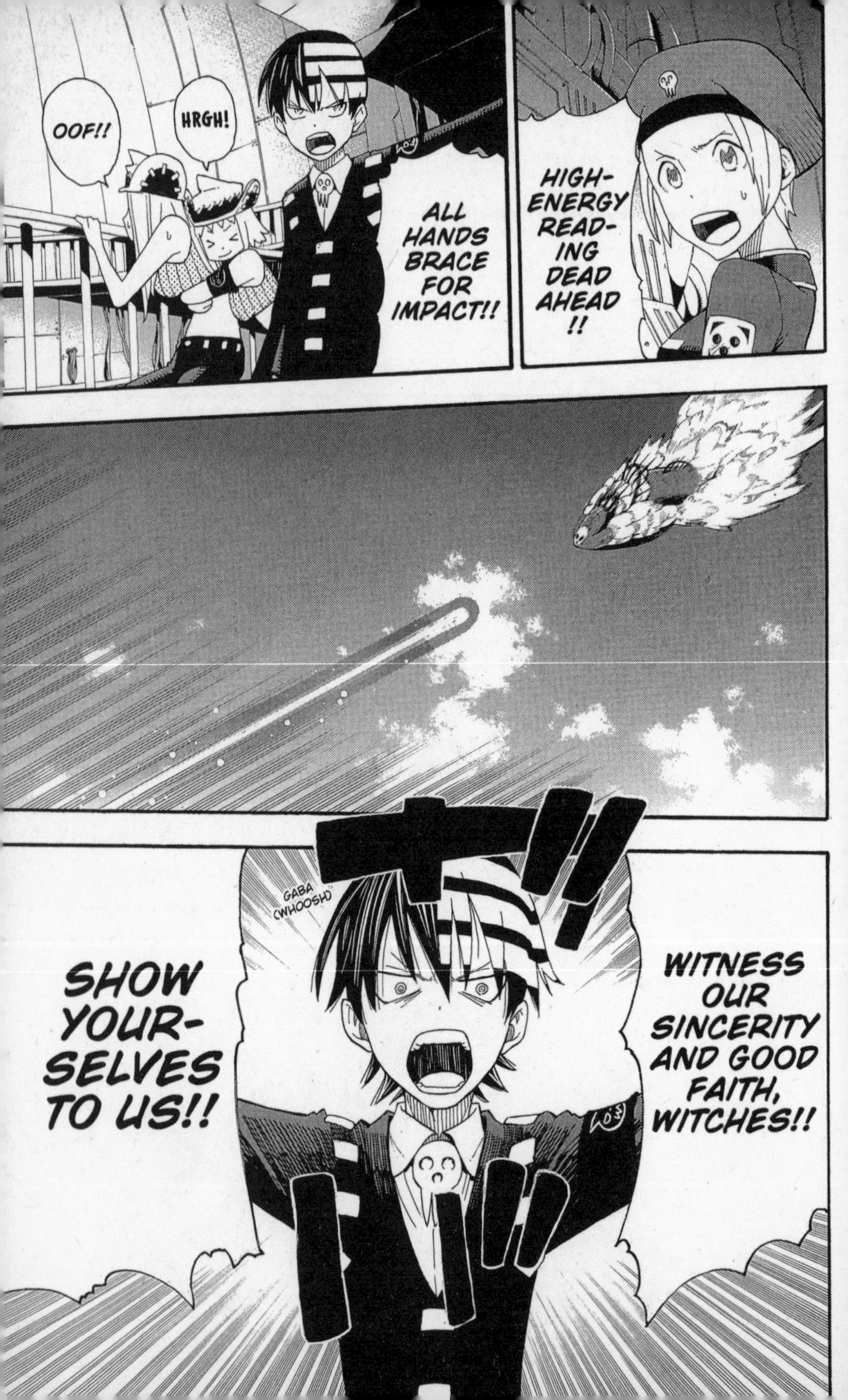
HIGH-ENERGY READING DEAD AHEAD!!
ALL HANDS BRACE FOR IMPACT!!
HRGH!
OOF!!
WITNESS OUR SINCERITY AND GOOD FAITH, WITCHES!!
GABA (WHOOSH)
SHOW YOURSELVES TO US!!

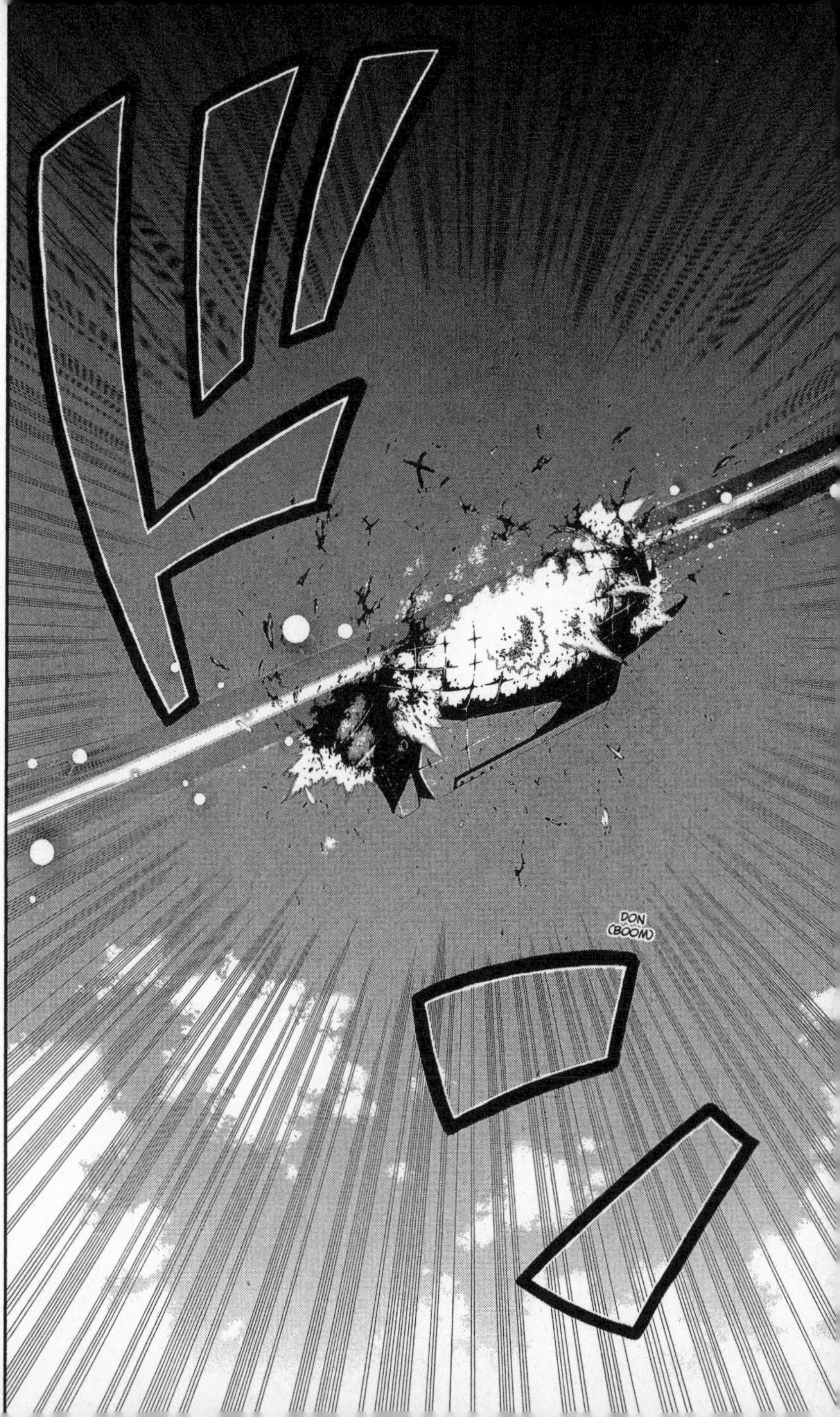
DON
(BOOM)

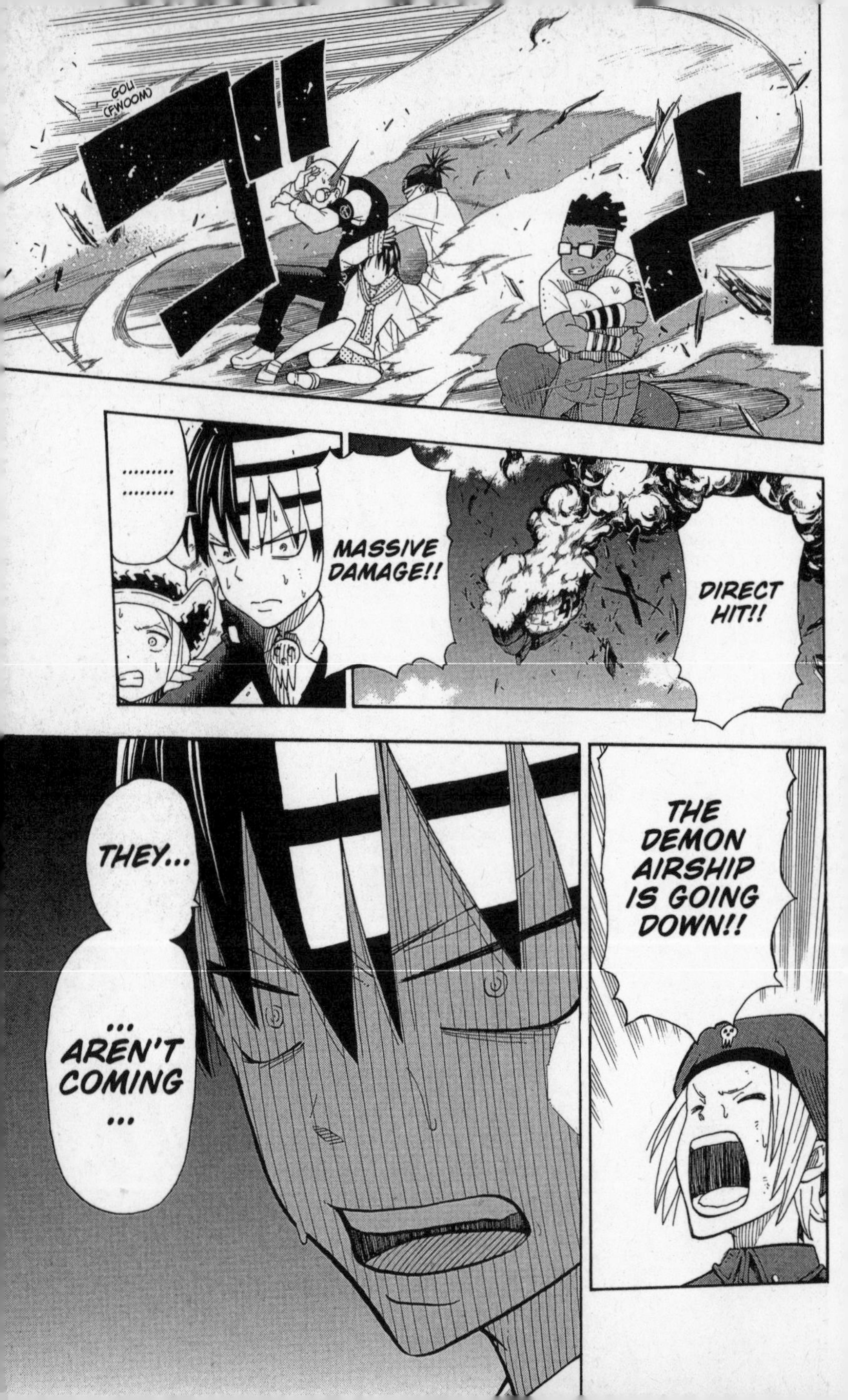
GOU
(FWOOM)
DIRECT HIT!!
MASSIVE DAMAGE!!
....
....
THE DEMON AIRSHIP IS GOING DOWN!!
THEY...
...AREN'T COMING...

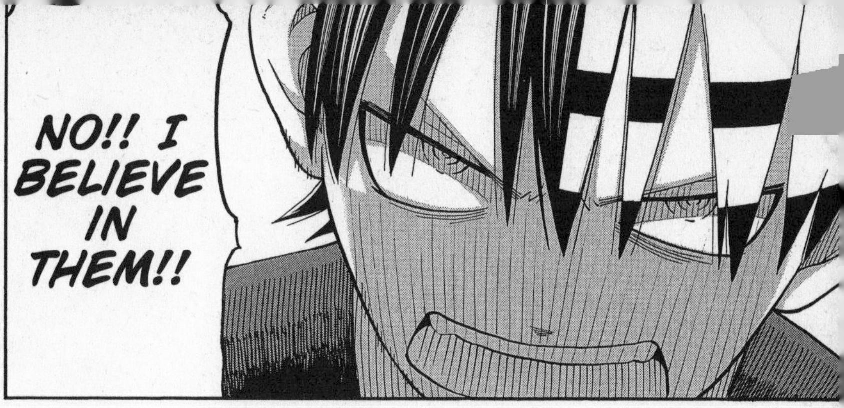
NO!! I BELIEVE IN THEM!!
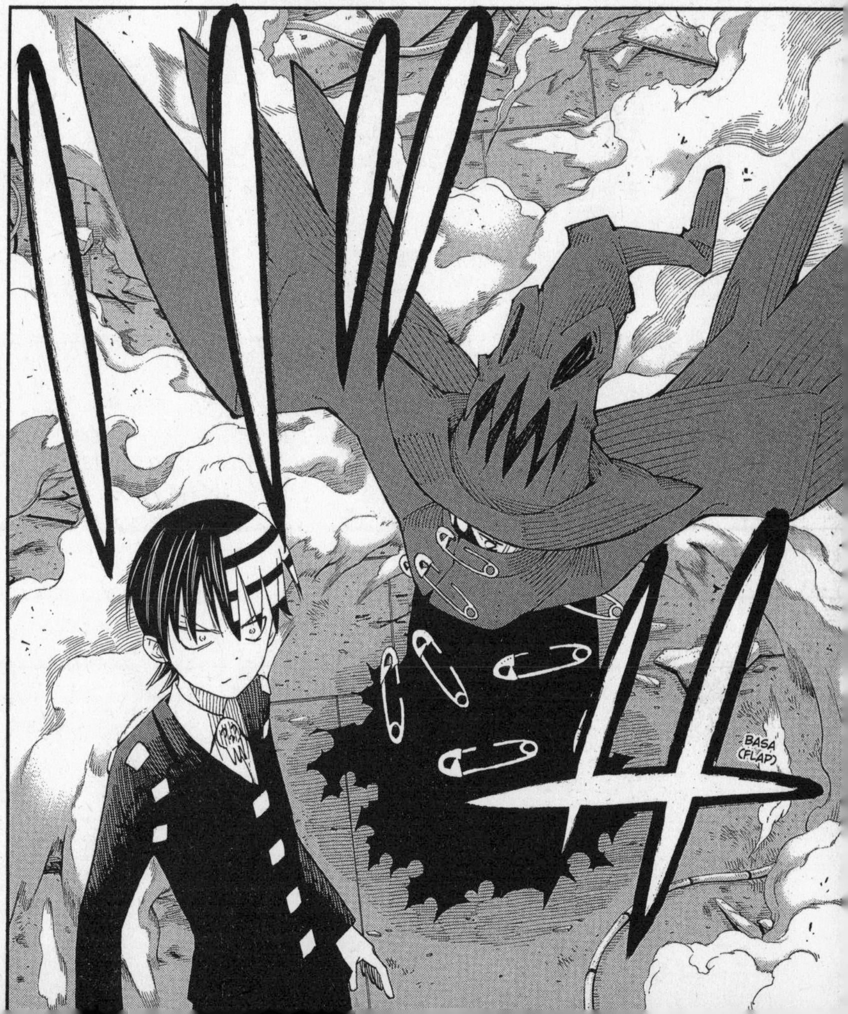
BASA (FLAP)

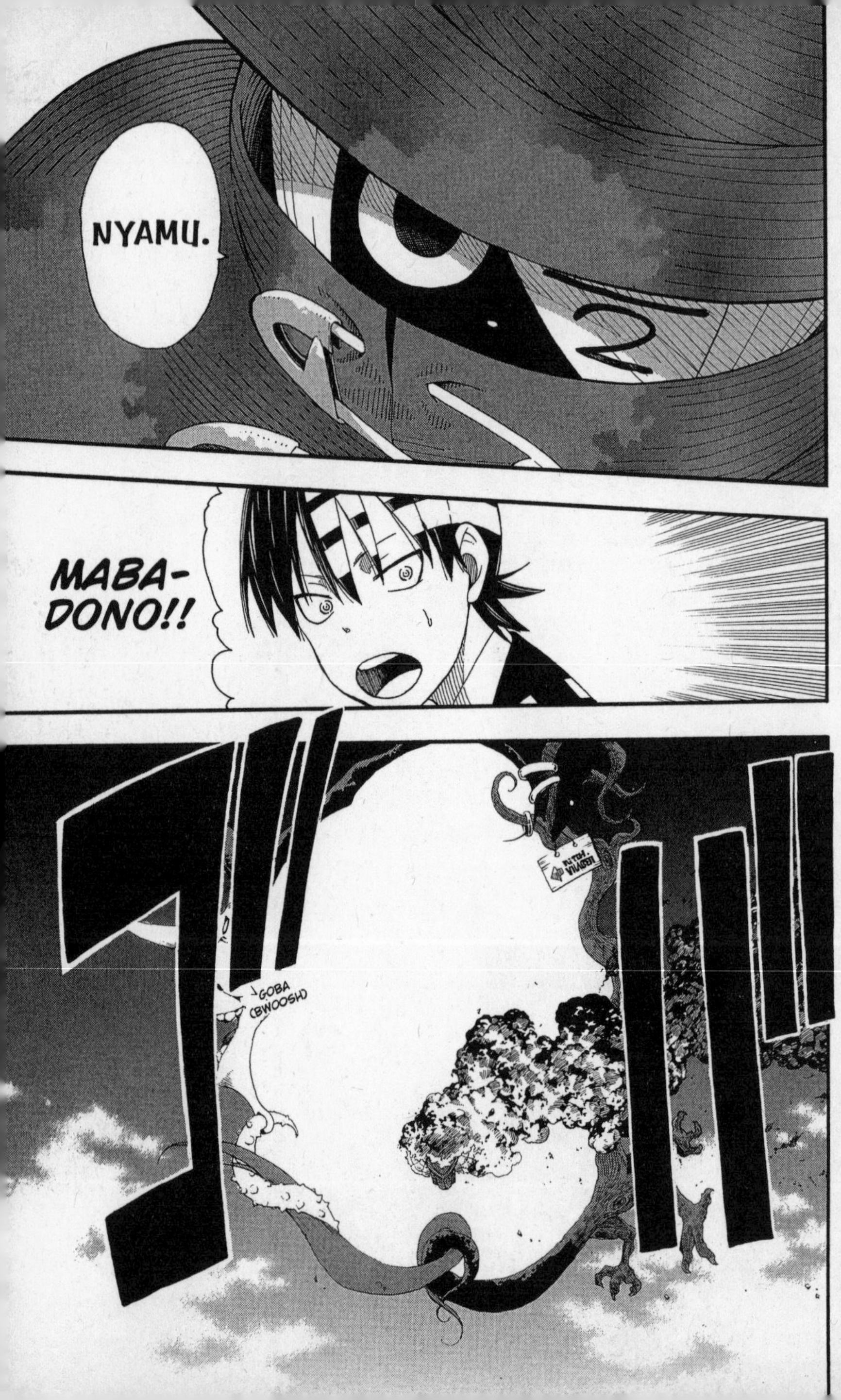
NYAMU.
MABA-DONO!!
GOBA (BWOOSH)

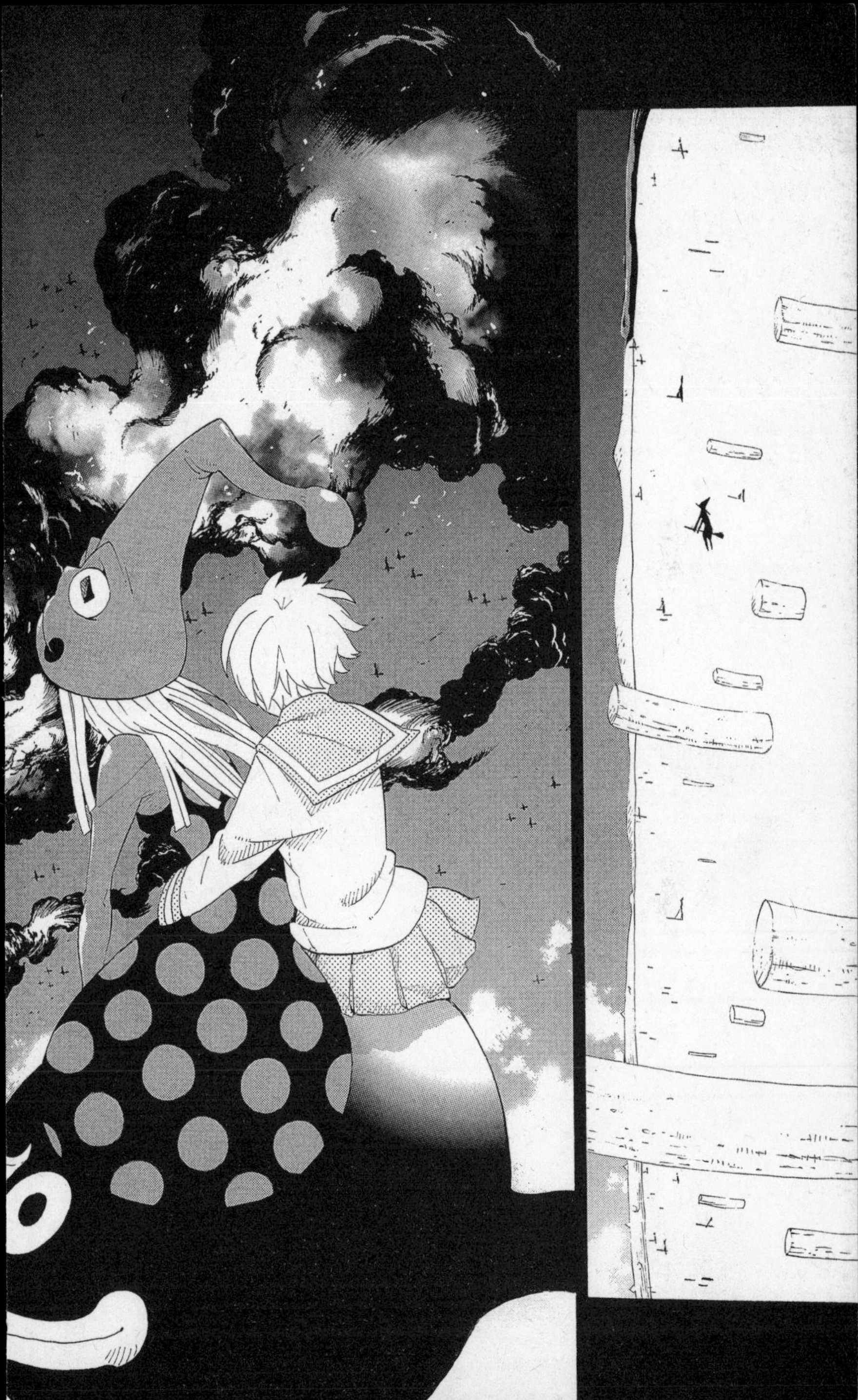

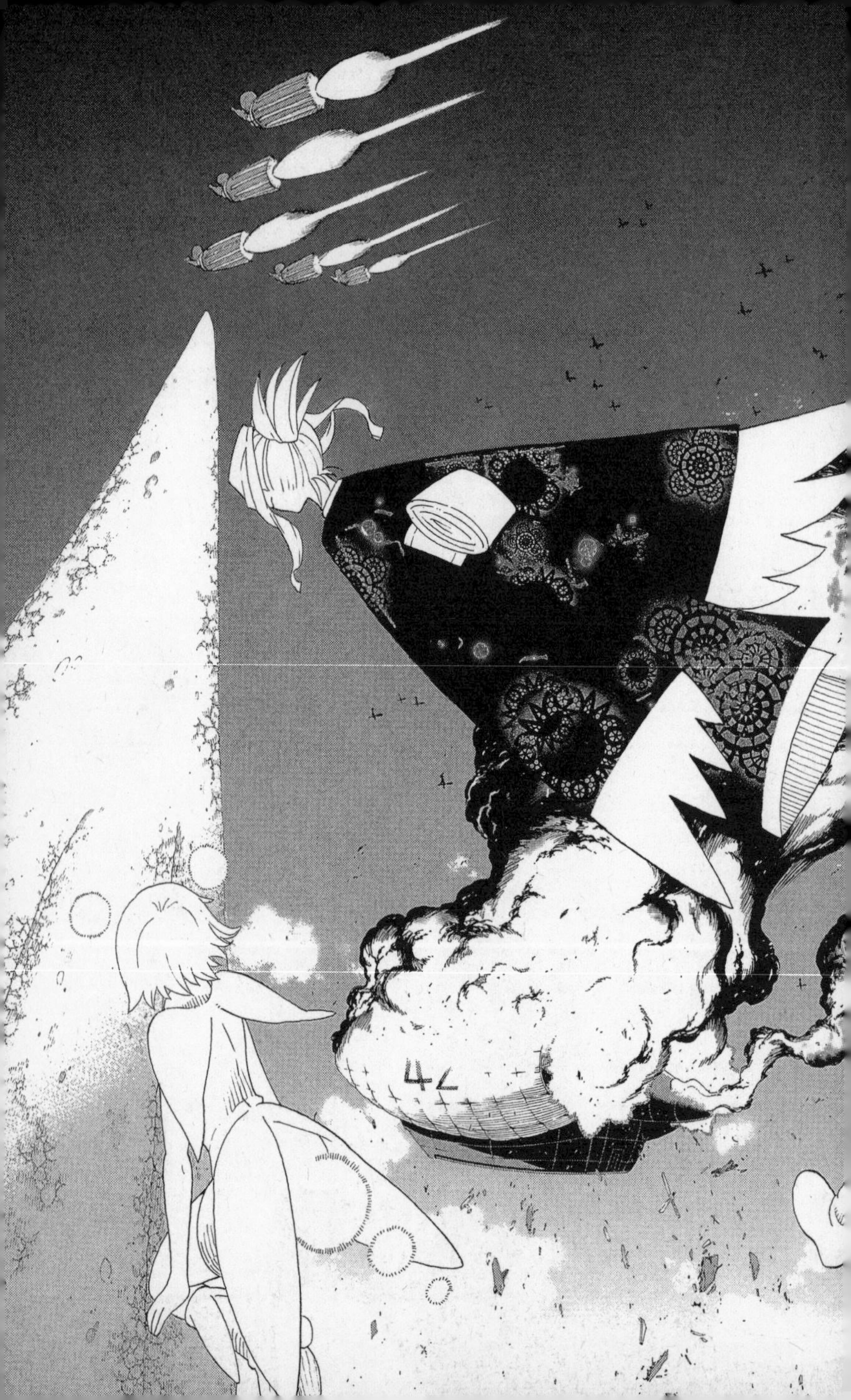
42

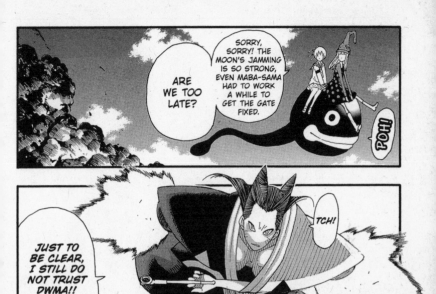

SORRY, SORRY! THE MOON'S JAMMING IS SO STRONG, EVEN MABA-SAMA HAD TO WORK A WHILE TO GET THE GATE FIXED.
ARE WE TOO LATE?
POH!
TCH!
JUST TO BE CLEAR, I STILL DO NOT TRUST DWMA!!
YOU CAME, MABA-DONO...
DAMN! THAT'S CRAZY!!
WE TRAVELED HERE IN AN INSTANT.
WHEN DID THIS HUGE GUY GET HERE!?
HOO-RAY!! THEY CAME, SENPAI!!
PYON (BOING) !!
PYON
ISN'T THAT WONDERFUL?

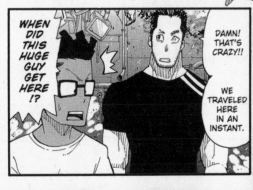

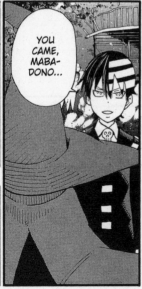

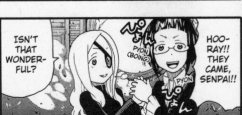

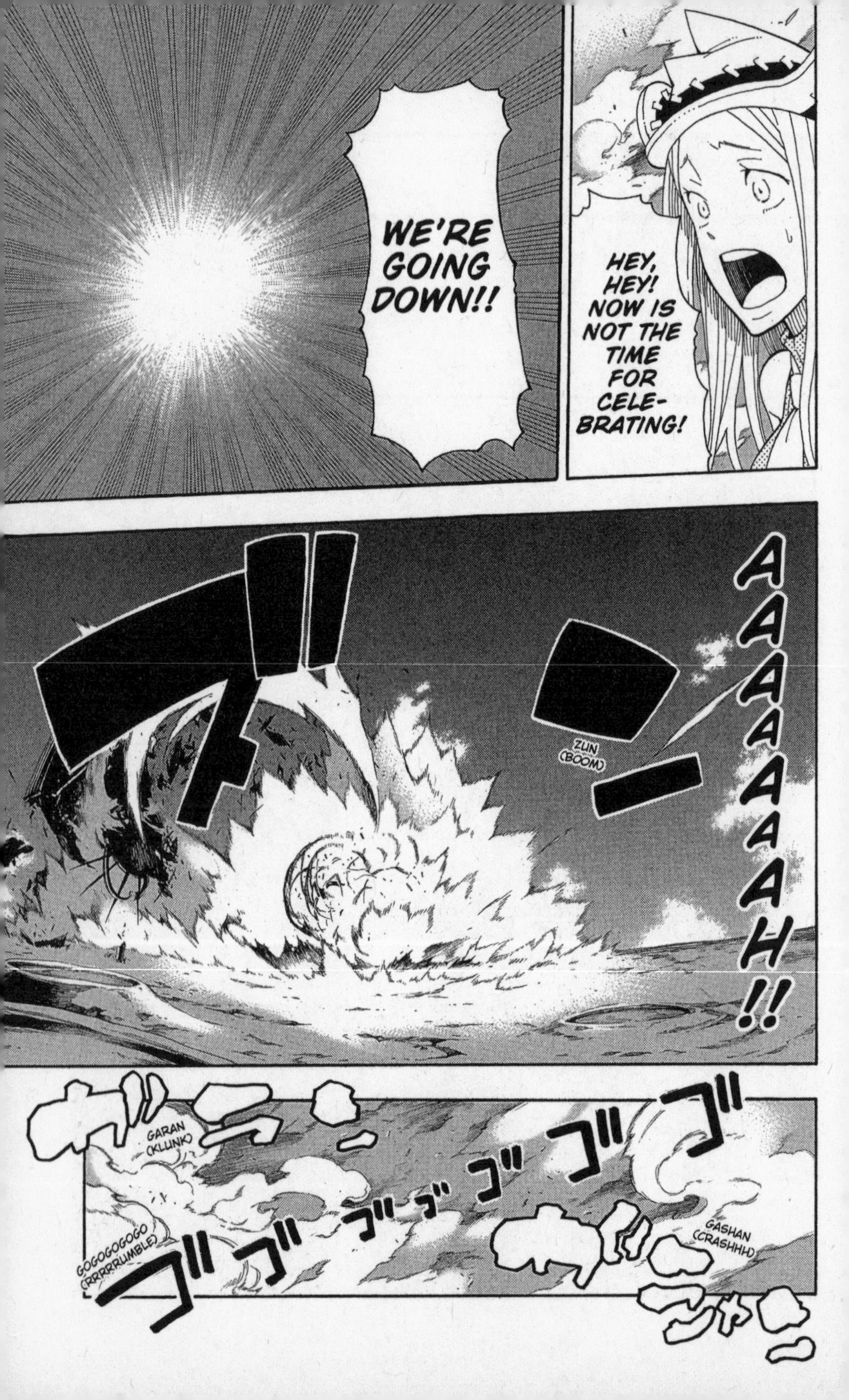
HEY, HEY! NOW IS NOT THE TIME FOR CELE-BRATING!
WE'RE GOING DOWN!!
AAAAAAAH!!
ZUN (BOOM)
GARAN (KLUNK)
GASHAN (CRASHHH)
GOGOGOGOGO (RRRRRUMBLE)

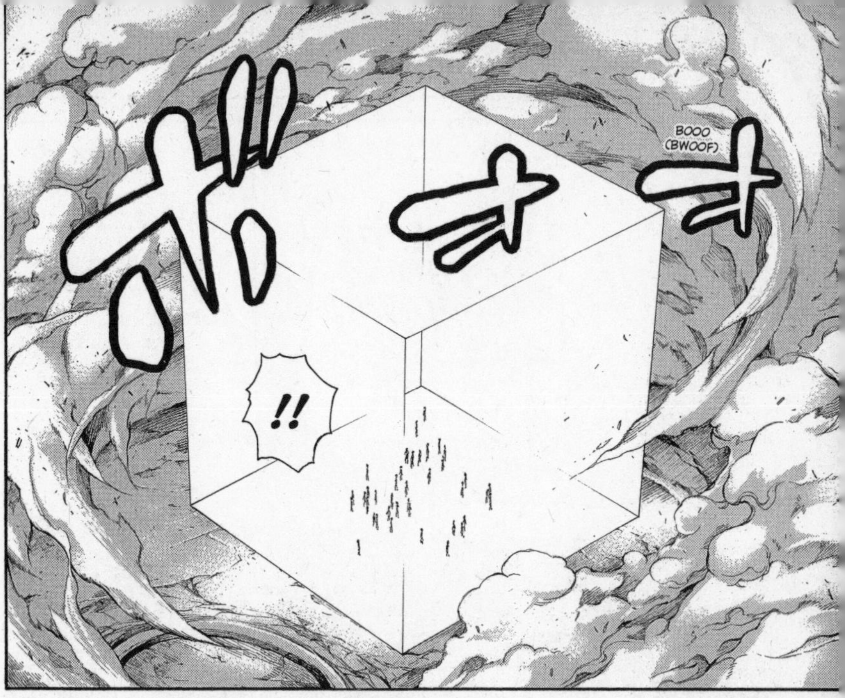
ボォオ
BOOO (BWOOF)
!!

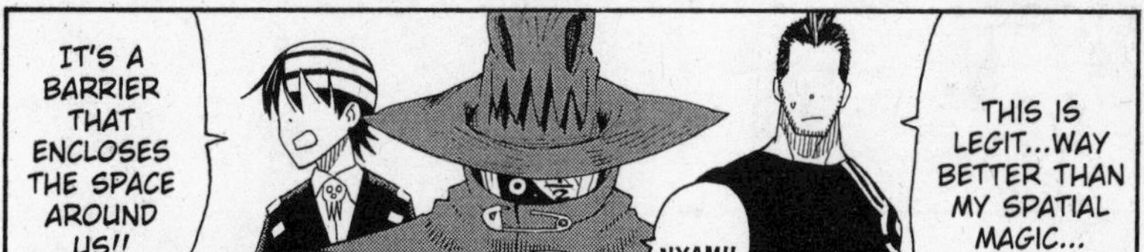
THIS IS LEGIT...WAY BETTER THAN MY SPATIAL MAGIC...
NYAMU.
IT'S A BARRIER THAT ENCLOSES THE SPACE AROUND US!!

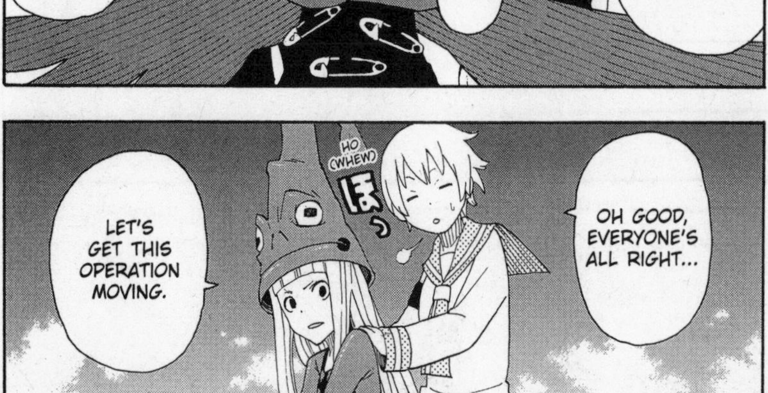
OH GOOD, EVERYONE'S ALL RIGHT...
HO (WHEW)
ほっ
LET'S GET THIS OPERATION MOVING.

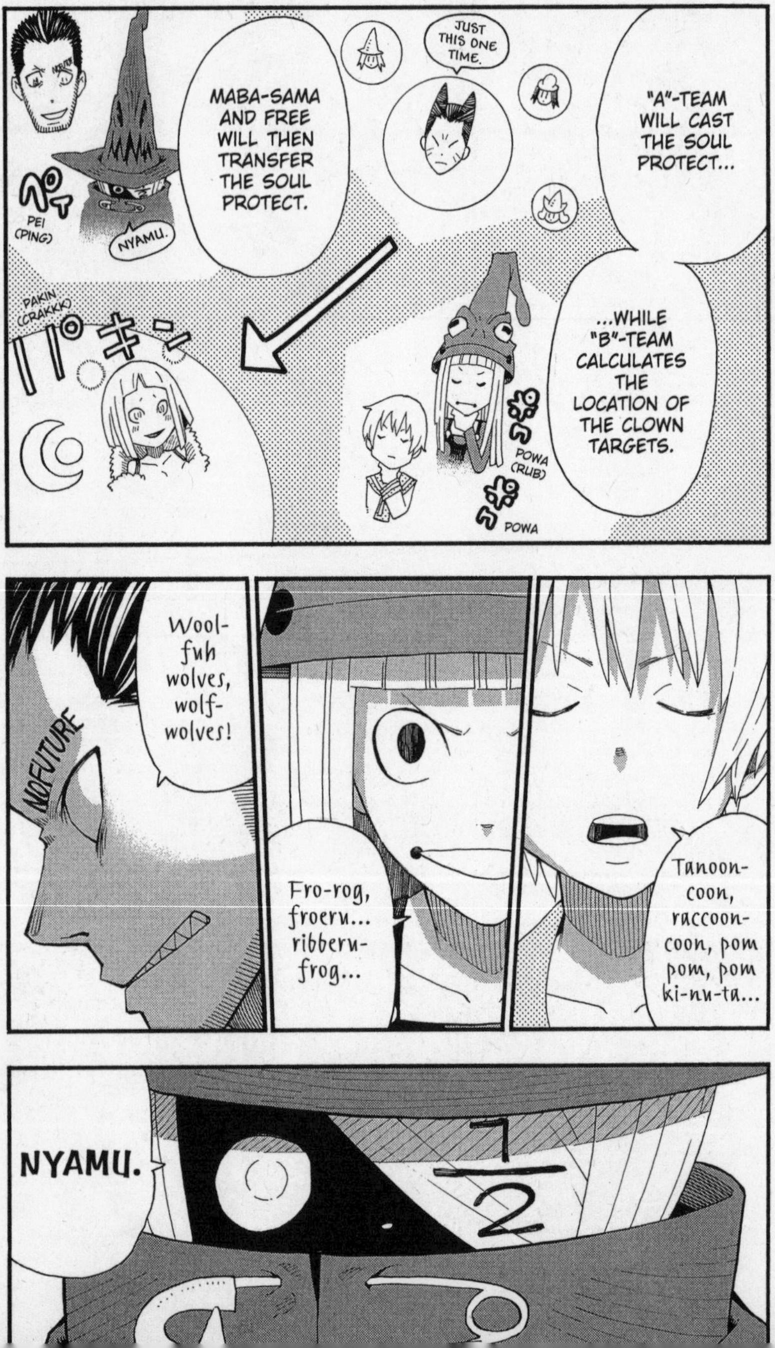
"A"-TEAM WILL CAST THE SOUL PROTECT...
...WHILE "B"-TEAM CALCULATES THE LOCATION OF THE CLOWN TARGETS.
POWA (RUB)
POWA
JUST THIS ONE TIME.
MABA-SAMA AND FREE WILL THEN TRANSFER THE SOUL PROTECT.
PEI (PING)
NYAMU.
PAKIN (CRAKKK)
Tanoon-coon, raccoon-coon, pom pom, pom ki-nu-ta...
Fro-rog, froeru... ribberu-frog...
Wool-fuh wolves, wolf-wolves!
NOFUTURE
NYAMU.
1/2

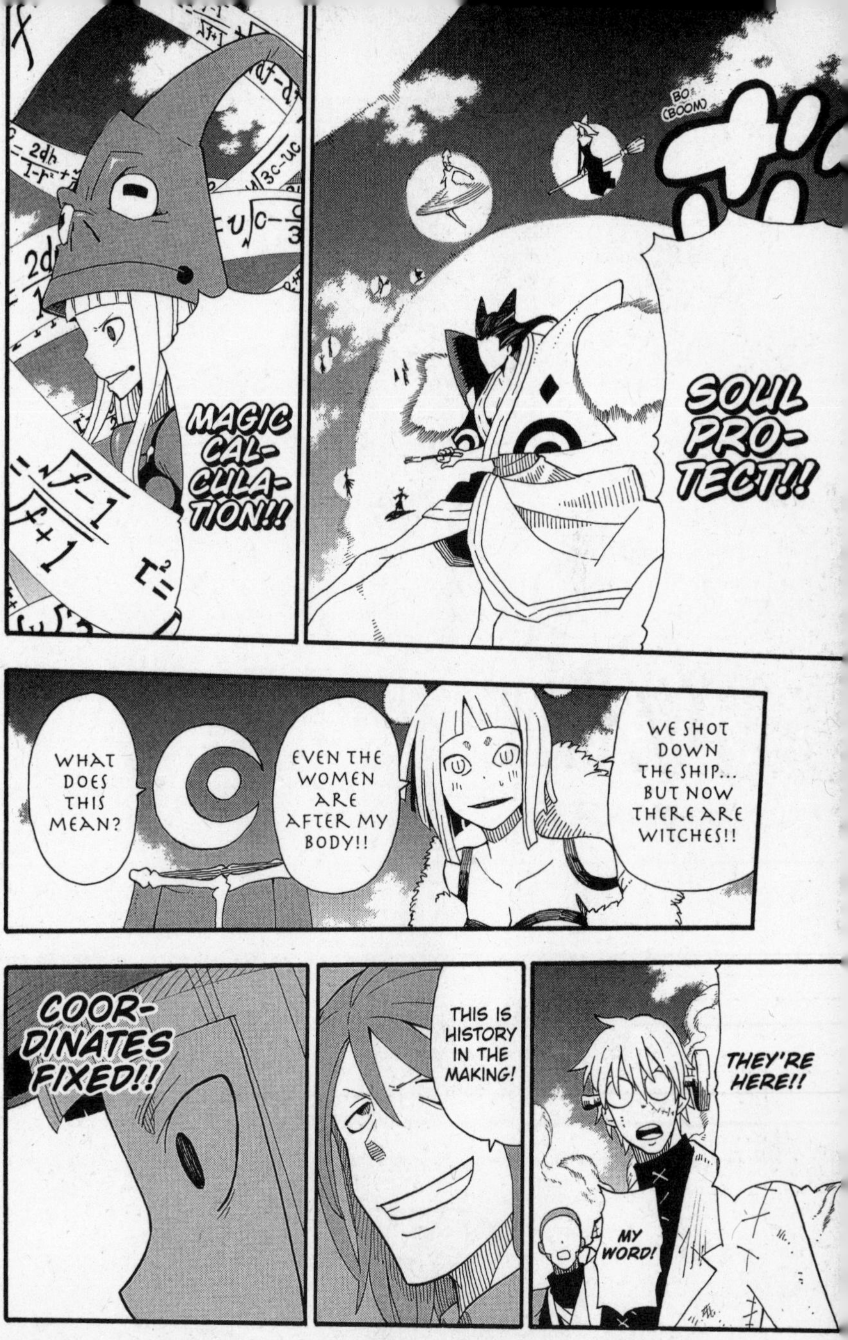
BO (BOOM)
SOUL PRO-TECT!!
MAGIC CAL-CULA-TION!!
WE SHOT DOWN THE SHIP... BUT NOW THERE ARE WITCHES!!
EVEN THE WOMEN ARE AFTER MY BODY!!
WHAT DOES THIS MEAN?
THEY'RE HERE!!
MY WORD!
THIS IS HISTORY IN THE MAKING!
COOR-DINATES FIXED!!

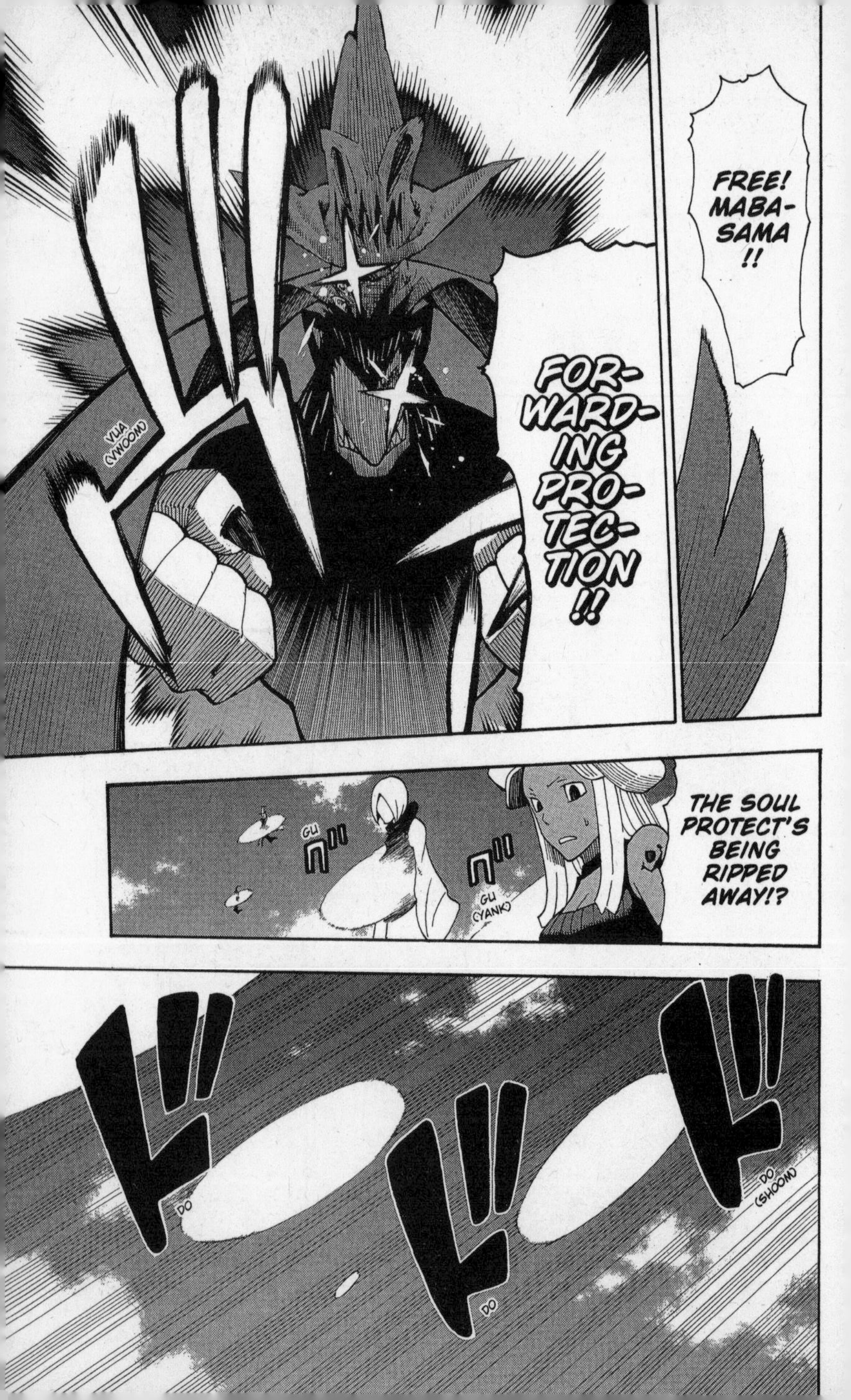
FREE! MABA-SAMA !!
FOR-WARD-ING PRO-TEC-TION !!
VUA (VWOOM)
THE SOUL PROTECT'S BEING RIPPED AWAY!?
GU
GU (YANK)
DO (SHOOM)
DO
DO

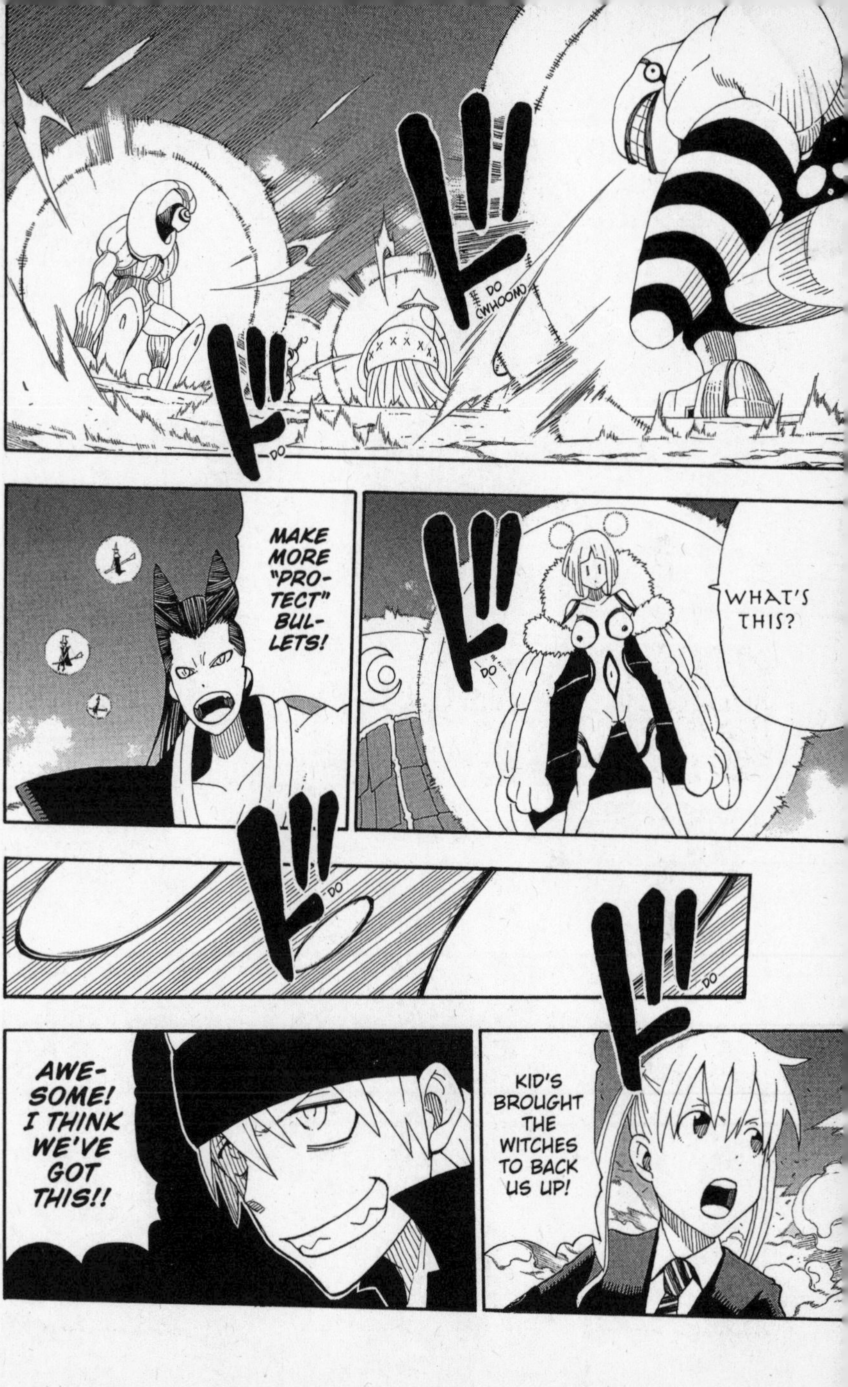
DO (WHOOM)
DO
WHAT'S THIS?
DO
MAKE MORE "PRO-TECT" BUL-LETS!
DO
DO
KID'S BROUGHT THE WITCHES TO BACK US UP!
AWE-SOME! I THINK WE'VE GOT THIS!!

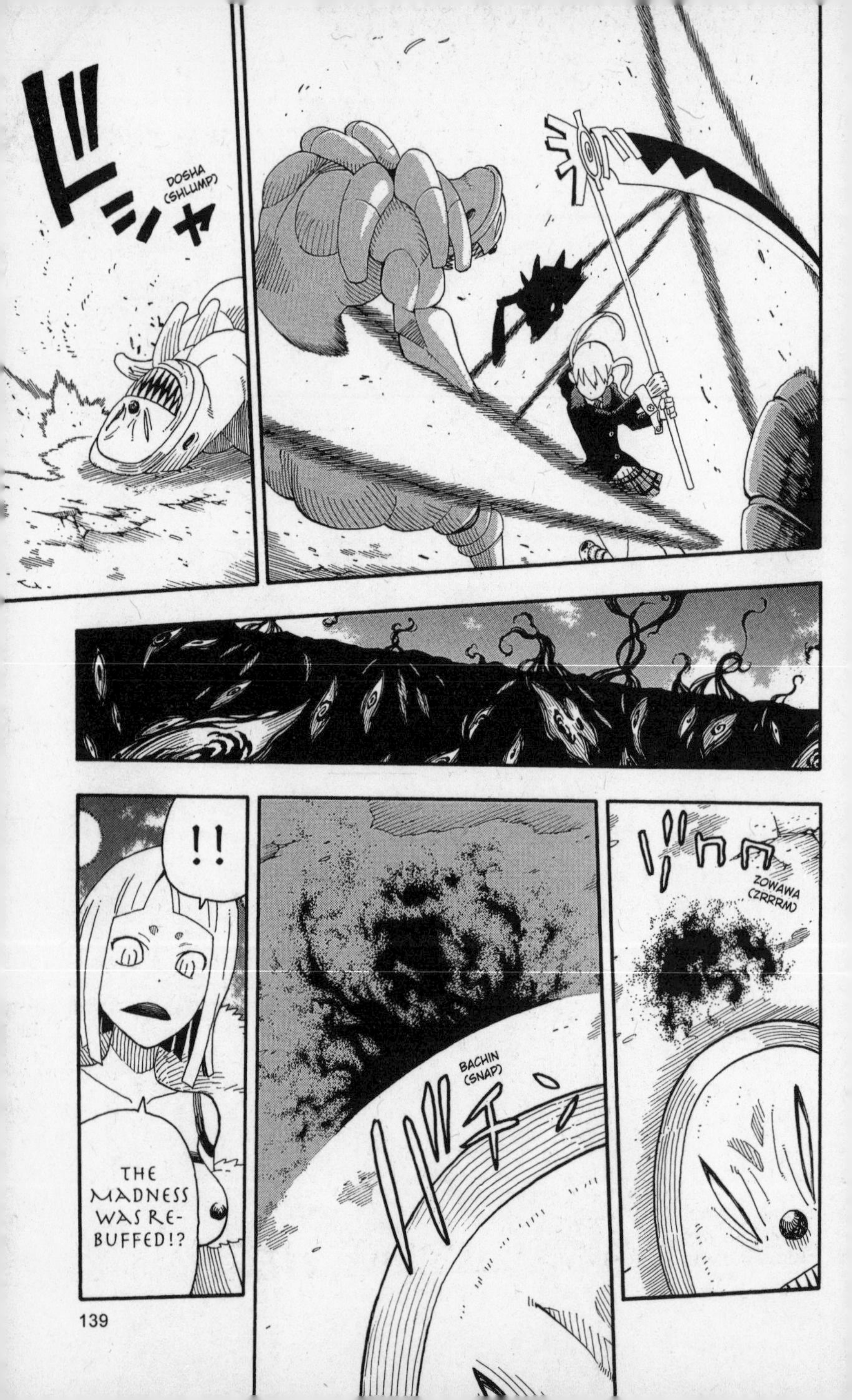
ドシャ
DOSHA (SHLUMP)
ゾワワ
ZOWAWA (ZRRRM)
バチン
BACHIN (SNAP)
!!
THE MADNESS WAS RE-BUFFED!?

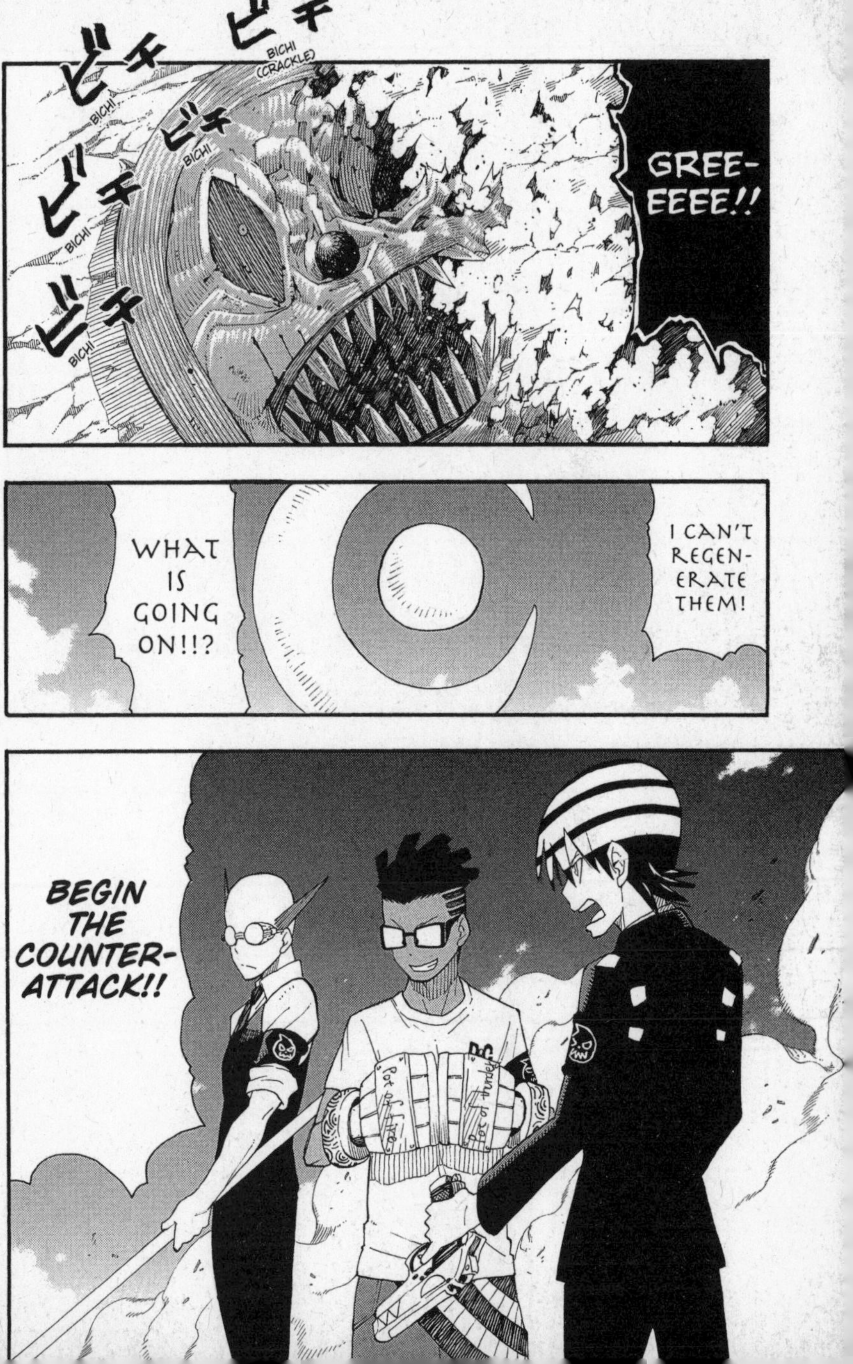
ビチ
BICHI (CRACKLE)
ビチ
BICHI
GREE-EEEE!!
ビチ
BICHI
ビチ
BICHI
ビチ
BICHI
I CAN'T REGEN-ERATE THEM!
WHAT IS GOING ON!!?
BEGIN THE COUNTER-ATTACK!!

SOUL EATER

GN-GUH-GAH!!

KISHIN-SAMA'S MADNESS IS BEING BLOCKED!?

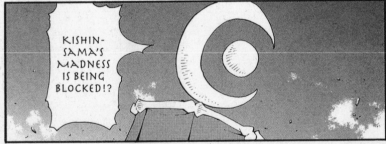

IT'S WORK-ING!!

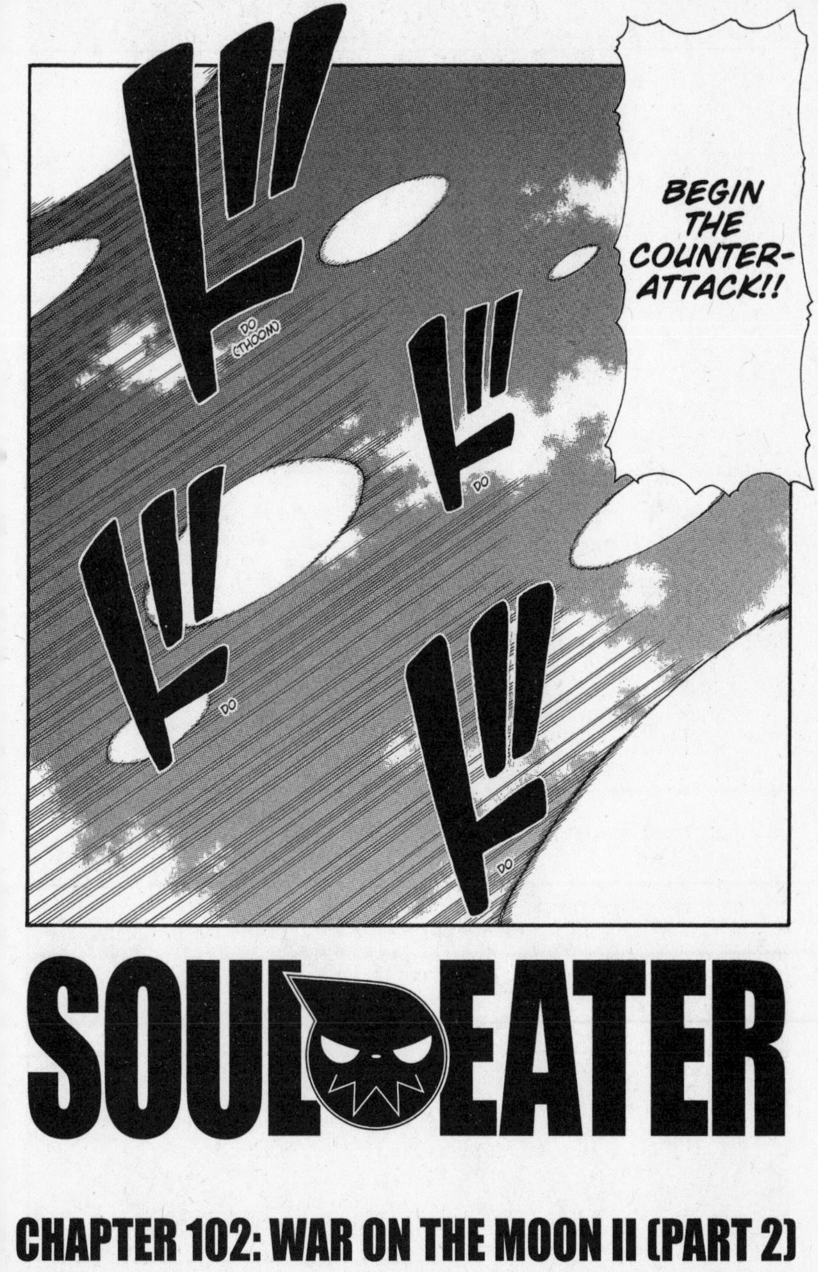
BEGIN THE COUNTER-ATTACK!!
DO (THOOM)
DO
DO
DO

SOUL EATER

CHAPTER 102: WAR ON THE MOON II (PART 2)

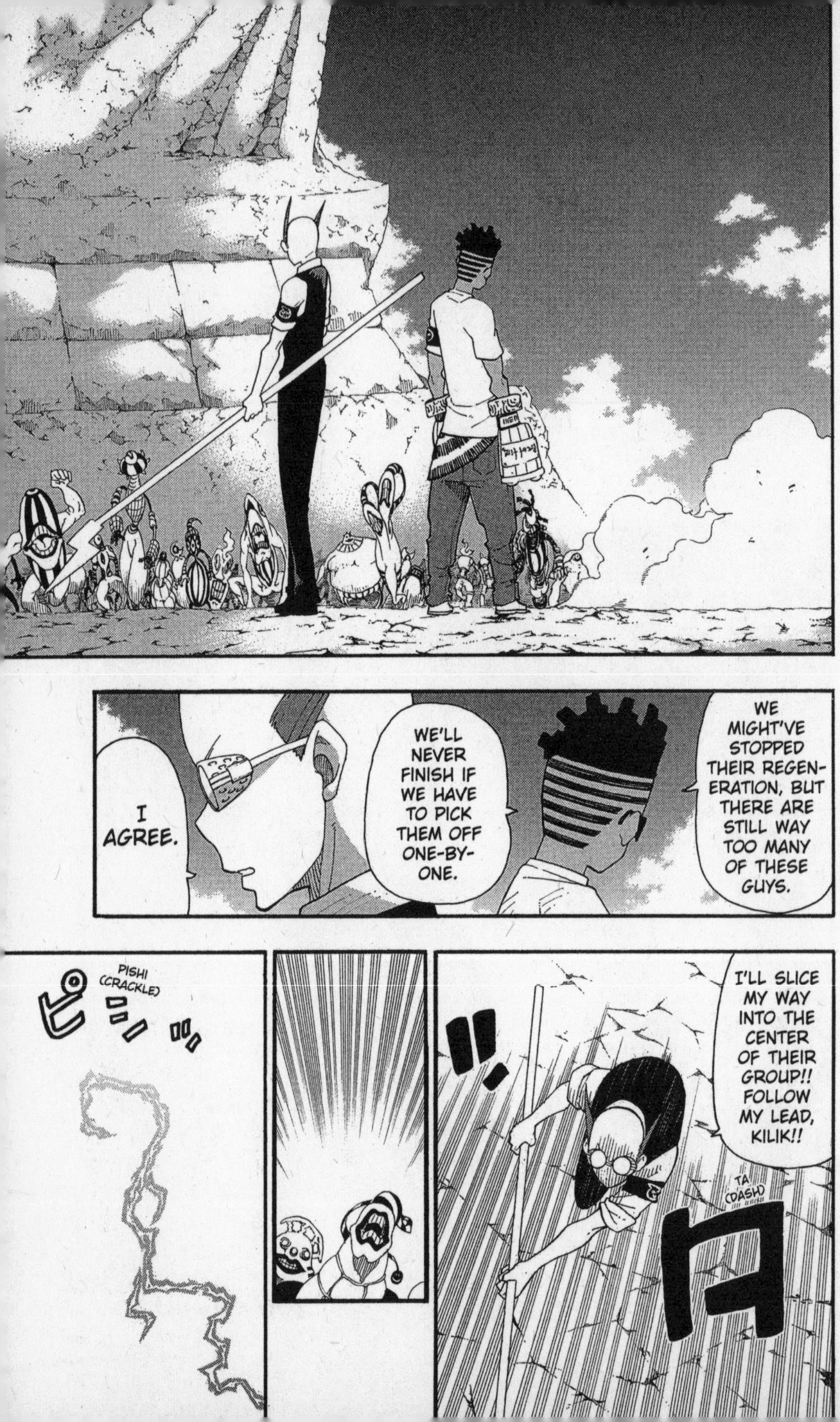
WE MIGHT'VE STOPPED THEIR REGEN-ERATION, BUT THERE ARE STILL WAY TOO MANY OF THESE GUYS.
WE'LL NEVER FINISH IF WE HAVE TO PICK THEM OFF ONE-BY-ONE.
I AGREE.
I'LL SLICE MY WAY INTO THE CENTER OF THEIR GROUP!! FOLLOW MY LEAD, KILIK!!
TA (DASH)
PISHI (CRACKLE)

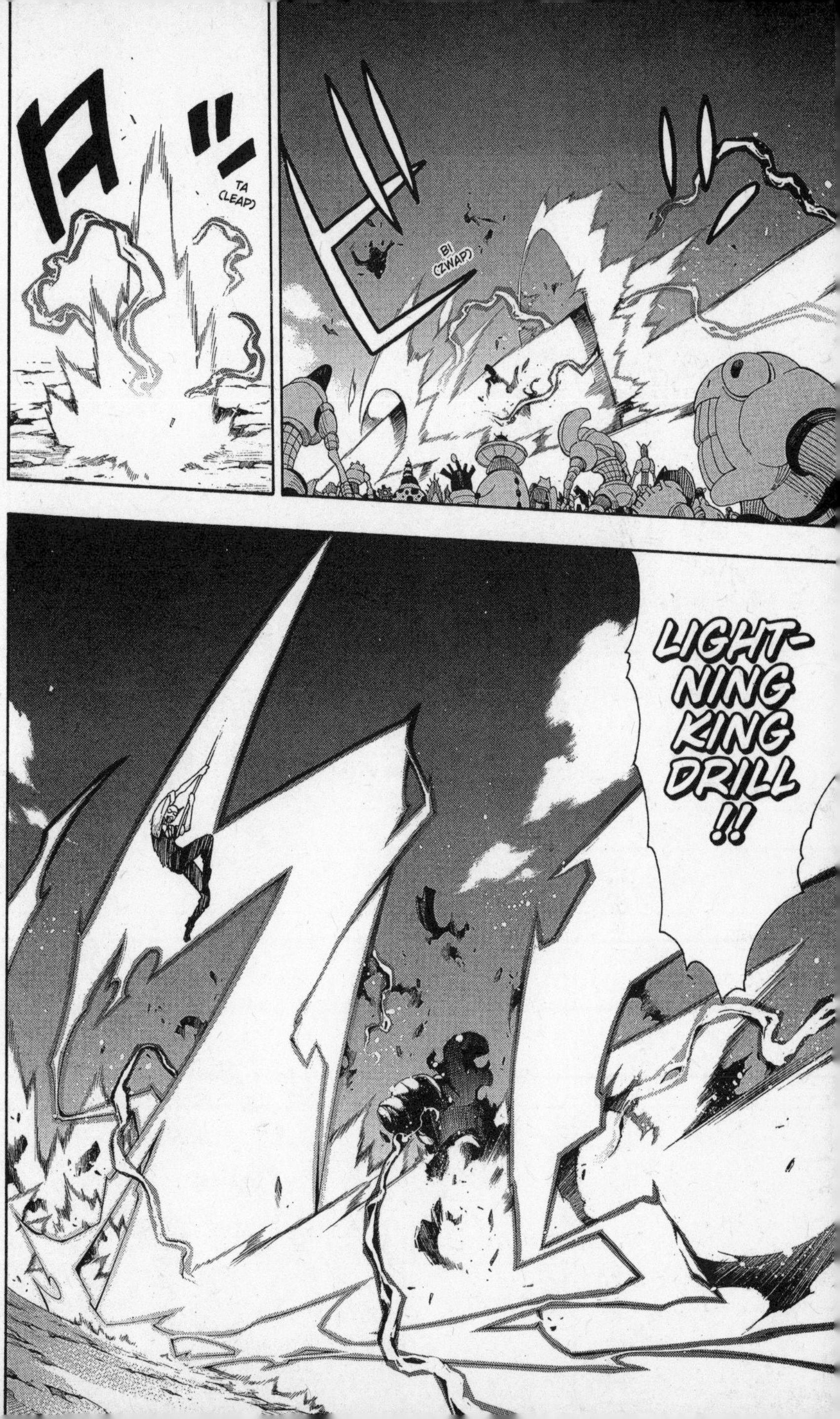
BI (ZWAP)
TA (LEAP)
LIGHTNING KING DRILL!!

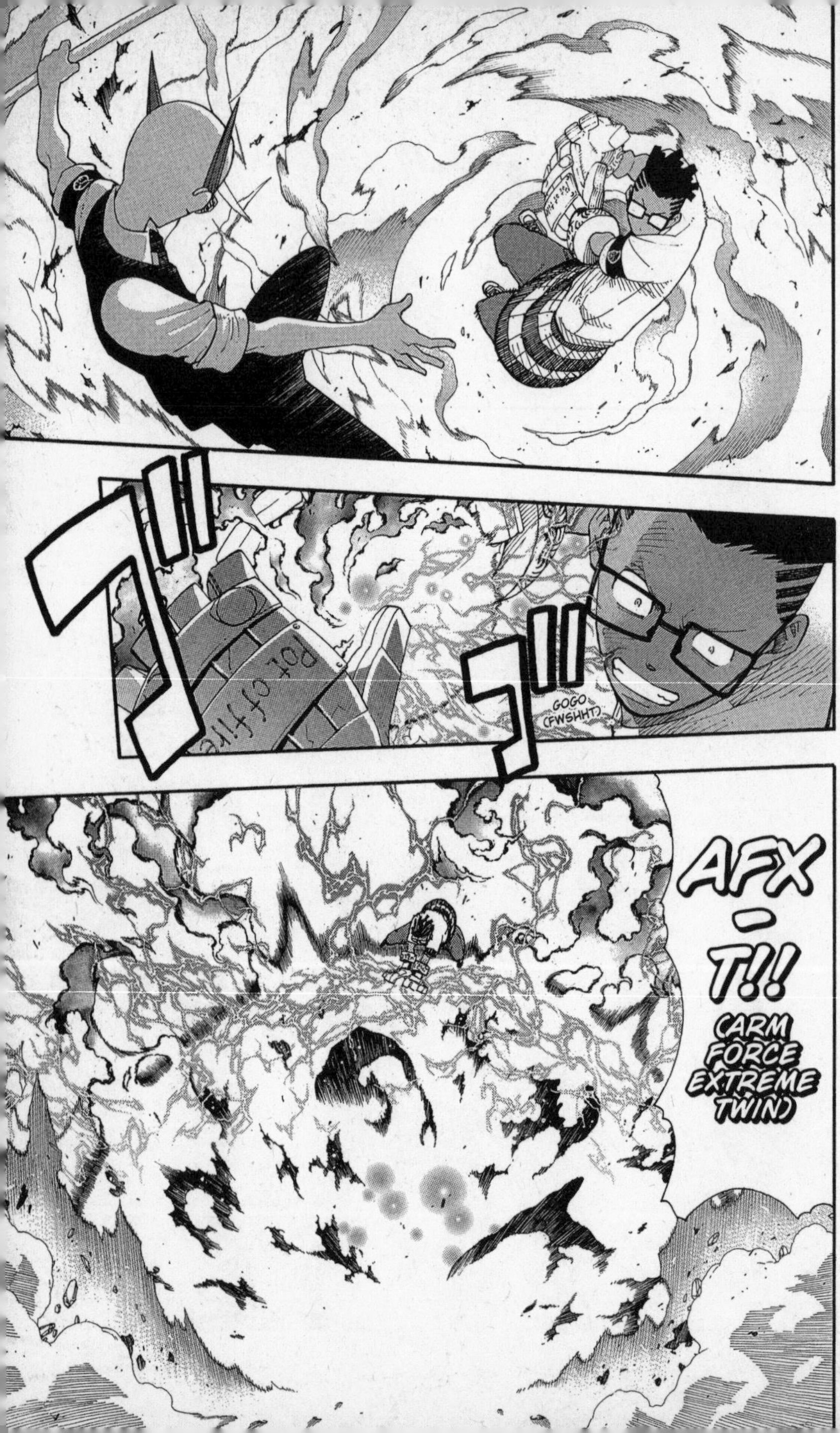
GOGO (FWSHHT)
AFX-T!!
(ARM FORCE EXTREME TWIN)

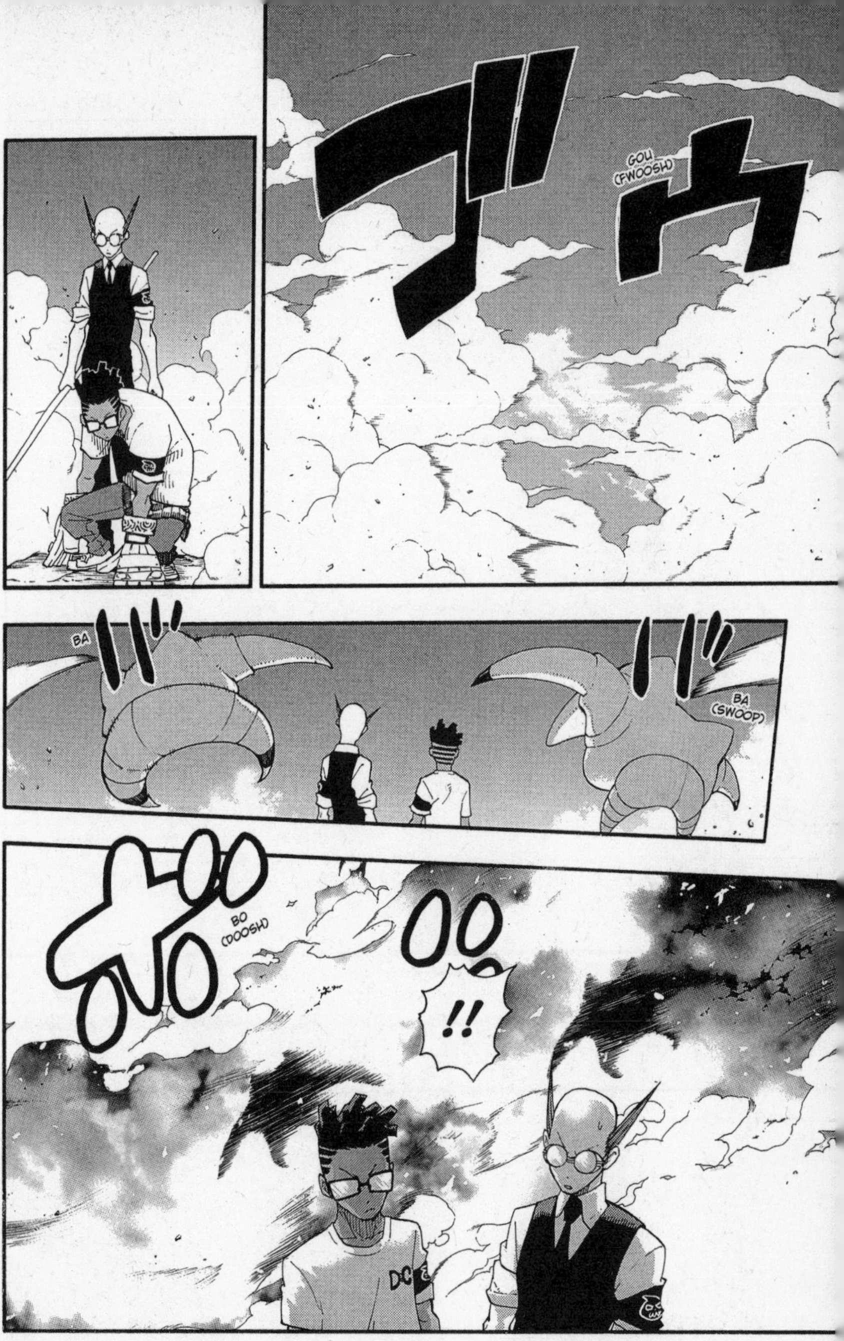
GOU (FWOOSH)
BA (SWOOP)
BA
BO (DOOSH)
!!

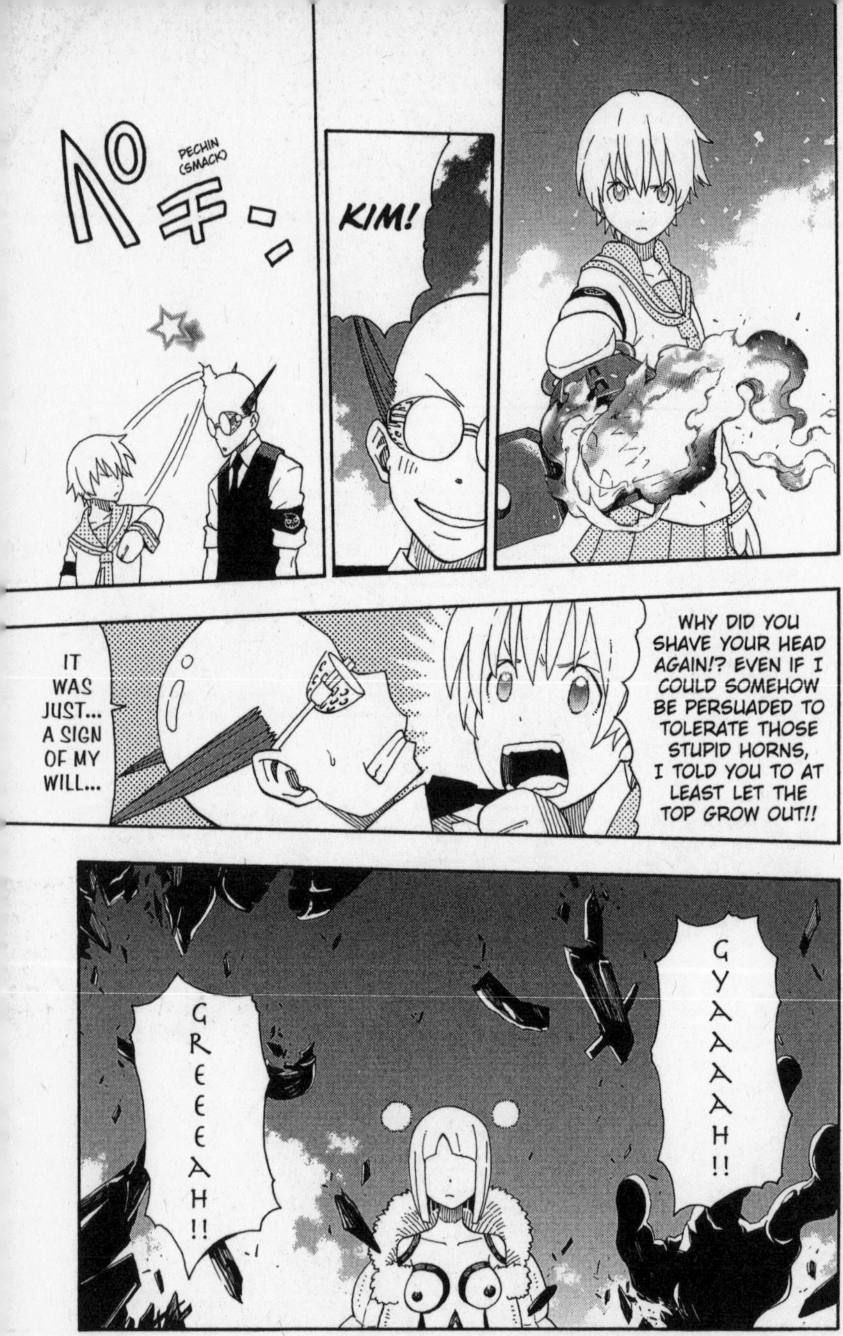
KIM!
PECHIN (SMACK)
WHY DID YOU SHAVE YOUR HEAD AGAIN!? EVEN IF I COULD SOMEHOW BE PERSUADED TO TOLERATE THOSE STUPID HORNS, I TOLD YOU TO AT LEAST LET THE TOP GROW OUT!!
IT WAS JUST... A SIGN OF MY WILL...
GYAAAAH!!
GREEEAH!!

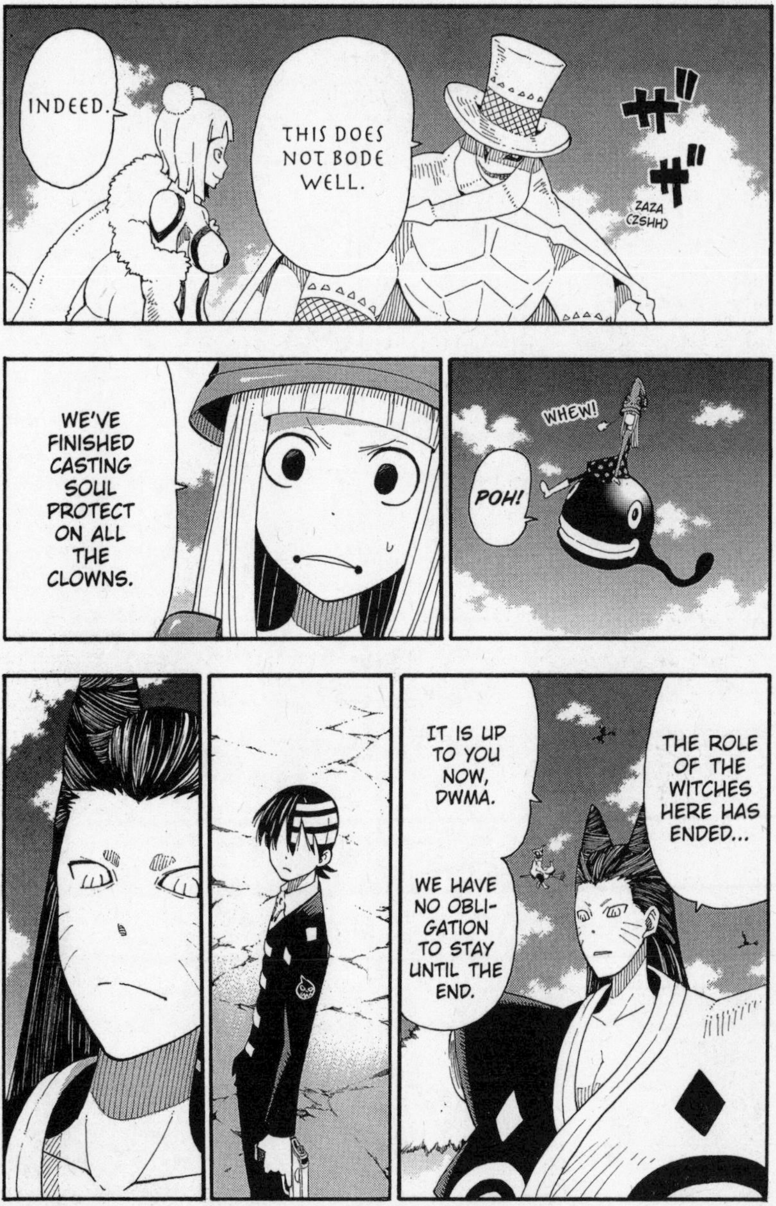
ZAZA (ZSHH)
THIS DOES NOT BODE WELL.
INDEED.
WHEW!
POH!
WE'VE FINISHED CASTING SOUL PROTECT ON ALL THE CLOWNS.
THE ROLE OF THE WITCHES HERE HAS ENDED...
IT IS UP TO YOU NOW, DWMA.
WE HAVE NO OBLI-GATION TO STAY UNTIL THE END.

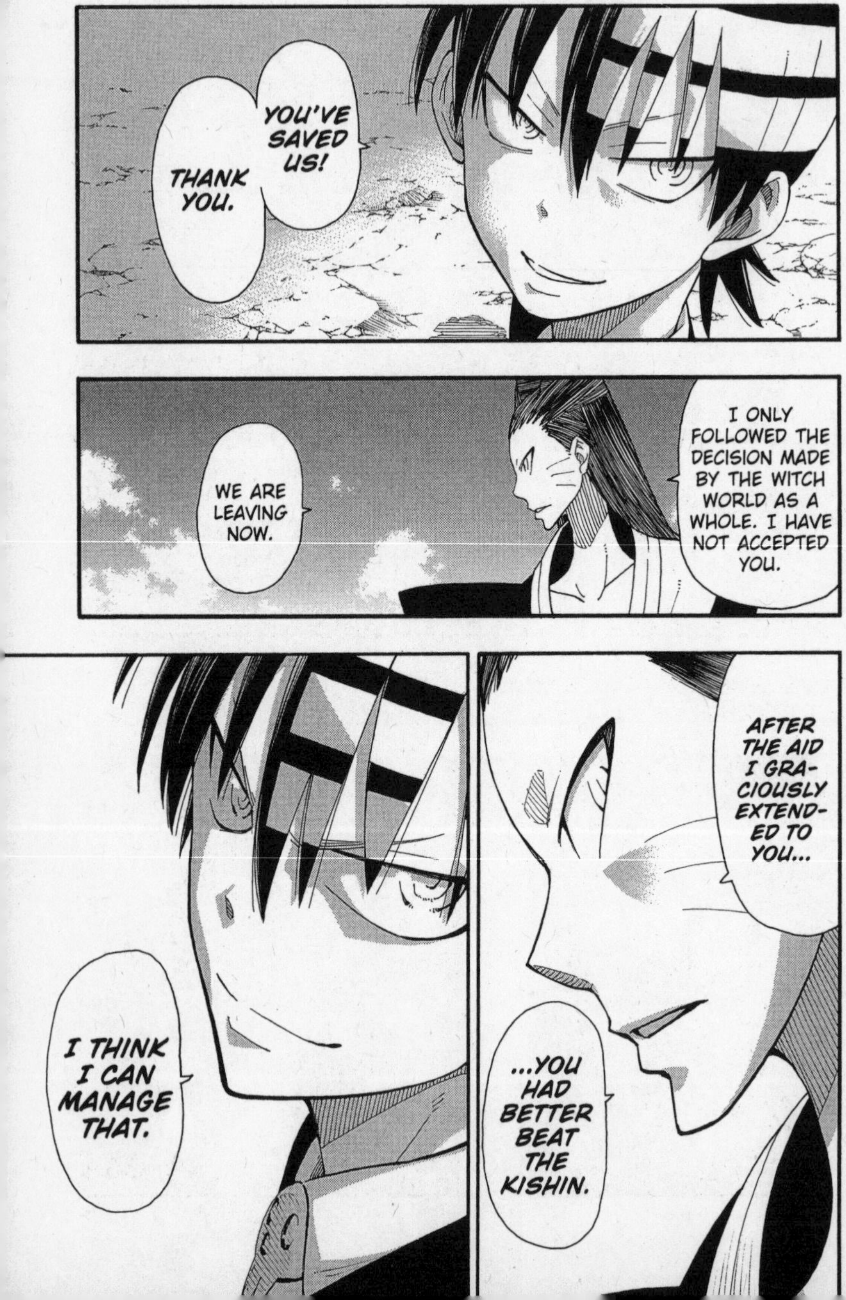
YOU'VE SAVED US!
THANK YOU.
I ONLY FOLLOWED THE DECISION MADE BY THE WITCH WORLD AS A WHOLE. I HAVE NOT ACCEPTED YOU.
WE ARE LEAVING NOW.
AFTER THE AID I GRA-CIOUSLY EXTEND-ED TO YOU...
...YOU HAD BETTER BEAT THE KISHIN.
I THINK I CAN MANAGE THAT.

GA

GA

GA
(SLASH)

HEH!

NOFUTURE

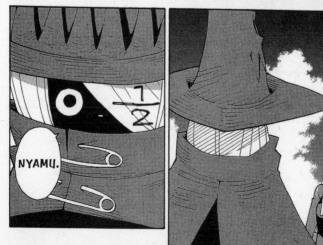

NYAMU.

MABA-
SAMA...
WE CAN'T
RETURN TO
THE WITCHES'
REALM YET,
SO WE'LL
STAY HERE.

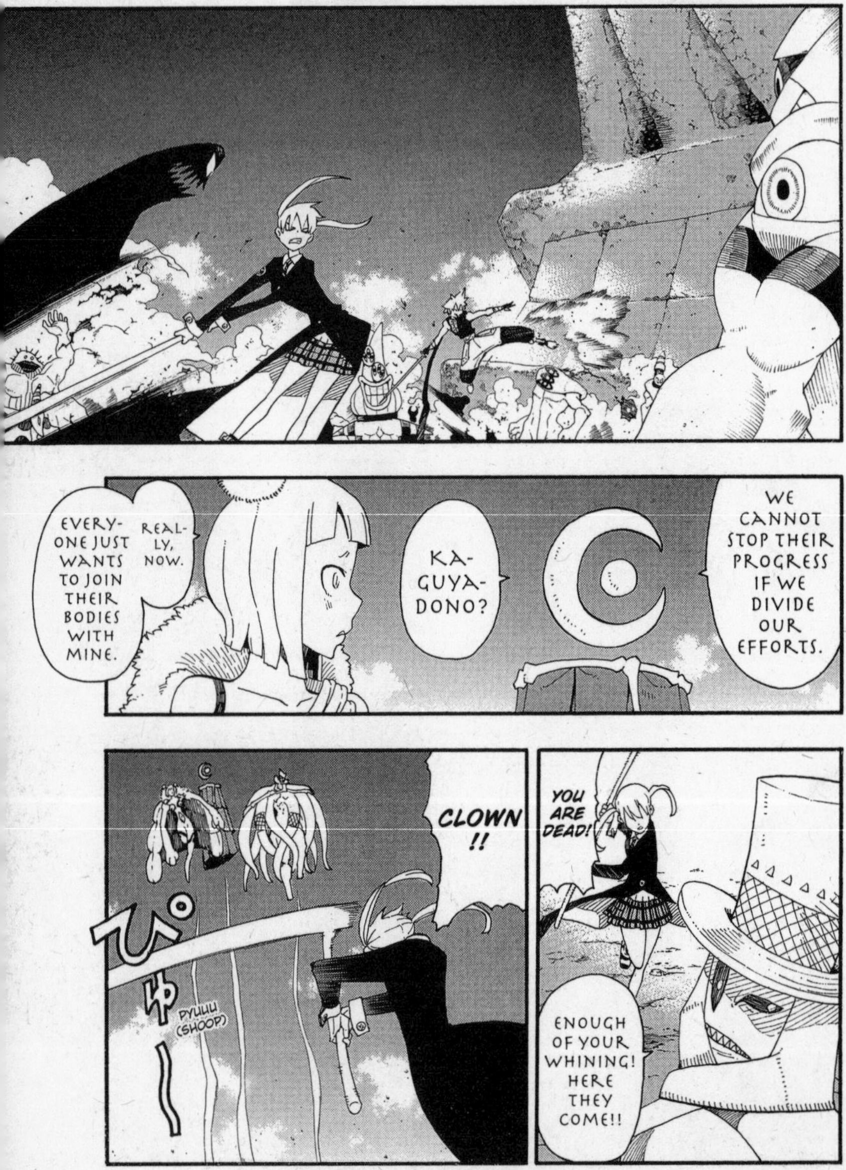
WE CANNOT STOP THEIR PROGRESS IF WE DIVIDE OUR EFFORTS.
KA-GUYA-DONO?
REAL-LY, NOW.
EVERY-ONE JUST WANTS TO JOIN THEIR BODIES WITH MINE.
YOU ARE DEAD!
ENOUGH OF YOUR WHINING! HERE THEY COME!!
CLOWN!!
ぴゅー
PYUUU (SHOOP)

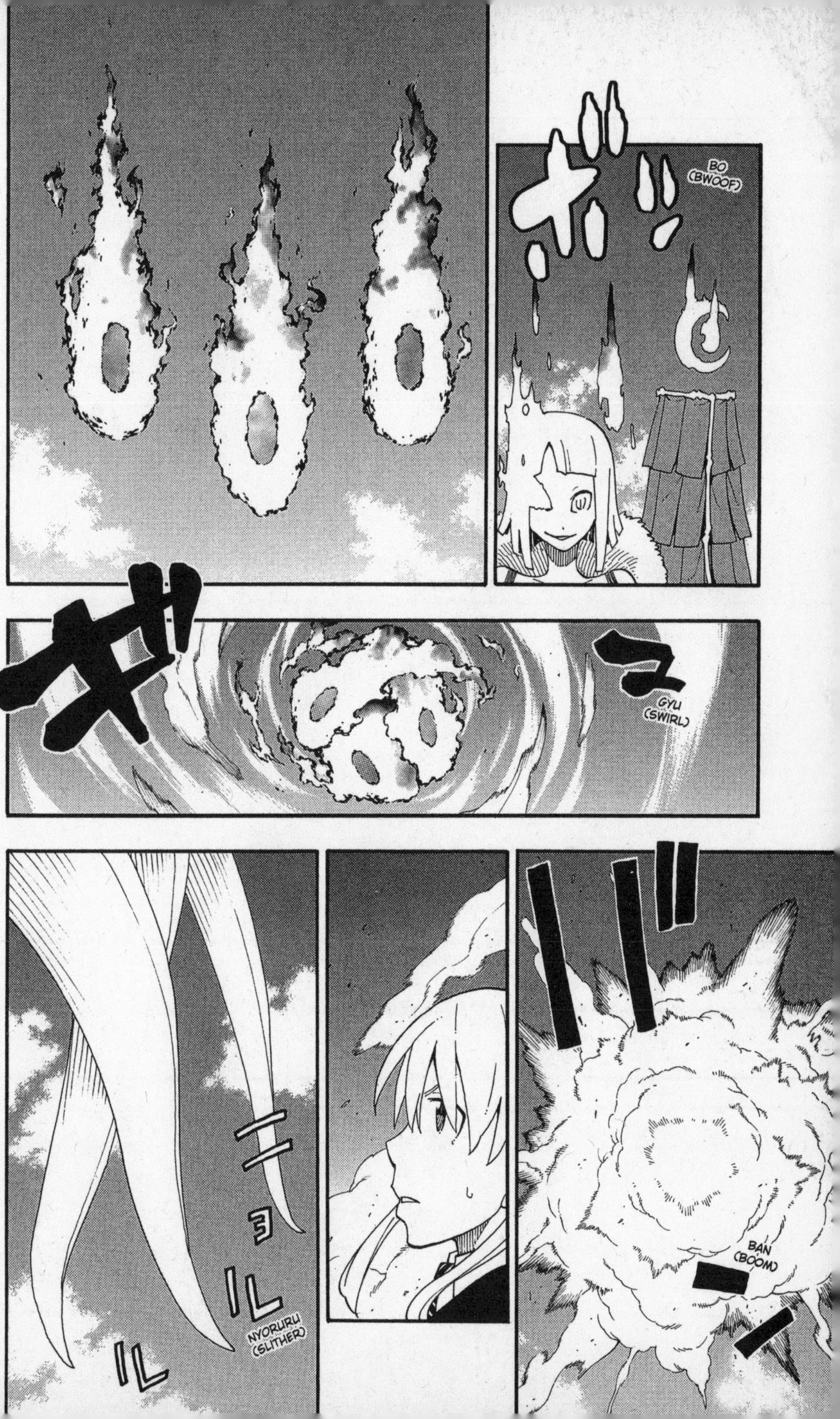
BO
(BWOOF)
GYU
(SWIRL)
BAN
(BOOM)
NYORURU
(SLITHER)

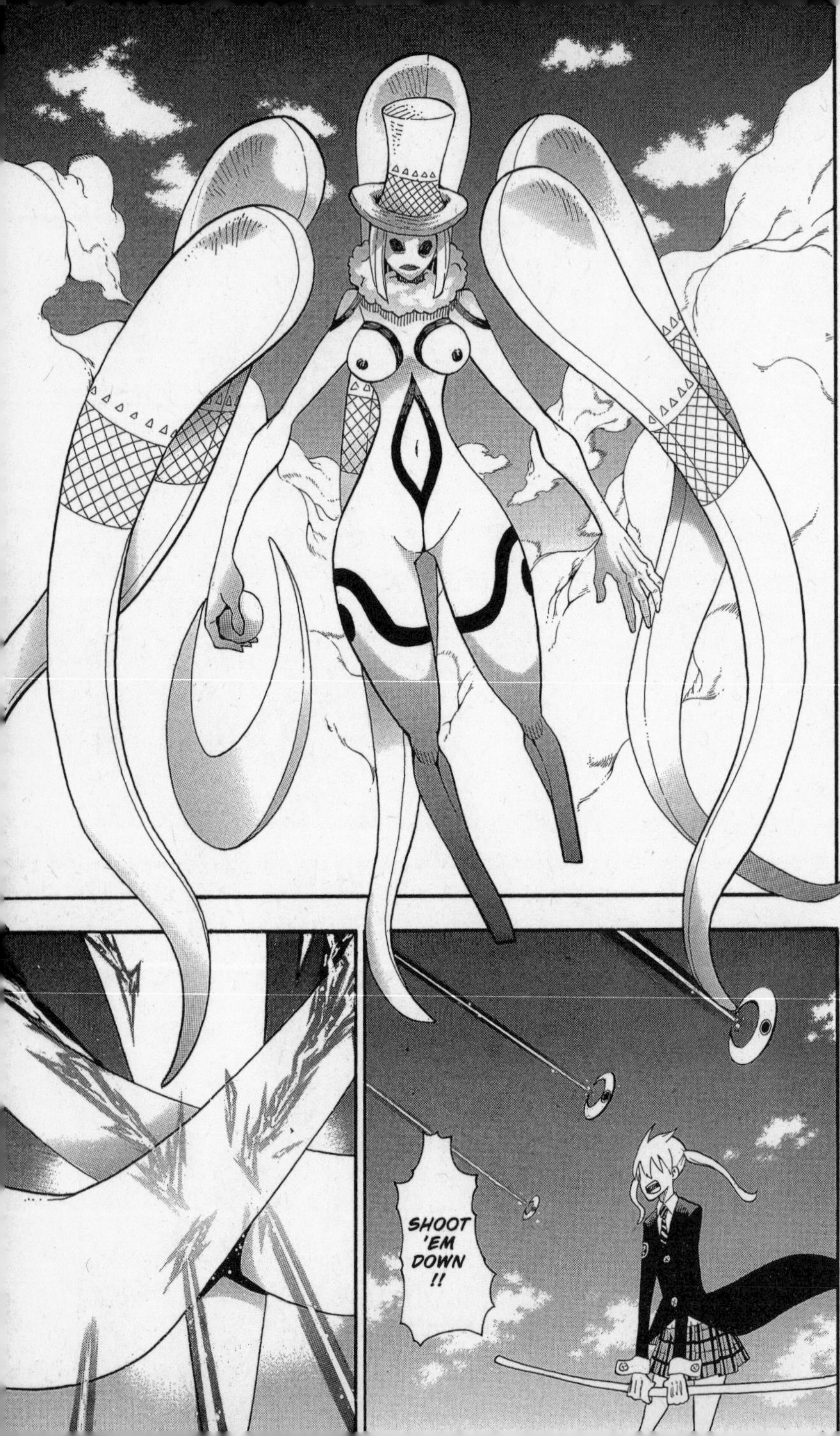
SHOOT 'EM DOWN !!

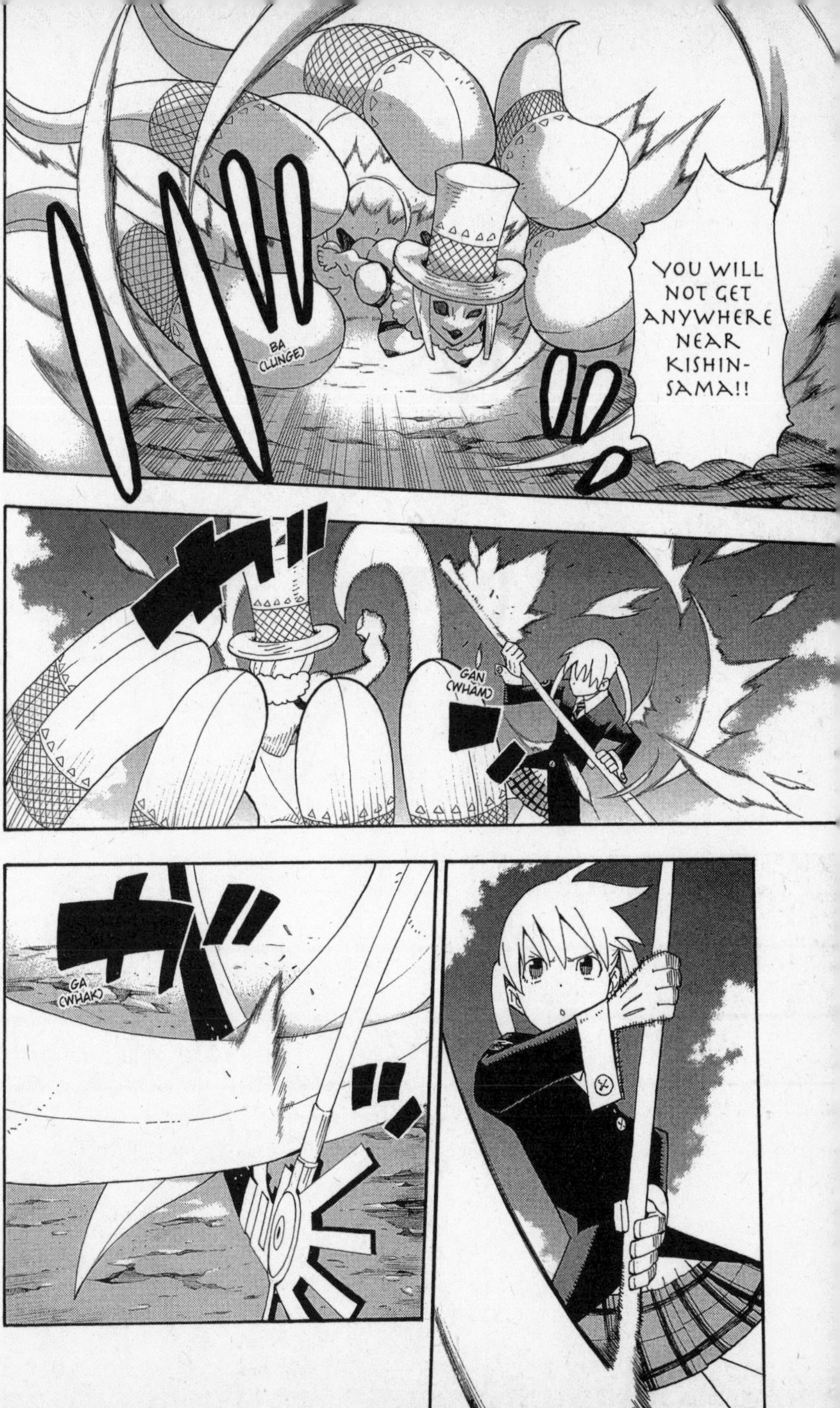
YOU WILL NOT GET ANYWHERE NEAR KISHIN-SAMA!!
BA (LUNGE)
GAN (WHAM)
GA (WHAK)

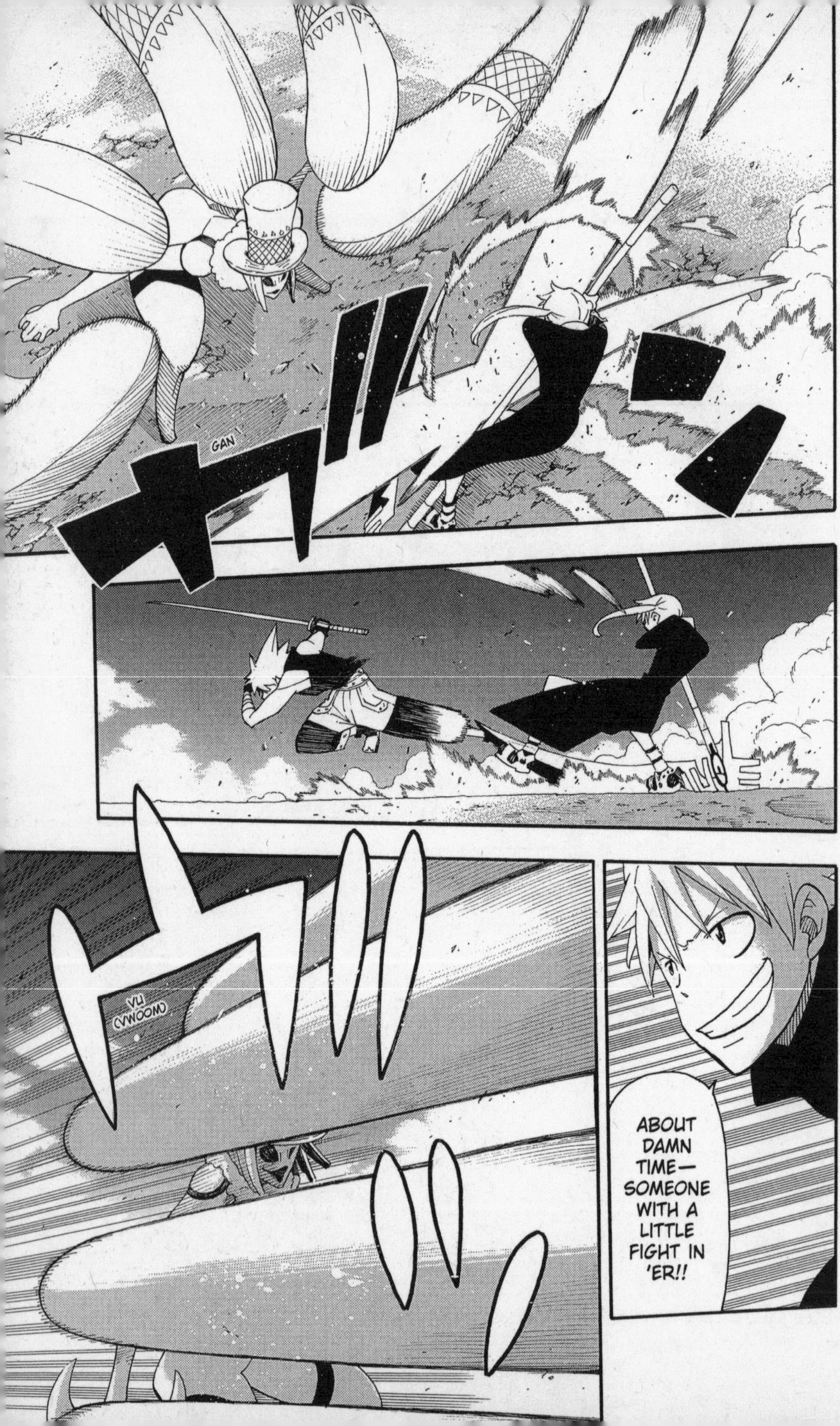
GAN
ABOUT DAMN TIME—SOMEONE WITH A LITTLE FIGHT IN 'ER!!
VU (VWOOM)

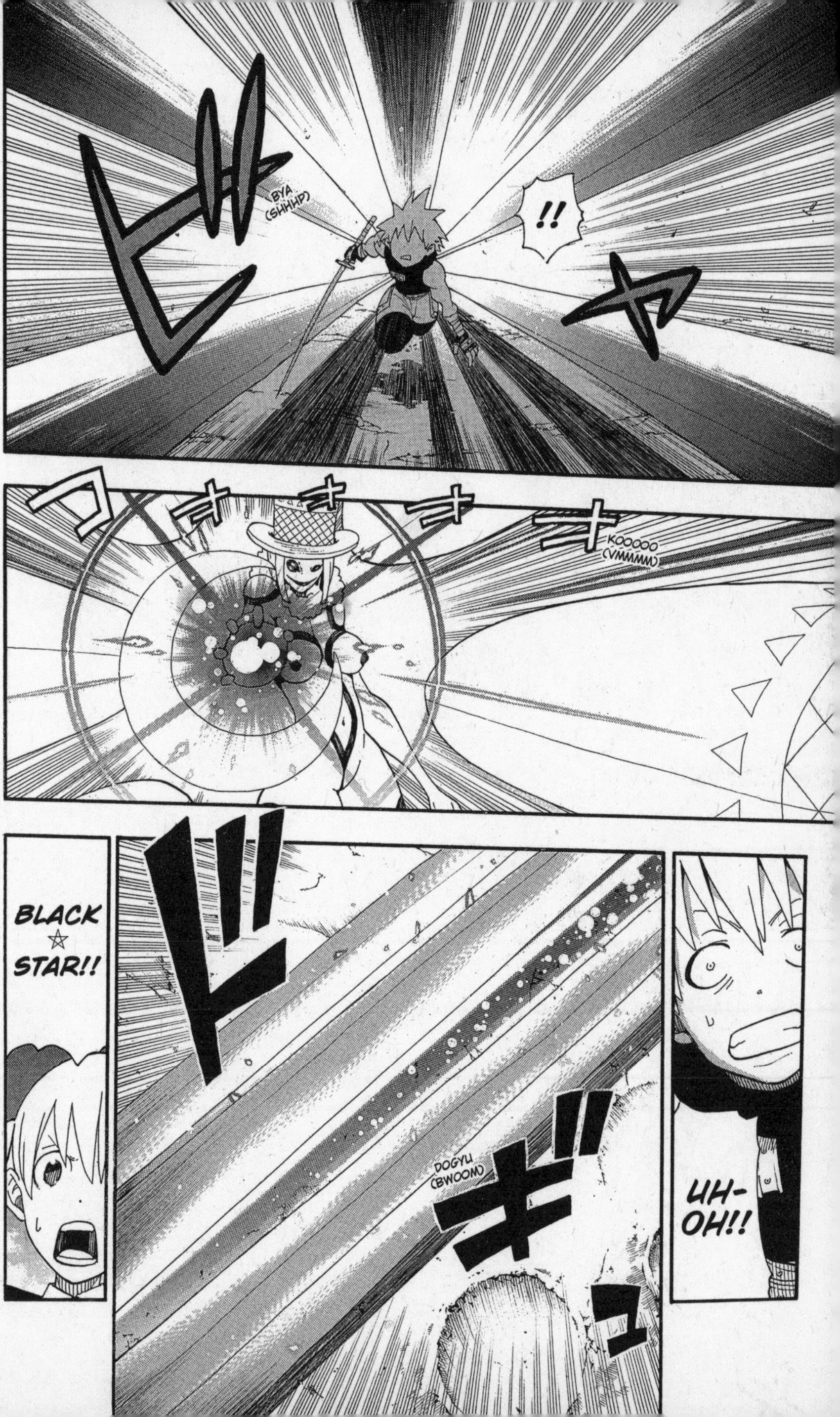

!!
BYA (SHHHP)
KOOOOO (VMMMMM)
UH-OH!!
DOGYU (BWOOM)
BLACK ☆ STAR!!

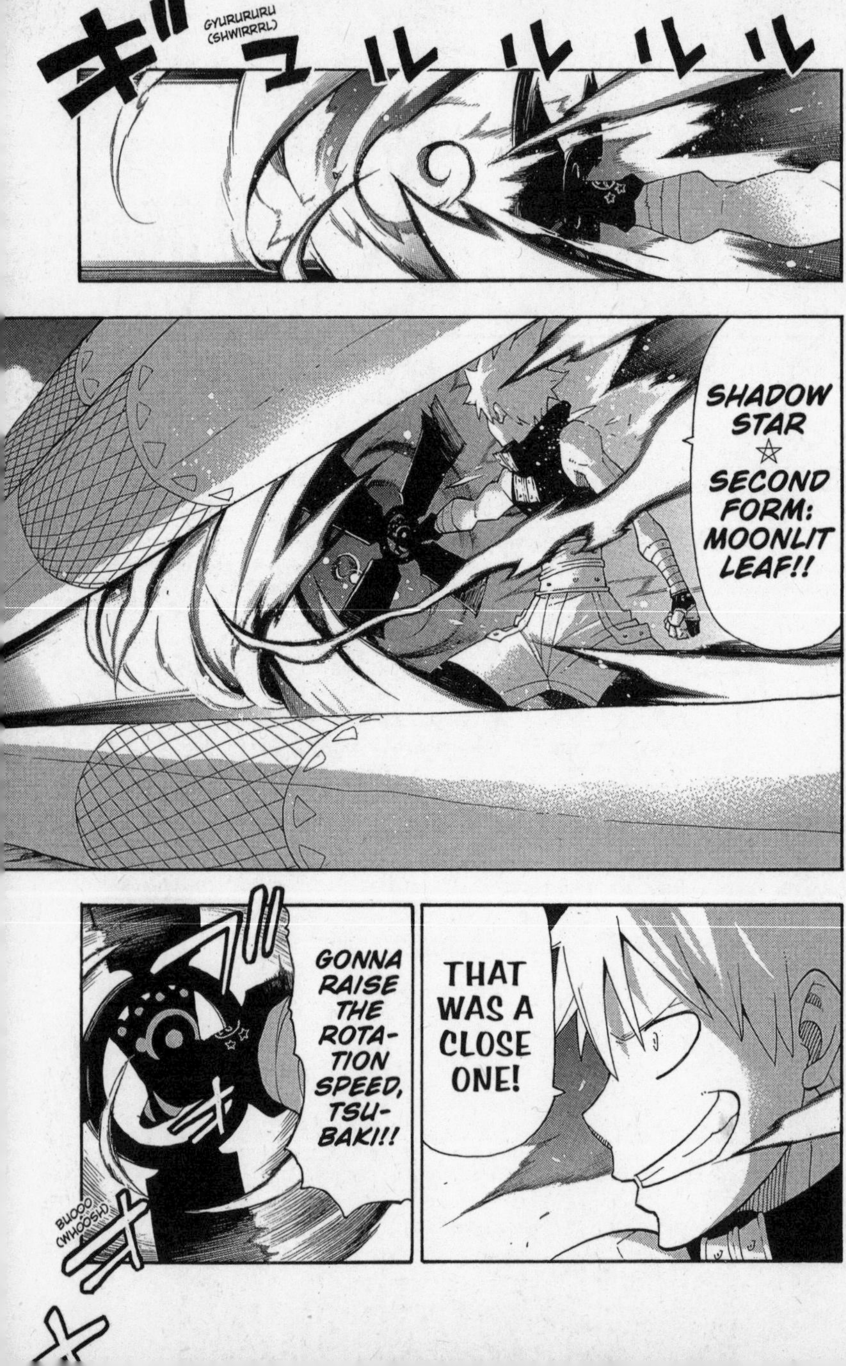
GYURURURU (SHWIRRRL)
SHADOW STAR ☆ SECOND FORM: MOONLIT LEAF!!
THAT WAS A CLOSE ONE!
GONNA RAISE THE ROTATION SPEED, TSUBAKI!!
BUOOO (WHOOSH)

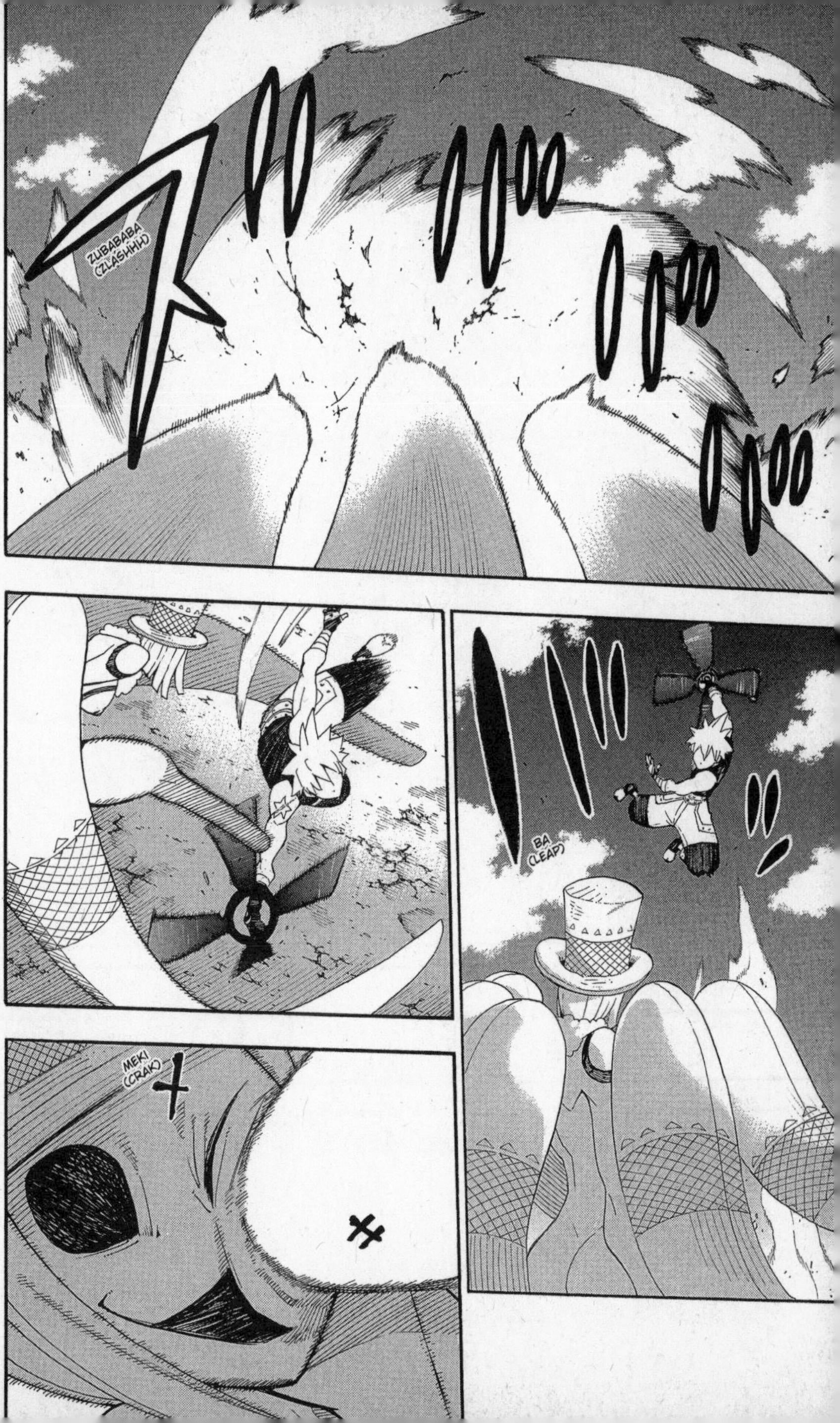
ZUBABABA (ZLASHHH)
BA (LEAP)
MEKI (CRAK)

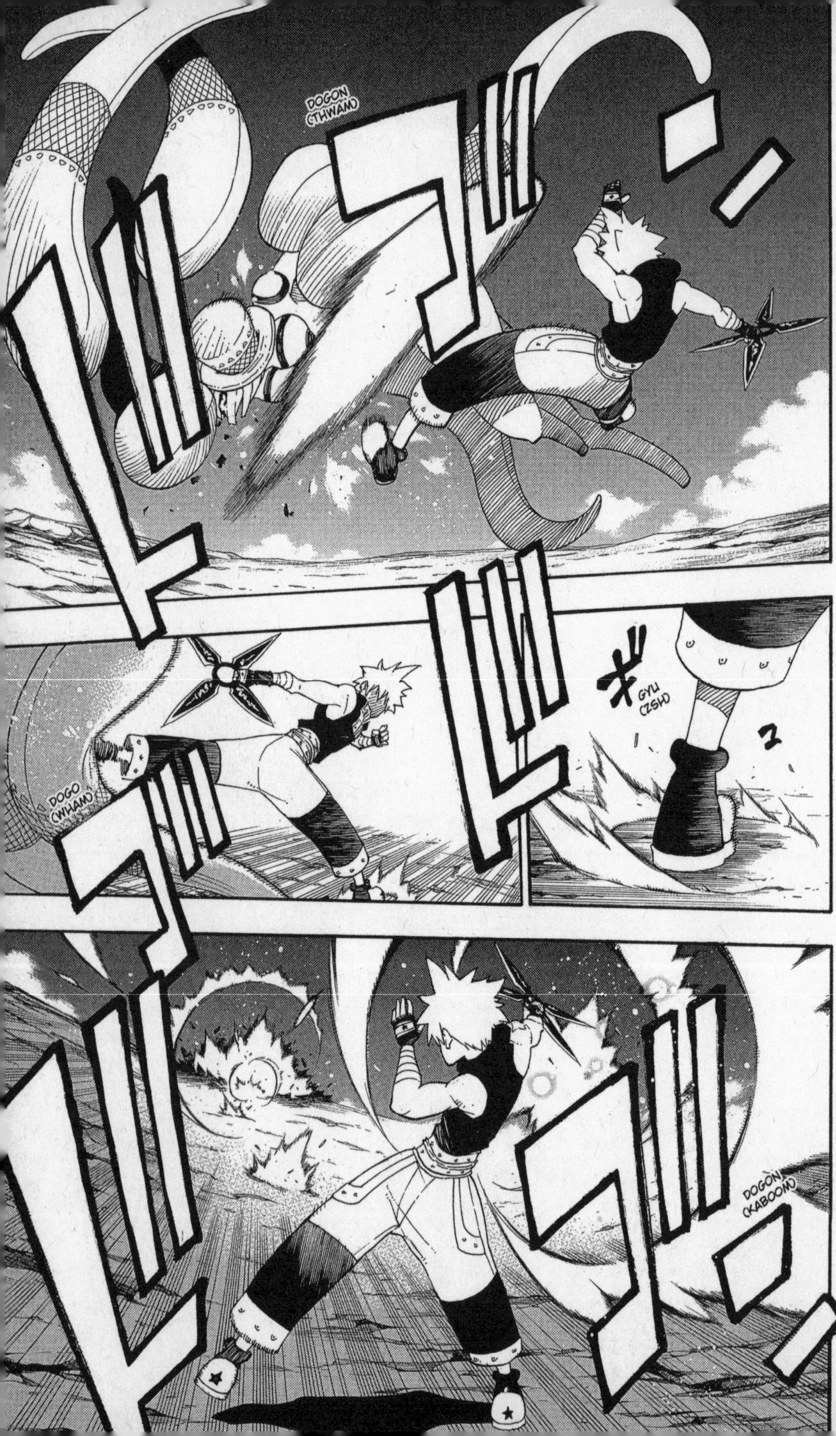
DOGON (THWAM)
GYU (ZSH)
DOGO (WHAM)
DOGON (KABOOM)

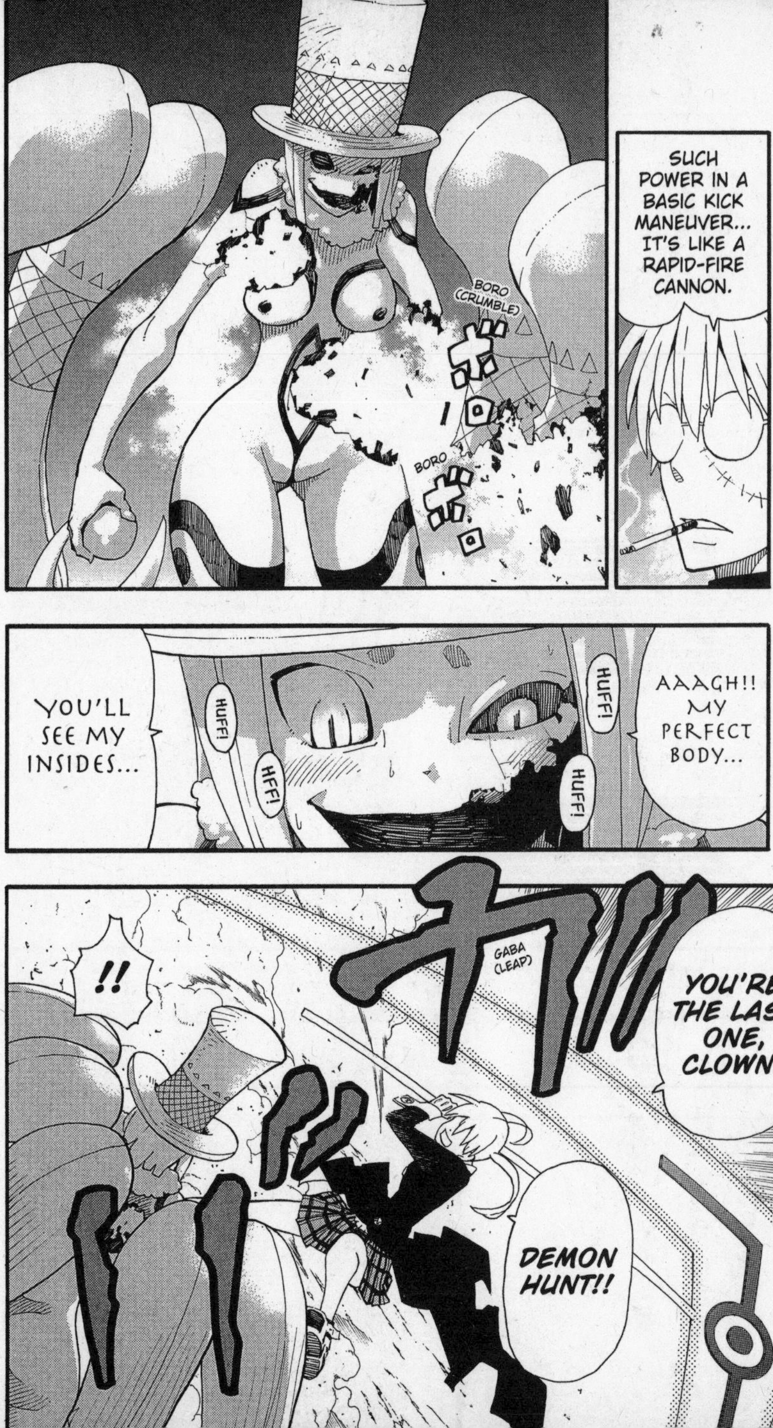
SUCH POWER IN A BASIC KICK MANEUVER... IT'S LIKE A RAPID-FIRE CANNON.
BORO (CRUMBLE)
BORO
AAAGH!! MY PERFECT BODY...
HUFF!
HUFF!
HFF!
HUFF!
YOU'LL SEE MY INSIDES...
YOU'RE THE LAST ONE, CLOWN!
GABA (LEAP)
!!
DEMON HUNT!!

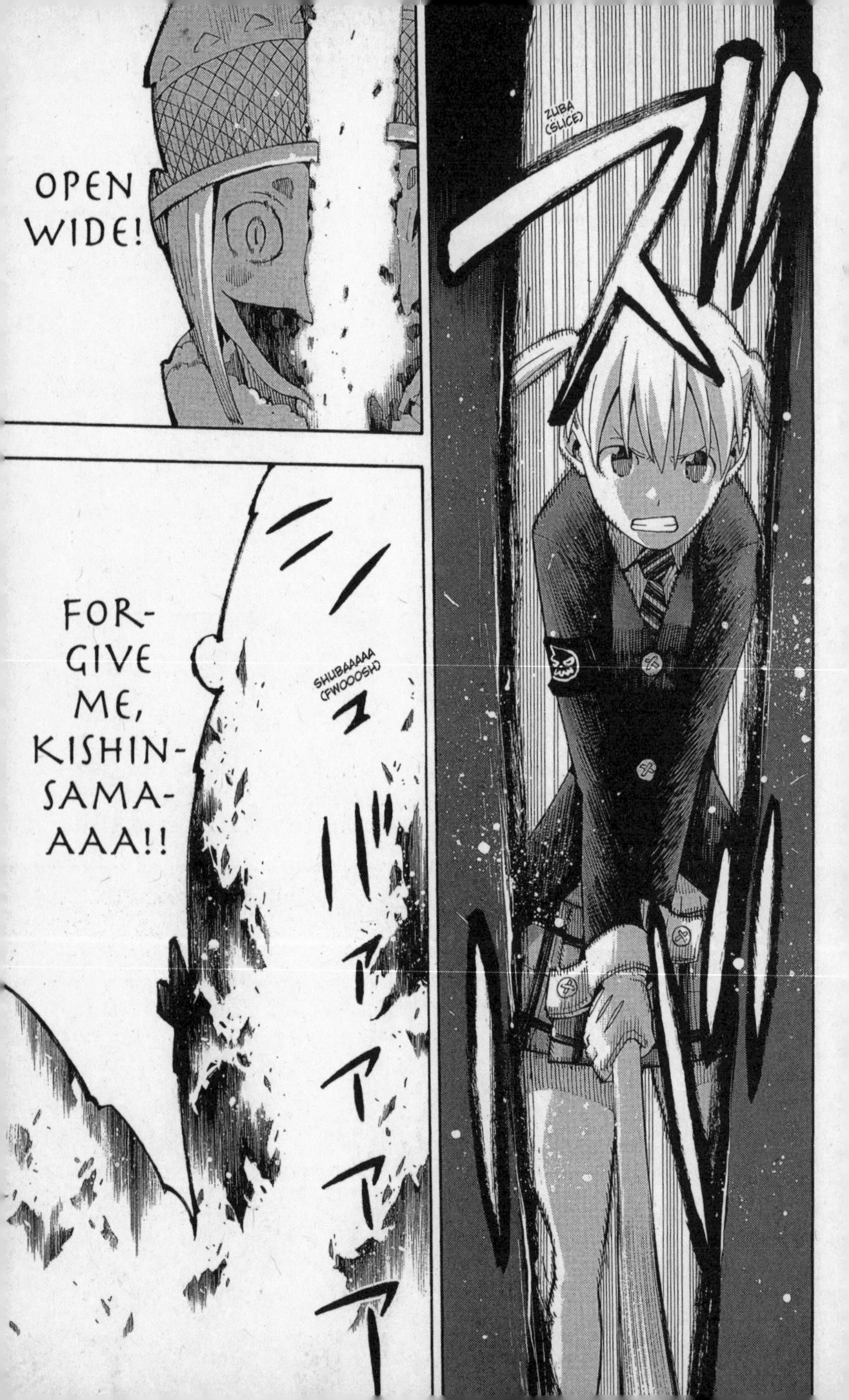
ZUBA (SLICE)
OPEN WIDE!
FOR-GIVE ME, KISHIN-SAMA-AAA!!
SHUBAAAAA (FWOOOSH)

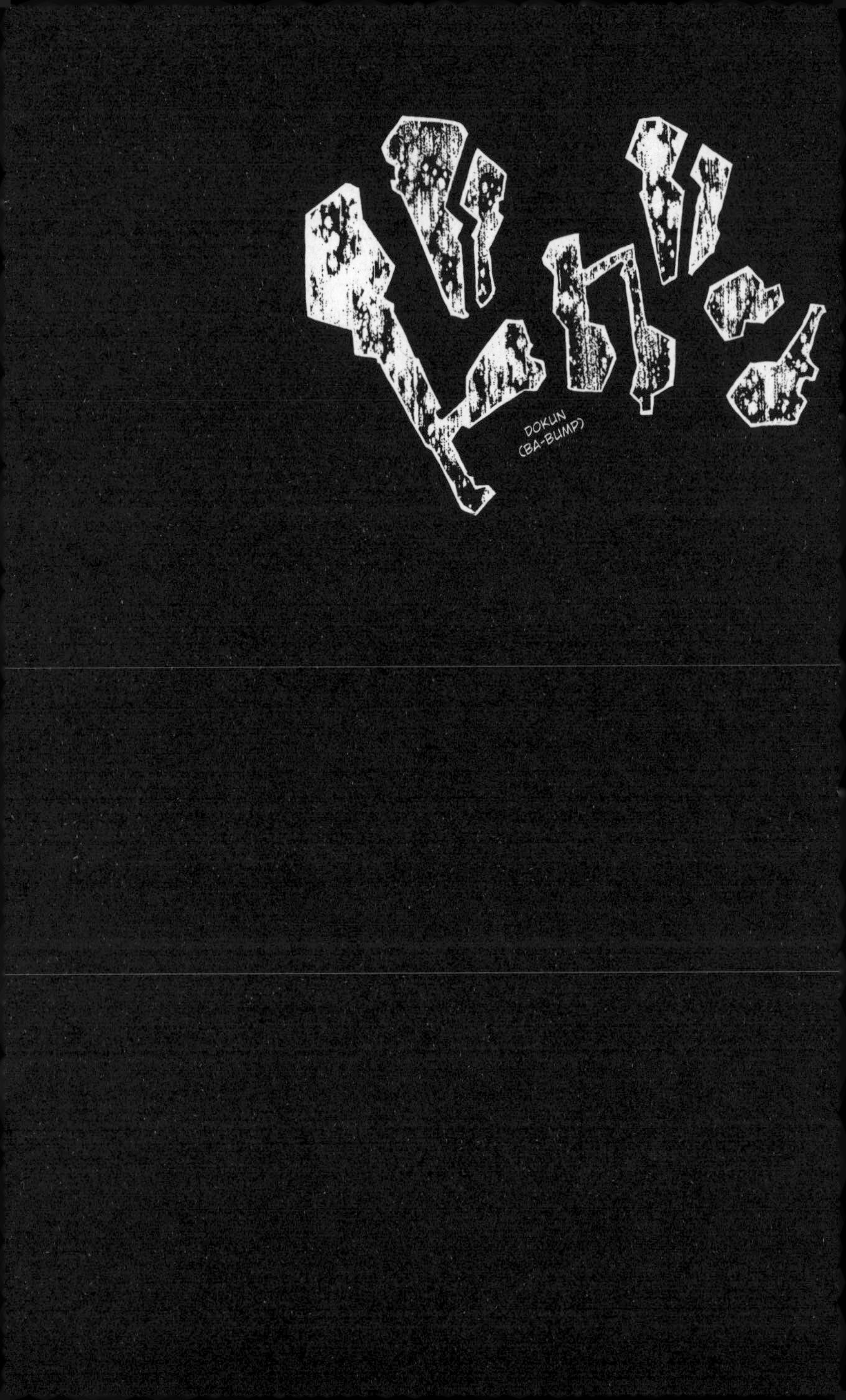
DOKUN
(BA-BUMP)

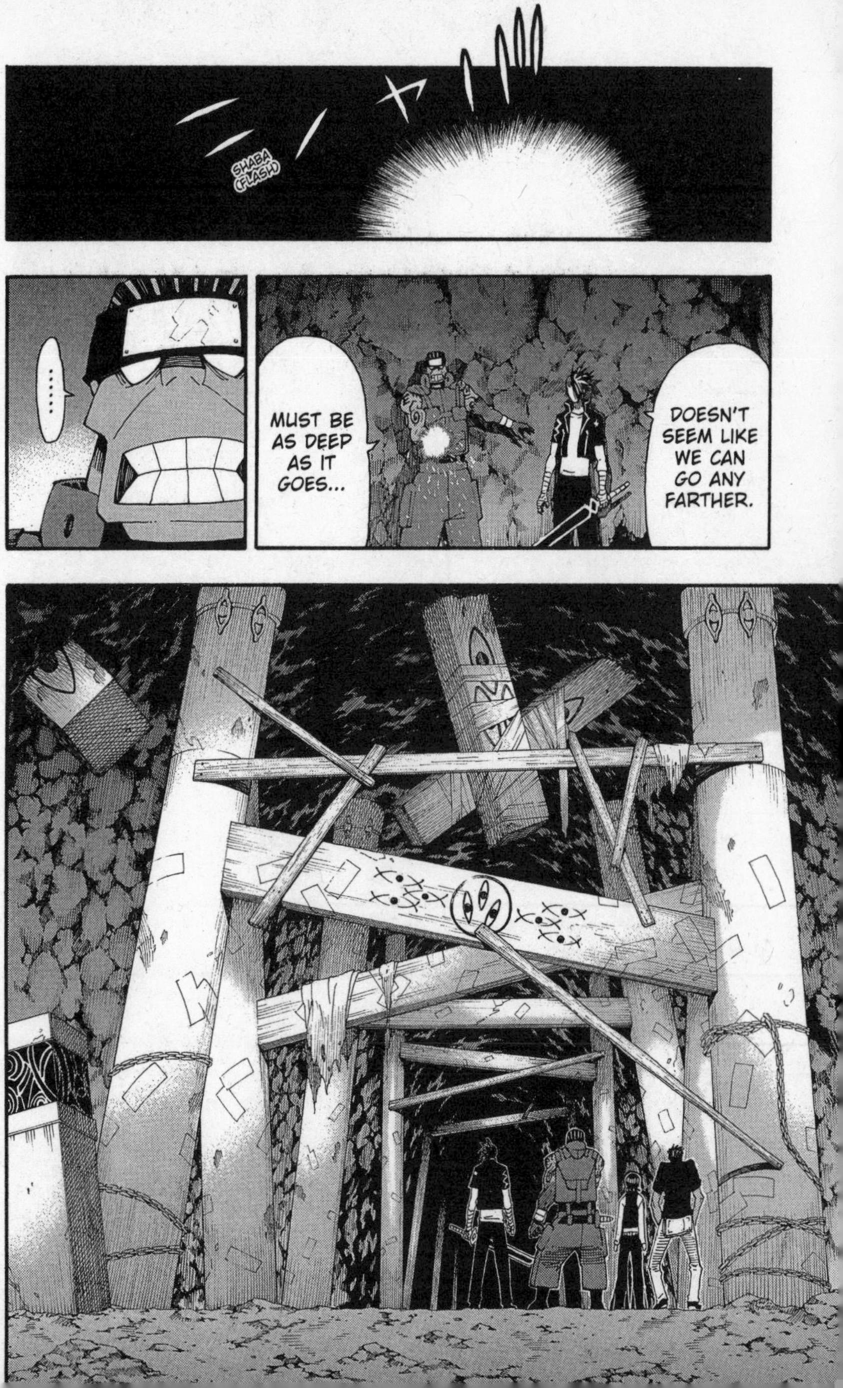
SHABA (FLASH)
DOESN'T SEEM LIKE WE CAN GO ANY FARTHER.
MUST BE AS DEEP AS IT GOES...
......

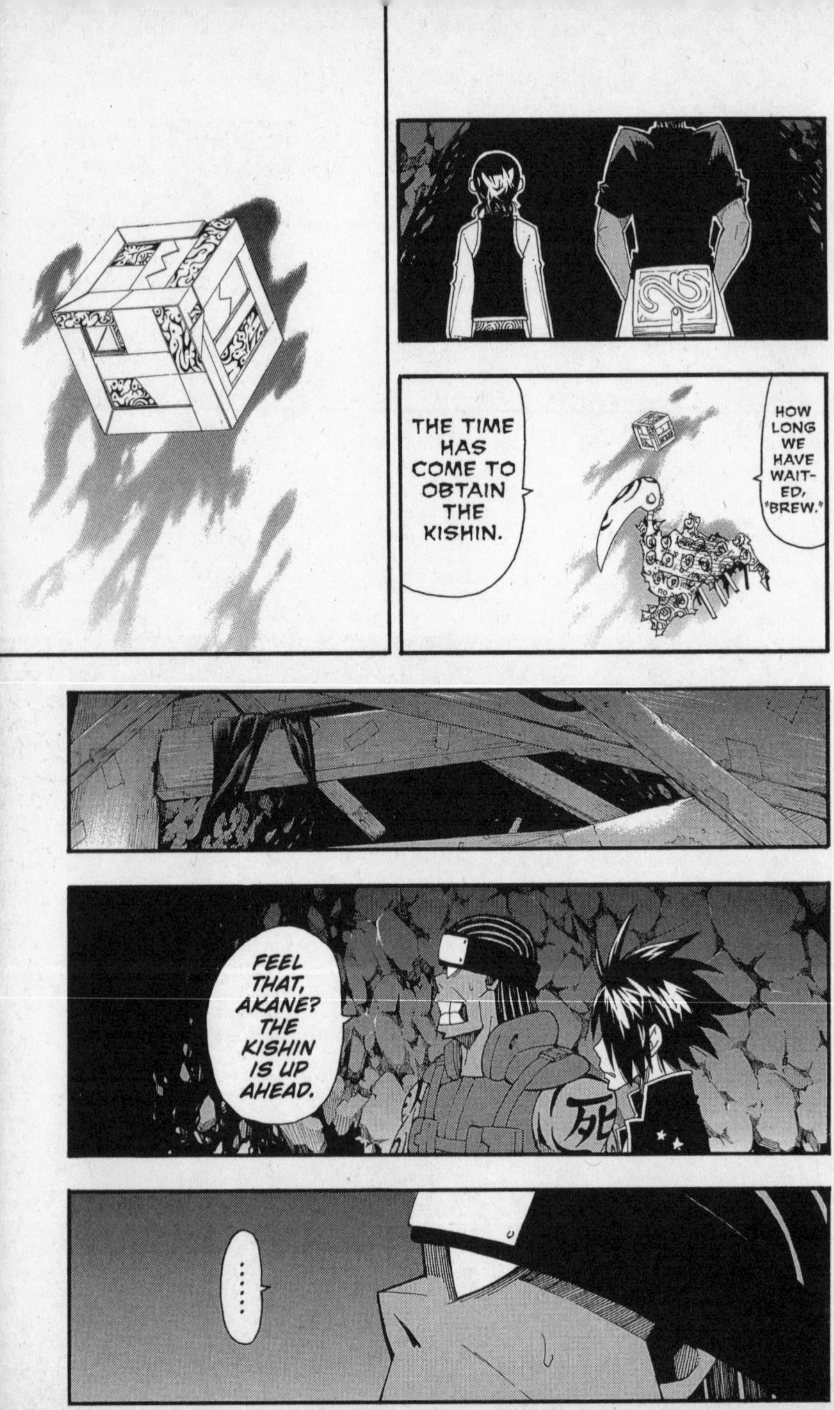
HOW LONG WE HAVE WAIT-ED, "BREW."
THE TIME HAS COME TO OBTAIN THE KISHIN.
FEEL THAT, AKANE? THE KISHIN IS UP AHEAD.
......

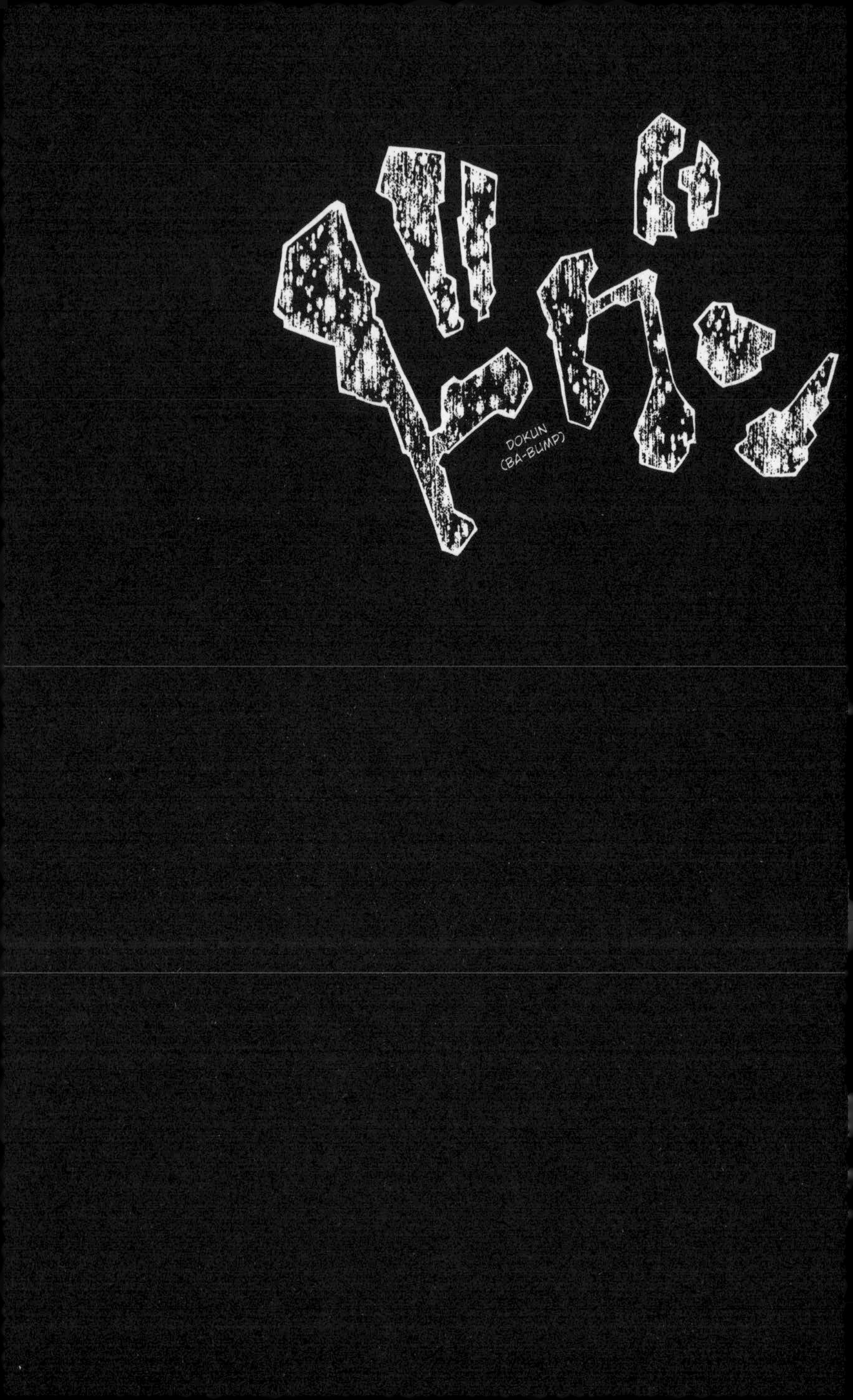
DOKUN
(BA-BUMP)

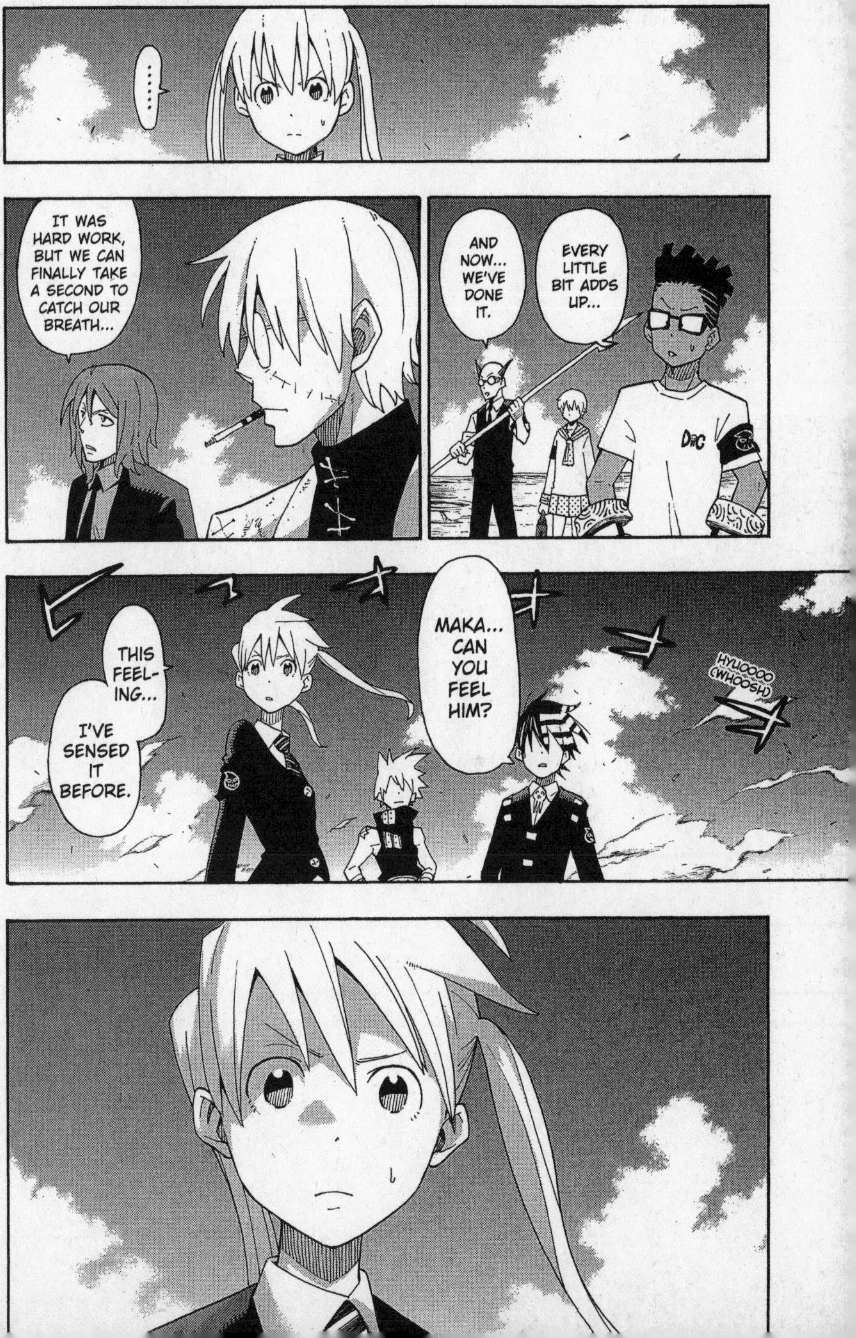
……
EVERY LITTLE BIT ADDS UP...
AND NOW... WE'VE DONE IT.
IT WAS HARD WORK, BUT WE CAN FINALLY TAKE A SECOND TO CATCH OUR BREATH...
HYUOOOO (WHOOSH)
MAKA... CAN YOU FEEL HIM?
THIS FEEL-ING...
I'VE SENSED IT BEFORE.

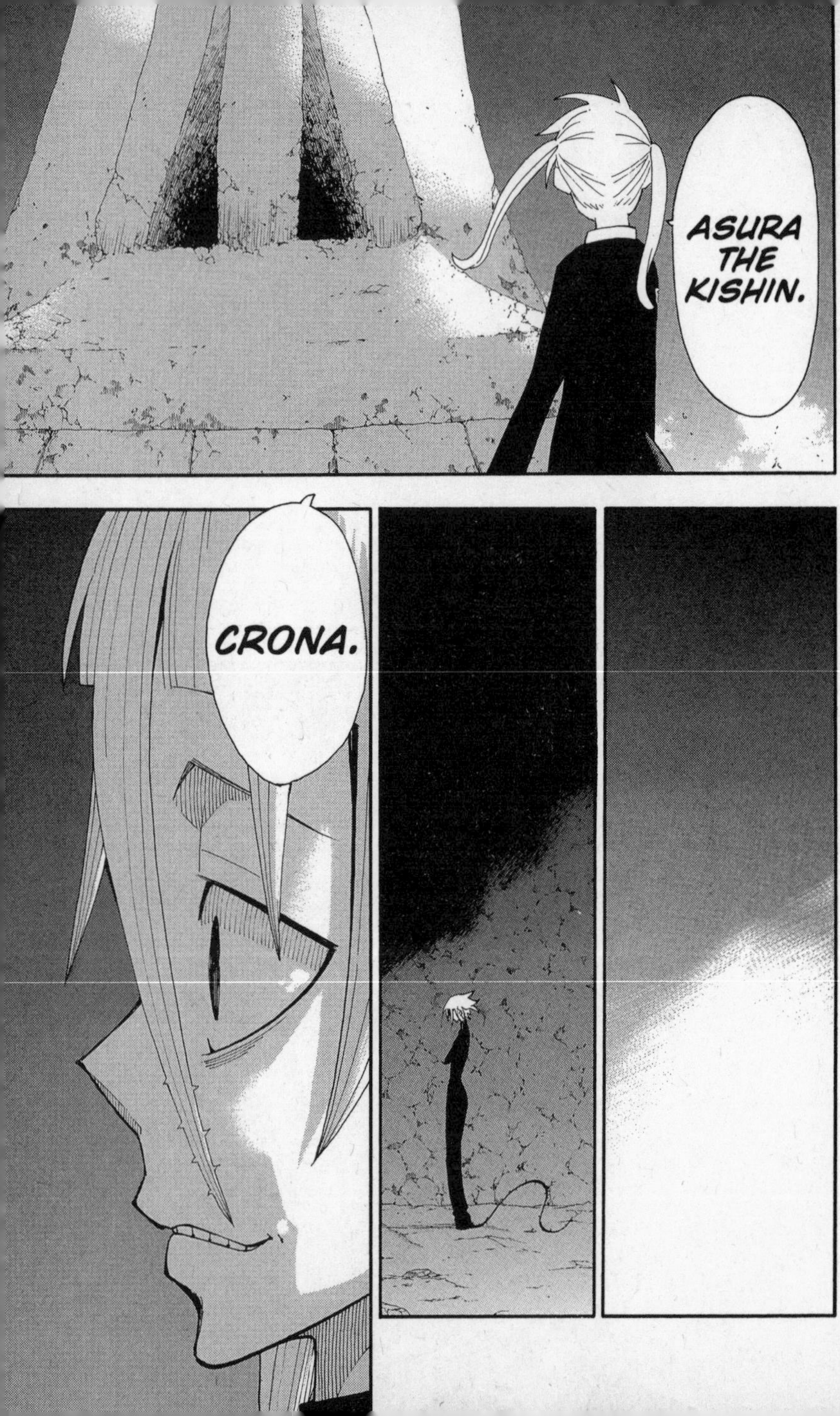
ASURA THE KISHIN.
CRONA.

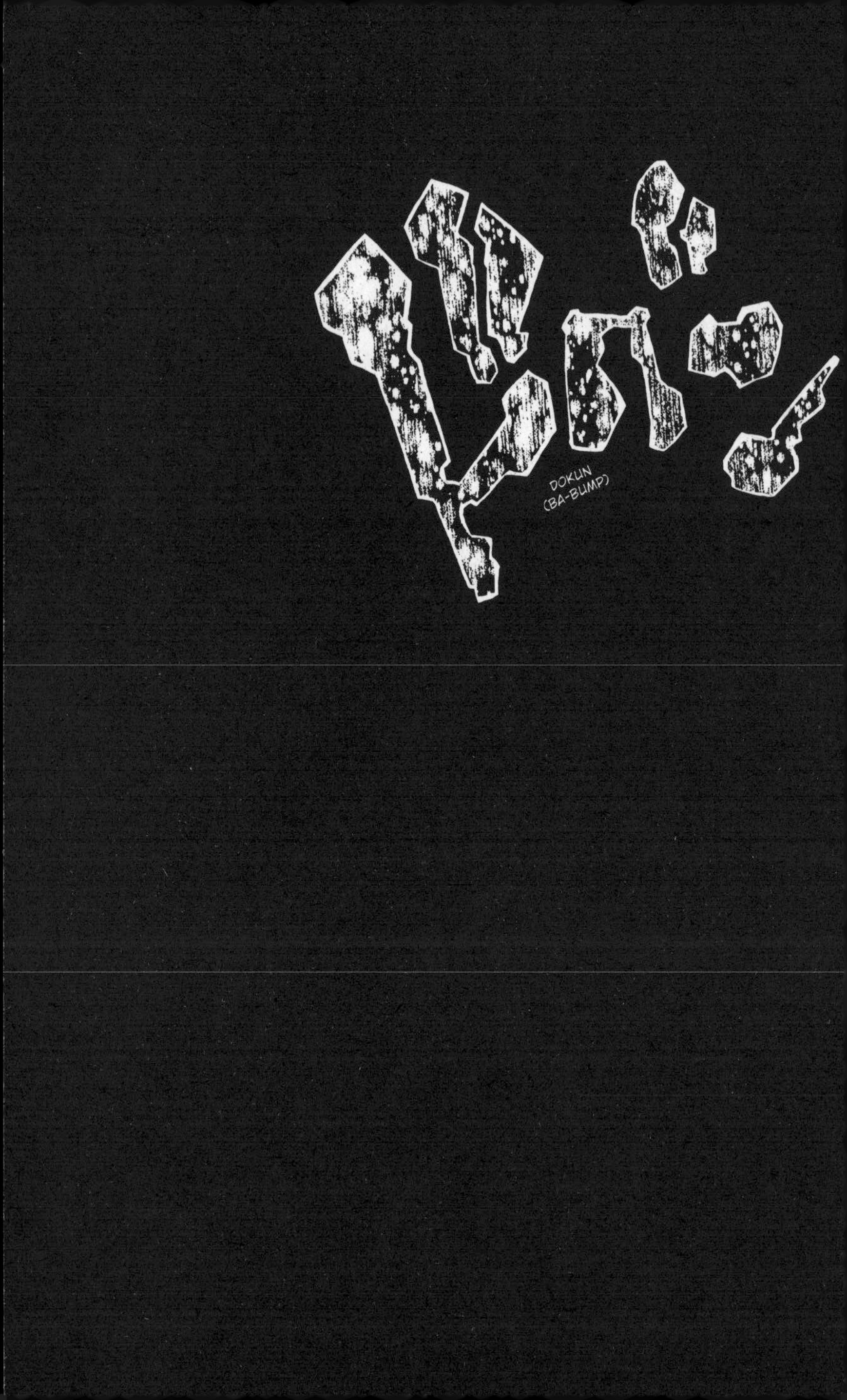
ドクン
DOKUN
(BA-BUMP)

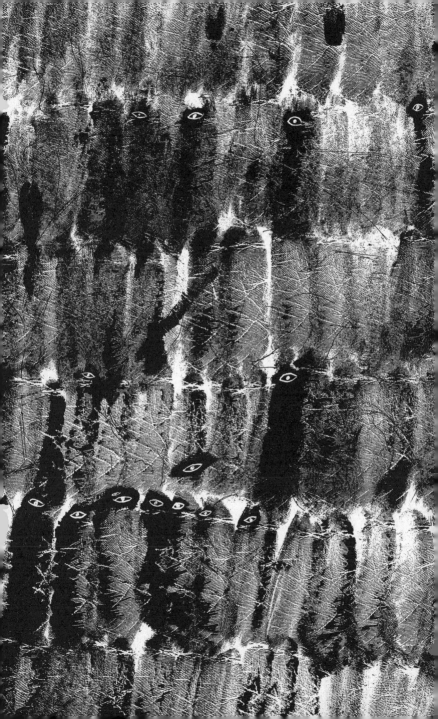

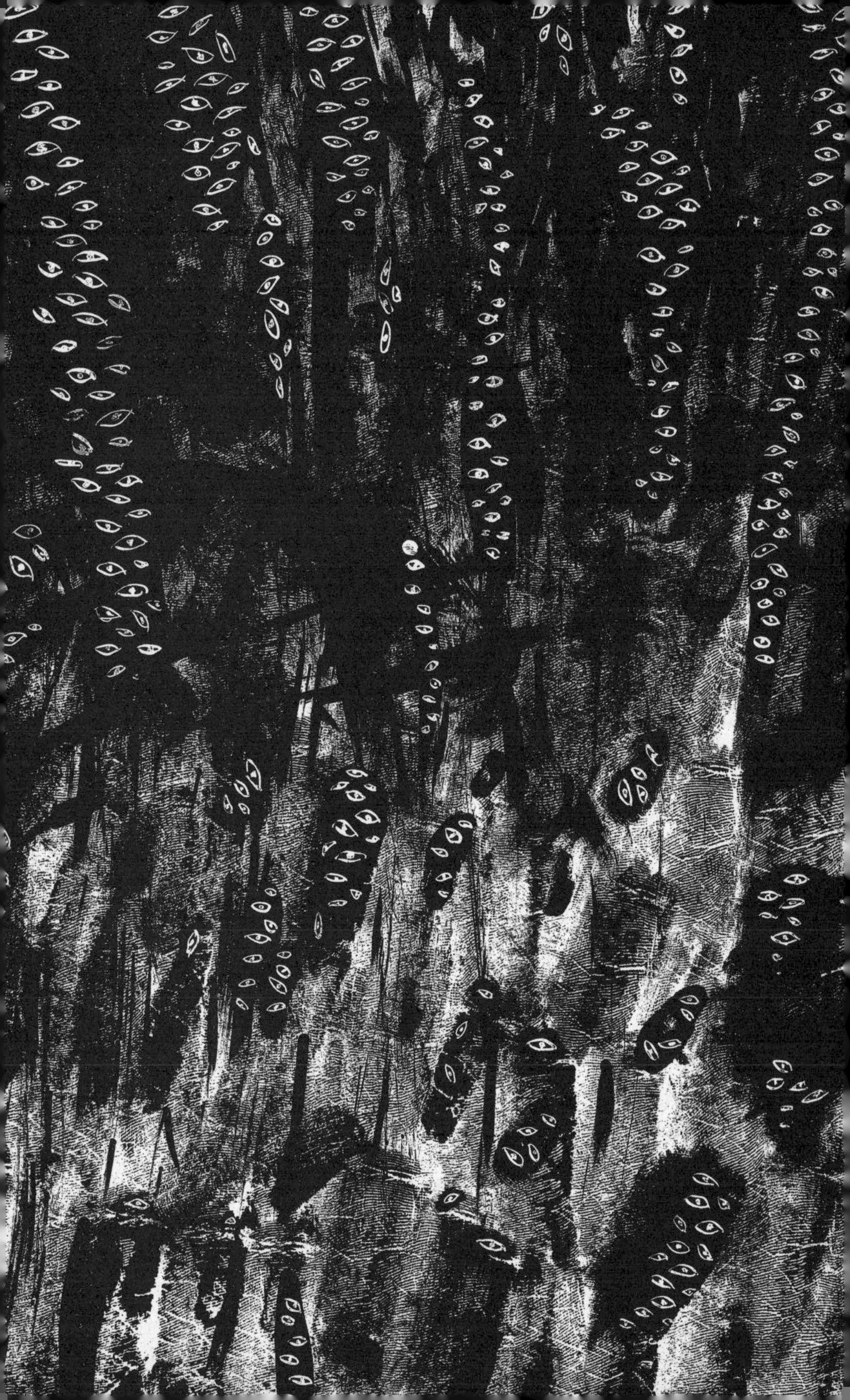

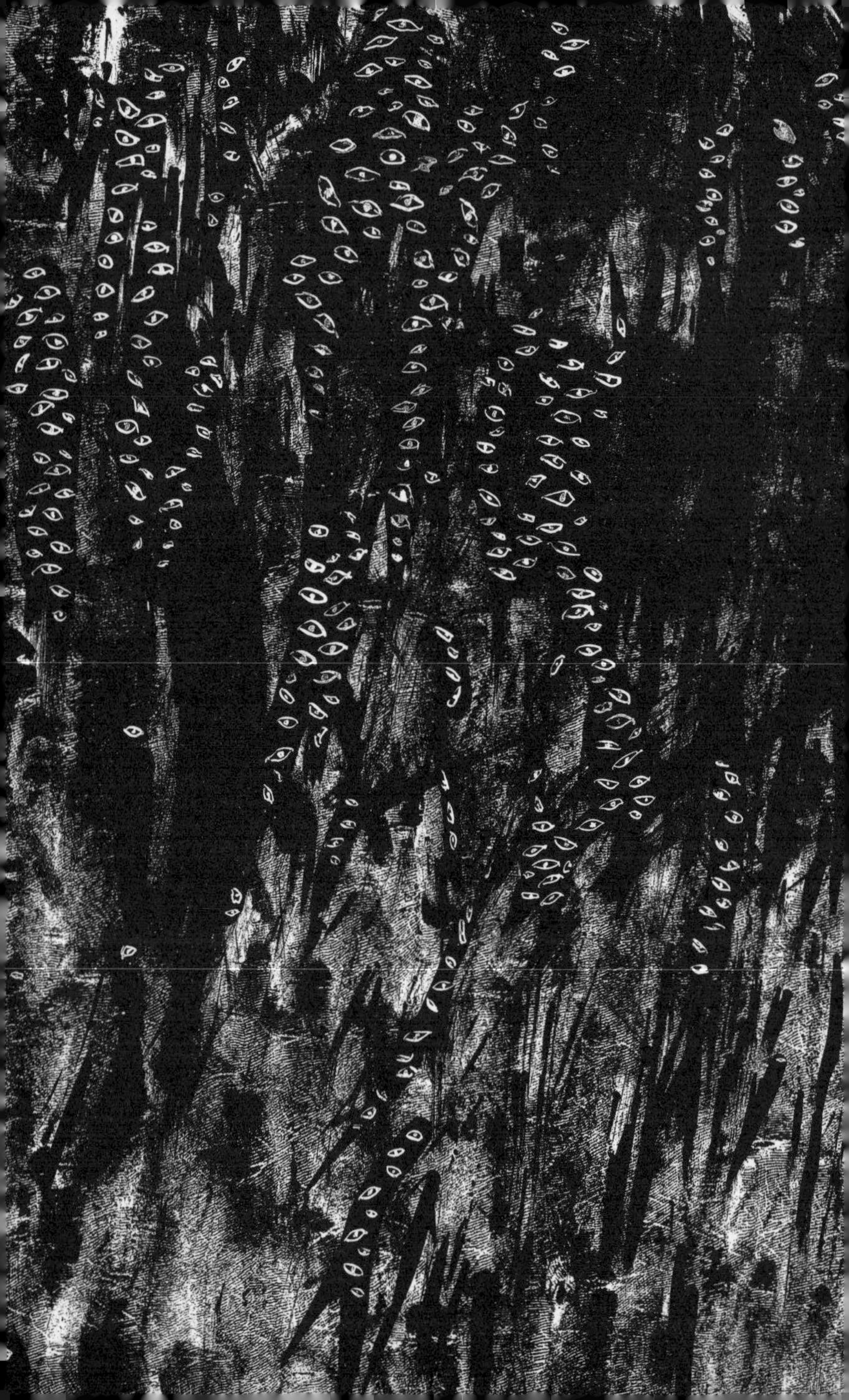

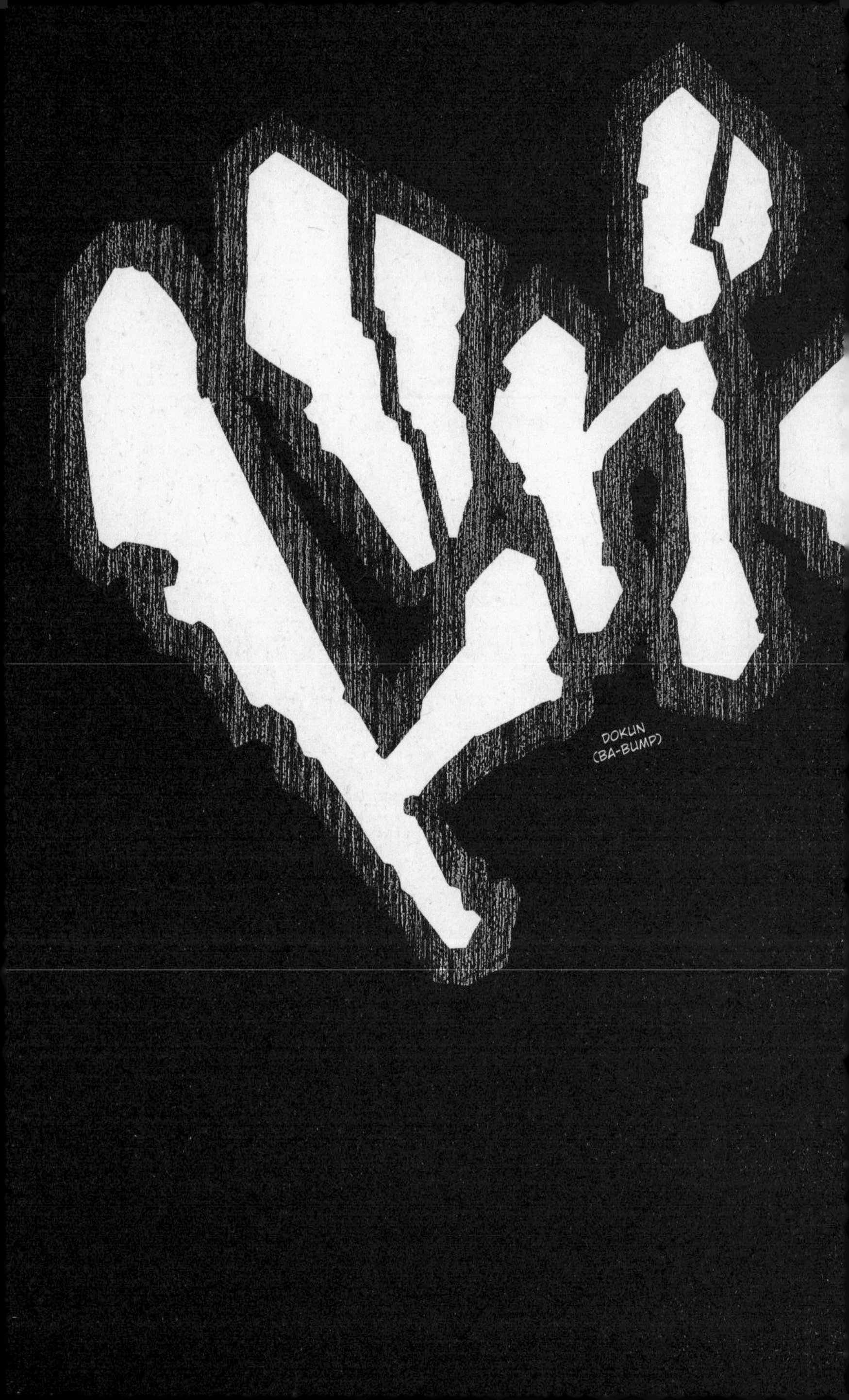
DOKUN
(BA-BUMP)

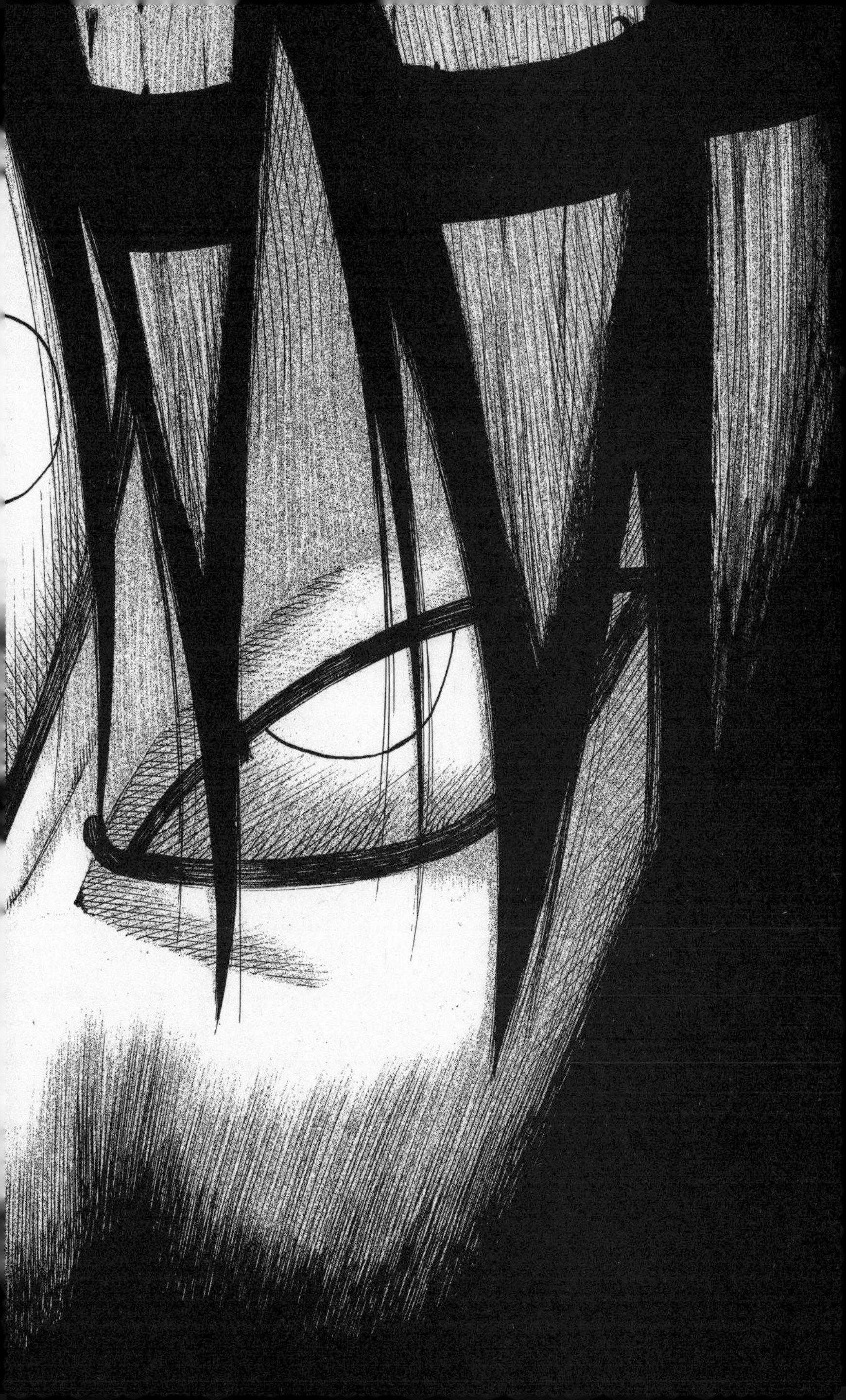

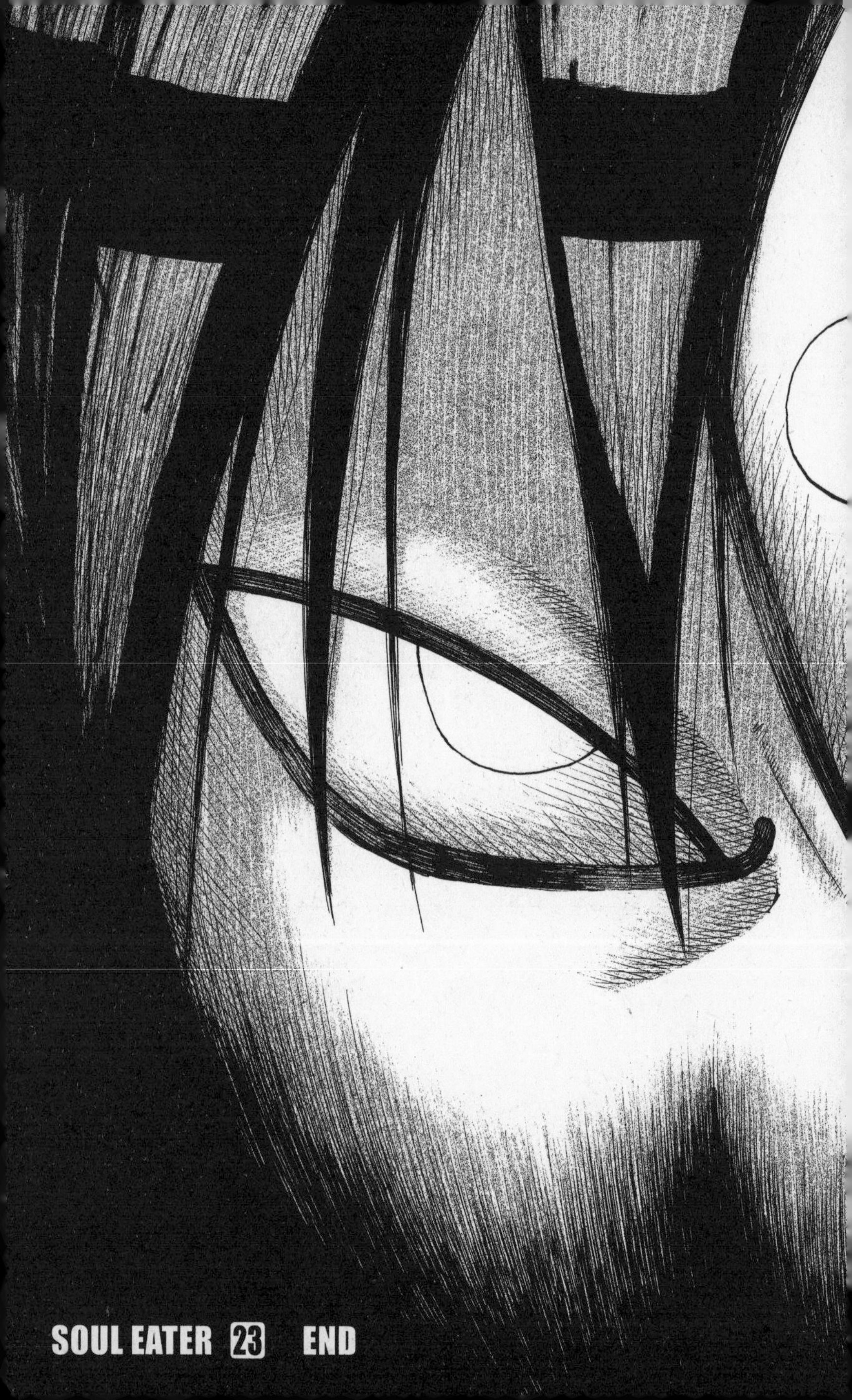
SOUL EATER 23 END

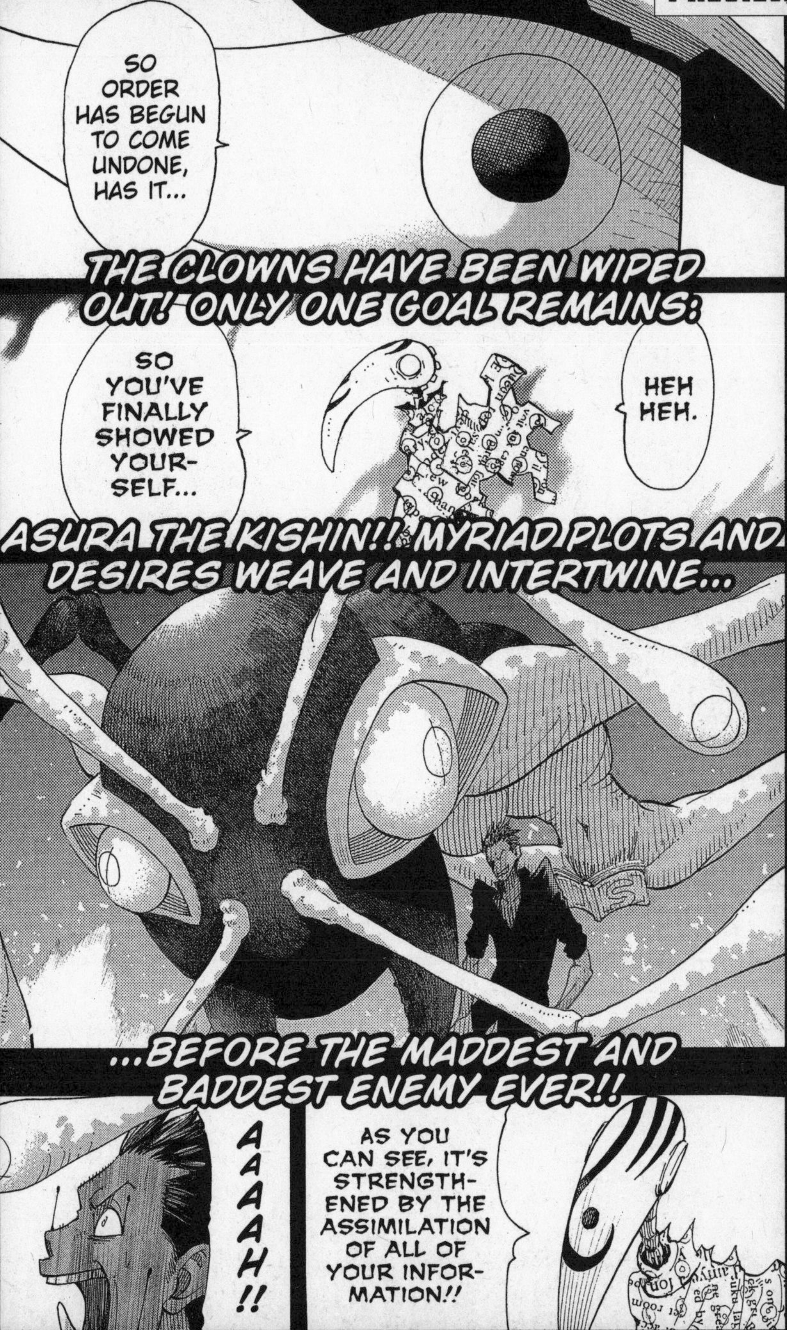
SO ORDER HAS BEGUN TO COME UNDONE, HAS IT...
THE CLOWNS HAVE BEEN WIPED OUT! ONLY ONE GOAL REMAINS:
HEH HEH.
SO YOU'VE FINALLY SHOWED YOUR-SELF...
ASURA THE KISHIN!! MYRIAD PLOTS AND DESIRES WEAVE AND INTERTWINE...
...BEFORE THE MADDEST AND BADDEST ENEMY EVER!!
AS YOU CAN SEE, IT'S STRENGTH-ENED BY THE ASSIMILATION OF ALL OF YOUR INFOR-MATION!!
AAAAAH!!

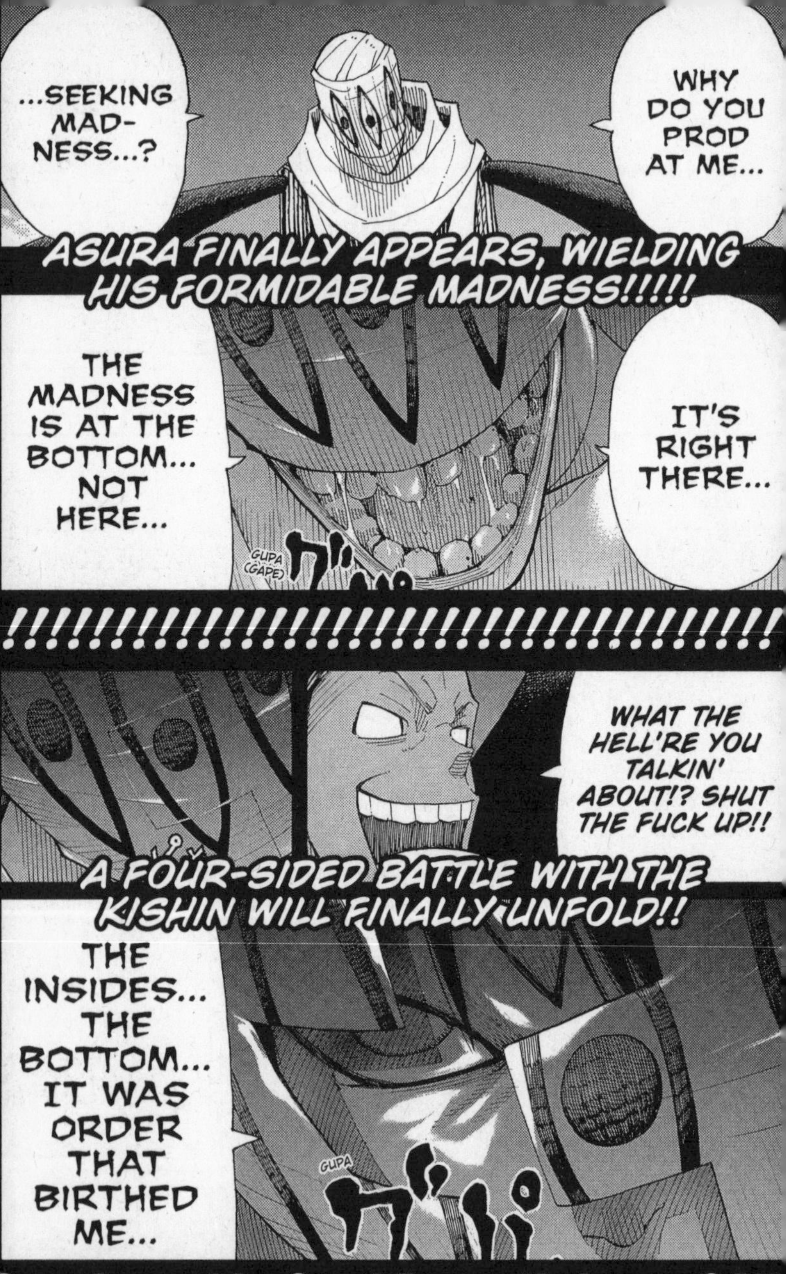
WHY DO YOU PROD AT ME...
...SEEKING MAD-NESS...?
ASURA FINALLY APPEARS, WIELDING HIS FORMIDABLE MADNESS!!!!!
IT'S RIGHT THERE...
THE MADNESS IS AT THE BOTTOM... NOT HERE...
GUPA (GAPE)
!!
WHAT THE HELL'RE YOU TALKIN' ABOUT!? SHUT THE FUCK UP!!
A FOUR-SIDED BATTLE WITH THE KISHIN WILL FINALLY UNFOLD!!
THE INSIDES... THE BOTTOM... IT WAS ORDER THAT BIRTHED ME...
GUPA

Continued in Soul Eater Volume 24!!

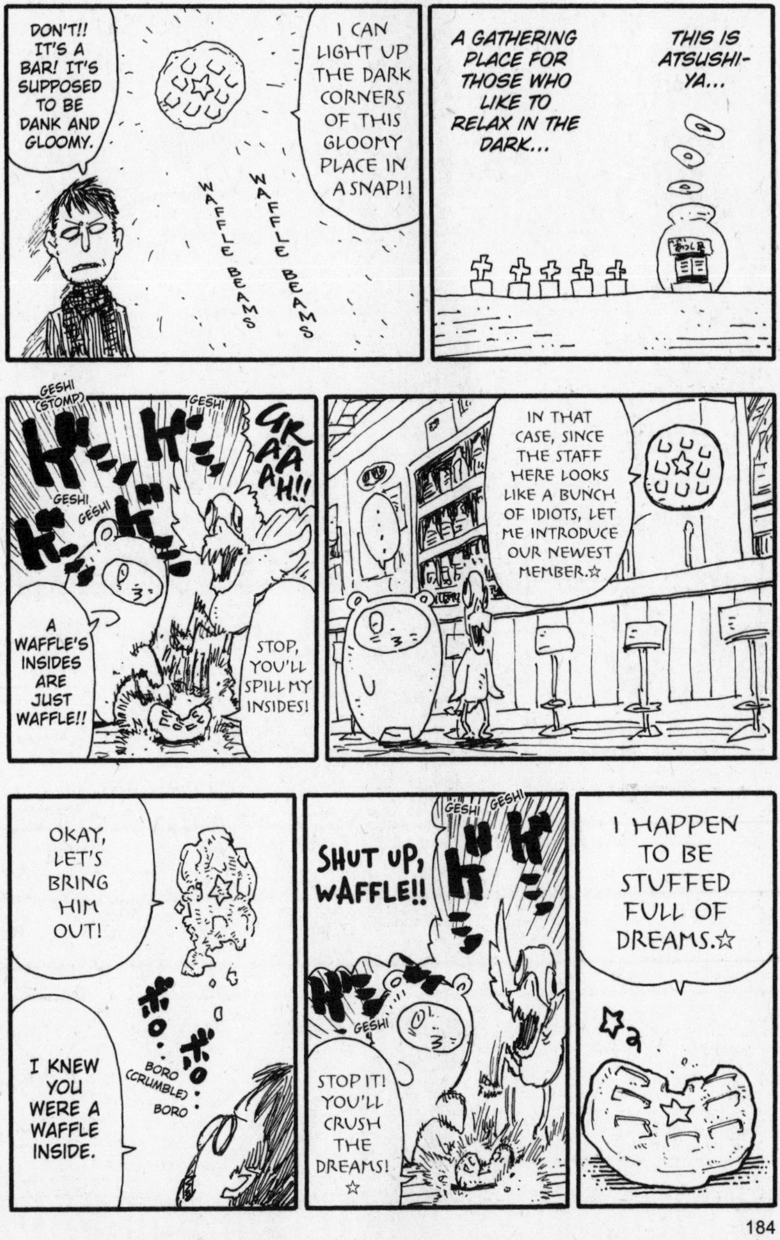
THIS IS ATSUSHI-YA...
A GATHERING PLACE FOR THOSE WHO LIKE TO RELAX IN THE DARK...
I CAN LIGHT UP THE DARK CORNERS OF THIS GLOOMY PLACE IN A SNAP!!
WAFFLE BEAMS
WAFFLE BEAMS
DON'T!! IT'S A BAR! IT'S SUPPOSED TO BE DANK AND GLOOMY.
IN THAT CASE, SINCE THE STAFF HERE LOOKS LIKE A BUNCH OF IDIOTS, LET ME INTRODUCE OUR NEWEST MEMBER.☆
GRAAAAH!!
GESHI
GESHI (STOMP)
GESHI
GESHI
STOP, YOU'LL SPILL MY INSIDES!
A WAFFLE'S INSIDES ARE JUST WAFFLE!!
I HAPPEN TO BE STUFFED FULL OF DREAMS.☆
GESHI
GESHI
SHUT UP, WAFFLE!!
GESHI
STOP IT! YOU'LL CRUSH THE DREAMS! ☆
OKAY, LET'S BRING HIM OUT!
BORO (CRUMBLE) BORO
I KNEW YOU WERE A WAFFLE INSIDE.

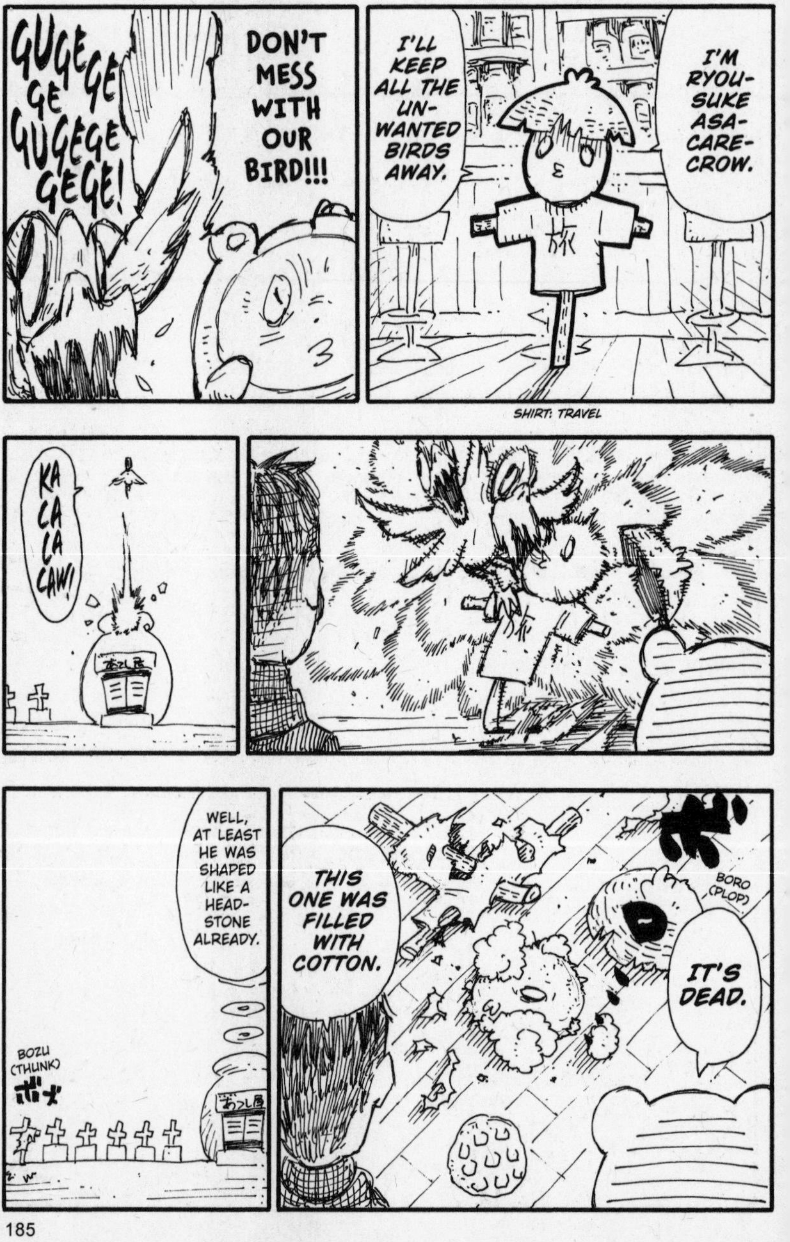
I'M RYOUSUKE ASA-CARE-CROW.
I'LL KEEP ALL THE UN-WANTED BIRDS AWAY.
SHIRT: TRAVEL
DON'T MESS WITH OUR BIRD!!!
GUGEGE GE GE GUGEGE GEGE!
KA CA LA CAW!
BORO (PLOP)
IT'S DEAD.
THIS ONE WAS FILLED WITH COTTON.
WELL, AT LEAST HE WAS SHAPED LIKE A HEAD-STONE ALREADY.
BOZU (THUNK)

Translation Notes

Common Honorifics

no honorific: Indicates familiarity or closeness; if used without permission or reason, addressing someone in this manner would constitute an insult.

-san: The Japanese equivalent of Mr./Mrs./Miss. If a situation calls for politeness, this is the fail-safe honorific.

-sama: Conveys great respect; may also indicate that the social status of the speaker is lower than that of the addressee.

-dono: Like -sama, using -dono is an indication of respect for the addressee.

-kun: Used most often when referring to boys, this indicates affection or familiarity. Occasionally used by older men among their peers, but it may also be used by anyone referring to a person of lower standing.

-chan: An affectionate honorific indicating familiarity used mostly in reference to girls; also used in reference to cute persons or animals of either gender.

-senpai: A suffix used to address upperclassmen or more experienced coworkers.

-sensei: A respectful term for teachers, artists, or high-level professionals.

Page 23
As in earlier volumes, the witch's chant, **"Joma Joma Wachi Suchi,"** is Japanese written in reverse. Rearranged, the greeting spells, "Witches, Witches, Heya! 'Sup?" (In Volume 3, the closing words of the witch mass, "*Joma Joma Dublahsa*," mean "Witches, Witches, Farewell")

Page 147
Kilik's **"AFX-T"** attack is a reference to the legendary British electronic music artist, Aphex Twin.

READ THE LATEST INSTALLMENT SIMULTANEOUSLY WITH JAPAN!

NEW CHAPTERS AVAILABLE MONTHLY FROM YOUR FAVORITE EBOOK RETAILER AND IN THE YEN PRESS APP!

DING-DONG!

DEAD-DONG!

DON'T BE LATE FOR THE "NOT" CLASS AT DEATH WEAPON MEISTER ACADEMY!

OLDER TEEN
OT

Yen Press

SOUL EATER NOT!

ATSUSHI OHKUBO

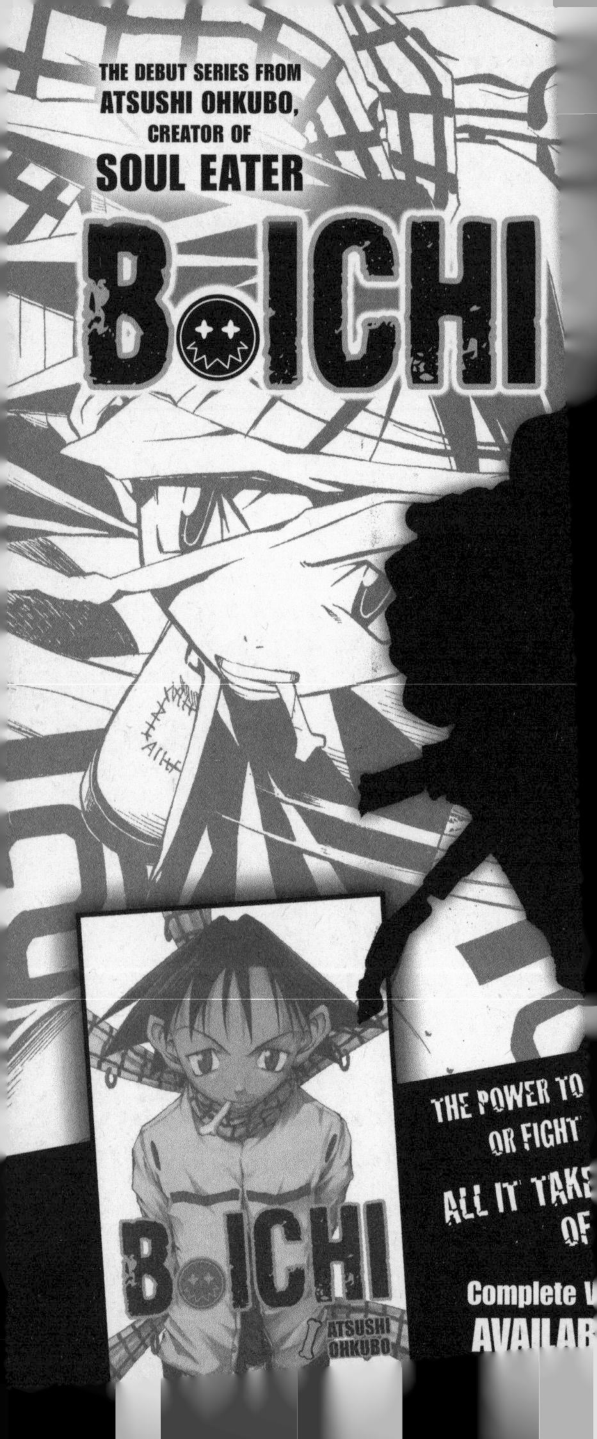
THE DEBUT SERIES FROM
ATSUSHI OHKUBO,
CREATOR OF
SOUL EATER
B ICHI
THE POWER TO
OR FIGHT
ALL IT TAKE
OF
Complete V
AVAILAB
B ICHI
ATSUSHI
OHKUBO

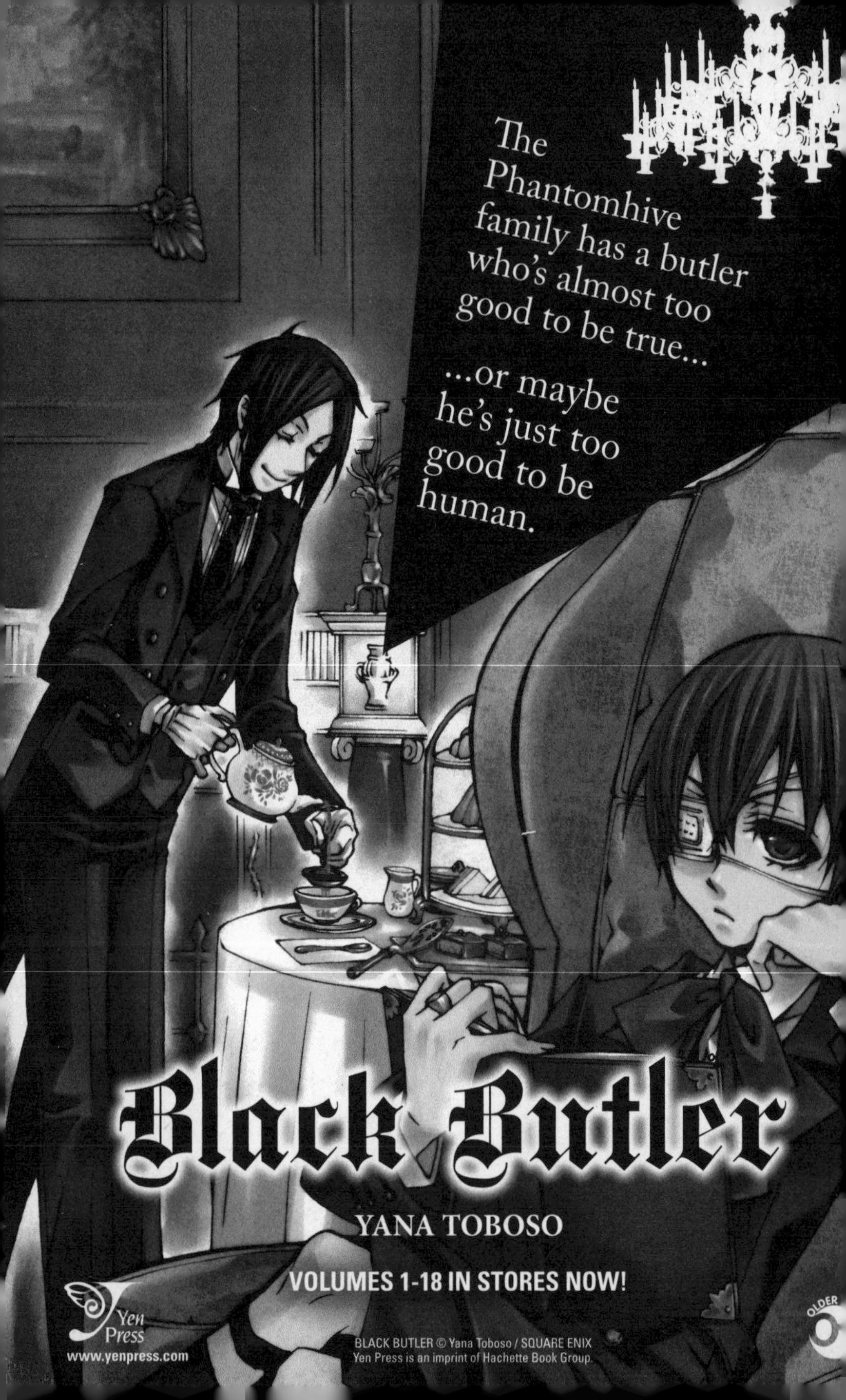

The Phantomhive family has a butler who's almost too good to be true...
...or maybe he's just too good to be human.
Black Butler
YANA TOBOSO
VOLUMES 1-18 IN STORES NOW!
Yen Press
www.yenpress.com
BLACK BUTLER © Yana Toboso / SQUARE ENIX
Yen Press is an imprint of Hachette Book Group.
OLDER

SOUL EATER ㉓

ATSUSHI OHKUBO

Translation: Stephen Paul

Lettering: Abigail Blackman

SOUL EATER Vol. 23 © 2012 Atsushi Ohkubo / SQUARE ENIX. First published in Japan in 2012 by SQUARE ENIX CO., LTD. English translation rights arranged with SQUARE ENIX CO., LTD. and Hachette Book Group through Tuttle-Mori Agency, Inc.

Translation © 2014 by SQUARE ENIX CO., LTD.

Yen Press
Hachette Book Group
1290 Avenue of the Americas
New York, NY 10104

www.HachetteBookGroup.com
www.YenPress.com

Yen Press is an imprint of Hachette Book Group, Inc. The Yen Press name and logo are trademarks of Hachette Book Group, Inc.

First Yen Press Edition: November 2014

ISBN: 978-0-316-40698-7

10 9 8 7 6 5 4 3 2 1

BVG

Printed in the United States of America